A
HOWARD
NEMEROV
READER

A
HOWARD NEMEROV
READER

University of Missouri Press
Columbia and London

Copyright © 1991 by Howard Nemerov
University of Missouri Press, Columbia, Missouri 65201
Printed and bound in the United States of America

5   4   3   2   1   95   94   93   92   91

Library of Congress Cataloging-in-Publication Data

Nemerov, Howard.
  [Selections.   1991]
  A Howard Nemerov reader
    p.   cm.
  Includes index.
  ISBN 0-8262-0776-6
  I. Title.
  PS3527.E5A6   1991b
  817'.54—dc20   90-20174
                                            CIP

∞™ This paper meets the requirements of the
American National Standard for Permanence of Paper
for Printed Library Materials, Z39.48, 1984.

Designer: Kristie Lee
Typesetter: Connell-Zeko Type & Graphics
Printer: Thomson-Shore, Inc.
Binder: Thomson-Shore, Inc.
Typeface: Elante and Sabon

Frontispiece photograph by Herb Weitman

to Frances McIntosh

CONTENTS

ABOUT THE AUTHOR

The Edward Mallinckrodt Distinguished University Professor of English at Washington University in St. Louis, Howard Nemerov has had an illustrious career as a teacher since 1946. In that year, after having served as a pilot in the Royal Canadian and United States air forces, he was hired to teach World War II veterans about literature at Hamilton College in New York. After a long tenure at Bennington College and a shorter one at Brandeis University, Nemerov joined the faculty at Washington University in 1969.

Nemerov is a member of the American Academy of Arts and Letters and is a fellow of the Academy of American Poets and of the American Academy of Arts and Sciences. Among the dozens of awards he has received are the first Theodore Roethke Memorial Award (1968), the National Book Award (1978), the Pulitzer Prize for Poetry (1978), the Bollingen Prize for Poetry (1981), the National Medal for the Arts in Poetry (1987), and the first Aiken/Taylor Prize for Poetry from the *Sewanee Review* and the University of the South (1987).

From 1963 to 1964, Nemerov served as Consultant in Poetry to the Library of Congress, and when that post was elevated to that of Poet Laureate of the United States he again served, this time as the nation's third Poet Laureate, from 1988 to 1990.

The author of over three dozen works of fiction, poetry, and criticism, Howard Nemerov is one of America's most distinguished men of letters.

BOOKS BY HOWARD NEMEROV

The Image and the Law: Poems (1947)

The Melodramatists: A Novel (1949)

Guide to the Ruins: Poems (1950)

Federigo, Or, the Power of Love: A Novel (1954)

The Salt Garden: Poems (1955)

The Homecoming Game: A Novel (1957)

Mirrors and Windows: Poems (1958)

A Commodity of Dreams and Other Stories (1959)

New and Selected Poems (1960)

The Next Room of the Dream: Poems (1962)

Poetry and Fiction: Essays (1963)

Journal of the Fictive Life (1965)

Poets on Poetry (editor, 1965)

The Blue Swallows: Poems (1967)

Stories, Fables & Other Diversions (1971)

Reflexions on Poetry and Poetics: Essays (1972)

Gnomes and Occasions: Poems (1973)

The Western Approaches, Poems 1973–75 (1975)

The Collected Poems of Howard Nemerov (1977)

Figures of Thought: Speculations on the Meaning of Poetry and Other Essays (1978)

I.
POETRY

FROM
The Image and the Law
(1947)

Observation of October

An old desperation of the flesh.
Mortification and revivification
Of the spirit. There are those
Who work outdoors, and others
Who pull down blinds against the sun.

A cold October day I find
Fear of death in the weather, for
Those in the streets are hurrying,
And those at home take hot baths
Or pace the floor and refuse to go out.

And many, winter approaching,
Go early to bed at night, refuse
To admit their friends or read the papers,
And sleep curled up. There are, I think,
Simplicities in every life.

Autumnal

October: the falling leaves resume the earth,
Recording time upon the sodden floor;
All energies and foreign heats retract

And luminous at night, in rain, the mold
Decays. It is a timely paradox
To be considered by who works in stone.

Fading the flesh delineates the bone,
Indicts your face, a precious artifact,
That so your legal beauty may be known.

Mortal and inconclusive every fall
By repetition further unredeemed
Tears at the rotting fabric of this world

And falls away: in the destructive hour
False permanence of stone can speculate
In splendid light, illumination and

Reconnaissance of always failing time.
How should we be the emblem of our tomb?
Always we fail with time to fall: and yet

Love might construct a form so true, so tense
As to survive its own antithesis,
Achieving an ironic permanence

With, for a pulse, repetitive despair.
Fading, the flesh delineates the bone
As surely, certainly, as autumn leaves

Describe a tree when they resume the earth.
Then do not fear your beauty will be known
Only by fever, attempted by decay:

Love is the form of stone, statue and law
As far locked from corruption of the sun
As Buddha smiling in the seamless rock.

                    . . . for my wife

FROM
Guide to the Ruins (1950)

Succession

Furnished and clean, this room does not betray
The traces of another tenancy,
Discourages what charges you might lay
Against its suspect calm. But lingering by
The door the woman hints a history—
The priest, your predecessor, "went away"
(So much you might have gathered; did he die?
Was it a year ago or yesterday?)

Left alone with the horrible brass bedstead,
Imagine the Father to come in at night,
Undo his collar, lie upon the bed
(His naked feet incongruously white)
And close his eyes against the icy light
For half-an-hour's nap, his dreaming head
Reworking all the daytime in a rite.
Rising, he dines on onion soup and bread.

So much you see, but cannot see his face,
And have no further wish to follow him ·
Where he has gone, for now the room awaits
The thud of your belongings and your name—
How easily it will encompass them!
Behind the door the sycophantic glass

Already would reflect you in a frame
That memorizes nothing but its place.

Hypocrisy! you'll get to know them well,
Wallpaper, closet, bureau and the bed,
Their repetitions in the glass, that tell
A ceaseless inventory of the bled
Stuff of your life. While in your lonely head
The poor gone priest cries vanity and hell.
O murderous usurper! Is he dead?
Has any man late heard the passing bell?

Like kings of Egypt, dreaming death a dream
In which their men and women still would come
To minister as always to a whim,
You may make of this place a kind of home:
Straighten the wrinkled window blind, make dumb
The dripping tap, let neither drop nor dram
Derange the composition of the room,
The furnished room, the garment without seam.

Madrigal

She is the darkness where I wander
Who was the light that found my way.
What time and choice have torn asunder
Come together in no day.

Blackness her great beauty bringeth
Upon me, and I go my way
Singing as one lonely, that singeth
Unregarding and astray.

Night time on her also is fallen,
Shadow clouds her perfect way.
For her the winter sun rides sullen
And shines not on the dark day.

To such a year no springtime riseth,
Nor is no excellence in May,

But darkness in the sky abideth
Where the world wanders astray.

The Ecstasies of Dialectic

Her laughter was infectious; so, some found,
Her love. Several young men reasonably
Regret inciting her to gratitude
And learning of her ardent facility.

She has gone, back it may be to the world,
To ply her silken exercise elsewhere.
Now is occasion for the medication
(As possible) of ills not all of the heart,

And certain hints, conveyed in sermon or
By private word, are reasoning the weight
Of pleasures, pains. Thus her capable joys
Are debased by her ignominious communications.

"The flesh, the rouged cheekbones of Babylon,
The unclean loins, the thief of legal delight,
O ye generations!" "The spider that eats up
Her mate!" "The test-tube of iniquity!"

Despite the wisdom of Christian Epicures
Many of the affected more regret
Her going than her legacy. They huddle
At street corners, before drugstores, and moon

Over the hour of pestilent delight,
The yellow taste good times will always have.
"The proof of the apple is in the worm," they say,
And hug their new knowledge of life and death.

FROM
The Salt Garden
(1955)

Dandelions

These golden heads, these common suns
Only less multitudinous
Than grass itself that gluts
The market of the world with green,
They shine as lovely as they're mean,
Fine as the daughters of the poor
Who go proudly in spangles of brass;
Light-headed, then headless, stalked for a salad.

Inside a week they will be seen
Stricken and old, ghosts in the field
To be picked up at the lightest breath,
With brazen tops all shrunken in
And swollen green gone withered white.
You'll say it's nature's price for beauty
That goes cheap; that being light
Is justly what makes girls grow heavy;
And that the wind, bearing their death,
Whispers the second kingdom come.
—You'll say, the fool of piety,
By resignations hanging on
Until, still justified, you drop.
But surely the thing is sorrowful,

At evening, when the light goes out
Slowly, to see those ruined spinsters,
All down the field their ghostly hair,
Dry sinners waiting in the valley
For the last word and the next life
And the liberation from the lion's mouth.

A Harvest Home

To stand on the long field in fall,
To feel the silence of the sun
Bending the earth toward afternoon—
So hot and mute the human will
As though the angry wheel stood still
That hub and spoke and iron rim
Might fall, might burn away in air
And rot in earth before the ear
Had lost the last, grinding scream;
So much the moment was a snare
For time to pull from and be torn
Screaming against the rusty brake—
Until four crows arise and shake
Their heavy wings across the way,
Four shadows dragging on the shorn
Beard of the field, on the baled hay.
So afternoon resumes its slow
And ancient ceremonious bow
Down to the field and so beyond
The gate, the houses and the pond,
Out where the tracks run west and trains
Cry out, leaning in the long curve
Away, away. The owl complains
In darkness, and at dawn the jay
Proclaims the colors of the day.
All tendrils of the lonely nerve
Stand out in sunlight, and will serve.

The Goose Fish

On the long shore, lit by the moon
To show them properly alone,
Two lovers suddenly embraced
So that their shadows were as one.
The ordinary night was graced
For them by the swift tide of blood
That silently they took at flood,
And for a little time they prized
   Themselves emparadised.

Then, as if shaken by stage-fright
Beneath the hard moon's bony light,
They stood together on the sand
Embarrassed in each other's sight
But still conspiring hand in hand,
Until they saw, there underfoot,
As though the world had found them out,
The goose fish turning up, though dead,
   His hugely grinning head.

There in the china light he lay,
Most ancient and corrupt and grey.
They hesitated at his smile,
Wondering what it seemed to say
To lovers who a little while
Before had thought to understand,
By violence upon the sand,
The only way that could be known
   To make a world their own.

It was a wide and moony grin
Together peaceful and obscene;
They knew not what he would express,
So finished a comedian
He might mean failure or success,
But took it for an emblem of
Their sudden, new and guilty love

To be observed by, when they kissed,
   That rigid optimist.

So he became their patriarch,
Dreadfully mild in the half-dark.
His throat that the sand seemed to choke,
His picket teeth, these left their mark
But never did explain the joke
That so amused him, lying there
While the moon went down to disappear
Along the still and tilted track.
   That bears the zodiac.

FROM
Mirrors and Windows
(1958)

Sandpipers

In the small territory and time
Between one wave and the next, they run
Down the beach and back, eating things
Which seem, conveniently for them,
To surface only when the sand gets wet.
Small, dapper birds, they make me think
Of commuters seen, say, in an early movie
Where the rough screen wavers, where the light
Jerks and seems to rain; of clockwork dolls
Set going on the sidewalk, drawing a crowd
Beside the newsstand at five o'clock; their legs
Black toothpicks, their heads nodding at nothing.
But this comedy is based upon exact
Perceptions, and delicately balanced
Between starvation and the sea:
Though sometimes I have seen one slip and fall,
From either the undertow or greed,
And have to get up in the wave's open mouth,
Still eating, I have never seen
One caught; if necessary he spreads his wings,
With the white stripe, and flutters rather than flies
Out, to begin eating again at once.
Now they are over every outer beach,

Procrastinating steadily southwards
In endlessly local comings and goings.

Whenever a flock of them takes flight,
And flies with the beautiful unison
Of banners in the wind, they are
No longer funny. It is their courage,
Meaningless as the word is when compared
With their thoughtless precisions, which strikes
Me when I watch them hidden and revealed
Between two waves, lost in the sea's
Lost color as they distance me; flying
From winter already, while I
Am in August. When suddenly they turn
In unison, all their bellies shine
Like mirrors flashing white with signals
I cannot read, but I wish them well.

Runes

". . . *insaniebam salubriter et moriebar vitaliter.*"
St. Augustine

I

This is about the stillness in moving things,
In running water, also in the sleep
Of winter seeds, where time to come has tensed
Itself, enciphering a script so fine
Only the hourglass can magnify it, only
The years unfold its sentence from the root.
I have considered such things often, but
I cannot say I have thought deeply of them:
That is my theme, of thought and the defeat
Of thought before its object, where it turns
As from a mirror, and returns to be
The thought of something and the thought of thought,
A trader doubly burdened, commercing
Out of one stillness and into another.

II

About Ulysses, the learned have reached two
Distinct conclusions. In one, he secretly

Returns to Ithaca, is recognized
By Euryclea, destroys the insolent suitors,
And makes himself known to Penelope,
Describing the bed he built; then, at the last
Dissolve, we see him with Telemachus
Leaving the palace, planning to steal sheep:
The country squire resumes a normal life.
But in the other, out beyond the gates
Of Hercules, gabbling persuasively
About virtue and knowledge, he sails south
To disappear from sight behind the sun;
Drowning near blessed shores he flames in hell.
I do not know which ending is the right one.

III

Sunflowers, traders rounding the horn of time
Into deep afternoons, sleepy with gain,
The fall of silence has begun to storm
Around you where you nod your heavy heads
Whose bare poles, raking out of true, will crack,
Driving your wreckage on the world's lee shore.
Your faces no more will follow the sun,
But bow down to the ground with a heavy truth
That dereliction learns, how charity
Is strangled out of selfishness at last;
When, golden misers in the courts of summer,
You are stripped of gain for coining images
And broken on this quarter of the wheel,
It is on savage ground you spill yourselves,
And spend the tarnished silver of your change.

IV

The seed sleeps in the furnaces of death,
A cock's egg slept till hatching by a serpent
Wound in his wintry coil, a spring so tight
In his radical presence that every tense
Is now. Out of this head the terms of kind,
Distributed in syntax, come to judgment,

Are basilisks who write our sentences
Deep at the scripture's pith, in rooted tongues,
How one shall marry while another dies.
Give us our ignorance, the family tree
Grows upside down and shakes its heavy fruit,
Whose buried stones philosophers have sought.
For each stone bears the living word, each word
Will be made flesh, and all flesh fall to seed:
Such stones from the tree; and from the stones, such blood.

V

The fat time of the year is also time
Of the Atonement; birds to the berry bushes,
Men to the harvest; a time to answer for
Both present plenty and emptiness to come.
When the slain legal deer is salted down,
When apples smell like goodness, cold in the cellar,
You hear the ram's horn sounded in the high
Mount of the Lord, and you lift up your eyes
As though by this observance you might hide
The dry husk of an eaten heart which brings
Nothing to offer up, no sacrifice
Acceptable but the canceled-out desires
And satisfactions of another year's
Abscess, whose zero in His winter's mercy
Still hides the undecipherable seed.

VI

White water now in the snowflake's prison,
A mad king in a skullcap thinks these thoughts
In regular hexagons, each one unlike
Each of the others. The atoms of memory,
Like those that Democritus knew, have hooks
At either end, but these? Insane tycoon,
These are the riches of order snowed without end
In this distracted globe, where is no state
To fingerprint the flakes or number these

Moments melting in flight, seeds mirroring
Substance without position or a speed
And course unsubstanced. What may the spring be,
Deep in the atom, among galactic snows,
But the substance of things hoped for, argument
Of things unseen? White water, fall and fall.

VII

Unstable as water, thou shalt not excel
—Said to the firstborn, the dignity and strength,
And the defiler of the father's bed.
Fit motto for a dehydrated age
Nervously watering whisky and stock,
Quick-freezing dreams into realities.
Brain-surgeons have produced the proustian syndrome,
But patients dunk their tasteless madeleines
In vain, those papers that the Japanese
Amused themselves by watering until
They flowered and became Combray, flower
No more. The plastic and cosmetic arts
Unbreakably record the last word and
The least word, till sometimes even the Muse,
In her transparent raincoat, resembles a condom.

VIII

To go low, to be as nothing, to die,
To sleep in the dark water threading through
The fields of ice, the soapy, frothing water
That slithers under the culvert below the road,
Water of dirt, water of death, dark water,
And through the tangle of the sleeping roots
Under the coppery cold beech woods, the green
Pinewoods, and past the buried hulls of things
To come, and humbly through the breathing dreams
Of all small creatures sleeping in the earth;
To fall with the weight of things down on the one
Still ebbing stream, to go on to the end

With the convict hunted through the swamp all night.
The dog's corpse in the ditch, to come at last
Into the pit where zero's eye is closed.

IX

In this dehydrated time of digests, pills
And condensations, the most expensive presents
Are thought to come in the smallest packages:
In atoms, for example. There are still
To be found, at carnivals, men who engrave
The Lord's Prayer on a grain of wheat for pennies,
But they are a dying race, unlike the men
Now fortunate, who bottle holy water
In plastic tears, and bury mustard seeds
In lucite lockets, and for safety sell
To be planted on the dashboard of your car
The statues, in durable celluloid,
Of Mary and St. Christopher, who both
With humble power in the world's floodwaters
Carried their heavy Savior and their Lord.

X

White water, white water, feather of a form
Between the stones, is the race run to stay
Or pass away? Your utterance is riddled,
Rainbowed and clear and cold, tasting of stone,
Its brilliance blinds me. But still I have seen,
White water, at the breaking of the ice,
When the high places render up the new
Children of water and their tumbling light
Laughter runs down the hills, and the small fist
Of the seed unclenches in the day's dazzle,
How happiness is helpless before your fall,
White water, and history is no more than
The shadows thrown by clouds on mountainsides,
A distant chill, when all is brought to pass
By rain and birth and rising of the dead.

XI

A holy man said to me, "Split the stick
And there is Jesus." When I split the stick
To the dark marrow and the splintery grain
I saw nothing that was not wood, nothing
That was not God, and I began to dream
How from the tree that stood between the rivers
Came Aaron's rod that crawled in front of Pharaoh,
And came the rod of Jesse flowering
In all the generations of the Kings,
And came the timbers of the second tree,
The sticks and yardarms of the holy three-
masted vessel whereon the Son of Man
Hung between thieves, and came the crown of thorns,
The lance and ladder, when was shed that blood
Streamed in the grain of Adam's tainted seed.

XII

Consider how the seed lost by a bird
Will harbor in its branches most remote
Descendants of the bird; while everywhere
And unobserved, the soft green stalks and tubes
Of water are hardening into wood, whose hide,
Gnarled, knotted, flowing, and its hidden grain,
Remember how the water is streaming still.
Now does the seed asleep, as in a dream
Where time is compacted under pressures of
Another order, crack open like stone
From whose division pours a stream, between
The raindrop and the sea, running in one
Direction, down, and gathering in its course
That bitter salt which spices us the food
We sweat for, and the blood and tears we shed.

XIII

There sailed out on the river, Conrad saw,
The dreams of men, the seeds of commonwealths,

The germs of Empire. To the ends of the earth
One many-veined bloodstream swayed the hulls
Of darkness gone, of darkness still to come,
And sent its tendrils steeping through the roots
Of wasted continents. That echoing pulse
Carried the ground swell of all sea-returns
Muttering under history, and its taste,
Saline and cold, was as a mirror of
The taste of human blood. The sailor leaned
To lick the mirror clean, the somber and
Immense mirror that Conrad saw, and saw
The other self, the sacred Cain of blood
Who would seed a commonwealth in the Land of Nod.

XIV

There is a threshold, that meniscus where
The strider walks on drowning waters, or
That tense, curved membrane of the camera's lens
Which darkness holds against the battering light
And the distracted drumming of the world's
Importunate plenty.—Now that threshold,
The water of the eye where the world walks
Delicately, is as a needle threaded
From the reel of a raveling stream, to stitch
Dissolving figures in a watered cloth,
A damask either-sided as the shroud
Of the lord of Ithaca, labored at in light,
Destroyed in darkness, while the spidery oars
Carry his keel across deep mysteries
To harbor in unfathomable mercies.

XV

To watch water, to watch running water
Is to know a secret, seeing the twisted rope
Of runnels on the hillside, the small freshets
Leaping and limping down the tilted field
In April's light, the green, grave and opaque
Swirl in the millpond where the current slides

To be combed and carded silver at the fall;
It is a secret. Or it is not to know
The secret, but to have it in your keeping,
A locked box, Bluebeard's room, the deathless thing
Which it is death to open. Knowing the secret,
Keeping the secret—herringbones of light
Ebbing on beaches, the huge artillery
Of tides—it is not knowing, it is not keeping,
But being the secret hidden from yourself.

FROM
The Next
Room of
the Dream
(1962)

To Clio, Muse of History

On learning that The Etruscan Warrior
in the Metropolitan Museum of Art
is proved a modern forgery

One more casualty,
One more screen memory penetrated at last
To be destroyed in the endless anamnesis
Always progressing, never arriving at a cure.
My childhood in the glare of that giant form
Corrupts with history, for I too fought in the War.

He, great male beauty
That stood for the sexual thrust of power,
His target eyes inviting the universal victim
To fatal seduction, the crested and greaved
Survivor long after shield and sword are dust,
Has now become another lie about our life.

Smash the idol, of course.
Bury the pieces deep as the interest of truth
Requires. And you may in time compose the future
Smoothly without him, though it is too late

To disinfect the past of his huge effigy
By any further imposition of your hands.

But tell us no more
Enchantments, Clio. History has given
And taken away; murders become memories,
And memories become the beautiful obligations:
As with a dream interpreted by one still sleeping,
The interpretation is only the next room of the dream.

For I remember how
We children stared, learning from him
Unspeakable things about war that weren't in the books;
And how the Museum store offered for sale
His photographic reproductions in full color
With the ancient genitals blacked out.

De Anima

Now it is night, now in the brilliant room
A girl stands at the window looking out,
But sees, in the darkness of the frame,
Only her own image.

And there is a young man across the street
Who looks at the girl and into the brilliant room.
They might be in love, might be about to meet,
If this were a romance.

In looking at herself, she tries to look
Beyond herself, and half become another,
Admiring and resenting, maybe dreaming
Her lover might see her so.

The other, the stranger standing in cold and dark,
Looks at the young girl in her crystalline room.
He sees clearly, and hopelessly desires,
A life that is not his.

Given the blindness of her self-possession,
The luminous vision revealed to his despair,
We look to both sides of the glass at once
And see no future in it.

These pure divisions hurt us in some realm
Of parable beyond belief, beyond
The temporal mind. Why is it sorrowful?
Why do we want them together?

Is it the spirit, ransacking through the earth
After its image, its being, its begetting?
The spirit sorrows, for what lovers bring
Into the world is death,

The most exclusive romance, after all,
The sort that lords and ladies listen to
With selfish tears, when she draws down the shade,
When he had turned away,

When the blind embryo with his bow of bees,
His candied arrows tipped with flower heads,
Turns from them too, for mercy or for grief
Refusing to be, refusing to die.

The Dial Tone

A moment of silence, first, then there it is.
But not as though it only now began
Because of my attention; rather, this,
That I begin at one point on its span
Brief kinship with its endless going on.

Between society and self it poses
Neutrality perceptible to sense,
Being a no man's land the lawyer uses
Much as the lover does: charged innocence,
It sits on its own electrified fence,

Is neither pleased nor hurt by race results
Or by the nasty thing John said to Jane;
Is merely interrupted by insults,
Devotions, lecheries; after the sane
And mad hang up at once, it will remain.

Suppose that in God a black bumblebee
Or colorless hummingbird buzzed all night,
Dividing the abyss up equally;
And carried its neither sweetness nor its light
Across impossible eternity.

Now take this hummingbird, this bee, away;
And like the Cheshire smile without its cat
The remnant hum continues on its way,
Unwinged, able at once to move and wait,
An endless freight train on an endless flat.

Something like that, some loneliest of powers
That never has confessed its secret name.
I do not doubt that if you gave it hours
And then lost patience, it would be the same
After you left that it was before you came.

Vermeer

Taking what is, and seeing it as it is,
Pretending to no heroic stances or gestures,
Keeping it simple; being in love with light
And the marvelous things that light is able to do,
How beautiful! a modesty which is
Seductive extremely, the care for daily things.

At one for once with sunlight falling through
A leaded window, the holy mathematic
Plays out the cat's cradle of relation
Endlessly; even the inexorable
Domesticates itself and becomes charm.

If I could say to you, and make it stick,
A girl in a red hat, a woman in blue
Reading a letter, a lady weighing gold . . .
If I could say this to you so you saw,
And knew, and agreed that this was how it was
In a lost city across the sea of years,
I think we should be for one moment happy
In the great reckoning of those little rooms
Where the weight of life has been lifted and made light,
Or standing invisible on the shore opposed,
Watching the water in the foreground dream
Reflectively, taking a view of Delft
As it was, under a wide and darkening sky.

Lion & Honeycomb

He didn't want to do it with skill,
He'd had enough of skill. If he never saw
Another villanelle, it would be too soon;
And the same went for sonnets. If it had been
Hard work learning to rime, it would be much
Harder learning not to. The time came
He had to ask himself, what did he want?
What did he want when he began
That idiot fiddling with the sounds of things?

He asked himself, poor moron, because he had
Nobody else to ask. The others went right on
Talking about form, talking about myth
And the (so help us) need for a modern idiom;
The verseballs among them kept counting syllables.

So there he was, this forty-year-old teen-ager
Dreaming preposterous mergers and divisions
Of vowels like water, consonants like rock
(While everybody kept discussing values
And the need for values), for words that would

Enter the silence and be there as a light.
So much coffee and so many cigarettes
Gone down the drain, gone up in smoke,
Just for the sake of getting something right
Once in a while, something that could stand
On its own flat feet to keep out windy time
And the worm, something that might simply be,
Not as the monument in the smoky rain
Grimly endures, but that would be
Only a moment's inviolable presence,
The moment before disaster, before the storm,
In its peculiar silence, an integer
Fixed in the middle of the fall of things,
Perfected and casual as to a child's eye
Soap bubbles are, and skipping stones.

These Words Also

There is her mother's letter on the table
Where it was opened and read and put down
In a morning remaining what it never was,
Remaining what it will not be again.

These words also, earth, the sun brings forth
In the moment of his unbearable brilliancy:
"After a night of drink and too much talk,
After the casual companions had gone home,
She did this. . . ." How the silence must have grown
Austere, as the unanswerable phone
Rang in a room that wanted to be empty.

The garden holds its sunlight heavy and still
As if in a gold frame around the flowers
That nod and never change, the picture-book
Flowers of somebody's forbidden childhood,
Pale lemony lilies, pansies with brilliant scowls
Pretending to be children. Only they live,

And it is beautiful enough, to live,
Having to do with hunger and reflection,
A matter of thresholds, of thoughtless balancings.

The black and gold morning goes on, and
What is a girl's life? There on the path
Red ants are pulling a shiny beetle along
Through the toy kingdom where nobody thinks.

FROM *The Blue Swallows* (1967)

Landscape with Figures

What a dream of a landscape!
Cries Mrs. Persepolis, and I
Agree, my gaze follows hers
Out to the giant recumbent
Hills in their sullen haze
Brooding some brutal thought
As it were about myself &
Mrs. Persepolis, who are now
Alone in a closed garden
With various flowers and bees
And a feeble fountain that drips
On a stone in a heart-shaped
Pool with a single leopard-
Like toad immobilized all
Morning at his predatory
Meditation, making me think
Mrs. Persepolis not too old
With her bright voice and
Wrinkling skin at the wrist
Patterned in sunburnt diamonds
But still a game old girl
(And I a game old guy) good
For a tumble in the August

Grass right at the center
Of the dream of a landscape

Till I see her glittering eye
Has taken this thought exactly
As the toad's tongue takes a fly
So that we laugh and the moment
Passes but Mrs. Persepolis
As the bees go about their business
And we go in to have lunch
(How cold the house, the sudden
Shade! I shiver, and Mrs.
Persepolis shivers too, till
Her bangles bangle) my dear
Mrs. Persepolis, beautiful
Exile from childhood, girl
In your rough and wrinkled
Sack suit, couldn't you cry
Over that funny moment when
We almost fell together
Into the green sleep of the
Landscape, the hooded hills
That dream us up & down?

The Blue Swallows

Across the millstream below the bridge
Seven blue swallows divide the air
In shapes invisible and evanescent,
Kaleidoscopic beyond the mind's
Or memory's power to keep them there.

"History is where tensions were,"
"Form is the diagram of forces."
Thus, helplessly, there on the bridge,
While gazing down upon those birds—
How strange, to be above the birds!—
Thus helplessly the mind in its brain

Weaves up relation's spindrift web,
Seeing the swallow's tails as nibs
Dipped in invisible ink, writing . . .

Poor mind, what would you have them write?
Some cabalistic history
Whose authorship you might ascribe
To God? to Nature? Ah, poor ghost,
You've capitalized your Self enough.
That villainous William of Occam
Cut out the feet from under that dream
Some seven centuries ago.
It's taken that long for the mind
To waken, yawn and stretch, to see
With opened eyes emptied of speech
The real world where the spelling mind
Imposes with its grammar book
Unreal relations on the blue
Swallows. Perhaps when you will have
Fully awakened, I shall show you
A new thing: even the water
Flowing away beneath those birds
Will fail to reflect their flying forms,
And the eyes that see become as stones
Whence never tears shall fall again.

O swallows, swallows, poems are not
The point. Finding again the world,
That is the point, where loveliness
Adorns intelligible things
Because the mind's eye lit the sun.

The Mud Turtle

Out of the earth beneath the water,
Dragging over the stubble field
Up to the hilltop in the sun
On his way from water to water,

He rests an hour in the garden,
His alien presence observed by all:
His lordly darkness decked in filth
Bearded with weed like a lady's favor,
He is a black planet, another world
Never till now appearing, even now
Not quite believably old and big,
Set in the summer morning's midst
A gloomy gemstone to the sun opposed.
Our measures of him do not matter,
He would be huge at any size;
And neither does the number of his years,
The time he comes from doesn't count.

When the boys tease him with sticks
He breaks the sticks, striking with
As great a suddenness as speed;
Fingers and toes would snap as soon,
Says one of us, and the others shudder.
Then when they turn him on his back
To see the belly heroically yellow,
He throws himself fiercely to his feet,
Brings down the whole weight of his shell,
Spreads out his claws and digs himself in
Immovably, invulnerably,
But for the front foot on the left,
Red-budded, with the toes torn off.
So over he goes again, and shows
Us where a swollen leech is fastened
Softly between plastron and shell.
Nobody wants to go close enough
To burn it loose; he can't be helped
Either, there is no help for him
As he makes it to his feet again
And drags away to the meadow's edge.
We see the tall grass open and wave
Around him, it closes, he is gone
Over the hill toward another water,
Bearing his hard and chambered hurt

Down, down, down, beneath the water,
Beneath the earth beneath. He takes
A secret wound out of the world.

Summer's Elegy

Day after day, day after still day,
The summer has begun to pass away.
Starlings at twilight fly clustered and call,
And branches bend, and leaves begin to fall.
The meadow and the orchard grass are mown,
And the meadowlark's house is cut down.

The little lantern bugs have doused their fires,
The swallows sit in rows along the wires.
Berry and grape appear among the flowers
Tangled against the wall in secret bowers,
And cricket now begins to hum the hours
Remaining to the passion's slow procession
Down from the high place and the golden session
Wherein the sun was sacrificed for us.
A failing light, no longer numinous,
Now frames the long and solemn afternoons
Where butterflies regret their closed cocoons.
We reach the place unripe, and made to know
As with a sudden knowledge that we go
Away forever, all hope of return
Cut off, hearing the crackle of the burn-
ing blade behind us, and the terminal sound
Of apples dropping on the dry ground.

Two Girls

I saw again in a dream the other night
Something I saw in daylight years ago,
A path in the rainy woods, a shaft of light,

And two girls walking together through shadow,
Through dazzle, till I lost them on their way
In gloom embowering beyond the glade.
The bright oblivion that belongs to day
Covered their steps, nothing of them remained,
Until the darkness brought them forth again
To the rainy glitter and the silver light,
The ancient leaves that had not fallen then.
Two girls, going forever out of sight,
Talking of lovers, maybe, and of love:
Not that blind life they'd be the mothers of.

FROM
Gnomes and Occasions
(1973)

Lines & Circularities

on hearing Casals' recording of the Sixth Suite

Deep in a time that cannot come again
Bach thought it through, this lonely and immense
Reflexion wherein our sorrows learn to dance.
And deep in the time that cannot come again
Casals recorded it. Playing it back,
And bending now over the instrument,
I watch the circling stillness of the disc,
The tracking inward of the tone-arm, enact
A mystery wherein the music shares:
How time, that comes and goes and vanishes
Never to come again, can come again.

How many silly miracles there are
That will not save us, neither will they save
The world, and yet they are miraculous:
The tone-arm following the spiral path
While moving inward on a shallow arc,
Making the music that companions it
Through winding ways to silence at the close;
The delicate needle that navigates these canyons
By contact with the edges, not the floor;
Black plastic that has memorized and kept
In its small striations whatever it was told

By the master's mind and hand and bow and box,
Making such definite shudderings in the air
That Bach's intent arises from the tomb . . .
The Earth, that spins around upon herself
In the simple composition of Light and Dark,
And varying her distance on the Sun
Makes up the Seasons and the Years, and Time
Itself, whereof the angels make record;
The Sun, swinging his several satellites
Around himself and slowly round the vast
Galactic rim and out to the unknown
Past Vega at the apex of his path;
And all this in the inward of the mind,
Where the great cantor sings his songs to God . . .

The music dances to its inner edge
And stops. The tone-arm lifts and cocks its head
An instant, as if listening for something
That is no longer there but might be; then
Returns to rest, as with a definite click
The whole strange business turns itself off.

The Tapestry

On this side of the tapestry
There sits the bearded king,
And round about him stand
His lords and ladies in a ring.
His hunting dogs are there,
And armed men at command.

On that side of the tapestry
The formal court is gone,
The kingdom is unknown;
Nothing but thread to see,
Knotted and rooted thread
Spelling a world unsaid.

Men do not find their ways
Through a seamless maze,
And all direction lose
In a labyrinth of clues,
A forest of loose ends
Where sewing never mends.

September, the First Day of School

I

My child and I hold hands on the way to school,
And when I leave him at the first-grade door
He cries a little but is brave; he does
Let go. My selfish tears remind me how
I cried before that door a life ago.
I may have had a hard time letting go.

Each fall the children must endure together
What every child also endures alone:
Learning the alphabet, the integers,
Three dozen bits and pieces of a stuff
So arbitrary, so peremptory,
That worlds invisible and visible

Bow down before it, as in Joseph's dream
The sheaves bowed down and then the stars bowed down
Before the dreaming of a little boy.
That dream got him such hatred of his brothers
As cost the greater part of life to mend,
And yet great kindness came of it in the end.

II

A school is where they grind the grain of thought,
And grind the children who must mind the thought.
It may be those two grindings are but one,
As from the alphabet come Shakespeare's Plays,
As from the integers comes Euler's Law,
As from the whole, inseparably, the lives,

The shrunken lives that have not been set free
By law or by poetic phantasy.
But may they be. My child has disappeared
Behind the schoolroom door. And should I live
To see his coming forth, a life away,
I know my hope, but do not know its form

Nor hope to know it. May the fathers he finds
Among his teachers have a care of him
More than his father could. How that will look
I do not know, I do not need to know.
Even our tears belong to ritual.
But may great kindness come of it in the end.

To D____, Dead by Her Own Hand

My dear, I wonder if before the end
You ever thought about a children's game—
I'm sure you must have played it too—in which
You ran along a narrow garden wall
Pretending it to be a mountain ledge
So steep a snowy darkness fell away
On either side to deeps invisible;
And when you felt your balance being lost
You jumped because you feared to fall, and thought
For only an instant: That was when I died.

That was a life ago. And now you've gone,
Who would no longer play the grown-ups' game
Where, balanced on the ledge above the dark,
You go on running and you don't look down,
Nor ever jump because you fear to fall.

The Painter Dreaming in the Scholar's House

in memory of the painters Paul Klee
and Paul Terence Feeley

I

The painter's eye follows relation out.
His work is not to paint the visible,
He says, it is to render visible.

Being a man, and not a god, he stands
Already in a world of sense, from which
He borrows, to begin with, mental things
Chiefly, the abstract elements of language:
The point, the line, the plane, the colors and
The geometric shapes. Of these he spins
Relation out, he weaves its fabric up
So that it speaks darkly, as music does
Singing the secret history of the mind.
And when in this the visible world appears,
As it does do, mountain, flower, cloud, and tree,
All haunted here and there with the human face,
It happens as by accident, although
The accident is of design. It is because
Language first rises from the speechless world
That the painterly intelligence
Can say correctly that he makes his world,
Not imitates the one before his eyes.
Hence the delightsome gardens, the dark shores,
The terrifying forests where nightfall
Enfolds a lost and tired traveler.

And hence the careless crowd deludes itself
By likening his hieroglyphic signs
And secret alphabets to the drawing of a child.
That likeness is significant the other side
Of what they see, for his simplicities
Are not the first ones, but the furthest ones,
Final refinements of his thought made visible.
He is the painter of the human mind

Finding and faithfully reflecting the mindfulness
That is in things, and not the things themselves.

For such a man, art is an act of faith:
Prayer the study of it, as Blake says,
And praise the practice; nor does he divide
Making from teaching, or from theory.
The three are one, and in his hours of art
There shines a happiness through darkest themes,
As though spirit and sense were not at odds.

II

The painter as an allegory of the mind
At genesis. He takes a burlap bag,
Tears it open and tacks it on a stretcher.
He paints it black because, as he has said,
Everything looks different on black.

Suppose the burlap bag to be the universe,
And black because its volume is the void
Before the stars were. At the painter's hand
Volume becomes one-sidedly a surface,
And all his depths are on the face of it.

Against this flat abyss, this groundless ground
Of zero thickness stretched against the cold
Dark silence of the Absolutely Not,
Material worlds arise, the colored earths
And oil of plants that imitate the light.

They imitate the light that is in thought,
For the mind relates to thinking as the eye
Relates to light. Only because the world
Already is a language can the painter speak
According to his grammar of the ground.

It is archaic speech, that has not yet
Divided out its cadences in words;
It is a language for the oldest spells
About how some thoughts rose into the mind
While others, stranger still, sleep in the world.

So grows the garden green, the sun vermilion.
He sees the rose flame up and fade and fall
And be the same rose still, the radiant in red.
He paints his language, and his language is
The theory of what the painter thinks.

III

The painter's eye attends to death and birth
Together, seeing a single energy
Momently manifest in every form,
As in the tree the growing of the tree
Exploding from the seed not more nor less
Than from the void condensing down and in,
Summoning sun and rain. He views the tree,
The great tree standing in the garden, say,
As thrusting downward its vast spread and weight,
Growing its green height from dark watered earth,
And as suspended weightless in the sky,
Haled forth and held up by the hair of its head.
He follows through the flowing of the forms
From the divisions of the trunk out to
The veinings of the leaf, and the leaf's fall.
His pencil meditates the many in the one
After the method in the confluence of rivers,
The running of ravines on mountainsides,
And in the deltas of the nerves; he sees
How things must be continuous with themselves
As with whole worlds that they themselves are not,
In order that they may be so transformed.
He stands where the eternity of thought
Opens upon perspective time and space;
He watches mind become incarnate; then
                    He paints the tree.

IV

These thoughts have chiefly been about the painter Klee,
About how he in our hard time might stand to us
Especially whose lives concern themselves with learning

As patron of the practical intelligence of art,
And thence as model, modest and humorous in sufferings,
For all research that follows spirit where it goes.

That there should be much goodness in the world,
Much kindness and intelligence, candor and charm,
And that it all goes down in the dust after a while,
This is a subject for the steadiest meditations
Of the heart and mind, as for the tears
That clarify the eye toward charity.

So may it be to all of us, that at some times
In this bad time when faith in study seems to fail,
And when impatience in the street and still despair at home
Divide the mind to rule it, there shall some comfort come
From the remembrance of so deep and clear a life as his
Whom I have thought of, for the wholeness of his mind,
As the painter dreaming in the scholar's house,
His dream an emblem to us of the life of thought,
The same dream that then flared before intelligence
When light first went forth looking for the eye.

Myth & Ritual

You come down to a time
In every poker game
Where the losers allow
They've lost, the winners begin
Sneaking into their shoes
Under the covered table;
You come down to that time,

They all go home. And hard
As it is to imagine
A fat and rowdy ghost
Pee in his empty glass
So as not to miss a hand,
That's how it happens; Paul
Is gone, and Stanley is gone,

The winners have risen with cash
And checks and promising papers
And drifted through the cold door
Forever, while the host,
Like some somnambulist
Or sleepy priest, empties
Their ashes into the dawn.

The Rent in the Screen

to Loren Eiseley

Sweet mildness of the late December day
Deceives into the world a couple of hundred
Cinnamon moths, whose cryptic arrow shapes
Cling sleeping to a southward-facing wall
All through the golden afternoon, till dusk
And coming cold arouse them to their flight
Across the gulf of night and nothingness,
The falling snow, the fall, the fallen snow,
World whitened to dark ends. How brief a dream.

FROM
The Western Approaches
(1975)

Fugue

You see them vanish in their speeding cars,
The many people hastening through the world,
And wonder what they would have done before
This time of time speed distance, random streams
Of molecules hastened by what rising heat?
Was there never a world where people just sat still?

Yet they might be all of them contemplatives
Of a timeless now, drivers and passengers
In the moving cars all facing to the front
Which is the future, which is destiny,
Which is desire and desire's end—
What are they doing but just sitting still?

And still at speed they fly away, as still
As the road paid out beneath them as it flows
Moment by moment into the mirrored past;
They spread in their wake the parading fields of food,
The windowless works where who is making what,
The grey towns where the wishes and the fears are done.

The Western Approaches

As long as we look forward, all seems free,
Uncertain, subject to the Laws of Chance,
Though strange that chance should lie subject to laws,
But looking back on life it is as if
Our Book of Changes never let us change.

Stories already told a time ago
Were waiting for us down the road, our lives
But filled them out; and dreams about the past
Show us the world is post meridian
With little future left to dream about.

Old stories none but scholars seem to tell
Among us any more, they hide the ways,
Old tales less comprehensible than life
Whence nonetheless we know the things we do
And do the things they say the fathers did.

When I was young I flew past Skerryvore
Where the Nine Maidens still grind Hamlet's meal,
The salt and granite grain of bitter earth,
But knew it not for twenty years and more.
My chances past their changes now, I know

How a long life grows ghostly towards the close
As any man dissolves in Everyman
Of whom the story, as it always did, begins
In a far country, once upon a time,
There lived a certain man and he had three sons . . .

The Dependencies

This morning, between two branches of a tree
Beside the door, epeira once again
Has spun and signed his tapestry and trap.
I test his early-warning system and
It works, he scrambles forth in sable with

The yellow hieroglyph that no one knows
The meaning of. And I remember now
How yesterday at dusk the nighthawks came
Back as they do about this time each year,
Grey squadrons with the slashes white on wings
Cruising for bugs beneath the bellied cloud.
Now soon the monarchs will be drifting south,
And then the geese will go, and then one day
The little garden birds will not be here.
See how many leaves already have
Withered and turned; a few have fallen, too.
Change is continuous on the seamless web,
Yet moments come like this one, when you feel
Upon your heart a signal to attend
The definite announcement of an end
Where one thing ceases and another starts;
When like the spider waiting on the web
You know the intricate dependencies
Spreading in secret through the fabric vast
Of heaven and earth, sending their messages
Ciphered in chemistry to all the kinds,
The whisper down the bloodstream: it is time.

Again

Again, great season, sing it through again
Before we fall asleep, sing the slow change
That makes October burn out red and gold
And color bleed into the world and die,
And butterflies among the fluttering leaves
Disguise themselves until the few last leaves
Spin to the ground or to the skimming streams
That carry them along until they sink,
And through the muted land, the nevergreen
Needles and mull and duff of the forest floor,
The wind go ashen, till one afternoon
The cold snow cloud comes down the intervale

Above the river on whose slow black flood
The few first flakes come hurrying in to drown.

The Consent

Late in November, on a single night
Not even near to freezing, the ginkgo trees
That stand along the walk drop all their leaves
In one consent, and neither to rain nor to wind
But as though to time alone: the golden and green
Leaves litter the lawn today, that yesterday
Had spread aloft their fluttering fans of light.

What signal from the stars? What senses took it in?
What in those wooden motives so decided
To strike their leaves, to down their leaves,
Rebellion or surrender? and if this
Can happen thus, what race shall be exempt?
What use to learn the lessons taught by time,
If a star at any time may tell us: *Now*.

FROM
Sentences
(1980)

The Makers

Who can remember back to the first poets,
The greatest ones, greater even than Orpheus?
No one has remembered that far back
Or now considers, among the artifacts
And bones and cantilevered inference
The past is made of, those first and greatest poets,
So lofty and disdainful of renown
They left us not a name to know them by.

They were the ones that in whatever tongue
Worded the world, that were the first to say
Star, water, stone, that said the visible
And made it bring invisibles to view
In wind and time and change, and in the mind
Itself that minded the hitherto idiot world
And spoke the speechless world and sang the towers
Of the city into the astonished sky.

They were the first great listeners, attuned
To interval, relationship, and scale,
The first to say above, beneath, beyond,
Conjurors with love, death, sleep, with bread and wine,
Who having uttered vanished from the world
Leaving no memory but the marvelous
Magical elements, the breathing shapes
And stops of breath we build our Babels of.

Walking the Dog

Two universes mosey down the street
Connected by love and a leash and nothing else.
Mostly I look at lamplight through the leaves
While he mooches along with tail up and snout down,
Getting a secret knowledge through the nose
Almost entirely hidden from my sight.

We stand while he's enraptured by a bush
Till I can't stand our standing any more
And haul him off; for our relationship
Is patience balancing to this side tug
And that side drag; a pair of symbionts
Contented not to think each other's thoughts.

What else we have in common's what he taught,
Our interest in shit. We know its every state
From steaming fresh through stink to nature's way
Of sluicing it downstreet dissolved in rain
Or drying it to dust that blows away.
We move along the street inspecting shit.

His sense of it is keener far than mine,
And only when he finds the place precise
He signifies by sniffing urgently
And circles thrice about, and squats, and shits,
Whereon we both with dignity walk home
And just to show who's master I write the poem.

FROM
Inside the
Onion
(1984)

At the Tomb of the Unknown Celebrity

You see how strange it is about the soul,
Hardly a one among the lot of us
Who witnessed his eccentric visit thought
Of him as anything other than he seemed,
Borne to us across an emptiness of space
And evanescing into it again
After the light went out, the lights went up,
Leaving us swept with empty empathy.

But now it turns out that he had a soul,
Or was one, dead in the middle of the way
Exactly, gone from the now here to the no where,
The undercover agent loved by us all
As by us all unknown, a stranger in
The unsuspected skin, his actor's art
Perfected to vanishing in the alien part.

Wintering

A prism hung in a window to the south
Spangles the room, the kitchen, the hall beyond,
With rainbows from the time of Orion's rise

Until the sun climbs up so high in May
His angle gets too thin to manage anything
More than a splinter of spectrum on the floor
Beneath the sill; but who needs rainbows then,
With the sun his radiant self all summer long?

No diamond from deep earth could celebrate
So well our long engagement with the world
As faceted glass dangled against the pane
To swing advantage from the sun's long swing
Low through the darkness and the burning cold
Until, sweet chariot, he brings us up
Again, poking the crocus through the snow
Again, and once more turns might into may.

This Present Past

The tulip's cup falls open helplessly,
The redbud's petals are already dust,
The trees are dropping all their various dreck
Pertaining to generation; once again
The spring has gone, as we complain it does
Year after year, before we had the time
To take it in.
               But brief as flowering
Has always been, our power to attend
Is briefer by far, and intermittent, too.
We look at the iris, say how beautiful,
And look no more, nor watch the fail and fall
Of its bruised flags. So runs the world away,
As blown about upon the rainy wind
The keys of the maple's kingdom copter down.

Adam and Eve in Later Life

On getting out of bed the one says, "Ouch!"
The other "What?" and when the one says "I said
'Ouch,'" the other says "All right, you needn't shout."

Deucalion and Pyrrha, Darby and Joan, Philemon and Baucis,
Tracy and Hepburn—if this can happen to Hepburn
No one is safe—all rolled up into two,
Contented with the cottage and the cottage cheese
And envied only by ambitious gods . . .

Later, over coffee, they compare the backs of their hands
And conclude they are slowly being turned into lizards.
But nothing much surprises them these days.

FROM
War Stories:
Poems About
Long Ago
and Now
(1987)

On an Occasion of National Mourning

It is admittedly difficult for a whole
Nation to mourn and be seen to do so, but
It can be done, the silvery platitudes
Were waiting in their silos for just such
An emergent occasion, cards of sympathy
From heads of state were long ago prepared
For launching and are bounced around the world
From satellites at near the speed of light,
The divine services are telecast
From the home towns, children are interviewed
And say politely, gravely, how sorry they are,

And in a week or so the thing is done,
The sea gives up its bits and pieces and
The investigating board pinpoints the cause
By inspecting bits and pieces, nothing of the sort
Can ever happen again, the prescribed course
Of tragedy is run through omen to amen
As in a play, the nation rises again
Reborn of grief and ready to seek the stars;
Remembering the shuttle, forgetting the loom.

Models

1.

The boy of twelve, shaping a fuselage
Of balsa wood so easy to be sliced
Along the grain but likely to get crushed
Under the razor when it was cut across;

Sanding the parts, gluing and lacquering
And pasting on the crosses and the rings
The brave identities of Fokker and Spad
That fought, only a little before his birth,

That primitive, original war in the air
He made in miniature and flew by hand
In clumsy combat, simulated buzz:
A decade away from being there himself.

2.

The fuselage in the factory was aligned on North
So that the molecules lay along the axis,
Or so they said, to make the compass read
A right magnetic course; and after an attack

You headed the aircraft to what you hoped was North
And fired one more burst at the empty night
To set the shaken compass true again:
It straightened the molecules, or so they said.

The broken circle with the centered cross
Projecting the image at infinity
Quivered before him in the vacant air
Till it lay on the target like a haloing light.

3.

And memory, that makes things miniature
And far away, and fit size for the mind,
Returned him in the form of images
The size of flies, his doings in those days

With theirs, the heroes that came out of the sun
To invent the avant-garde war of the air—
Richtofen, Rickenbacker, and the rest—
Where if you were shot it would be in the back,

Where the survivors, by their likenesses
Before and after, aged decades in a year,
Cruel-mouthed and harsh, and thought the young recruit
Not worth their welcome, as unlike to last.

More Joy in Heaven

This bird that a cat sprang loose in the house,
Still flyably warm and wet from the cat's mouth,
Beat like a heart set fluttering with fear;
The bird's heart first, but ours beat after it.

Some comedy came of this, the saner sort
Opening doors, the others batting at cats
With brooms, or flying towels at the bird
To muffle it safe from enemy and self;

Who after getting confused among the drapes
And flopping back from a window, from a wall,
Found out the empty daylight of a door
Left open, and left, thinking the good thoughts

It would tell its children in our children's books
About an ultimate kindness to the world
Where once, in a legend of the Golden Age,
One ecosystem beat the other, once.

The Shadow Side

The evening sunlight coming down the meadow
And slanting through the window strikes to light
A silver service that her father sent

Down from the Enlightenment and across the sea
To cast its complicities of light and shadow
On the white wall in halo and silhouette.

Some things remain the same, the silver bowls
And swan-necked coffee urn with the fluted sides,
But shift their shapes now as their shadows pass
Along the wall, while evening on the meadow
And evening in the room make indistinct
The silver highlights sinking into gloom

Until it is full night and the new-made widow
Remains unmoved and dark and derelict
In the museum of wreckage and regret
Left of a life subjected to earth's shadow.

PREVIOUSLY UNCOLLECTED

Larkin

Imagine Larkin going among the dead,
Not yet at home there, as he wasn't here,
And doing them the way he did *The Old Fools*,
With edged contempt becoming sympathy
Of a sort, and sympathy contempt for death.

It's a quirky spirit he carried through the arch
To aftertime, making a salted fun
Of the holy show and grudging his respect
For all but truth, the master of a style
Able to see things as he saw through things.

He was our modern; in his attitude,
And not in all that crap about free verse.
He understood us, not as we would be
Understood in smartass critical remarks,
But as we are when we stand in our shoes and say.

Our Roman, too; he might not have cared to be,
But what I mean is this: you wander through
The galleries entranced with shepherdess and nymph,
The marble or alabaster faery and fay,
Then suddenly you come on him, the stone

Of his face scored up and scarred with the defeat
An honorable life has brought him to,
And know that backing up the tales we tell

Is mortal this, the what-it's-all-about,
So that you turn away, the lesson told,

That's it. Dear Warlock-Williams, might you weep?
The penetrative emptiness of that gaze
Kindly accusing none, forgiving none,
Is just the look upon the face of truth,
Mortality knowing itself as told to do,

And death the familiar comes as no surprise —
"Ah, Warlock-Williams, are you here as well?"
With Auden, with Hardy, with the other great and dead,
Dear Larkin of the anastrophic mind,
Forever now among the undeceived.

Trying Conclusions

I

There is a punishment too smart for Hell,
And it is this: some people here on earth
Have been so hot at prayer that when they come
At last to bliss eternal they cannot stop
Blessing, beseeching, praising His Holy Name.

They would spend eternity hunkered on their knees
Without a cushion, save that the Infinite
Of his wisdom and mercy pities them in the end.
They are the ones He will send to be born again.

II

What rational being, after seventy years,
When Scripture says he's running out of rope,
Would want more of the only world he knows?

No rational being, he while he endures
Holds on to the inveterate infantile hope
That the road ends but as the runway does.

II.
SHORT
STORIES

FROM
A Commodity
of Dreams and
Other Stories
(1959)

Yore

Over the lavish *Forgeterie* of the Beauldvoir Hotel rose the bone-china moon, rubbing all things to a hard beauty that looked permanent. Tomorrow would be the war, and everywhere in the hotel people accordingly rose and fell in value; meanwhile here was the moon swinging over the lovely gardens and the pool.

Alone at a marble-topped table, Mr. Luc le Mesurier bent his ancient head, baldness tipped in moonlight, toward the small ivory radio which murmuringly kept him company; from time to time he drew out of his coattail and consulted his memorandum book, a thin, tall volume bound in calfskin. Here with a gold pencil he made a note now and again, or placed a mark against the name of some acquaintance, or crossed off a name entirely; then with a slight contortion and a sigh he would turn to slip the book back into the tail of his coat, but always a remark made by the radio could cause him to get it out again almost at once.

Mr. Luc le Mesurier was a lean, elegant old gentleman, whose subtly gleaming black and white clothes fitted him like a second skin; when he arose, as he now did to welcome his expected companions, the tails of his coat curled slightly but deftly up and back as though they belonged to his own muscular arrangements. The

61

dark tan of his face left off at the brow, for on bright days at the Beauldvoir Beach he was accustomed to wear, besides a black loincloth, a skullcap against the sun, and for this reason he looked, as he bowed and nodded, like an old priest or haloed saint.

After turning off the radio he drew out a chair for Mme. Mastaba, who with care placed her enormous backside between its arms and pressed down. The black sequins of her dress writhed with moonlight as, emplaced, she shook herself into comfort. Mr. Aiken Drum, the American millionaire, sat beside her and opposite to the place which Mr. le Mesurier now resumed. Mr. Aiken Drum was a large shaggy man with a full head of gray hair, rather unkempt. In this company Mr. le Mesurier resembled a whangee cane placed on exhibition, beside a knobkerrie stick and a pillow—an exhibition, perhaps, in a black museum, of instruments employed in the commission of long-forgotten crimes.

"It is hard to believe," said Mr. Aiken Drum, "but it has happened at last."

"It was bound to come sooner or later," said Mr. le Mesurier. "I suppose none of you knows where Great Coco is? This is something the announcer has neglected to inform us of so far."

"It will be very quickly over," averred Mme. Mastaba. "Atom bombs, hydrogen bombs, very quickly over."

"No, no, this will not be very quickly over," said Mr. Aiken Drum somberly enough yet with a certain tone of pride. "It will be a long, bitter struggle. At least," he added, "we have seen my daughter married before it began."

Felicia Drum had been wed that very afternoon to Layamon Brute, Marquess of Yore; the Bishop of Norfolk had been flown in to preside. It was now in the interval between the service and the wedding supper that the three elderly friends had gathered in the *Forgeterie,* at a table beside the pool.

"She does not love him, poor thing," said Mme. Mastaba. "A great shame."

"Well, no," replied Mr. Drum. "But she is a good girl, is Felicia, and knows that first things come first."

"He will perish in this war," said Mr. le Mesurier.

"Well," said Mr. Drum, spreading wide his hands, "that of course can't be helped." He snuffled slightly, and brushed the end of his nose with delicacy on the back of his wrist. "They will be down in a few minutes. Let us be cheerful."

A waiter now took their orders. Mr. le Mesurier had been drinking a wine which he persuaded the others to try, a very fine wine expressed from seaweed, tasting something like iodine, dry, reddish-brown and puckering. As an afterthought, he instructed the waiter to find out where in the world was Great Coco.

"It will doubtless be an island," he said, "for the announcer speaks of 'the air base *on* Great Coco.'"

"Who would have thought," said Mme. Mastaba, "we should have lived to see the day when we had to feel responsible for an air base on Great Coco?"

"But reality is always improbable," observed Mr. le Mesurier.

Great Coco, the waiter told them, was in the Bay of Bengal.

"I am scarcely any the wiser for that," said Mme. Mastaba.

Mr. le Mesurier suddenly snapped on the radio again. After a silent moment they heard a chorus of young voices repeating the Hail Mary over and over again with the swaying emphasis of a roller coaster which takes a deep breath at the top of its initial climb, then rushes downward.

"No news as yet," said Mr. le Mesurier, turning the radio off.

"But that is more frightening than anything I have heard so far," said Mme. Mastaba. "During the First World War I was at the School of the Sacred Heart in Grenoble."

"I really cannot understand," said Mr. Aiken Drum, "why man cannot learn to live at peace with his fellow man."

"It is possibly because, my dear," returned Mme. Mastaba, "man living at peace with his fellow man would use considerably less oil than he will have to use under the present circumstances."

"My dear Andrea," said Mr. Aiken Drum in a dignified manner, "I did not want this war to happen."

With a slight wiggling motion Mr. le Mesurier now reached around to his coattail and drew forth his memorandum book.

"I was reflecting before you came," he said, "on where in the world one might go next. Doubtless everything will be destroyed in a few weeks, or the hotels will have no food and the servants will have been conscripted. Tananarive, possibly? But there will of course be an air base there as well. Mukalla? Porto Alegre? Toby

Lustig has a small inn at Misurata, but will it still be there? And will any sort of transport be available? On the other hand—Kristiansund? Or a farm near Stornoway? Ireland may be neutral; a visit with Salvadi at Castlebar? I fear life will not be made easy for the traveler."

"I shall go to my cousin at Denderah," said Mme. Mastaba. "No one ever bothers with the Upper Nile."

"And I return to the States tomorrow," said Mr. Drum. "Not exotic, but quite safe if one stays far from the cities. You are both invited. It is the children I am worried about."

"They will be evacuated, poor things, in droves," said Mme. Mastaba.

"It was my children I meant," said Mr. Drum. "Felicia and Layamon."

"She will go to Yore, I suppose," said Mr. le Mesurier, "and he to join his squadron."

"But they are coming in now," said Mme. Mastaba, raising her massive white head and peering toward the entrance.

2

Over the black water of the pool, moon-whitened in rippled streaks, an orchestra hidden in an island grove began to play The Wedding March. Felicia Drum advanced on the arm of her new husband the Marquess of Yore, the pair of them preceded by a small headwaiter who continually turned toward them to bow as he directed their path to the table. The girl, though she had put aside her white veil, still wore the wedding dress of white satin and a white cap of the same material. She looked pale and sullen, but charming. Layamon Brute wore the somewhat Germanic-looking blue dress uniform of the Royal Air Force, with embroidered silver wings on the breast, three equal stripes of a Wing Commander on each sleeve, and upon his head the dully gleaming helmet with its high, horsehair crest, under which his thin, ruddy, pleasant face with its small red mustache did not appear especially adequate. A saber in scabbard swung at his side. Amid applause from the many guests at the tables beside the pool the bridal couple were seated with their elders just as the March came to an end.

"Exactly like a chamber pot," said Layamon of his helmet, which he took off now and placed in the center of the table.

"It does form a strange costume for an aviator," observed Mme. Mastaba. "I thought they wore something more *sportif.*"

"I am afraid," said Mr. Aiken Drum, "that this war will not much be a wedding present for you two." He shook his head seriously, and Felicia, who at seventeen remained very uncertain about the great world, considered for a moment the idea that her father had really arranged the war with the object of giving her pleasure, and that he now rather regretted having gone to all that trouble. Under the fleeting influence of this notion she smiled brightly at him, to show appreciation.

"It can't be helped, sir," said Layamon quietly. "Felicia will stay with Mother at Yore. I shall pack off to my Group as soon as we get back." He looked tenderly at his bride. "Not much of a show for you, my dear," he said.

Felicia looked back with an appearance of equal tenderness and leaned over to whisper something in his ear. What she whispered was "You know what you can do with your stiff upper lip," but the others, unable to hear, interpreted the Marquess's sudden rigidity of expression as pleased surprise. After a moment he whispered back in her ear, pushing aside with his nose her brown hair, "I shall die in this war. You won't be troubled with me for very long." To which Felicia replied aloud, and with a slight smile, "We can't help that, can we?" It seemed to her that she was being unnecessarily cruel, but apart from having been both annoyed and fatigued by the long ceremony, she felt quite bewildered about the nature of the feelings that would henceforth, it seemed, be officially demanded of her. She had seen in the *Tatler* pictures of Yore, towering and ancient amid great trees, and it seemed to her that in order to live up to such a possession she would have to be somewhat haughty, inscrutable, full of cold, cryptic sentences and surprised at nothing, like a great lady in the movies. It was also true that she did not love her husband, but this was only because she did not know from any personal experience what love was, and also perhaps because he failed to frighten her, even when wearing the helmet with the horsehair crest.

A waiter brought more wine, the delicious, bitter wine from

seaweed. Mr. le Mesurier turned on the radio again, and now an announcer was describing in a tense, professionally anxious voice the preparations for reprisal that were going on all over the world: the battleships and carriers getting up steam at Guam and Pearl and Scapa Flow; the huge aircraft engines beginning to turn on the runways at Reykjavik and Disco and Yell and distant Thule; vast, uneasy populations beginning to move through the Balkans, through Turkey, through India; the air of the world laced with radio messages; the President of the United States would speak to Congress.

"The King of Thule," said Mme. Mastaba. "We used to sing that song at school. There was a golden cup, a silver cup?"

"This is the century of dreams come true, is it not?" Mr. le Mesurier with doubtful relevance observed.

London and Paris, the announcer said, were under attack from the air. There was no news from these places, there was radio silence from these places.

"What a strange phrase," said Felicia, "as though *radio silence* were more golden than other kinds."

"It is a technical term," said the Marquess.

"A technical term," said Mr. le Mesurier, "meaning silence."

"But look," said Mr. Aiken Drum, suddenly reaching out and turning off the radio, "the floor show is about to begin."

"Now there is radio silence indeed," said Mme. Mastaba.

Across the water the orchestra had begun to play once again, a brilliant fanfare followed by a dreamy, muted tune.

"It can hardly be a *floor* show," said Felicia, "unless the performers walk on water, which I understand is not done even in the century of dreams come true."

"My dear girl," her father replied, "you do not know everything about the world as yet."

While he spoke the music became louder, and gradually the depths of the pool beside them began to glow increasingly with light. Soon the reflections of the moon, and the black surface itself, disappeared from view and were replaced by a softly brilliant fairy-land of coral castles and coral foliage underwater. Small, brightly striped fish swam slowly about, and there was even the submerged hull of a ship, with broken masts and tattered rigging, half sunken in sand covered with waving green moss. It was altogether a beau-

tiful and strange sight, which Felicia had certainly not been expecting, and it made her feel for a moment privileged to mystery.

"It is a floor show of the ocean floor," said Mme. Mastaba.
"They have it only here, at the Beauldvoir. I have seen it many
times. It is very beautiful."

3

Now through the softly radiant water, from the doorway of a
distant castle, came swimming a dozen mermaids, naked and
white as pearls. They moved effortlessly forward with sinuous
twistings of their tails, and soon formed into a circle, around
which they swam for some minutes.

"How do they stay under so long?" asked Felicia.

"They are said to be perfectly real mermaids," Mme. Mastaba
replied, "imported from the Seychelles Islands. Only here do they
have them. Nowhere else in the world."

"At the Beauldvoir you know you are getting the real thing,
expensive as it is," said Mr. Aiken Drum.

"All the same," Mr. le Mesurier said, "I am inclined to think
they are not real. Rather, the legs of those girls have been slipped
into the hinder skins, the tails, you understand, of very large fish—
glued there, you know."

"Ugh," said Felicia.

"But how, in that case, do they stay under for so long?" asked the
Marquess. "Unless of course it is a trick," he added, anxious not to
appear naïve.

"Ah," said Mr. le Mesurier, "that I cannot tell you."

"I will tell you," said Mme. Mastaba with a certain emphasis.
"It is because they are real mermaids, imported." She frowned at
Mr. Luc le Mesurier. "You men," she said disdainfully.

"But there are no such things as mermaids," said Felicia petu-
lantly, feeling nevertheless as though she were betraying her whole
sex for nothing more than a cheap rationalistic idea picked up at
school.

"There are these mermaids," replied Mme. Mastaba.

"There are more things in heaven and earth, Horatio, than are
dreamed of in your philosophy," said Mr. Aiken Drum.

"Horatio?" inquired Mme. Mastaba.

At this moment the music left off, and a galleonlike ship, man-
ned in statuesque poses by a crew of perhaps a dozen men, moved
slowly from behind the orchestra's island into the center of the
pool; the spectators could see for an instant the outstretched hands
of a number of waiters, porters and bellhops who must have given
it a strong push. This ship came to a stop on the still water, its
paper sails billowed out as though with a stiff breeze. One could
see it wholly, down to the keel, seeming to hang in a medium
scarcely existing, so clear and smooth the water; and down below
the mermaids slowly swam about.

Now in the silence there broke forth the sound of a number of
pianos dispersed around the place, a loud, confused rumbling and
tinkling and clanging; and a blond young man climbed to the high
poop of the vessel, placed one hand over his heart and, in the crook
of the elbow thus formed, the golden crown he had been wearing.
So poised, he began half to sing and half to declaim a long recitative interwoven with passages of balladry, to which the pianos
formed a remote and intermittently allusive background. Because
of those pianos and because of the fact that the young man did not
sing extraordinarily well—he looked stupid, unhappy and rather
helpless despite his breastplate, crown, scepter and golden hair—
the group at the table did not easily distinguish at first what he was
singing about; Felicia thought possibly he sung in German or
some other foreign tongue. Presently, however, she got used to it,
and it became clear that he was a prince "from an island beyond
the foam" and that his wicked stepmother had prevailed with the
king his father to have him exiled. Not only this, but because of his
father's power no other nation would give him refuge, and in all
the wide world he had only this ship for home, to sail the seas with
till he died. His song was very lonely and sad even though he did
not sing well, and presently the mermaids themselves rose to the
surface and poked their heads through to listen. ("Ah," said the
Marquess with satisfaction, as though he had been holding his
own breath. "They are real nevertheless," said Mme. Mastaba.)

And now there came through the clear water from the coral
castle in the distance a new mermaid. This one wore, like the
young prince, a crown, and she too rose to the surface to hear his
song. Upon seeing this creature the young man became more passionate in his declamation; nowhere in the world, on land or at

sea, was there woman half so beautiful as she. He stretched forth his scepter, and in a burst of exalted and flourishing song declared that she alone must be his bride. The pianos rumbled loudly at this.

"He is quite Wagnerian, with his bare knees," said Mr. le Mesurier.

The mermaid princess now made her reply, singing in a voice cool and steady as a night wind off the water. She was indeed a beautiful woman, or mermaid, with very white skin and with long, black hair which even though wet curled in reptilian folds about her breasts and back. She would be his bride, she sang, but she could never leave the sea which was her home. She pitied his exile, but alas, they were doomed, the two of them, to eternal separation by the elements they breathed.

The young prince, hearing this, declared, still singing, that if he could not have her to wife the world held nothing more to please him—an exile and alone, condemned to sail forever across the seven seas. To have her love what might he better do than die, so be he died in her white arms? All this he sang in a voice which was evidently becoming somewhat distressed with fatigue.

The mermaid princess sternly yet perhaps a little coyly forbade him the death he so eloquently sought; while she sang she provocatively waved those white arms, making her breasts move just below the surface of the water. The hero, with an artificial vehemence and ferocity very convincing, insisted. She again imperiously denied. This went on, in the form of a duet, for some time.

"It is a little boring, *tout ce* Papageno-Papagena," said Mme. Mastaba, "but the spectacle is brilliant."

Felicia agreed. Charmed at first, she had very quickly become bored as the two lovers passed this theme back and forth between them, while the pianos went on like stones bouncing down a hill. The whole scene rapidly began to seem ridiculous, not least because the labored, healthy earnestness of the young man contrasted so unfavorably with the cool, queenly demeanor and effortless voice of the mermaid. Because she was bored, Felicia paid, finally, not much heed to the course of all these antics, and was in fact lighting a cigarette at just the moment when—with a theatrical scream of loving anguish and a somewhat awkward splash—the young prince cast away scepter and crown and leaped into the water, into the embrace of his mermaid sweetheart. And she? What did she do? Felicia was quite in time to see that she, her long white arms fixed firmly around her lover's middle, her silver tail flashing in one powerful turn and dive, dragged him away below. The audience, leaning over the edge of the pool, had a clear view of his silent writhings, kickings and strugglings, accompanied by chains of bubbles from the air in his clothing and one final chain of bubbles from the air in his lungs; after this—it had taken over a minute—he lay still at the entrance of the coral castle, until presently a cortege of mermaids swam down and carried him away, while on distant pianos empty octaves bounded angrily up and down their deserted, echoing stairwells. Then all was over, and the underwater light began to fade. It was oddly noticeable that scepter and crown, made of some light materials, still floated on the surface; but soon all was dark on the water, dark and opaque and resuming the reflection of the moonlight.

"So you see," said Mme. Mastaba, laughing, to the Marquess, "the mermaids were real, after all."

Felicia saw that her husband had got very red in the face. So he had not been expecting it either, she thought, and made herself smile as at some remote and secret thought.

"How did you like it, my dear?" inquired Mr. le Mesurier, putting his bony old hand upon hers. Felicia turned the smile in his direction.

"I thought it was quite sweet, really," she said, "but maybe just a little too long."

Mr. Aiken Drum coughed.

"It is doubtless on account of the expense," he said. "They prolong it deliberately, to make the most of the materials."

"I find it," said Mr. le Mesurier, "an ominously romantic conception. That is, after all, not the kind of world we live in today. It is more like—like this Valkyrie's headpiece," he added, indicating the Marquess's helmet with the horsehair crest.

"Ah, but there will always be romance," said Mme. Mastaba, profoundly sighing. "No matter what they do to the poor world, there will be romance."

"It is hard to believe," said Mr. Aiken Drum, "it is hard to believe that we are at war once again. Reality is harsh, after this fairyland." He gestured broadly toward the dark pool beside them.

"It cannot go on forever," said Mr. le Mesurier. "Before we know it we shall meet again, perhaps here in this very place."

"We are old," said Mme. Mastaba. "The world may never again be as we know it. But there will be romance for the young, will there not, Felicia?"

But Felicia had not heard. She sat very straight, with the smile of a great lady playing distantly upon her face, and was caught in a vision, wherein she saw her husband and herself, he wearing the helmet that lay there on the table, flying alone in the silent aircraft, high in the dark night, back to the stone towers and the stately trees of Yore. In her mind's eyes, then, she saw herself walking endlessly through silent corridors hung with portraits, and down the sweeping curve of a grand staircase, all in the silence. The silence continued, it seemed for years.

"What are you thinking, my dear?" asked the Marquess.

Abruptly Felicia came to the surface of her dream. "I was thinking," she said with a laugh both grand and gay, "that if there's anything in the world I love, it's reality."

And though the Marquess seemed confused for a moment, the elders laughed indulgently. Then they all had more of the bitter wine from seaweed.

A Commodity of Dreams

In a little black house in the woods the dreamer lived; and I met him when I was lost, hungry and ill tempered. But I still had wit enough about me to realize, as I rushed forward to ask directions, how odd it was that there should stand, before a little black cottage in the woods, a uniformed and armed personage, whose appearance suggested some combination of beadle, commissionaire and constable; he wore a black greatcoat with golden buttons, a leather belt from which hung, on one side, a great pistol, and on his head, incongruously, was a silk hat. He stood at ease, and did not actually change his posture as I came up, but seemed to grow slightly more tense and to take, with rapidly flickering eyes, a kind of professional survey of me, which finally fixed on the binoculars slung about my neck.

"Bird-watching," I said in explanation. "I've got lost. Perhaps you could direct me to the road." There was a silence, which lasted a few seconds until I got nervous enough to add, "Any road, of course," and to realize, as the silence settled back, how silly this must sound.

"Ah," he said finally, and, following with my eyes the slight turn of his head, I saw, a few yards off to the side of the cottage, a modern building of brick and concrete mostly sunken in the earth, like a hurricane cellar, or a bomb shelter. It occurred to me that I had come across some highly secret military installation or experimental center.

"Maybe," said the guard, who looked in the fading light to be an old, probably feeble man and had drooping white mustaches which made a pathetic assertion at the front of his somewhat shrunken face. "But you'd best come see the Master, all the same."

"Oh, that's not necessary at all," I said politely, struggling with a slight feeling of annoyance. "I'm sorry to have to bother you—" But I was talking to the empty doorway; he had gone inside. In a moment a lantern appeared in his place, and behind it, lighted

72

from below, a little, sandy man—not only with sandy hair, that is, but of a very light, pebble-grained appearance, washed out, desiccated, leached away by some receding torrent and left, it appeared, to crumble at his leisure. A scientist, certainly, was my thought, and this is some government work he has been put away here to do secretly.

"Come in, won't you," he said, and this phrase of peremptory hospitality left me no choice, for he turned away at once. As we went within, the old guardian of the place slipped by me and resumed his post.

"You'll have tea, of course," said the sandy man, leading the way with the lantern into a room otherwise lighted only by firelight. "I'll get another cup." And he vanished into some shadowy, low-ceilinged area beyond the fireplace.

"I've only come to ask my way," I called after him, but this explanation, and even the voice in which I offered it, sounded curiously weak in the silence and the gloom.

"We'll soon set you straight," came the reply out of the darkness. "I have to be careful, though, of course."

Careful? Of what? And yet, surely a military or government man would have said, as they always do, *we*—"*We* have to be careful."

My host now returned, carrying a cup and saucer of very delicate china, through which the firelight shone. We stood for a moment, then, as there seemed little else for it, sat down in opposed chairs, and regarded each other in the fire's light.

"Sugar? You're an American, you very likely don't take milk? Perhaps you don't even care for tea?"

"A cup of tea would be fine," I said. Looking more closely at the man, I found, in addition to his sandy quality of failure and debilitation, some effect of sharp cunning, of pertinaciousness, in his small, close-set features: little eyes, of an indistinguishable color, a small, pointy nose. "It's nice of you to take the trouble," I added, "but I've really got to be getting on right away."

As Englishmen so often do, he took no notice of what I said, but went right along on his own line with another question which was not a question but an assertion.

"You'll have been up seeing the waxwings. Pretty little things; I often watch them myself." And he handed me across a plate of little cakes.

"It'd be very strange, waxwings in March," I said with a smile. How shrewd the little man was. Doubly shrewd to choose waxwings; though they don't winter in Britain they should have sounded plausible to an American because they do winter far north in the United States. And triply shrewd to pass the cake at the same moment, as a distraction. And yet, since I had seen through it, by luck and an odd shred of information, it all looked pretty silly, too.

"And the mustached warbler," he went on, without returning my smile.

"Look," I said, "I am obviously a bona-fide bird-watcher, or I wouldn't have known about the waxwings. And now you've put me on my guard I am certainly not going to consent to any mustached warbler other than the one who stands outside your door. I don't know what it is you do up here, and I've no idea of pushing my way in to find out—in fact, though it is good of you to give me tea, I ask nothing better than to be shown off your property and on to a public highway just as soon as it can be arranged."

"That's all very well," he said in a kind of mean and aggrieved way. "We welcome legitimate visitors, you know, at the proper hours. There was no need to come up out of the woods at nightfall."

I repeated, tersely, to all this, that I had got lost, that I had explained myself once, twice and again. "And that should be enough," I concluded.

"Yes, I suppose so," he said, strangely disconsolate. And we sat there for a few minutes not knowing exactly what to say. I wanted to go, and I felt I ought to go; but there was no point in going without directions. Also I was tired, and the tea was welcome, and whatever the spirit might say the body was very unwilling to stir itself. For his part, he seemed to be going through some intricate calculation about me, outwardly signified by keen stares, shakings of the head, even slight mumblings into the teacup, until I decided he was simply wrong in the head.

"You Americans are very self-centered people, aren't you?" he finally came forth. "Egotistical, not very interested in others?"

"I am not very interested," I said, "in sentences beginning *You Americans*."

"You haven't even asked me what sort of place this is."

"If I had, you would most likely have said, 'You Americans are always sticking your noses in other people's business.' I assume," I added, "that whatever you've got in that bomb shelter outside is a military secret."

This seemed to please him, for he laughed. At least he tittered for such a time, and at so high a pitch, that it got on my nerves, and I said, "It must be depressing to have a military secret so ineffably dull that you can't persuade people to ask what it is." This stopped the tittering, all right. He looked very sad all of a sudden, and said, "Yes."

That *yes*, dull as it was, put a stop to conversation for the time being, except for his presently adding, "Not military, though," after which the silence again closed in. But it was enough, with the tea and the mystery, to get my attention; for if military secrets interested me not at all, civilian ones vastly did. I began to see that this middle-aged, dried-up, not superficially attractive person had a secret, whatever it was, for the one purpose only of revelation— what else are secrets good for?—and that, hidden away (for secrecy's sake!) up here in the forest, he must have but small audience, occasional and stray, whose want of curiosity would appear to him as a major disaster.

"I am, you see, a dreamer," he said at last, with a curious mixture in his tone of pride, apology and the most awful humiliation. "A dreamer," he repeated, somewhat more aggressively.

Did he mean a poet? an inventor? a mystic? hermit? Would he, when he led me (as he surely meant to do) into his brick workshop, show me an epic, a new cosmogony, the first flying machine, a plan to establish universal peace or predict the future?

"There's no reason why I shouldn't show you around," he said, and with evident effort brought himself to add, "If you like, that is."

"Oh, I really can't stay," I said, rising, for I was still annoyed at his absurdity and determined to show no interest whatever.

"It wouldn't take you but a few minutes," he said with a sad petulance, "but I suppose you're very busy . . ."

This attitude made me a little ashamed; I saw also something pleasingly silly in the spectacle of two grown men in a cottage in the woods at nightfall, one saying to the other, "I suppose you're very busy."

"It's not that I'm not interested," said I. "For a few minutes, maybe. It's really very kind of you."

He led, and I followed his lantern out the front door, where the old gentleman in the silk hat immovably stood. It was by now quite dark. The lantern stopped and swung about suddenly, and I bumped into my host, who merely said, "I'm sor—sorry, Mr. Uh?" while the lantern bobbed down and up as if he were bowing. So we exchanged names there in the dark; his was Captain Lastwyn. He even gave me his card, which I put in my pocket. When he turned again and held up the lantern, I saw, beside the doorway of the brick building, a black sign with gold letters which read:

Museum & Library
of
Dreams
WEEKDAYS 10-4   CLOSED SUNDAYS
ADMISSION 6D.

"It's all a trifle irregular, in your case," he said, "so we'll not trouble about the sixpence."

"Oh, no," I said, determined by now that every form of our little farce should be gone through with. "I insist on paying in the usual manner."

"Well, sir, you are very kind," he said, with embarrassing deference, in accepting the coin. The exchange of money, however, seemed to put us in a different, more manageable relation, and by the time he had opened the door of his cellar and we had descended into it, by the time he had switched on the light—there was electricity laid on here, though none had been evident in the cottage—and turned to address me, he had a new authority in his manner.

"Perhaps you'd care to sign the guest book?" leading me to a register on a deal table to one side. I signed, noting the last entry before mine to be dated three weeks before. It was, certainly, an odd spot for a museum.

"How very interesting," I said, insincerely, and for want of something to say. For so far as I could see, except for some pictures on the walls, two reading tables with chairs, and a long glass cabinet in the center of the room, the entire establishment consisted of filing cabinets, which neatly lined the walls and here and there jutted out into the room to form alcoves.

"Ah, well," he said, correctly interpreting the falsity in my tone, "it reveals itself, the museum does, only rather slowly. You'll scarcely have time to form an impression." Again he made me feel a little ashamed, for being caught sneering at his pathetic exhibition. "Perhaps you'd best start by having a look over here," he said, indicating the glass cabinet.

I went over and looked in. At the center was a neat typewritten card which read: "Objects and Facsimiles of Objects of Frequent or Striking Appearance in the Dreams of Capt. Frank Lastwyn, R.A. (ret.)." To both sides the "objects" were neatly mounted with pins and glue on a kind of gray cloth, very professional and museumlike in style. There was, for example, a little silver cup, rather bent, such as is given to parents at the birth of a child; there was a gull's feather; a snuffbox; a tiny crucifix on a golden chain; a woman's hat, very old and dirty; a horse's hoof; a table napkin comically knotted to resemble a rabbit; a schoolbook, a battered Greek primer open at a line drawing of two naked wrestlers; a stuffed woodcock with the beak missing. I moved around to the other side, and there were more objects: the cover of a golf ball, a dinner plate with a red, open-mouthed fish painted on it; a pair of gold spectacle rims with the glass broken out; a piece of rough rock and masonry with a hole in it; and a number of other things I can't remember.

"You've no idea the trouble I was put to getting some of these things," said my guide, who followed at my shoulder while I inspected the things. "That crucifix, there, belonged to a young lady—in my youth, you know. She died. And by the time I knew I needed that piece, of course, you know how it is—her family had moved, her brother was dead too, no one seemed to know where her younger sister had moved to or even what her name was—she had married, you see. But I persisted, and as it turned out she had the crucifix, was glad to have someone who remembered to give it up to. We had a cry over it.

"That hat, now—took me four years, from the time I first dreamed of that hat, till I remembered it was hers, my young lady's. Just came to me, one afternoon. *That* one—" pointing at the hat in the cabinet—"that one's a facsimile, of course; no one would have saved a thing like that. But it's an exact likeness; it was on a market day in Bedford I saw it, recognized it straight off, and bought it up.

"The rock and masonry piece, here, doesn't exactly belong. It's from the Roman Wall over yonder, that they dug up in thirty-nine. Not that I didn't dream of the Wall, and often, mind you, but I never dreamed that exact piece." He smiled rather confidingly at me, and added poetically that he kept at it because remembering one's dreams was, after all, something like "digging up a Roman Wall, especially a piece with a hole in it."

"Yes," I said, turning to face him. "So you really are a dreamer, after all? I thought you meant you were some kind of inventor, or possibly an artist—you know impractical."

"Oh, no. I never had any talents along those lines, sir," he gravely replied.

"And these, I take it, are the dreams?" I gestured at the line of filing cabinets. "What a vast lot of them there must be."

"It is not, actually, that there are so many dreams," he said. "It is the cross-filing that takes up the space. Of actual dreams there are, I should say, only slightly more than three thousand at this moment. But it did, one day, occur to me that if the collection were to be of any real use it had to be articulated, indexed, catalogued for ready reference." He smiled at me once again, a rather touching smile. "There was trouble, if you like—and cost, as well. The typing alone—I had to give up recording new dreams, as a regular thing, for several months, while I made copies of the old ones. But it was all most instructive. I had the town librarian in, for the filing. A nice woman, but she could make nothing of it; she would have stuck things away under the headings she was accustomed to—dreams of domestic science, poetry, fiction . . . She was an odd one. At last I lost my patience with her. 'My dear lady,' I said—but there's no point in my telling you all this, is there? Perhaps, instead, you'll examine a sample of the kind of things we did?"

Captain Lastwyn opened a drawer, hunted swiftly through the folders neatly ranged there, pitched decisively on one and brought it out to the nearest table, where he spread it out, continuing meanwhile to talk about filing.

"I got, finally, a very nice girl, university trained, who had done inventories for one of the big shops—Harrod's, I think. She understood right away what I was about, and we worked it out together. Have a look here."

At his direction I sat down before the open folder, which contained, in typescript, with a date, the following record:

> I am in the hallway of a strange house, with stone flagging on the floor. My feet are bare. At the end of the hallway I see daylight, and the surf of the sea breaking up on the flags. Mrs. Page, whom I cannot see clearly, says in a loud voice, "Time to trump the geese." I wake up, very fearful.

"Yes," I said. "I see—" conscious in a bemused way that there was so much I did not see at all.

"That is the reading copy," he said, turning the page. "Now here is what I like to call my Variorum edition."

On the next page the dream appeared again, but here heavily annotated. Captain Lastwyn ran his finger down the margin.

"The stone flagging, you see, occurs in numerous dreams of this period; their index numbers and dates are given here; so also with Mrs. Page. Here, in red ink, we refer to dreams in which Mrs. Page appears in combination with some other person. Dreams of the sea are catalogued so; and here is a list of references to other dreams which end with my waking in fright.

"Completeness, you see," he said, drawing himself up and walking a few paces away. "Completeness at all times, and absolute control over the materials. That is the object. And that, too," he added, relaxing, "is what takes up so much space."

"What a fascinating hobby," I murmured, continuing to look at the page because I did not just then wish to meet his eyes.

"Of course, if you like to look at it that way," he said, in a resumption of his former grumpy tone.

"I didn't mean *hobby* as a reflection on it," I said.

"It takes up all my time," said he simply.

"I'm certain, in fact, that it is a work of great potential and value."

"Ah, as to that, only the future can tell." He rummaged in a filing cabinet at some distance and brought over three or four more folders.

"These are very recent," he announced in a tone of some little artistic vanity. I dutifully read through them all, admired the cross-indexing, the cataloguing—the completeness and control. When I used these words, Captain Lastwyn evidently became quite pleased with me.

"You've been, I gather, psychoanalyzed?" I said at last.

At this he looked not quite offended but rather blank.

"No," he said. "I never saw the need." Then, as though feeling the incompleteness of this, he added, "It would rather spoil the beauty of the dreams themselves, I've always thought."

"Do you have many visitors," I asked, "to your museum?"

"No, not a great many," he confessed. "A few stray walkers, like yourself. And on Saturday afternoons, in fine weather, a number of people from the town come out. But they haven't," he added hesitantly, "the serious view. Want me to read palms, and so forth."

"Well, you are rather off the beaten track here, aren't you? Still," I said, "I should think, when word got around a bit, there'd be clusters of psychiatrists and such out here, and maybe a few novelists and poets—sort of picking up images where they could, you know. You'd become a fad."

"There's the danger," said Captain Lastwyn seriously.

"Danger?" I echoed. "But surely you want people to know? You *seem* to want people to know."

"Well, sir," he said, walking nervously up and down behind me, "I do, and I don't."

As I had nothing to say to this I sat still, idly turning the pages of one of his folders, then of another, reading a sentence here and there: "I am at school again . . ." "I wake in a mood of deep despair . . ." "'You must eat until you see the fish on the plate,' says my mother . . ." Ah, you strange, strange man, I thought, you strange little sandy sandman, you are about to tell me something, you are pacing up and down and up and down, but soon you will decide.

There was the scrape of a chair across the tile floor; in a single motion Captain Lastwyn placed it before me, across the table, and straddled it. His chin rested on the back, his wishy-washy eyes looked into mine, I noticed for the first time that he had a thin, sandy mustache, and he said, "I haven't had much of a life, you know, in the ordinary sense."

Oh, dear, was my thought at this inauspicious beginning.

"But then," he continued, "who has? I mean, what is it all about, what does it leave you with, after the shouting, what do you remember of it?"

These questions clearly required no answer from me.

"I lost my wife quite early on; we had one child, a boy, who was killed in the desert in forty-three. I was shot up early in the war myself, and invalided out. My being a professional soldier in the first place was accident; I'm not really the type, you can see that—or if not accident, then just the way such things are arranged . . . or were." He paused. "We were what used to be called a good family," he added, "and we always had one son in the army. It was natural, you see."

"Yes," I said, to help him over this point, where he seemed to want to stick.

"Funny—" he took it up in a new tone—"how you're brought up well, on such and such an amount of money; you become used to living in a certain way—but because there are, all that time, five of you, brothers and sisters, each one, at last, can have only at most one fifth of that. *And* things getting dearer every day, *and* at the same time meaner. Funny."

"Things are getting harder everywhere," said I.

"Ah, it's not that, not that alone," he quickly said. "They know what they're doing, of course." *They* being, presumably, the Government. "It's that all our lives it's the same way; we're cut down and down and down.

"When I came back here—that was the keeper's cottage, the one I live in now—when I came back, I thought about such things a great deal. Oh, yes, a great deal. But thought did nothing; thought is like everything else, a cheat. I began to dream."

"You began to dream," I affirmed, like a chorus in *The Mikado*.

"I wanted, do you see, to save something out of it all." He put this with peculiar vigor, as though such an idea could be got across by brute strength alone. "I know, I know, dreams can't make us immortal—but can't they double our lives, our experiences—triple them, multiply them by, who knows, an indefinite factor?"

I said, truly, that I had never thought of this before.

"*If*—" and he raised an emphatic finger—"*if* we truly possess them."

"Ay, there's the rub," I said.

"Think, then," went on Captain Lastwyn, seeming actually to glitter with a kind of dry, sandy light of exaltation suitable to his nature, "if we do not forget, do not let go, but hang on—" he clenched his fist in midair—"hang on to the end!"

"What then?"

"Why, we've had," and he seemed to look for a sufficient expression, hesitated, lost it, and concluded simply, "we've had so much *more*."

"More what?"

"Life."

"Ah."

"I began to dream." He returned to the attack. "I taught myself, by practice, to remember. I kept a pad and pencil by the bed, and in the morning I would copy out what happened there—" and he waved back over his shoulder as though to some definite place. "It was quite easy, after a while, though now and then I find something in me doesn't want to remember."

"How did you overcome that?" I asked, thinking of all that psychiatry had to say about *resistances,* and glad to have, for a change, some constructive question.

"Ordinary strength, sir," he said in a modest yet perceptibly military way. His shoulders straightened slightly. "All things yield in time, one learns that in the service, though the mind doctors," he added, exactly catching my thought, "won't allow it." And now he leaned forward to me, to say quietly, with intensity, "I have seen it all—again."

"Again?"

"The little boys and girls, my home, the way we used to live, the little things which happened that one doesn't remember. I've had them all back, I have them all back."

"Here?" I asked, indicating the files.

"Here, and inside me." He bowed his head a little, and added, "I have seen my father smile again, and spoken to my mother— though we said only silly things." As he raised his head I was not surprised to see tears in his eyes. "It was all out of control," he added, "and jumbled up. But it was there, and I saw it.

"You can understand," he added in a firmer voice, "why I'd not be interested in psychoanalysis. It is my dreams I want, and I want them for themselves."

"Yes, I understand," said I, hovering for a moment, a little insanely myself, between criticism and sympathy.

"I can dream at any time I want, now," he said brightly. "I can drop off in the middle of the day. In a few seconds I can spend hours elsewhere."

"It is a marvelous power," I said, and we sat in silence for a few moments until I added, "But what about all this?" meaning, generally, the museum and library.

"Yes, all this," he agreed glumly. "It started simply enough. I wanted to have a record, you see. After all, the idea was not to lose it once one had got it back. And it is history, isn't it, like anything else?" He pronounced the word *history* with a certain reverence.

I had, on this, a brief, confused impression of pyramids, battles of Marathon, Yankee Stadium, long rows of thick volumes, lonely stacks of documents . . . "Yes," I said, "that it is."

Captain Lastwyn seemed pleased at this but sank back after a moment into his gloom, and said somberly, "But it costs money, it takes time, one can't simply let things go, they must be kept up in order, mustn't they?"

"Completion and control," said I.

"And then there's the danger of theft," he said. "Which is why I keep Rennett with me—" gesturing toward the cottage—"he used to live here, in the old days. He was the head keeper when my father lived."

"Insurance—" I began.

"What could replace it?" he asked mildly. "It's not worth anything that money can pay for."

"But just in case," I insisted. "If it burned down, for instance . . ."

"If it went," he said, "I should go too." He looked at me keenly, as keenly as those faded eyes could, and said, "I have terrible fears about it, you know."

"I know," said I.

"I'm proud of it and want people to see it. It is something to have done in this world, isn't it? Not much, but something—a man with his history, complete, like this? And yet, I have the most dreadful fears."

"That people may steal it?" I asked, smiling.

"That people are stealing it, with every look they give. That I have somehow, very painfully, thrown myself open to the world."

"At sixpence a throw," I reminded him.

"But I must, don't you see," he said half apologetically and yet with a certain quick effect of anger. "I can't support it all on my own."

"But you admit you don't take in many sixpences. It couldn't be much support."

"No."

"So that the whole enterprise is more or less going to pieces at this moment?"

"Yes."

"And you won't advertise it a bit, to scholars and such?"

"No," he said stubbornly, and though his head was bowed I had the idea he was again crying, or nearly. "I don't want—scholars. I shall carry on while I am able. And after that—" He let it go here, and stood up. "I've kept you rather long," he said. "Didn't mean to bore you with my woes. Sometimes, you know, one wants to talk."

"I know," said I, also getting up. "I suppose you have a fund for maintenance? If someone should make a donation?"

"No, I haven't," he said, watching me closely while I got out my wallet.

"You should have," I said. "Let me begin it." I held out a pound note. "I am interested in the work and would like to see it go on."

"Well, sir, you are very kind," he said again, and took the money. Again it seemed that our relation had changed, and we stood in a silence very constrained.

"I'll show you to your bus stop," he finally offered, and I agreed that it was time I went. I took one last look at the Museum & Library of Dreams before he turned off the light, and then we set off down a crooked path through the woods, he leading the way with the lantern held high, and I following.

It was a short walk; evidently I had first approached his house from the other side, the road being only over the hill. But in the darkness of the country night I somehow felt more deeply than I had inside the poignant oddity of Captain Lastwyn's life, its desperate and compromised endeavor to salvage the ruins and hulks of time, keep them somehow safe, and exhibit them for sixpence.

We came out at a bus stop in a little lane arched over with branches. Beside the bus signal was a replica of the sign at the museum door. Captain Lastwyn shifted the lantern to his left hand, evidently with some idea of shaking hands. But he seemed to think better of it, and we stood there.

"You'll get your bus here all right," he assured me. I thanked him, and said he need not wait with me. But he seemed unwilling to leave and, finally, after some pawing of the ground, asked me if I thought he was a happy man. "As much, I mean, as any of us can be said to be? In your opinion?"

"Why, yes," I said after a pause intended to look like deep consideration. "You have, as you said, your history, complete, and that's more than most of us can say."

"Yes," he said gravely. And we stood there some more, until after a few minutes we saw the lights of the bus approaching.

"When I die," Captain Lastwyn said to me by way of farewell, "I have arranged to leave it all to the British Museum."

"Indeed?" I asked, as the bus drew to a stop. And as I stood on the step and the bus began to move he grinned broadly all of a sudden and called after me, with his first and last show of humor.

"What'll they make of it, those poor beggars, do you think?"

"I've no idea," I shouted back, turning away.

The inside of the bus was crowded, so I went up on top, where I was able to settle into a front seat and watch the deep lanes unroll in the headlights.

The British Museum, I thought. That was probably the place for it; they must have stranger things even than dreams stored away in that great marble and granite barn, among the plundered and boughten confusion of empires. They would, at the British Museum, look at it all twice, and imperturbably file it away under *Dreams* . . . which was probably where everything, after all, belonged. We were all, I thought sleepily, going down in history, whether as Tamerlane or Genghis Khan, Beethoven, St. Francis or Nesselrode who invented the pudding. Or as Capt. Frank Lastwyn, R.A. (ret.), or as anonymous nobodies, such as myself. And ho-hum to it all.

The conductress appeared, and when I stated my destination, said, "Yer on the wrong bus."

"Wrong bus?"

"Going the wrong way. You should have crossed the street." She was very kind about all this, but clearly she doubted my ability to cross the street unaided.

"Where does this bus go, then?"

"The other way. Ampthill."

I considered this, being very sleepy and under no necessity of going back to my hotel this night.

"I could, I guess, get a meal and a room at Ampthill?"

"You could," she said doubtfully, for now I was behaving queerly, like a foreigner.

"Very well, to Ampthill, then," I said, and gave her a note to change. While she counted out the money I thought again of Captain Lastwyn. How typical that his final effect on my destiny should be to put me on the wrong road; or on the right road but going the wrong way. Then I remembered that I had never, after all, told him where I was going, but foolishly got on the first bus which presented itself.

"Yer change," the conductress said, a little nastily.

"Oh, yes, thanks," I said, taking the money and looking into her face, a very pretty but very tired face framed in terribly peroxided hair, and with clear blue eyes. Behind it, clearly, was a thought which began, These Americans . . . ! while on my side I was thinking, These dreamers . . . ! And the huge bus blundered along among the branches of the leafy lane.

The Ocean to Cynthia

All afternoon they sailed beside the gray cliffs and castles of Ireland, and the girl Elizabeth was at Mr. Bower again with her idea that it was better to die than live. Clearly she was mad, and he regretted having got himself involved, though it was that quality of madness, with its hint of the erotic behind the mortal abandon, which in the first place had attracted him. Now she had him there by the rail, aft, where the motion of the vessel was most apparent, and the two of them would rise dizzily into the empty sky, then sink as suddenly till they stood beneath the black and cresting tops of the waves, which, only fifty feet away, seemed that they might at any moment fall on the liner and overwhelm it in their continuously thundering weight. It was a bad place for the discussion of a suicide pact; the ocean, from this view of it, exercised a frightful fascination, and Mr. Bower, with one arm as if protectively about the girl's shoulders, kept his free hand tightly clutched on the rail, which shuddered suggestively with the vibration of the engines; it actually seemed to him that—in a careless moment, so to say—he might throw himself overboard. Also he feared catching cold from standing so long in the chill wind, with spray and a hint of rain in the air; age with its prudence rebuked the lover's recklessness, and he kept thinking of his overcoat and tweed cap in the cabin below.

"To get it over with," this bitter girl was saying. "Look, there's no one looking. Now!" She actually urged his body strongly against the rail.

"My dear," he cried. "My dearest girl, be sensible. You don't really want to; you're just teasing yourself with the idea."

"You promised," Elizabeth said, "because you 'loved me more than the world.'" The theatricality of this quotation filled Mr. Bower with the sort of self-disgust to which, however, he had long been inured, and he merely shuddered, part with cold.

"It was because I wanted you to be happy," he said. "Dearest Elizabeth, you were so sad."

"Because you wanted me to come to you last night," Elizabeth replied. The strength of the wind made it necessary for them to shout these intimacies at each other; even so the words would be whipped into fragments which flew off over the sea.

"I wanted to bring you out of it," he said, "that pathological state of mind."

"We know what you wanted," she cried back. "And now you've got it."

"Don't talk like that, my child—" Mr. Bower admired this priestly form of address, even at the top of his voice—"you know I'll always love you."

" 'Better than the world'?"

The great waves smashed at the side of the ship and broke away beneath them in dirty marble flags like the flying draperies of a statue. The girl clung to him and pressed against his mouth the cold skin of her cheek, wet and salt to taste.

"Tony, Tony," she said, sobbing in such a way that he felt the crisis, for the time being anyhow, must be over, "don't leave me alone, Tony."

"Of course I won't, ever," he proclaimed, patting her tenderly on the shoulder but keeping his other hand firmly all the same on the rail.

For a moment the cold sun broke raggedly through cloud and shone on them: it was like the epiphany of all the movies; and across the glinting, tossing black of the waters great white birds, gannets, flew low and fast.

"Look, aren't they beautiful!" he cried, turning her to see these bulky, long-winged wanderers, while the sun obediently lighted the lonely, magical cliffs and castles of the coast as though to tell this poor child in his embrace that the world could be the scene after all of wonderful adventure. Presently he was able to send her away below to powder her nose, after which she was to meet him in the Moorish Court for cocktails.

"We'll talk it over sensibly," he assured her, wondering what sensible things might be said—other than "No! No!"—on the subject of their jumping together into that loud, insane sea.

2

Morbid thoughts, morbid thoughts! While Mr. Bower sat waiting in the Moorish Court, as the tourist saloon was called, he
sipped at a Bols gin which he hoped would avert the consequences
of his having stood so long in damp and cold not merely physical
in their effects—he could not help imagining himself, embraced
with that sad young lady, drifting hither and yon in the black
water, their hair streaming, their faces eaten by fish—it was all
very poetical, no doubt, and he wanted no part of it.

At the same time, while his spirit was soothed by the gin as by
the string quartet of the Moorish Court, which at this hour played
sentimental "semiclassical" music to the tea drinkers and cocktail
drinkers, Mr. Bower could not help some rather self-pitying reflections on the subject of suicide. To be rid of one's life—there was
something theoretically proper (and really rather moving) in the
thought, so long as it was thought in the ornate vulgarity of the
Moorish Court and not outside, face to face with the wild abyss.
And that this girl Elizabeth should love him, Anthony Victor
Bower, of all the world, enough to want to die with him—that
suggested a fascination in his very nature, which age had no power
to diminish. For a moment he could feel toward her a tenderness
and romantic ardor such as had not come his way in many years,
which put him nostalgically in mind of the first girl he had ever
loved, Cynthia, whom he had got with child and deserted at the
very start of his career, which was that of a seducer of women.

But this girl, Elizabeth, was insane; she really wanted him to
jump! Anthony had even thought briefly of pushing her overboard, if she so badly wanted to die—that was how far matters
had gone—but had refrained chiefly because he could think of
himself as a scoundrel but not as a criminal. He imagined again
the huge waves of the sea, shuddered, and ordered a second gin. At
this moment he was joined by a criminal.

This was a portly, apoplectic-looking gentleman who dressed as
a priest of Rome and called himself Father Frank. He and Mr.
Bower had chanced to travel by the same ship a number of times
during many years and recognized each other as alike predators of
the sea; not that they were friends on this account, for the counterfeit priest was contemptuous of Mr. Bower as an amateur, while

Mr. Bower, though he did not care much for religion, felt horrified at Father Frank, who profaned the cloth with the object of black-mailing women. Still, a kind of neutral acquaintance was imposed on them whenever they met on the high seas, and Father Frank had to be invited to a chair and a glass of gin.

"Prosperous voyage, Father?" asked Mr. Bower; it was his standard joke with this colleague.

"Good hunting to you," Father Frank replied in kind, raising his glass.

"As a matter of fact, I am expecting a young lady just now," Mr. Bower said, and the priest made a conventional gesture at rising to seek another table. "No, by all means join us, do," Mr. Bower insisted. "It occurs to me that you may have the power of assisting me to avert a rather unpleasant thing."

This time Father Frank's motion to depart was not conventional at all; however, Mr. Bower clutched at his arm.

"Please," he said.

"I don't want any part of your trouble, old son," said Father Frank.

"I should be eternally indebted to you," Mr. Bower said, "for only a trifling effort on your part."

What this trifling effort was to consist in he outlined quickly.

"You see," he said, bringing his narrative after a few minutes to its climax, "she actually wanted me to jump with her."

The false priest laughed contemptuously. "Maybe one day you will," he said. "You never know."

"Never mind that," Mr. Bower said. "The point is, the poor girl is obsessed with the idea of death. She is a widow already, her husband died on their honeymoon in America, and she is bringing the body back home—she made me go down to the baggage room with her to see the casket, that's how much it's preying on her mind. We kissed first down there," he confessed in a suddenly altered voice.

"And you swore to die with her—to drown?"

"Well, you know how that is."

"Well, I don't, my dear Bower. An oath is a serious thing."

"Come off it, do," said Mr. Bower savagely to this wolf in lamb's clothing, "or I'll report you to the purser."

"That would fix us both," replied Father Frank. "Supposing I put on the show for you, is there any guarantee it would work? Is the girl religious?"

"I've no idea."

"For ten pounds."

"That's a good deal of money, Father."

"You may jump in the ocean for all of me," the other replied with a civil smile, "but put it this way—five pounds down, now, and if you drown yourself tonight, why, you needn't pay the balance."

Elizabeth appeared just as Mr. Bower was passing over the five pounds.

"It is for charity," he said. "The Father has touched my better nature—for the orphans and poor."

"Are you a Roman?" she asked. "I didn't know that."

"No, I'm not," Bower replied. "But it is a good cause. Father Frank and I are old friends. Father, this is Mrs. Brayle I was telling you of."

"May I offer my sympathies," said the Father, "in your bereavement."

"I don't believe in God," Elizabeth said.

"Now, dear, now, Elizabeth," said Bower, but the Father raised a warning hand.

"Why shouldn't she say so, if it's the fact?" he demanded. "You seem to think a priest should be protected from the truth. It's better to be perfectly frank, isn't it?" he said to Elizabeth with a lively smile, as though placing them both over against Bower. Elizabeth smiled back somewhat stiffly.

"It's what I've always thought," she said, now taking a chair between them. The fresh air had improved her color, perhaps her disposition, Bower thought, and she looked *so* pretty, there was such an appeal in her thinness, delicacy, even in the rather sober poverty of her clothing, which was bride-new and yet not quite *good*, that he wished very much to lean over and squeeze her knee in amiable assurance; restraining himself, however, as not being quite right in this wish when they were *before a priest*. For by imperceptible revisions of countenance Father Frank had now so entered into his role that Bower absurdly felt some emanation from his presence of the real power to rebuke and forgive; and this he continued to feel even despite his knowledge of the facts and his compelled admiration for a technically polished performance.

The element of reality in this performance depended, he knew, upon Father Frank's once having been a priest, though long unfrocked for reasons which Mr. Bower had neither heard nor expected to hear; consequently the details were all quite exact, being marked by a dignity both grave and jovial and by no excessive austerity, since, as the Father had said once, it would be easier to counterfeit a saint than a priest, but less profitable and far more likely to awake suspicion. In the conduct of his present profession Father Frank had two or three dangers to face, which kept him constantly alert. The first of these Mr. Bower shared; it was the risk of becoming too well known to the authorities, and they neither of them traveled by the same line more than once in two years. The second danger was that of meeting real Catholic priests; not that the Father was incapable of handling doctrine and lingo, but the Church is in some respects, to its officers, like the Regular Army, a large but intimate association in which one was always likely to be asked "What about old So-and-So who was stationed at Karachi five years ago?" etc., an embarrassment which the impostor skillfully evaded, when necessary by getting in first with his own questions. His third peril was a personal one; he liked the drink, did Father Frank, and had to be very careful of himself while working—though, as he had told Mr. Bower, "People can think only one thought at a time, and the more they think of a real bad priest who drinks the less they will think of his not being a priest at all. It is, as a matter of fact, a fair instance of the doctrine of casuistry, whereby a venial sin is substituted for a mortal one."

That was the kind of remark which not merely shocked but a little terrified Mr. Bower, who as a tourist-class seducer was also a sentimentalist, and did not like to hear religion spoken of except in distant and poetical ways, preferring to keep unsullied by the technicalities of obedience his half-belief in a Being unspecified who would bring all things right in the end, subdue the proud and exalt the meek, and, in the intermission of these activities, find time also to forgive Anthony Victor Bower, who, whatever his faults, really did love each and every one of those women who for twenty-five years had moved across his vision like ducks in a shooting gallery.

What a disgusting life I lead! he thought, and, simultaneously, But I am really a very nice fellow after all.

They ordered a gin for Elizabeth, and soon after another round for all, Mr. Bower paying.

"My dear child," Father Frank said, after having in a few minutes got on an easy footing with the girl, "you needn't think of me as a priest but simply as an older man and, I hope, a friend." He too, Mr. Bower noted, very nearly patted the girl's knee, but at the last instant his hand remained suspended above it: the blessing of the patella, thought Mr. Bower irrelevantly, and considered briefly the polished flesh beneath the silk stocking.

"But I do want to talk to you seriously for a moment, if you will let me," insisted the priest.

"Go ahead, then. I shan't stop you," said Elizabeth with derisive carelessness, and she smiled quickly, secretly, at Mr. Bower, a loose, rather dreamy smile which he found both erotically appealing and desperate to insanity. She is gone, he thought nervously. Nothing can touch her.

"This gentleman here," began Father Frank, indicating Mr. Bower, "though he is not of our persuasion, has nevertheless seen fit to repose his confidence in me as a priest, and has told me something of your unhappy circumstances, my dear, together with that decision of yours which I cannot too strongly reprehend—but it is difficult for me, sitting in this comfortable lounge, even to believe you can be serious, or final, in thus deciding once and for all against life and in favor of the other. I tell myself that something—which you will call fear and I will call, if you like, a good angel—would always hold a person back, at the last instant, from the satisfaction of that dreadful wish."

"I really don't give a damn," Elizabeth said in a neutral voice which embarrassed her lover and frightened him at the same time with its impudent despair. To behave that way before a priest! It was precisely the measure of her childishness and distance from reality.

"I tell myself that," evenly continued the priest, "though it is true that everywhere, every day, people do this terrible thing. It is not so much to die, themselves, personally, that they wish; it is to deny life, and by a puerile obstinacy make it impossible for God to save them."

"I don't believe in a God," Elizabeth said again.

"God may believe in you," said the father with a smile of dialectical triumph. "After all, what is so insupportable about your life? You have lost your husband—many women lose their husbands. Sometimes, you know, life appears as not all happiness. What of it?"

"He had left me," Elizabeth said. "He was—what you call it?—killed trying to escape." This joke had a dreadful effect on her, so that she was laughing with her mouth while her eyes cried.

And I can understand why, thought Mr. Bower, you poor, dreadful child. He felt filled with a vague, generous pity for all the sad world, while at the same time he thought what an embarrassment it would be if the girl made a scene here, with the quartet playing an arrangement of "Tales from the Vienna Woods."

"You and this gentleman," said Father Frank with a new sternness in his voice, "have sinned. Understand that I am not overlooking the fact—you are both at this moment in a state of mortal sin. Maybe you don't view that as desperate, but I do. You have come together carnally without blessing, without sanction, without so much, poor as it would be, as the scratch of the registrar's pen. Consider, young lady, if that in itself may not be responsible for your present despair—remorse, natural remorse, which by mysterious ways might yet light in your souls the beginning of grace. You know, both of you, that you have sinned. Oh, this is not theology, my friends; I am merely stating what you both have natural knowledge of. I want to use that natural knowledge to help you."

And he really does, at that, thought Mr. Bower, becoming aware in some surprise of the depths of sincerity which must go to the making of any good impersonation. Despite himself he felt vague yearnings which began with the formula: If I had my life to live over again . . .

"I hate the world," Elizabeth said, tears running down her face. "Cruel, miserable, bitchy world where you're to blame for everything."

"That hatred of the world," said Father Frank, "is the beginning of wisdom. In it is our first awakening to the command of our Creator, who did not put us here to enjoy ourselves. Consider," he added, "that this life is like an ocean voyage, a vessel filled with delicacies—of which we become weary, nevertheless—and borne up irrationally on the waters of utter death."

"Another gin, all of us," said Mr. Bower. "And don't cry, Elizabeth."

"You are fortunate indeed, young lady," said Father Frank, "that this man with whom you have committed fornication is, after all, an honorable and upright person. Though he was tempted, and fell, upon coming to his senses he has resolved on the only right course—and it is to make his decision public and in some sense binding that he has employed a third person, myself, to say openly that he will marry you as soon as we reach Southampton—or on this ship itself, tonight, if I can persuade the officials that the ceremony will be confirmed by a civil ceremony tomorrow, ashore."

Elizabeth giggled sadly. "It's very nice of you to bother," she said to either or both of them.

"You see, dear," Mr. Bower said tenderly. "Things do sometimes come right in the end."

"I can't conceal my opinion, though," said the priest, "that you both have a great deal to beg forgiveness for. I don't at all condone your behavior but am simply making the sorry best of a bad situation."

"We are grateful to you, Father, I'm sure," said Mr. Bower.

"He won't really, will he? Marry me?" asked Elizabeth. "You've cooked this up, both of you, to keep me safe till we dock." Her eyes, glittering with suspicion and tears, went first to one and then the other.

"I put it to you, Anthony Bower, as a gentleman," said the priest.

Mr. Bower's eyes too filled with tears at the image of himself in his sacrifice.

"Elizabeth," he asked, "do you love me?"

"You ask me that?" she cried out. "You've had what I could give. I'll do anything, I don't really want to die—anything. But don't let us talk about love."

"I love you, my dear," Mr. Bower replied, and truly at this moment meant it, so that his generous nature expanded with sympathy, pity, romantic ardor—all those feelings which ran so near the surface in him that he had always been convinced, when cuddling ladies naked in bed, that he really saved them from the dire and miserable world.

"I will marry you, Elizabeth," he said outright. "I will try to make you happy." And really he believed this, seeing suddenly, unexpectedly, something like the very truth emerging from falsehood. False priest, false lover, between them they had cooked up—

the phrase was Elizabeth's—a resolution which he could regard as satisfactory, at least for the time being; so that instead of going down into old age in increasing loneliness, watching the failure of his charm, he might be comforted in bed and at his board by this young and pretty girl whom by this means he had saved, in all probability, from death. In what was nearly a religious thought he saw himself redeeming the past, and silently he named a litany of names: Cynthia, Joan, Louise, Helen . . . etc., etc. It was a prayer, perfunctory and powerful.

"I'm glad I didn't die," Elizabeth said, with a return of that secret, crazy smile. She took out her compact, made a little exclamation, and began intently to repair her stained face.

"You consent, then?" insisted Father Frank.

"Yes, I do," said the girl, continuing to examine her face in the mirror.

Father Frank looked significantly across at Mr. Bower, who nodded reassuringly and framed with his lips the word *later*.

"We should have some champagne," he said, and waved at a waiter.

The priest pursed his lips indecisively and wistfully while champagne was selected. But he rose to his feet.

"I will speak to the proper authorities," he said, "and meanwhile, you two, be steadfast."

He frowned severely down at them, while his eyes twinkled with benign merriment, and off he went. In his new resolve, Mr. Bower wished that the authorities were actually going to be consulted; which was, however, too much for Father Frank to be expected to do for ten pounds.

The champagne arrived, and they drank to each other while the quartet played selections from *Midsummer Night's Dream,* the *Barcarolle* and other such pieces.

"The coffin," Elizabeth said suddenly. "I must return it to his parents. They will be waiting."

"You needn't tell them anything," Mr. Bower assured her.

"You don't know anything about me," she said.

"Nor you about me—I have not been a very good person all my life," he replied.

"Aren't we shabby, though?" she said, laughing.

"Not at all."

3

On the strength of the champagne they neither of them wanted dinner but decided instead to walk on deck.

"To look at the sea," she said, "without wanting to throw yourself in."

Giggling like children, they agreed to climb the forbidden passage to the first class, and cautiously emerged on a well-lighted but empty boat deck.

"They are all at supper now," said Mr. Bower, pressing his fiancée's arm. "We have the place to ourselves."

The sea had calmed, and the moon come out between clouds. Ireland had been left behind, and here, so high above the water, the scene was no longer threatening even though the waves were still moderately strong.

"My darling," cried Mr. Bower above the voice of the waves. "Be happy."

"I'll try," she cried back. The cold wind whipped at their hair and carried off their words.

The stopped to embrace, standing under the high white bellies of the lifeboats. Here there was a break in the railing, and Mr. Bower was possessed of a sudden irrational desire to carry both of them overboard now, while they were happy. He trembled with this feeling and the tension produced by his terrified resistance to it. Happiness never lasts, he thought, and pressed the girl closer to him.

"Elizabeth," he cried, "I'm so happy I could die."

She broke gently from him and stood back a trifle.

"You really mean it," she said, and then, somewhat histrionically, "'My love is not of time nor bound to date.'"

"What?" loudly asked Mr. Bower, who seemed to hear these words flying past his ears as from a great distance and at high speed.

She repeated the verse, and drew out from her dress a locket.

"My mother," she replied; "someone wrote that to her."

They leaned their heads close together over the open locket and looked at the picture of the young man with wavy hair and bristling mustache who had written in a cramped hand beneath his face, "My love is not of time nor bound to date."

"But it was, after all," Mr. Bower said in a low voice.

"Was what?"

"The 'Ocean to Cynthia,'" he said. "A poem."

"Cynthia was my mother's name," she said. "You know poetry too."

"Yes," Mr. Bower said, "yes, I know everything."

He took her in his arms again and gently moved with her between the lifeboats. He kept his eyes shut, and seemed to hear the sound of the sea become louder.

"No!" she cried in his ear. "No! No!"

"Everything," he shouted back, and they moved together as though dancing toward the free fall and the wild marble water singing below.

FROM
Stories, Fables & Other Diversions (1971)

The Outage

In families that cared for customary ways the telling of the story was assigned to the oldest man present—grandpa it might be, or great-uncle—with only his wife allowed to correct him or bring him back if he strayed; his wife, or else, if he were widowed, one of the other old women. He would begin after the traditional holiday dinner, at the time of drawing of curtains and lighting of lamps, with the families arrayed around him. The middle generation, the fathers and mothers and uncles and aunts, some of whom could remember and some of whom only thought they remembered, were expected to contribute to the recital only their choral assent at the high moments; while the children—well, the children had to ask questions, and on this occasion their questions would be received with good humor, though not invariably answered. In return, they shared in the convention by pretending to be hearing the story for the first time, though only the youngest of them really were.

The grandfather began.

"Once long ago," he said, "there was electricity. It was not a thing, such as table or chair, but a force, a very great force; it was not a thing, but it did many things. One of the things it did was fill

99

houses with light. We used to be able to press that little black doohickey on the wall there, and this room would become bright enough to read in right away; the light would come from those pear-shaped glass things called bulbs that you see hung from the ceiling; or sometimes from long glass tubes that would flicker prettily at first before they settled to a steady shine.

"That wasn't all electricity could do—there were a great many more things than that—but it was the most wonderful and the one we most took for granted. Whenever you walked into a room that was darker than you wanted it to be, you would press one of those things set into the wall—right by the door, for convenience—and the room would immediately light up, spread with an even, unwavering light.

"One thing the electricity did, it made the world of those days practically free of demons and ghosts. They always existed, of course, but by turning on the lights you automatically made them leave the house; so that for all practical purposes it was as if there weren't any."

The children began looking at one another a little doubtfully in the firelight, the lamplight, and from the shadows around the grown-ups' knees. It was a nice idea for a story, their glances seemed to say, but how seriously ought it to be taken?

"With this electricity," the grandfather went on, "you could also run a great many different machines. You know what machines are, you see them every day on your way to school, standing out in the weather with a kind of hulking patience—cars, trucks, and so on; in some spots you can see the fine colors they had before they rusted so. Those particular machines didn't quite *run* by electricity, but they had to be started by electricity. . . . I like to think that if electric power came back they would some of them be right and ready to go, just like that. It used to be such a fine thing to see, on the big roads, the lanes of traffic streaming away in both directions as far as the eye could see, and all the colors of the speeding cars that flashed in the sunlight . . . or else at night the headlight beams driving their moving cones of light into and through the shadows . . ."

"Tell them more about in the house," his wife reminded him. She thought perhaps he was becoming too rhapsodic.

"In the house?" the old man said, "Well, in the house I used to lie awake some nights counting up the number of items we owned that ran by electricity. The power came in the house from those rubbery-looking ropes and cords and cables you still see carried on poles along the street, and once it got into the house this power was good for almost anything: it cooked, it ironed, it washed, it kept people warm and kept their food cold; if you had the right machines it would even sharpen pencils, or tell time, or make ice cubes—it would freeze the water into miniature blocks—or run typewriters, or do the sewing . . ."

There is some trouble in narrating things you have experienced to people who have never known their like at all: you never know when you are leaving out some essential point, and you never know what strange shape your understanding takes inside another mind. The children were attentively trying to imagine a sort of stuff that oozed or crept along or through those rubbery-looking ropes and came into your house and went right to the ironing-board and *did the ironing*. But the only way they had of doing this was to imagine mother standing there with iron in hand, and then subtract from that picture mother, iron—maybe ironing-board as well?—which left the clothes and—and what?

But the old man had his story to tell, it was all present to his memory, and he went right on, getting vaguer as he went, about all the marvelous things that could be done by electricity—only by this time he had for the most part dropped that word and was speaking instead of *power,* and *the power.* Also it was observable, though not by the children, that he was moving ever further from his own experienced knowledge, and talking instead of such things as mains and generators and transformers and dynamos; of hydraulic stations and even of what he called The Central Power Station and the Hydroelectric Grid, which last seemed to be like a gigantic invisible spider's web—without a spider—that began in one place and went all over the world.

"Now that's enough, Arthur," the old woman put in after a while of this sort of thing. "It's only confusing the children, and you're not getting on with the story."

"I just wanted to give the whole picture," said the grandfather. "I wanted the children to see it as it was. But all right, all right."

"The story," he began anew, "is simply told, for its climax is not, as in an ordinary story, the happening of something, but, instead, the happening of nothing. We had all these things I've been telling you of, and then, instantly, on this very day, and almost at this time of day, in fact—there it all wasn't. It was gone. Just as the wives were beginning to cook the supper, as the men were coming home from work and looking forward to the evening news on the TV— you never even let me tell them about television," he said complainingly, "but that glass-fronted chest over there in the corner, with the plants on top—you children may not believe this, but it used to light up and pictures would come out on the glass part, moving pictures. People would be there dancing and singing and telling you what was happening everywhere . . ."

"You mean there used to be people in that box?" a child asked, and another child snickered, but softly, imagining how tiny those people would have had to be.

"No, not exactly *in* the box," grandfather said, and stopped. But an uncle permissibly intervened to save the situation by saying rather impressively, "It was done by what they used to call a *cathode ray tube*." Several people murmured "*cathode ray tube*" in a ragged chorus, and renewed silence seemed to show that this explanation satisfied.

"Now what you want to imagine if you can," the grandfather resumed, "is the bewilderment and the helplessness. What's most important to see is that none of us so much as knew what had happened. We assumed, of course, that it was an ordinary power failure and would be put right in a matter of minutes or at most a few hours. There even used to be a joke about such things, which happened once or twice a year, that some little man in overalls had just absent-mindedly pulled out the one plug on which the rest of the system depended—and for all we knew, or know now for that matter, it might as well have been that simple and stupid. For we had always been assured that no such thing could ever really happen, and even if we hadn't been assured we'd have gone on assuming it couldn't, simply because—well, because it couldn't. And when it did," he added with a touch of vehemence, "one of the things that happened was that our way of finding out what had happened vanished along with everything else."

With this he entered, in a different tone, on what seemed to be for him the noblest and loftiest and most sorrowful part of memory. No longer stopping to explain, he spoke of the wonders and the terrors that ensued: the giant aircraft cruising over a land sud-

denly become dark and incapable of giving direction; the few
islands of light from self-contained emergency systems; the liners
out at sea, themselves such systems, glittering with self-generated
brilliance that made them proudly and pathetically independent
for a time; the portable radios that answered their worshippers'
questions only with static; the dark and cooling houses; the car
headlights beamed into the living rooms all night and fading before the dawn; the cold realization, disbelieved for days but gradually and relentlessly imposing itself upon belief.

"If there was one thing about that time more tragic than the
rest," he said, "or so I've heard, for I'm not sure I remember any
such thing myself, it was that once, a few days later, everything
came on again. Came on with a great, silent rush. But we had left
every switch we had, all of us, in the on position—so that we'd
know at once, you see—and it seems, or so they say, that by this
folly we sucked the power out of the system faster than it could
deliver, so fast that in five minutes it failed again and was gone,
who knows, forever. All we could do, all we can do, is wait. And
though I realize that though some of this sounds like a fairy tale to
the younger of you, the whole point of the story, of telling the story
every year on the day, is that we are waiting still. That TV set over
there is on right now, and it will stay on while we live, in memory
and hope. For we believe that what has gone must one day return."

"But why didn't they start all over making the electricity work?"
asked one of the older boys. The grandfather looked at him earnestly, and took his time about replying.

"I can't say for certain," he began in an impressively careful way,
"that nothing of the sort was ever done. If it was, it either didn't
work or else it just hasn't reached this region yet. Think for a moment, young man, of the magnificence of what it was we lost in a
moment of time. People accustomed to having such powers in their
hands are proud, too proud to fly Ben Franklin's kite again, as the
saying is. We have another saying hereabouts, as well: if a king is
accidentally locked out of his castle he doesn't build a hovel with
his hands. He waits."

There was a silence, possibly of emotion on the old man's side,
likely of some small embarrassment in other parts of the room.
Perhaps it was to get them past the moment that the grandmother
broke in once again:

"You haven't told them about the telephones," she reminded him.

"O yes," the old man said, brightening, "the telephones. They were the strangest things of all, because in the middle of the general panic and blackness and stillness they went on working. They worked for quite a while, I don't know why any more than I know why they finally faded and went dead."

The grandmother patiently said, "You haven't told them yet what telephones were." And the old man told the children what he could about that. He pointed to a telephone on a table back in the shadows, he explained how by turning that little wheel seven different times you could talk to anyone in town you wanted to; how in fact with different combinations of numbers you could talk to anyone in the whole world.

"What did you say to them?" a child wanted to know.

"What did you say to them?" This made the grandfather a little indignant. "Why, the same things you'd say to—to anyone in the world. Hello, how are you, and whatever else you wanted to know, that's what you said to them."

"But it all got strange," he continued. "Even while the telephones were still working, I can remember, the voices at the other end seemed to be getting weaker all the time. You had to shout, and get the other person to shout, to be understood. And after that it got even more uncertain. You'd often feel—it's hard to express it, but you'd often feel the other person wasn't really any longer the person you meant to talk to at all, but someone else entirely. People said very strange things anyhow, in those days, but especially on the phone. We were all so lonely, you see, especially at night, and as often as not you'd pick up the phone when it rang and you'd just hear somebody crying or saying Help me, please help me, but there wouldn't be anything you could do about it if they wouldn't say who they were or where or what kind of help they needed.

"Once in a great while," he added, "you do still hear of people picking up a phone and getting a response, but it doesn't seem to be in a language they understand."

During all this a little boy had crept over and picked up the phone.

"It sounds like the wind," he said, holding it correctly to his ear, "like the wind blowing down a dark tunnel."

"You'd better put that down, son," said a grown-up. "It's not a thing for kids to play with."

"Well," said the grandfather, "of course there's more, there's much more. You children will read about it when you're older, about the sufferings and so on, about that first winter without. I've just given you the bare outline, and why we tell the story every year, which is to pass on to you the memory and the hope.

"But why didn't they ever fix it?" the older boy insisted. And the grandfather looked at him solemnly, rather sternly.

"They just didn't, is all," he said at last. "If they had done I wouldn't be telling you all this, now, would I?"

"But who is They?"

"That is a good question, young man," the elder replied, "and one day, when you're full grown, you may be the one to find the answer. Who knows, you may be the one to find the switch, wherever it is, and turn it on. Stranger things have happened in the world. Meanwhile, I've told you the story, as I was bound to do. I didn't say I could answer every question that might come up. I'm tired, too. And it's time for children to be thinking about bed. Under the covers is the only place children can be safe during the hours of darkness."

Which frightened some and tickled others among the children; one of whom, before falling asleep, expressed the sense of the meeting as it had come through to her:

"It's a funny kind of story," she said, "funny ha ha and funny peculiar both, only I don't know if you're supposed to believe it like Jesus or like Santa Claus."

Unbelievable Characters

It was a Sunday afternoon in the late fall. I had come home from college for the weekend, and now, after a heavy dinner, I stood out on the lawn in the last of the good weather, raking the last of the leaves and burning them on the gravel drive. My father had gone up for a nap, my mother and her brother, Uncle Snevely, were still sitting with their second and subsequent cups of coffee. It was a brilliant day, blue and gold, with the heat of noon just beginning to chill as the shadows of the spruces lengthened on the grass; and there was no wind, so that the smoke from the burning leaves, after its first flame and fuss, rose straight up, gray, blue, black, like a signal fire, dissolving overhead.

When I first noticed the skywriter, he was just rounding off the B in ROB and was lazily turning away from his work, really in order to start his run up on the next letter, but a little as if he were a painter standing back from the easel for a critical look. At first I thought he was going to spell my name, which is Robert; then I thought perhaps he was going to spell out, over the suburbs and the city, some tremendous instruction: ROB—BURN—MURDER. I leaned on the rake to watch. But of course the tines of the rake simply bent under at that, so I more or less pretended to be leaning on the rake, while the skywriter completed the word: ROBIN. The "I" had a little kink halfway; he might have stopped to scratch himself, or his knee might simply have straightened and caused him to kick the rudder bar.

Just about then Mother and Uncle Snevely came out on the terrace and sat down a few feet away. It had been such a mild fall that the garden furniture was still out, though the cushions had been removed, and the iron chairs looked old and naked, like the trees.

"I can't resist the smell of burning leaves," said Mother. "I think of when I was a little girl."

"We used to bury each other in the leaves," Uncle Snevely said. "Like the Babes in the Wood." After a moment he added, "It might have been better for me if." And he stopped. Not that his sentence trailed off; no, it definitely stopped. That was Uncle Snevely's way. He had to get it in that he was a failure and realized it, but that he was not going to say any more of it unless invited to, because he wanted you to know that *he* knew he was a bore as well as a failure, and that the one depended on the other, and that he had some dignity left.

"Oh, now, Snevely," said Mother.

I called their attention to the skywriter, who had now got as far as ROBIN HOO, which was already enough to solve the mystery of what he was about: an ad for Robin Hood bread.

"It's awfully beautiful," said Mother. "Even an ordinary little ad can be beautiful sometimes."

Especially, I thought, if you write the ordinary little ad across several miles of sky.

"If you call that skywriting," said Uncle Snevely, "it's pretty plain you've never seen skywriting, that's all."

No one picked this up, which was not a rare thing with Uncle Snevely's openings, and we all watched the tiny black cross in the sky, the buzzing pen-nib, roll leisurely toward the completion of its message. It was beautiful, after all, the white solid jet of smoke, its edges struck to gold and black by the sun and shadow, streaming away in such a definite line; and there was always the millionth chance, too, I suppose, that this time the airplane was really on fire, that the smoke would turn black and begin to plunge away down the sky.

"Oh, look," cried Mother. "He's misspelled bread. Bred."

"It's just another advertising trick," I said. "Though the way people brutalize the language these days, spelling through t-h-r-u and night n-i-t-e. . . ." I let it go, not only because the others weren't listening, but because I was just repeating a notion my English teacher had a sort of fix about, and I didn't care one way or the other what people did with the language.

Sure enough, the cute little man in the plane came back and put a caret between the E and the D, and then put an A up above. The suspense was over, though I didn't really imagine all the eager spellers on the ground rushing forth to buy Robin Hood bread as a result.

"The finest man I ever knew was a skywriter," said Uncle Snevely. "A *chevalier sans peur et sans reproche*."

I did my best to pretend that some leaves wanted raking thirty or forty feet away, but Mother said:

"I think you've done enough for now, Robert. Come sit down and talk with us."

This meant come sit down and listen to us, but there was no easy way out, so I did.

"Robert will be interested in this story," said Uncle Snevely, "since he is so interested in aviation."

It was true that I wanted to fly, and intended to join the Air Force after college—I never did, by the way—but it did not follow that I was interested in anything Uncle Snevely had to say. The odd truth was that I was a little frightened of him.

I don't mean being afraid of anything he might do or say to *me*, because he was a very mild, maybe even helpless, little man, who had never been good for anything in his life and never would be good for anything, and was a drinker as well. I was frightened of his sadness, his general air of inadequacy, something awful and weepy about him which I identified with the smell on his breath and the constant liquid fullness in his eyes. I had high ideals for myself and had put in all this time reading good books and preparing myself for citizenship in the community, and I didn't want to run the risk of catching whatever it was that Uncle Snevely had.

He was a drinker, this was understood, but even about his vice there was something crippled. He wasn't a drunk, he didn't even on any occasion that I remember *get* drunk. Simply, he had to have that sort of nourishment constantly handy if he was to get through the day. When he visited us, which he did for about two to three weeks each fall and spring, he always had some kind of glass within reach. From five o'clock on this would be cocktail or highball; we weren't by any means a nondrinking family, except for me, and I had sometimes, though rarely, seen my father in a condition to which Uncle Snevely probably could not have attained. But with Snevely the stuff was like insulin to a diabetic; he didn't need much of it at a time, but if he needed little he needed it often. And because he wanted so much, at the same time, to be at least reasonably respectable, perhaps even because he thought, poor helpless man, of setting me a good example, his drinking through the morning and afternoon was carried on under a variety of disguises. He would carry a glass of milk through the house, sipping a bit wherever he stopped to chat or read the paper, and the milk would have, say, rum in it. He would go for a glass of water—"Got a frog in me throat," he would say, apologetically and cheerfully—and stop in the pantry on his way back to put gin in the water. Gin, being colorless, was of course a great help to him, but he didn't rely altogether on that; his coffee after lunch, for instance, would have had whiskey in it. And I remember how one afternoon the year before, when I'd come in hot from playing tennis, I saw this half-empty bottle of Coke on the coffee table in the living room and I drank it down, finishing just as Uncle Snevely came back. He looked at me, and he looked at the empty bottle, and then marched straight on through as if that had nothing to do with him. I didn't notice anything except a slightly odd taste till I got upstairs and lay down for a few minutes to rest before taking my shower, and slept through supper.

Right now, on the flagstones beside his right foot, there was a glass of rather thick and viscous-looking water. Moreover, having a cold, he came provided with a pocket atomizer, which, I had maintained to my parents the night before, blew Scotch mist into his nostrils. My father had laughed a little at this, but Mother had become very reserved:

"I don't consider that a very nice joke at all," she had said.

"I wasn't joking," I said.

"It is not a remark for a young man to make about his elders," Mother replied. "You don't know everything about the world yet, you know. My brother has had a good deal of trouble in his time."

What this great deal of trouble was I never knew, but had heard of one, possibly the last, episode in it: Uncle Snevely, only a few years before, had forged a check in somebody else's name and been arrested. My father had persuaded the other person not to prosecute.

Sitting on the terrace, as Uncle Snevely began telling about his skywriter friend, I had a sort of vision of Uncle Snevely sitting at a desk somewhere—in some abstract cloud chamber of my imagination—laboriously, blatantly, and with a glass of gin beside him, forging that check. Of course he would do it badly; of course he would be caught.

The skywriter had begun on Robin Hood bread again, in another part of the sky. His first effort, meanwhile, had already blurred and become illegible.

"There was this fellow, when I was young and lived in New Jersey," said Uncle Snevely, "this fellow used to fly over, every calm day, from the airport at Teterboro, in a little old biplane he'd fly over, to practice his skywriting. And by skywriting I really mean *writing*. Not like this stuff—" he gestured on high—"which is nothing but printing, such as kids do in second grade.

"You are a young man, Robert, and because of all the wonderful things, the inventions, that have come into the world in the few years since you were born, you probably believe in Universal Progress."

"Well, no, as a matter of fact—" I began.

"But Progress is not, um, equal in all directions at once," continued Uncle Snevely, "and in the art of skywriting you might say there has been no progress at all, but actually Regress. In fact, skywriting, which used to be quite a big thing and attracted international attention, is now, you might really say, extinct, a lost art, like stained glass and mummies and, um, things of that nature. Mind you, I am not against Progress."

At this moment we observed, as though it had been summoned by the mention of progress, a jet plane drawing its double chalk-line up the sky.

"When I see that, for instance," said Uncle Snevely, pulling with "for instance" the jet plane smoothly into his discourse, "I always see a Great Hand with an Eraser coming after it through the sky. That Great Hand is a Symbol."

He sniffed, took out the atomizer, squirted some whatever-it-was into each nostril, took a sip of gelid-looking water, and resumed.

"I can well remember the first day we saw the skywriter," he said. "One of those long, still, seemingly endless summer days without wind, when, in that small manufacturing town out in the Jersey flats, the heavy air seemed like a kind of eternity, which would never move away, never be replaced by anything fresher— an eternity compounded of smells, smells, or even stinks, which I can understand might be offensive to someone passing through, but in which someone born and bred there, like myself, became a connoisseur: there was the smell of garbage, pig food; the smell of rusting iron in the sun's heat; the smell of decaying rubber tires; and, as the broth in which these ingredients could be picked out,

the faint smell of the salt ocean and the drying mud at low water—
all these were beautifully, yes, beautifully, blended into one dear
essence. Forgive me, Robert—I'm sure your mother understands.
It was, after all, the place of my boyhood and youth."

I looked at him, and his eyes, sure enough, were overflowing, as
they so easily did. Even ordinarily, the eyeballs seemed to float in a
medium which I thought of as made out of tears and alcohol,
which would seep out on very little provocation and run down his
flat cheeks.

"It was on such a day, toward the end of summer, that we looked
out the office window and first saw the skywriter. I was, by the
way, as a young man, more, um, serious than I may seem to be
now, I had ideals and ambitions and industry and a certain amount
of brains to go with 'em. I worked in the biggest of the local facto-
ries, a place which made the old Triplex typewriter—they went
under in the crash, in Twenty-nine—and I had already got to be
assistant to the manager of the ribbon division.

"By the time we noticed him, this skywriter had already drawn
three parallel lines across the air, and was beginning what you
might call his penmanship exercises—*e's, l's,* and *o's*—for the day.
They used to have not only a better grade of smoke, back there,
one which lasted longer, at least in still air, and didn't spread out as
though you were writing on blotting paper, but also the airplane
itself, for some reason I have never understood, was a handier instrument, and the device for squirting the smoke made a finer nib
than they use now."

"Those old airplanes," I said, "were more maneuverable, because they were slower. A medium turn, in a jet, would take you
over six miles of sky."

"I suppose there is some such reason for it," Uncle Snevely said.
"Anyhow, this old biplane seemed just right for the purpose, and
everyone in the office, as I suppose most everyone all over town,
watched with great attention while the fellow finished his practice
warm-up and then wrote out in Copperplate style: *A thing of
beauty is a joy forever,* and *Beauty is Truth; Truth Beauty, that is*
. . . But there, it seemed, he ran out of ink, or smoke, and flew
away to the east, leaving behind him those noble thoughts so neatly written across the sky, words which remained there through the
afternoon in scarcely dissolving strokes, until they were outlined

in bold relief by the rays of the late sun at evening. We had all been severely told to get back to our desks, but the thing had captured our imaginations, and I especially kept raising my head every few minutes to stare at those majestic messages, which seemed to stir in me what I may well call a divine discontent, not only with the ribbon division and my assistantship, but also with the idea and the whole life implied in those things."

"I don't remember any skywriter like *that*," Mother said, not in contradiction but rather wistfully.

"One forgets, one forgets—so much," answered Uncle Snevely. "That may have been the year we thought you had tuberculosis, and you spent the summer in the Adirondacks, remember that?"

"Well," said Mother, "I do remember about the TB scare, and the Adirondacks, but surely I was never away the whole summer?"

"Well, anyhow," continued Uncle Snevely, "he was there, after that first time, nearly every day—every clear day without wind, of which there were a good many. He would write, most days, beautifully turned sentences, like, *To be or not to be, that is the question* and *Shall I compare thee to a summer's day?*, but on other days he would write down, or write up if you like, more puzzling things, sometimes things which were perhaps not altogether in good taste, such as *Conception is a blessing,* or *Don't laugh, lady, your daughter may be inside.* Once there hung over our heads for the whole afternoon the ominous symbols $E=mc^2$, the sense of which we of course were unable to make out, and he sometimes wrote in Latin, using an elegant uncial style: *Flectere si nequeo superos, Acheronta movebo.*

"I was courting at this time a young lady, Eunice Brown by name, who was a little above me socially, being the daughter of the manager of the ribbon division. I communicated to Eunice something of the emotions in me which were stirred up by those writings in the sky, she acknowledged similar stirrings in herself, and we wondered together if it might not be possible for us to meet the person responsible for so arousing us, and perhaps get him to write for Eunice and myself something from Edna St. Vincent Millay or Elinor Wylie.

"But at the same time, being an alert young fellow, I thought I saw a way to combine business and pleasure here. I suggested to Mr. Brown, who in turn suggested it to the front office, that this skywriter, if he could be persuaded to it, might write advertisements for the Triplex typewriter all over the sky above New York City, which would be an original, attractive and inexpensive means of reaching the greatest (and greatest typewriter-using) population in the world. This notion of mine, though it was Brown's notion by the time it reached the heights where policy was decided, found favor in the eyes of the mighty, and Brown's gratitude was enough to make me, as I had hoped, the delegate.

"So you may imagine not only my pleasure but my vanity as Eunice and I drove over to Teterboro; with a few words I had achieved so many things—a day off, with my young lady beside me, in her father's Pierce-Arrow with the top down, a day off which, moreover, actually bettered my reputation in the company whose representative I was; and, with all those things, the gratification of my private desire to become acquainted with the skywriter and know something of his art. I even imagined, as we drove along, a scene in which a lean young hero of the air offered me free flying lessons, on account of my great interest, and showed a willingness to accept me as his first pupil. The world seemed to open out, although at the same time my reason told me that at best I should approach no closer to this ideal than perhaps being allowed to compose the ads which the skywriter would weave the words of over New York City, before an audience of millions.

"Eunice was less aware than I of the complexity of motives involved in our visit; she had brought along a volume of Edna St. Vincent Millay, and was trying to decide on a favorite passage short enough to be performed by airplane.

"Romantic dreams," said Uncle Snevely, taking a new tone and interrupting himself as it were, "romantic dreams, I have always found, come true and not true in curious ways. Sometimes I think that on the drive over I should have paid more attention to what Eunice was thinking, and less to what I was thinking. They fell in love, Eunice and this man. Nelson St. Yves was his romantic name.

"And of course—of course," Uncle Snevely added, in what was for him a ferocious voice, "he turned out to be short and fat, and nearly forty years old, and in every way unsuitable except for, I guess, his most romantic name of Nelson St. Yves."

I may point out here that Uncle Snevely, even as a youth, could not have been strikingly the opposite of short and fat.

"He stood by his very dirty airplane, one of those left over from the First World War, the kind they called Jennies—"

"The Curtiss JN-4."

"Yes, I suppose its name was something like that. Anyhow, he was smoking a cigar, right next to the engine; he kept the cigar in his mouth even while he leaned in under the cowling to fiddle with things, wires and such, and he talked around the cigar with a kind of tired affability, a take-it-or-leave-it attitude which somewhat angered me, nervous as I was in the first place on account of the danger of fire or an explosion. After all, we had come all that way to be nice to him, and he seemed to be taking it as his due, the way a king would. But I suppose what I was feeling, what caused my irritation, was Mr. St. Yves' beginning to take notice of Eunice, and her beginning to respond to him (she was becoming less 'sweet' and more nervous, more what you might describe as a 'modern' young woman) so that I was being treated more or less as an extra.

"'So it's your neighborhood I've been working over,' said Nelson St. Yves. 'Glad you like the stuff. Some places, people can't put up with it—but they don't really own the sky, do they?' His laugh showed him to have very dirty teeth and many gold fillings.

"'You write such beautiful thoughts,' said Eunice, 'and you write them beautifully, too. There's something so solemn about living under a sky that has messages on it. Reverend Dyce used your skywriting in his sermon last week,' she added.

"'Well, that's normal,' the skywriter said. 'Though actually it's not the messages I care about. Most anything would do. It's the style that has to be perfected.'

"This was my chance to get in and say that if the messages didn't matter, why, the Triplex typewriter people were prepared to pay so and so much for him to go and write *their* messages over New York City, in a style as near perfect as he could make it. But Eunice had seen her chance, and taken it first, handing him the Edna St. Vincent Millay book and asking if Mr. St. Yves would possibly be so kind. . . .

"He stood there holding the book in his greasy hands.

"'Sure,' he said. 'Which line do you want me to write?'

"And Eunice, who had been so busy trying to make up her mind on just this one point, now blushed and said, 'Oh, I think you ought to be the one to choose.' And they stood there smiling at each other in a tender and exasperating way.

"'What will you give me if I pick your favorite line?' he asked, throwing Eunice into a pretty confusion because the answer obviously was supposed to be 'a kiss' and Eunice was not, or had not been till then, the easy kissing kind. To save her embarrassment I cleared my throat and began.

"'What the Triplex typewriter people are prepared to give,' I said, and outlined our proposals, which, after seeing Mr. St. Yves in person, I had begun to believe were not only fair, but actually more generous than necessary. So using my discretion I offered a sum substantially less than I was empowered to. He listened quietly, leaning against the lower wing of the plane, chewing at his cigar, and now and then running a hand over his not recently shaven chin.

"When I had finished, he said first that skywriting over a big city like New York was unprofitable—'unprofitable for the style, you get me?'—because of the numerous air pockets which interrupted the steady motion of the plane."

"There are no such things as air pockets," I broke in on Uncle Snevely here. "No one talks of air pockets any more. That's a superstition."

"Well, I am only telling you what the man said to me," Uncle Snevely replied a little huffily. "He said that he practiced out on the flats, over the salt marshes, because there were no, or very few, air pockets there. That's all I know."

"He must have meant convection currents," I said, feeling at the same time that by stooping to the criticism of this detail I implied that in other respects I was ready to believe my uncle's odd and silly story.

"Robert, don't interrupt your uncle," Mother said.

"But the main thing," Uncle Snevely resumed, with a sharp look at me, "was not the, um, convection currents—no, it was more surprising than that.

"'It's a nice-enough proposition,' said Nelson St. Yves, 'and I could use the few bucks. But, you see, I can't afford to lose my amateur standing; they're very strict about that.' And he went on to explain that his practicing so hard was in preparation for the International Championship Competition in Skywriting, which was going to be held that winter in Oberammergau."

"Snevely," said Mother, "Oberammergau is where they have the Passion Play."

"I'm sure he said Oberammergau," said Uncle Snevely, "but it doesn't matter, really."

"But I've never heard it mentioned in connection with sports," Mother persisted.

"Who's interrupting now?" I said.

"I raised the offer somewhat," said Uncle Snevely, "but rather halfheartedly, not only because I was rather disillusioned with the man, who seemed definitely casual and ill-bred, but because after all his amateur standing was obviously of the first importance to him, and I hadn't come prepared to argue about that.

"It was *all* rather disillusioning. Eunice's father, Mr. Brown, was a pretty good man, but strict, and when it turned out that instead of accomplishing something big I had merely been taking a day off on the company's time, at its expense, and in his automobile, not to mention with his daughter, he would not look favorably on me at all, especially since he had sold the whole scheme to the higher-ups as his own. So I was all for getting out of there, and making the best of a bad situation by showing up for work at least half the day. But while I was thinking how to make our excuses politely but definitely, St. Yves and Eunice were getting on fine, chattering about the sky, and flying, and messages, and Edna St. Vincent Millay, whose poetry the man continued to leaf through as they talked.

"'Why not come and see how it's done?' he said, to her and not to me. I coughed.

"'You mean—in the airplane?' Eunice was being girlishly delighted, and, I thought, somewhat scared. I coughed, and no one paid me any attention.

"'Why, I'd be just pleased as anything,' Eunice cried, and then turned to me with a serious face. 'It will be all right, won't it?' she said in a pleading way.

"'Your father didn't give me permission to let you go up in an airplane,' I said.

"'Are you her cousin?' asked St. Yves, 'or what?'

"'Oh, Daddy won't mind,' Eunice declared. 'Come, it'll be fun.'

"In the end, it was obvious to them that they had to take me, since there was just room. The airplane could be flown from either cockpit, and the front one was large enough for two. But this was something I didn't understand until too late. St. Yves suddenly became very polite and helpful to me, and insisted on my climbing up on the wing and thus into the bucket seat, very low, of the after cockpit; he strapped me in, answered my nervous questions—'Parachute? Never use 'em. Too close to the ground'—and showed me how to place my legs and feet to be out of the way of the duplicate set of controls. Then, when I was snugly tied down, and fitted with a dirty old helmet he had handy, he and Eunice climbed into the front cockpit together, with, on his side, much gentlemanly handing of her up and fussing lest her skirt get dirty. I was enraged, but I was also extremely nervous about going up in an airplane for the first time, and before I could settle myself enough to say anything a mechanic arrived to swing the propeller, the engine started with several bangs and a kind of jittery roar, and it was too late.

"That ride," said Uncle Snevely, and paused to take several sips from his glass. "That ride, I tell you, is something I will never forget. That rickety old airplane, for one thing, creaking and groaning, the engine sputtering and sometimes, even, just as we started down, stopping for a moment entirely—"

"Gravity feed," I said wisely.

"Whatever it was. Oh," said Uncle Snevely, "the difference between seeing something from far away and seeing the same thing close up, or for that matter inside it, and not really *seeing* it at all. Dreadful.

"The first part wasn't so bad, just flying over there. And the last part, just flying back, was a blessed relief—but in between, I tell you, I suffered.

"All that had looked so graceful and quiet from the ground, all that carving of immortal thoughts against the great background of the heavens, became, when you were involved, a hell of noise and motion and the smell of oil and whatever it was there was in that smoke he used. St. Yves would throw the airplane violently over on its side, my legs and ribs and even sometimes my head would knock against the cockpit wall; he would rise, and my stomach would sink; he would dive, and my stomach would come up to my chin; for a moment we would hang upside down, then nose over so that the brown marshes and my unrecognizable home town would swim madly up toward us, then suddenly we would be in a turn so intense that my cheeks felt as if they were being pushed down off my face. And, yes, finally, I was sick. I threw up, and could not avoid spattering the trousers of my best suit. But even that wasn't the worst. The worst was that it didn't stop, it went on. Surely, I thought, now that I've been sick it has to be over, there's nothing more can be demanded. But it just went on.

"No, I'm wrong, there was one thing which, at least in memory, was worse than that." Uncle Snevely made this assertion more impressive by drinking again. "That all this time you actually could not see what the man was doing. I presumed we were making letters, since that was what we had been taken up to do; but we were so close to the letters that no impression of the message could be formed whatever. Sometimes, even in my desperate condition, I got the idea that we must be dotting an *i,* or climbing the sickening curve of a *d.* And as I looked down I could see between my knees the stick which in obedience to St. Yves' hand was making us go through these insane contortions. The stick made very small motions this way and that, while we made these enormous motions this way and that. But even after we were through we didn't get a sight of the finished product; our track home kept us end-on to whatever we had written, for, as St. Yves said when we got safely back on the ground, we had been short of gas and couldn't spare the time to stand off and admire the work.

"'What did we write?' asked Eunice, who seemed not to have suffered at all, but to have enjoyed herself immensely.

"'Oh, you'll see, it'll still be there when you get home,' St. Yves said carelessly. And then out of somewhere in his flying costume— and this was in Prohibition—he quite openly got out a bottle of whiskey, and offered it around.

"I didn't drink, back then," Uncle Snevely said somewhat severely, eying his glass. "But what with the punishment I had just taken, and with the shock I received when Eunice, with no hesitation whatever, took a strong pull from the unsanitary mouth of that bottle, I felt justified there and then in tasting alcohol for the first time."

Uncle Snevely sat very straight, and seemed to pull round him more firmly the robes of an invisible dignity.

"So that is something else I owe to Nelson St. Yves," he said.

"He does not sound so much like a *chevalier sans peur et sans reproche* to me," said Mother.

"That was the ideal of him which I had formed," said Uncle Snevely. "He embodied the ideal in a reality which I may have found detestable, but that is not to the point. He was a knight of the sky, that was all there was to it, and he did not live, as we do, by earthly rules."

Uncle Snevely was quietly, automatically weeping again, but he went on.

"We drove back pretty much in silence, Eunice and I. I felt humiliated and still sick, and the whiskey which I imagined accusingly on my breath did not help me to recover my spirits at all; whereas Eunice seemed to glow with a quiet but intense happiness, a dreamy quality, as though some simple discovery like flying had all at once given her a new perspective on life, and expanded the limits of her vision.

"Long before reaching home, of course, we saw the results of our afternoon's work, pleasure, torment, however you look at it. In letters made fire by the setting sun it was written across our local heaven that *Euclid alone has looked on Beauty bare,* and by suppertime a good deal of indignation had been generated about it, too. Many people in our community did not like the idea of anyone, even a dead mathematician, looking on beauty bare; misunderstanding the very pure intention of the line in this way, they naturally were disposed to make a fuss about the effect of such a thing on their children's morals.

"Mr. Brown said nothing to me, probably because he did not know exactly what there was to say, and before he could make up his mind about that, he—and I—had other troubles. For during that weekend, as he told me on the Monday morning, Eunice had literally 'taken off' with Nelson St. Yves, and nothing was heard of the pair of them for about two months. Mr. Brown, it was plain, regarded this as largely my fault, and said that though he did not propose to take any outright action against me, such as having me fired, he would see to it, he said, that there would be no further advancement for me in any firm of which he was a member."

"If that is the end," said Mother, "I think it shows Eunice was not the girl for you, and you were fortunate to find it out in time."

"I'm sorry, Uncle Snevely," I said, "but I just don't believe sky-writing was ever the way you make out."

"That's extremely rude to your Uncle Snevely," said Mother.

"It wasn't the end, though," said Uncle Snevely. "Eunice came back and I married her when she was four months pregnant."

"Snevely!" cried Mother. "You never!"

"And as for you," said Uncle Snevely to me, "if you don't believe these simple things I have been telling, well, I am sorry for you."

He got out the atomizer again and squirted himself, then he took a long pull from his glass, which was almost empty.

"You won't want to hear about the circumstances of my marriage," he said, "my marriage, which has made me what I am today." He smiled at this pompous phrase, or at something. "She died at childbirth, and the child died, a little boy. I was going to be courageous, and make Eunice be, and call him Nelson. But that wasn't necessary.

"At her funeral he came back. He flew so low I thought he meant to crash at her grave, but his arm showed over the side of the cockpit and he threw some flowers, some lilies, very big ones. Then he went off a bit up the sky and wrote on it, *Sweets to the sweet, Farewell,* and flew off elsewhere. I called the airport at Teterboro, but he had not landed there."

"After all, even if you had found him, what would you have said to him?" I asked.

"I would have killed him," Uncle Snevely said. "I've never told anyone that story until today," he added, picking up his glass and rising. "Thank you both for your patience in listening. The sun's going in now, and I feel a trifle chill. Besides, it must be almost the cocktail hour."

And he padded off up the crazy pavement to the house, turning at the porch door to say, "I would have killed him, it would be kind of you to believe that."

"Of course Snevely never married," Mother said as soon as he had disappeared.

"The whole story is pretty absurd," I said. And when she didn't answer: "You agree, don't you?"

"You mustn't be so cruel as that," said Mother. "It obviously meant a great deal to him. When you are older, and understand more about the things people go through, the things that happen to them in this world, you will sympathize more readily—however it really happened, it must have been a terrible blow to him."

"However *what* really happened?" I cried, in some excitement. "You say yourself that he never married—there was no Eunice, there was no child, there was no tragedy. And of my own knowledge I can tell you that there never was any such skywriting as that, and that there was no Nelson St. Yves, an obviously fake name if I ever heard of one—"

"And no Teterboro, New Jersey, either, I suppose?" Mother said this with some spirit.

Then, as she arose and followed Uncle Snevely into the house, she said with her regained gentleness, "There is always something, Robert, always."

Uncle Snevely died that year, in the winter. He had been living in a furnished room in a town some two hundred miles away from us, and evidently having for once got thoroughly drunk he must have become incompetent to get back to that room, for he was found the next day in a snowdrift. Among his papers, which came to Mother, there was a picture of a girl, but no name on it. And at the funeral I rather hoped for an old Jenny to fly over, with a hand emerging to drop maybe a pint of whiskey, but none did; nor were there among the few mourners any strangers who might have been mistaken for Nelson St. Yves.

One thing more. I did write this up the following year for my course in English composition. I may not have phrased it exactly as I have here, but the order of things was pretty much the same. By that time I had given up wanting to be a pilot, and wanted to be a novelist instead, so although I was merely repeating what Uncle Snevely had told me I called the thing "a short story." Professor Selvyn wrote on it as follows (I looked it up just the other day) in his kinky, hurried, erratic hand:

Good beginning effort. Your greatest trouble—apart from your obvious [two words illegible here]—is that you do not create believable characters. All these characters are unbelievable. In rewriting, build up the mother. Make Eunice more believable especially. However, this is a good try; have you thought of printing it in the Blazon *[school literary magazine]? B.*

Below this, as an afterthought, someone else—I never found out who—had scribbled:

Have you noticed: Nelson St. Yves = Snevely + Son + St.?
I had not noticed, and I do not much care, though now that I am older and sympathize more I can see it as a sadly appropriate epitaph for Uncle Snevely that he should finish as one among a group of unbelievable characters.

The Native in the World

The climb from sleep was difficult, a struggle up a staircase of soft pillows into which he sank again and again, drowsily defeated, from which he clumsily climbed again to a sight of the room that, seen in the equivocal wisdom of sleep, seemed to him any room, or all the rooms, in which he had ever slept, or ever been at home. Perhaps (an instant afterward he could no longer remember)—perhaps the phrase 'at home' struck the first tone of clarity in his mind, for about it the room began to arrange itself, to become again the familiar fashion of his circumstance, rising and composing to his own composition of its features. One thing—the overturned chair by the desk, with his clothes crushed under it— remained obstinately unfamiliar; when had he done that? He searched his memory, but the incident had sunk under sleep; he could readily imagine himself coming in drunk and knocking the chair down in the effort to hang his clothes over it, but actually to remember doing it—that was a different thing.

He got out of bed, and as he stood up felt pain protest harshly in his forehead, making him dizzy with the angry sleep that would not readily dissolve. The clock said ten more or less exactly and it was dark outside. That meant twenty hours sleep; since two Tuesday morning. The dizziness surged higher as he bent in a methodical stupor to set the chair right and get his clothes. Going into the next room he started the phonograph and put on the Ricercare of the Musikalische Opfer; then settled back in the darkness of a far corner. The one voice strode through his mind with a more or less plaintive confidence that another would follow, and soon another did, then one more and another, and the rest were sunken in the ensemble and the scratch of the needle. He closed his eyes, and as if his consciousness rested on quicksand he was irresistibly sucked back toward sleep, his eyelids grew heavy in a sort of undertow that he could feel heavily about his head. A dream, some frightening and fast forgotten dream, jarred him out of sleep; he had a vague impression of fear, something was being thrown at him. He turned on the light, changed over the record and picked up a book that was lying on the couch: *Alcohol the Friend of Man*. It was a reassuring volume by a doctor of unspecified repute; one must, he thought, turning over the pages, combine theory with practice. It seemed to him, as he had so often said, that there was a way to drink seriously, and a way not to drink seriously. Of three years at Harvard he had spent the last two learning the former, and was glad to distinguish himself from many of his acquaintances whose drinking was of the rowdy-up-and-puke sort. If a man wish to drink himself into insensibility, he phrased it pedantically, that is his own business; but equally he should not become a charge on his fellow-beings, and there is no excuse for forgetting manners one instant before passing out.

The record was over, and he walked across the room to change it, a strange figure in white pajamas, barefoot, head slightly too large for his excessively small frail body. He already had on his silver-rimmed reading glasses; he must have picked them up from the desk without thinking. He came from the Middle West, but one would unhesitatingly have called him a Yankee, judging by his pedantic contemptuous manner, his manners so civil as to be rude whenever he gave a cutting edge to his voice. His own estimate of himself was quite accurate: that his aloofness was respected, also his enormous and casual erudition; that even full professors were chary of a too great freedom with him or with his papers; that it was generally said of him that he would go far if he did not drink himself to death; that his paper on Augustinianism in the 17th century would no doubt put him in line for a fellowship; and at last, that he was drinking himself to death, or near to it—a state which he conceived of dubiously as a slight chill in his personal weather, as though a cloud should slide over a hill on which he was sunning himself. As to his reasons—if a man wish to drink himself into insensibility, he thought again . . . and perhaps it is not even his own business, or perhaps it is a shady transaction in that business, into which he does well not to inquire too far; look what happened to Oedipus.

He had put on the Ricercare again, but now he turned it off in the middle and called Rico's number. He listened apprehensively to the empty buzz of the phone, three, four, five times: he could hear it as if he were in the room, but as if the room were still empty, the lonely stupid ringing. Damn Rico, he thought, damn the twisted little Cuban Jesuit gone wrong, and damn, he said, and damn with the ring of the phone, and damn again and hung up. The receiver clattered into its cradle, and he felt again how painfully slow it was to wake up, how fiercely he must fight to stay above the surface, so to speak, to force every last ache and hurt in body and mind to the service of wakefulness, to a nagging insistence on belief in being awake. Rico was probably out with Alan; Alan, he thought angrily, the little blond jew-boy who's trying to get me out of the way by advising me seriously to go see a psychiatrist. And Rico is helping him too.

He shuddered slightly, envisioning conspiracy and betrayal: the swift, sure, honest-eyed kiss of treachery, the bright, the clear, the trustworthy Judas; and the appalling thing was that it took place on such a pitifully small scale, the love life of a colony of worms. The disgust, and the hate, were waking him, slowly, as one fever will fight another and overcome it.

He took up the phone again and called Rhys. One could always talk to Rhys, no matter how far they had gone apart. Long ago, before the drinking, as he thought, they had been close friends, working furiously together, reading two and three books in an evening and listening to Bach from two to four in the morning. And then—there had been no break, not even a coolness; but they went their ways and saw rather less of each other. When he was drunk and wanted to talk out of turn, he often still climbed to Rhys' room, and he would talk wildly for fifteen minutes, often incoherently, and then Rhys would deliberate heavily, and say at last, "Well, John, it's difficult . . ." which in itself would be somewhat reassuring; and then they would exhaust a small stock of polite and cynically erudite remarks about obscure poets, or faculty members, and it would be over.

"Hello, Rhys? This is John—Bradshaw. . . . I hope I didn't disturb you?"

"Not at all," said Rhys, in the coldly amiable tones that meant he was disturbed.

"Look, Rhys, . . . you mustn't mind me; I'm not drunk, but I took twelve grains of amytal last night when I was. I've just managed to get out of bed and I'm a little—woozy." He was, in fact,

woozier than he had thought; there was that dull weight on his
forehead that was worse than pain, more unknown and more fearful therefore.

"What I wanted to know was could you meet me for a drink,
about fifteen minutes from now?"

"No, I can't," said Rhys. "You sound troubled. I don't know
medicine, but isn't twelve grains rather much?"

"The prescribed adult dose is a grain and a half. I wish you'd
come out for a drink. I want to talk to you. Really, you know, it
gets to be too much, sometimes . . . everywhere you go people are
such bitches. . . ."

"What the hell is wrong, John?"

"Oh,—look, I'm liable to ramble a bit—I'm not very awake and
the drug is still pretty strong—Oh goddam it Rhys, I've been betrayed, I—"

"Again?" A politely skeptical coolness.

Steady, he thought to himself; he was weak and falling again,
and before answering he bit his lower lip hard, till the blood ran, to
save himself from sleep.

"I mean it," he said stubbornly.

"Yes," said Rhys; and John recognized the tone Rhys used to
nice drunks. "Yes, people are . . . difficult sometimes."

"Rhys, I'm not drunk. I want to talk to you. Why won't you
have a drink with me?"

"Because I don't feel like it, John."

"Rhys, you think I'm drunk. I'm not, Rhys. It's the amytal. I
couldn't be drunk, Rhys, I just got up, I've slept since two this
morning."

"I know you're not drunk, John," said Rhys coldly. "I'm busy,
and I think you ought to go back to bed. You don't sound very
well."

"I only want to talk to you about Rico. You think I'm drunk."

"What's Rico done now?"

"I want to talk to you, Rhys."

"Well . . . ?"

"Not on the phone."

"All right then, good night."

"Rhys—"

"Good night."

He waited for the dead click at the other end, and then placed the receiver carefully down. That had been a shameful performance; he was not drunk, but he could not have been more maudlin in any case. Rhys would be nodding his head sagely at this very moment: poor John Bradshaw. Oh, damn Rhys. It was unfair of him. He might have had the common courtesy to listen to me, Rhys the careful, Rhys the undrunk, the dullard so proud of his dullness; one could summon up at will that favorite image of Rhys the damned, sitting deep in his armchair after a peculiarly bitter confessional period, sitting like a tolerant father-confessor, saying slowly between puffs at a cigarette, "Gawd, all you people live such exciting lives—it must be so difficult for you—you come and tell me about drinking and drugs and your homosexual experiences—and I sit here on my can, taking it all in, living my dull life . . . ." And he would sit there on his can, looking as old as he could, and staring into the fire, saying "they also serve," or some such. Poor Rhys! And so anxious, too, for you to know that he was only pretending dullness (which God knows he was not) and that he was a man of deep spiritual crises; as he would say, and so smugly, "My blowups all take place inside." All right. Let Rhys take that attitude. He wasn't required.

He got to his feet and walked slowly about the room, still thinking about Rhys, beating one little fist determinedly into the other hand and thinking with melancholy savagery, "cut away the non-essentials, cut them out." Rhys was a non-essential, Rhys always worrying about his writing, his piddling poetry, his painful anxiety that you read his newest work, that you pat him on the head, that you say nice things. . . . As for himself, he thought, there would be a book one day . . . a book after this long silence, after the non-essentials had been cut away and meditation had burned some great stone to form inside him, a book that would say all these things that had to be said, against the lying time, against the lying treacherous people, against Rhys, against Rico, against Alan, against (he sneered) all these smilers with their dull knives. One voice in his wilderness would not waste time crying out for help, for cries would only bring the wolves along faster. And through this, beneath the pain and the hate and the disgust and the still half-prevailing sleep, he knew that he was crying out.

He went into the bathroom and looked at the bottle of amytal.

There were at least twenty-five grains left; he smiled a little to remember the time when one grain could give him a solid night's sleep, the rapid necessity to step up the dose, the doctor at the hygiene building telling him pedagogically that he was by definition a drug-addict, his crazily epigrammatic crypticism to the doctor ("Jonathan Swift was by definition not a well man, and a neurotic to boot"), his cheerful announcement to Rhys (Rhys again): "You may call me De Quincey, I'm depraved." It was the precipitous, the plunging rapidity with which it had happened, this drug business, that astounded him and started slight inadmissible fears from their careful rest. How one thing led to another! in such seemingly inconsequential succession of one pettiness on the next, until, looking back from the most extravagantly fantastic heights of improbability, from the most unwarranted excesses and distortions, one was surprised and shocked to note how accurately and how unerringly every smallest act, word and gesture quietly conspired to build such a wildly rococo and out-of-the-way edifice—such a goblin's architecture that at one moment one shuddered to think how it drove one on to the end, and at the next dismissed the whole structure with a smile for its implausibility. He stared fixedly at the bottle, imagined himself reaching out for it, tried to imagine himself refusing, and could only get a more or less chromo reproduction of a man in a magazine advertisement with his head turned disaffectedly away from a cup of coffee saying: "Nope, I keep away from it. Keeps me up nights." This did not seem to him a satisfactory image of moral grandeur; with a smile he took up the bottle and locked it away in the filing cabinet on his desk. Then, puzzled, he looked at the key to the cabinet; what to do with that? He took it with him into the living room. He stood in the very center of the carpet, shut his eyes and turned around thrice, as though he were absurdly playing some children's game of blind man's buff; with his eyes still tightly closed, he threw the key straight before him, heard it tinkle in landing, then turned around twice more before opening his eyes. A glance about the room satisfied him that the key was not in evidence, not obviously anyhow. It might be days before he came across it. Unless the chamber-maid picked it up in the morning. He could imagine that she might hand it to him, asking whether he had lost it, and imagine himself saying no, I wonder how it could have got here . . . but one couldn't do that; all one's correspondence was in the filing cabinet, and notes for a couple of essays as well. Anyhow, it would be easy to find the key again, when it was really required. Meanwhile, one could . . . imagine it lost.

He decided to give Rico one more chance, and dialed his number again. The equivocal ringing—does it ring if you're not there to hear it?—angered him; he thought it possible that Rico and Alan were in the room, refusing to answer, he could hear them guessing who it might be, smiling complacently, drifting from smiles into their moonings and caressings, their adolescent, ill-informed lecheries—but no, neither one of them would have the strength to let the phone ring and keep on ringing; across each ugly infirm purpose would flash thoughts of importance, of some great person, some missed opportunity, the thought especially: it might be something better. And they would answer the phone. Rico particularly would answer the phone, compliant opportunist, affection's whore . . . had he ever done differently, or been anything else? Rico? who told (with pride) how he had been seduced by the house-maid when he was fifteen, and how three weeks later he had gone to his mother and got the girl discharged on some pretext.

No, they would answer the phone, he knew, and since they had not . . . Perhaps they weren't even together; he cut the call short and dialed Alan's room. Alan's roommate answered:

"Hello."

"Hello, is Alan there?"

"No, he went out half an hour ago."

"Was Rico with him?"

"I think he was going to meet Rico. Is there any message I can give him?"

"No thanks."

"Your name . . .?"

"No thanks," he said coldly and replaced the receiver. He thought desperately for a moment that he might call Rhys again, then rejected the idea. There was no sense in begging. He felt tired again; the weight in his forehead had turned into a headache, and his eyes tended to water. The slight exertion of walking about the room made him want to go to bed, but he refused, and to clinch his refusal, began to get dressed. A drink was probably what was needed, he thought. A drink, and an hour out of this room. There was the mood he had been in all too often lately: his room depressed him, almost as much as did a library, for example; and the best things in the room—the Matisse over the victrola, for example—they were so recognized, so much the very breath of this tepid climate that they became unbearable, and music was unbearable, and work as well, and it all seemed to him the ugly and ready-to-hand diversion afforded a man sentenced to life imprisonment. Not the ugly, but the commonplace disgusts, he thought. If they put Matisses in the street-cars, one would counter by hanging advertisements on one's walls. Yet he felt unsatisfied outside his room, again like a prisoner so acclimated as to shun freedom; a walk, however short, tired him inordinately, and climbing two flights to the room made his head throb as if the blood would burst out. He felt now that he required a drink; he would go to St. Clair's, nor did he disguise from himself the fact that half his motive was to find Rico, and that if Rico were not at St. Clair's he might be at Bella Vista, or McBride's, or the Stag Club, or he might be in town at the Napoleon or the Ritz or the Lincolnshire.

By the time he had finished dressing he found himself nearly exhausted. He had to sit down on the couch and turn out the light, and it was then that he began to think about the key to the filing cabinet. He felt that he had perhaps been foolish, with his infantile stratagem. He might need the key in a hurry, for his notes, or to answer a letter, or—no need to disguise the fact from himself—to get the amytal when he came in drunk; it had to be conveniently to hand, or he would get no sleep. He must recognize the fact by now, he argued: he required the amytal, he was a mature individual, still sane, heaven knows, more sane than most of his dull acquaintances, he would not over-dose. And anyhow, the test was in the will to stay off the stuff, not in locking it away, there was no help in that. To be able to keep it before his eyes, that bottle, to look at it steadily, and steadfastly not to take it—at least not more than was absolutely necessary—there was the thing. Besides, suppose he needed it in a hurry, sometime, and the key had got lost—there were any number of ways that could have happened: it might have fallen into a crack in the floor, might have slid under the carpet, might even have landed down the radiator gratings, irretrievable short of large-scale operations that would require the janitor.

Hastily he turned on the light, began to look around. It was not that he wanted any now, or would take any tonight; but this was the saner thing to do, he must know.

The key was discovered with ridiculous ease, under the bookcase. He picked it up and laid it carefully in the middle drawer of his desk. And unformed to speech or even to clear thought, but present in his mind, was that justification, that ritual against reason, of a postulated higher power, of unspecified nature, watching over the episode, the feeling, carefully swathed in obscurity: Providence didn't want me to hide the key, or I wouldn't have found it so easily.

Put vaguely at ease, he began to get on his overcoat, and then decided to call Rhys again, buoyed up by this same vague assurance that he would, by however narrow a margin, do the thing which was to be done, that the thing would be right because he did it. But there was no answer, and for some reason, he was more infuriated at this than at Rico's absence—a little relieved, too, for Rhys would have been annoyed; but angry, angry that Rhys should not be there, should have gone out after making some excuse to him. Betrayal, he thought, furiously and without power. Rhys too. Although loneliness was his habitual way, it was by preference, because it suited him to be alone, but this, the loneliness by compulsion, was a new thing. He felt a terrible isolation, the phone seemed to him now only an instrument of the Inquisition, to teach him his loneliness as it were by rote, and he had the sudden sense that whatever number he called, it would be closed to him by that instrument. In fact, he thought in satiric anger—in fact this whole room is given only to people who want to be left alone. It is made to teach them the measure—that is, the unmeasurable quality—of isolation, of being absolutely alone. Harvard College built it that way—they get a lot of lonely ones around here.

The brief walk in the cold, up Dunster Street and across the Square to St. Clair's, fatigued him excessively; he recognized that last night's dose had not nearly worn off, and that the cold had the unusual effect of making him want to lie down and go to sleep just wherever he was, in the street even. It was almost like being drunk, that disgusting soddenness with drink that made it Nirvana just to stop moving, anyhow, anywhere. He kept up his heart to a degree by repeating his little catechism of betrayal, his interdict on Rico

and on Rhys, all the fictions of his misery forming into churches
for his martyred self: here was a first station, where one knelt to
beg forgiveness for being rude to Bradshaw; and here a second,
where one knelt to do penance for being out when Bradshaw
called, here another for thinking Bradshaw drunk when he wasn't;
here another for the general sin of offending Bradshaw; and a last,
where one prayed for the grace of Bradshaw: Oh Bradshaw, we do
beseech thee . . . and a return for the petty humiliations, and a
hundred-fold paid back each error, and he knew it for pitiful, but
nevertheless went on, in a rage of cynical benevolence, to forgive
Rico, to forgive Rhys, to forgive them and cut them away from his
side, and to go on in the thorough lonely discretion of his anger.

When he entered St. Clair's the first person he saw was Rhys,
big, rather stout, and darkly dressed as usual, sitting by himself at
a corner table. Rhys waved and beckoned to the chair opposite,
and John sat down there.

"You're avoiding me," he said without thinking; his anger came
to a head and he wanted a fight.

"If I were avoiding you, would I come and sit in a bar?" asked
Rhys politely, and it was like being hit across the face.

"Then why did you tell me you couldn't go out?"

"I didn't say I couldn't go out. I said I didn't feel like going out."
Rhys was nettled, and showed it by getting more and more polite.

"If you don't want to see me, I won't sit here."

"Don't be silly. Sit around and have a drink."

Rhys, he thought, was playing for a dull peace and it was not to
be allowed; he must be disturbed, made to give himself away. He
ordered, and got, a large martini, and sipped it in an uneasy silence.

"You should have gone to bed. You look as if you were trying to
kill yourself." Rhys gave in and said something.

"What the hell would you care?" he asked rhetorically, hoping at
the same time that Rhys would say something friendly and reassuring.

"How is it possible for anyone to care? You're not very responsive to care, you know."

"Oh, some have managed." He lit a cigarette. It tasted very bad,
but it was against the sleep that even the drink seemed to drive him
at. The place where he had bit his lip was still tender, it hurt when
he spoke.

"You alienate even those," said Rhys. It was for him as though he had said 'where are you, John?' and reached out a hand in the darkness; it was such an unwelcome thing to be forced to find people when ordinarily they came and disclosed themselves.

They finished their drinks in silence and ordered more.

"Now what's this about Rico?" said Rhys at last.

John emptied his glass again, slowly, before answering. "It's only that from now on," he said, "I'm going to play dirty too. If you don't what chance have you got?"

"I always thought of Rico as more or less irresponsible," said Rhys, "but—"

"It's not only Rico, God knows. He can be excused: if you were bounced out of a parochial school in Cuba and landed at Harvard with the prospect of eight million bucks when you came out— *alors*. Not alone Rico, no. It's everyone. And you too, sir. Don't you understand: I'm playing your way now, the safe way you all play, don't give anything with one hand that you can't get back with both, any time. And if I can't beat these Jesuits at their own game—well, what the hell . . ." he shrugged his thin shoulders, deliberately blew smoke across the table between them.

Rhys determined to show no annoyance, to maintain objectivity. So he sat with hands out equally on the table, looking like the balance-pans of the blind goddess.

"Essentially stupid attitude to take," he said. "I mean—granting that people do present . . . difficulties at times—still, just how much have you got hurt?"

"Got hurt, hell. That's not—"

"You don't need to answer me," continued Rhys with a show of calm. "I'm just suggesting the question as something for you to worry about."

"Don't go on; you had it right the first time, when you said something about responsibility. You just make an ass of yourself when you put it on the piddling level of 'getting hurt.' It's only a question of how the essential non-pirate is to live in a world of pirates."

Rhys had no immediate reply to this, so they ordered more drinks and John continued:

"Romans and Orthodox Jews make the best pirates because even if they do put pretty far out to sea after plunder, they've both got a sailor's snug harbor to get to again. The Catholic can drop anchor in a church, the Jew carries his absolution along on shipboard. But they aren't the only ones, not by a long shot. It applies to everyone you know . . . piracy isn't so safe a game for them, but if you think for a minute—"

"I wish you wouldn't pretend to sit in judgment when you're looking so pitifully ill. You remind me not so much of the Christian Way as of Nietzsche."

And suddenly John felt the fatigue again, the wish to give it up; what was the use in arguing with Rhys. The drink was having an inordinate effect because of the amytal. He knew it would be difficult to get up, next to impossible to walk home.

"Hell," he said. "It's only an argument for you. Forget the whole thing." And then: "Will you take me home?"

"What's wrong? Not feeling well?"

"I'm sick to death of sitting here with you, listening to your well-fed brain. I want to leave and I can't do it by myself. I'm asking you: as one last favor, would you see me home? Let me assure you, sir, it will be the last. I shan't disturb you and your values again."

"Please don't be melodramatic with me, John," said Rhys in a quiet rage.

"Can't you see that's not the question?"

"Don't you think you'd feel better if you sat here without drinking for a few minutes?"

"Oh for heaven's sake, sir, don't be reasonable with me. I've asked you a question, will you—"

He felt a draught on his back from the open door. Shivering extravagantly, with the hope that Rhys would think him ill, he turned and saw Rico and Alan standing beside his chair.

"Wha's wrong, little one," asked Rico, slightly drunk, smiling with his beautiful teeth.

"Rico!" He held out his hand, forgetting Rhys, forgetting Alan. "Rico"—and more softly, as though drawing the other into conspiracy—"will you take me home? I can't go myself."

"Sure, little one. I can take you home. Come, give me your hand." Rico laughed, his laugh and his glance taking in the whole room, stranger and intimate alike, as though to disclaim all embarrassment and responsibility, as though to enlist their sympathy not for John but for self-sacrificing Rico who had to take him home.

"Come," he said. "Up on your feet."

He got to his feet slowly enough, his eyes half fading from their focus. The floor seemed to rock beneath him, his ears filled with noise, and it was as if he stood on a separate planet that rocked backwards and over in space, out of sight of Rhys who sat there with an embarrassed expression on his face. Then suddenly he knew he was heavily in Rico's arms, and in one instant synapse of sobriety he heard himself saying to Rhys, "I hate you more . . ." and Rico saying roughly, "Come on," pulling at his arm. Then the two little voices were again swept away in a wave of sound against his brain, formless sound at first, that resolved itself into a rhythm and at length into words spoken from far away: "Drink and drugs that done him in," or some such; and then—drink and drugs—he could no longer hear for noise, but the enormous voice of Rico was in his head saying "Come on, come on," and all at once they were in the street and the cold stung his eyes and the sweat on his cheeks.

Rico and Alan had taken him by the arms, close to the shoulder, and were dragging him along. Whenever he stumbled they set him right with a jerk that lifted his feet off the ground.

"Wait," he said. "Sick."

And while they stood silently by holding him, Rico holding his head forward, he was sick, with a horrible violence, in a little alley off Dunster Street. His stomach, almost empty to start with, twisted painfully at the finish, and he lost consciousness.

When he came to he was alone in his room with Rico. He could not see Alan anywhere. He rested on his bed and Rico was taking his clothes off. There was no longer any rest, or desire to sleep; there was only pain in his stomach and an actively hurtful weariness.

Rico finished stripping him, folded him in between the sheets. "You'll be OK in the morning," he said. "You were sick as a bitch. How d'you feel now?"

"Rico," he whispered. "Don't go away, Rico." He felt distantly that he was a child, in his child's bed at home; he had done a wrong thing, and Rico would be angry, with the efficient necessary anger of a mother.

"Kiss me, Rico," he said. "Kiss me good night." And then, as
Rico made no move to comply, he said: "You're mad at me . . . ?"
with a pathetic dubious note of shame in his voice, and Rico
stooped and quickly kissed him on the cheek.

"Now good night, little one."

"Don't go, Rico. Stay here tonight."

"I can't. You'll be all right now."

"But I won't, Rico. I won't. I'll be sick again." He grew panicky
with new fear. "I swear I'll be sick again," he said. "The minute
you leave. Don't leave, Rico."

Then, in a tone of malicious invalid craft, he said accusingly:
"You gave Alan the key to your room, didn't you?" Breathless, he
went on: "You told him to wait in your room, didn't you."

Rico's face gave him away; it was true, it could only be true.
"That's why you want to leave," he went on. "I know why." Quietly he began to whimper, and the tears rolled down his face. Then
in a desperate martyrdom he said in a choked voice: "I'll kill
myself if you go. I'll kill myself the minute you go out that door."

"Nonsense, what would you do it with, little one?" Rico was not
very good at situations like this; he felt vaguely that he should
comfort, should sacrifice himself a little and help; but he had no
intelligent means of doing it, being frightened not by a lie, but by a
lie that would involve him later.

"I'd take all the amytal. I would. It would be enough. You'd see
it would be enough. Rico, don't be a bastard. Don't go away."

"You mustn't do that, John. You mustn't think of it."

"And you can't find the amytal either. I hid it." There was a
terrible cunning in his voice, he was determined to have the drug.
It did not at that time matter to him whether it was a lethal dose or
not; it was to spite Rico, to hurt him, to say to him: 'See what
might have happened. The guilt would have been yours, you would
have murdered me.'

Rico went to the bathroom to look for the amytal.

"You can't find it, you can't," he mocked in a thin voice cracked
with approaching hysteria. "Go away, damn you. Go away."

Rico came back into the room.

"You won't do it, John."

"Get out."

"Promise me you won't do it."

"Get out."

"If you don't promise I can't do anything."

"I said get out."

Rico was faced with something beyond his comprehension, and he took the only way he understood.

"All right," he said sullenly. "I guess it's your life." And having thus washed himself clean in his own eyes, he walked out.

There was no question of decision, now he was alone. It was again that unfaced trust in a higher power, in some back world watching. With unnecessary stealth he got out of bed and, entirely naked, went to the desk, got the key and opened the filing cabinet. He took the bottle into the bathroom and poured all the pills into a highball glass, which he filled with warm water. This decoction he took back into the living room, where he sat down on the couch by the phone and began to drink. When the glass was empty there remained a considerable residue of damp powder at the bottom, so he refilled the glass and started again, more slowly, from time to time stirring the mixture with a pencil. At last he had finished. From experience, he knew there would be about fifteen minutes to wait.

He turned on all the lights, not feeling like getting into bed again. As he stood naked in the corner by the light-switch he was taken suddenly with a frenzy. The thing was done, it was done. Was it right? was it so at all? The indecision after the event frightened him, he imagined the maid finding him in the morning and with a certain sense of abject shame rushed to put his bathrobe about him. How to know? He questioned if he should be saved, and then, as he became somewhat more calm, there occurred to him another of those tests of providence, another cryptic question to which the oracle might smilingly equivocate over his special case.

He took up the phone and dialed Rhys' number. If Rhys answered he would explain and have him get a doctor. If there were no answer . . . and as he listened to the ring he felt certain there must be. It was not so much the test of fate, but the thought that he must speak again to Rhys, apologize, absolve, ask forgiveness.

There was no answer. Unwilling to believe, he put the phone down on the table and let it ring. The answer was given, but unsatisfactorily only more or less given, with the smiling ambiguity of power. He went to the window and opened it, then sat back on the couch. It is doubtful that he thought any more of death, of the probability or the certainty. He listened to the dried icy branches of the trees scratch together in the wind, down in the courtyard; and it is doubtful that he thought of leaving anything behind, of regret, or the irrevocability of death.

For his room, warm with the lights full on, seemed to him some tall citadel of the sun, with a certain congenial ease of sunlight upon it, and when the sleep came down, it drifted in like the cool sudden shadow of a cloud, that only made him shudder slightly.

The Idea of a University

On Sunday mornings President Ramshorn inspected his university, or at least went around it with one of his deans, this morning Dean Bildad of the Graduate School of Divinity. The president chose Sunday for his tour because almost no one was about, and there would be relatively little bowing and scraping to acknowledge.

Because it was the first Sunday of term, and maybe because of the presence of Dean Bildad, the occasion lent itself to wistful philosophizing on the themes of grandeur, achievement, and the passing away of men and worlds. The president began.

"What talent I've got," he said, "is for money. Don't think I don't realize that's why I'm here. Look at that now, Bill."

"That," still mostly hidden by foliage, was the new Aero Engineering Building, a long glass-and-metal shed slanting from the middle of the Park into the space between two old red-brick buildings given to the mellower studies of English and History.

"There didn't seem anywhere else to put it," said the president. "And even then they had to take down the Trysting Elm to get one of those fighters through the doors. But you've got to move ahead, you can't stand still."

"Place has changed," Dean Bildad said, "since we were undergraduates. World much harder to see around nowadays. Do you know that the kids can major in Hairdressing now? in Cosmetic Chemistry? in Fashion Design?"

"It was the Angel Azazel," President Ramshorn reminded him, "who taught men the art of war and women how to paint their faces. Book of Enoch. And of course I know everything that goes on here."

"Apocryphal," said Bildad, and the two men walked on in silence until he took up the theme again. "I've just remembered that when I studied Physics you weighed things with spring balances. A spring balance, now, is something I can understand. A touching

139

little instrument, with a homey charm all its own. I don't imagine they'd let a spring balance through the back door these days."

"No, they have somewhat more, ah, sophisticated methods now," the president vaguely allowed. "When I spoke of knowing everything, a moment back, I meant, of course, in a general way and with respect to its administration. Even Solomon, dear Bill, though quite correct in choosing wisdom, didn't know everything, but only everything pertaining to earthly rule."

"The world is too specialized," Dean Bildad agreed, if it was agreement. "No one—or so I'm told—can even know his own field any more."

"I certainly hope that isn't true," the president replied, "especially considering the salaries we pay some of these fellows nobody can quite say what they're about. What is slow light, Bill, would you know?"

Dean Bildad said it might maybe refer to the dawn of understanding in a student's head.

"I don't have to know exactly," the president went on, "but I would like to know if it means something just a shade off the standard figure—these scientists make their triumphs on what seems so little sometimes—or whether the stuff really does just creep across the floor. We've bought this fellow name of Mordecai Bosch, got him in out of Austria; well, he received the Nobel Prize for 'the invention of slow light,' that's what the citation said in the *Times*. Those Swedes must have had expert opinion; he's got to know what he's about—but how would you check? He doesn't teach, of course, he just thinks."

"You could ask him."

"Oh, I wouldn't want to do that," the president said; obviously he had already rejected this solution. "He's a very tetchy fellow, his English isn't good . . . They've had some trouble with him already, you see, because he hasn't got clearance. The Security Officer tried to explain to him, and did explain to his colleagues, that the Project wasn't to be mentioned in his presence till his clearance came through. So he sulked, Bosch did, for several days, and then began coming around during coffee breaks and committing breaches of security; it seems he thinks classified thoughts."

"What project would that be, now?"

"Well, Bill, I'm not allowed to say. But Defense thinks a great deal of it, I can tell you that."

Having completed their tour of the Park and its circumjacent buildings, they now boarded the president's limousine for a survey of the outlying precincts. Whitman, the Negro chauffeur, held open the door for them, and then resumed his place at the wheel.

"It's not only specialization," the president said, referring back a bit, "but integration."

Dean Bildad placed a finger before his lips, then indicated with it the Negro's back.

"Integration of disciplines," President Ramshorn went on, "confusion of fields. Fifty years back, Bill, a chemist stayed in one building and a physicist stayed in another building. Chemistry was cooking and Physics was playing with blocks. Atoms were bricks and there was no nonsense about three dozen invisible pieces inside them. Economists had never heard of anthropologists—no more had theologians—see what I mean? The world was more dignified, as well as simpler.

"I'll tell you, Bill," he went on, "a young fellow Clemence, in Math, at dinner the other night—Grace and I have them to dinner, you know—he was trying to explain to me what a Lobachevskian triangle would look like, and why; well, I tell you, I was morally affronted. Not because he drew it on the tablecloth, no, but because a triangle has got to add up to a hundred and eighty degrees, or the world is going to hell!" He slapped the seat beside him in emphasis, and added: "A razor made of glue!"

"What?"

"Time. He said that time was a razor made of glue. Brr."

The dean nodded.

"What you say is true in my bailiwick too, Fred. We've got a good school, I think, and in one way you might figure Christianity has never been more popular, especially with the intellectuals. But sometimes I wonder if it's Christianity. In our day a kid went to Divinity to be ordained, and go out to preach—theology, criticism, homiletics, Hebrew and Greek, that's what he studied. Then Comparative Religion got big. The utter silliness of a curriculum," he suddenly exploded, "that puts that sort of thing in a Divinity School just because it has 'religion' in the title. If I had my way,

Comp. Rel. would either be got rid of entirely or be taught as far as possible from our lot—on the Agricultural campus, maybe."

"You can't go back into the past, I guess," said the president.

The car was rolling through a rundown neighborhood of sagging frame houses bordering the railroad; Negro families were sunning themselves on the steps.

"Sooner or later," said the dean, "we'll have to buy up all this and clean it out. The town won't do it, and we need the land. The way it is now, our buildings are all dispersed over the landscape and the town pushes in between."

"This here?" President Ramshorn was surprised. "This does belong to the university," he explained. "It's our model slum."

"Is that—is it, well, ethical?" the dean inquired after a long pause.

"It's a very big project," answered the president. "Sociology wanted it badly, Economics wanted it for some studies they were doing, the Political Scientists found they could use it to good effect on local government, then the Anthropologists got in the act. . . . Finally everybody could see it as one huge integrated project, the Lasswell Foundation put up matching funds, we got the Department of Fine Arts to use faculty architects—and we went right ahead. Imported the tenants from Georgia. I assure you, Bill," he added earnestly, "it's an improvement in their situation, a real improvement. And of course it makes a situation where they can be studied. They've got their own churches, of course, if that's what you meant."

The car stopped beside an enclave of buildings new and old, large and small.

"Psychometrics," the president said. "I believe they study children."

"They are in my business too," the dean assured him. "They are trying to induce religious ecstasy in a selected group of divinity students and make electroencephalographs of the results; they say they are correlating Unitive Experience with variation of the Alpha rhythm."

"You don't say," said the president, and both men got out of the car.

Approaching the entrance of a white marble building without

windows, the two men were stopped by a sentry, one of two armed MPs who flanked the iron door.

"Sorry," he said. "Authorized Personnel only. I'll have to see your passes."

"Young man," said Dr. Ramshorn, "I am the president of this university."

"Can't anything be done about that, sir," the young man replied civilly enough.

"We didn't actually want to go in," said the president, "only to walk around."

"Not allowed," said the sentry.

"Young man," Dr. Ramshorn said, "I'll take your name and serial number, and I can promise you are going to hear about this; if necessary the Base Commander is going to hear about it. This is my university."

On hearing this the sentry presented arms, making an effect of deference and defense together.

"I wouldn't push it, Fred," advised Dean Bildad in a whisper. But now the president smiled.

"Good man, soldier," he said. "Strict obedience, letter of the law, no exceptions. Just testing," he added, "just testing."

Taking Dean Bildad by the arm, President Ramshorn, evidently pleased, turned him gently back toward the car.

"I bet we're the only campus in the country," he said, "with a Maximum Security Experimental Prison."

"An oddly elegant though appropriately tomblike arrangement," said Dean Bildad.

"It was built for the Art people," said the president, "to house the Caithness Collection. Then the Caithness Collection was torpedoed on the way over, but luckily the courts held that we had already accepted it formally and were paying the freight in an American bottom, so the insurance went to us. That's how we built the new all-denominational chapel," he added, "so you can see how everything adds up in the end."

"What do they do in there?" asked the dean, taking a glance back at the prison.

"Defense is doing studies in brain-washing, Bill. The Korea business got them mighty scared. They don't call it brainwashing, of course. I bet you couldn't guess the code name for the operation?"

"I guess I couldn't," said the dean.

"Operation Dry Clean," said the president, grinning, "because American brains couldn't stand the shrinkage, get it?"

"I get it."

"General Maclehose told me that. Got a keen sense of fun, General Maclehose."

Whitman held the door open, and the two got back in their limousine. Off they went toward the completion of their rounds.

"I like making this tour," said President Ramshorn. "Oh, I know we don't actually *do* much, but it kind of reassures me that everything is in its right place. And I get to know you fellows better, too. After all," he added with much seriousness, "a university gets its name because it is modeled on the universe. Whatever they have out there, we have here too."

But now it neared noon, and activity increased in and around the campus. For the last item on their tour, the president had Whitman halt the car briefly before the plate-glass front of their newest installation, the Random Access Computer Unit. Inside the window were visible several metal boxes, a couple of consoles, and a large typewriter which, with no evidence of human control or for that matter attention, was patiently printing something across and down an apparently endless roll of paper that fed in turn into a large but overflowing wastebasket.

Digressions Around a Crow

One afternoon in midsummer my son David appeared on the scene followed by a crow. Improbable spectacle, but there it was; the crow not flying, but walking at a distance of some six feet behind the child. A recent shower had left large puddles on the lane, and David walked through the puddles, while the crow detoured around them. My wife watched, I watched, as the two of them in line astern proceeded across the lawn. Suzy the dog and Alfred the cat also watched, somewhat alertly.

"This is my crow," David announced, with a prepared indifference. "He follows me everywhere." My wife Peggy, who responds to even the happiest emergencies with food, had already said, "He must be hungry, poor thing," and gone into the house.

"What is so special about you?" I said to my son, "that a crow should follow you?" I was chagrined. Given my long-standing sympathy with bird life of all domestically available sorts, it seemed to me as though a bird interested in forming human acquaintances might reasonably have come to me first.

"He just likes me, I guess," said David.

The crow was now walking and hopping tentatively about, investigating the gravel of the drive. He picked up a pebble, swallowed it, then coughed it up; he did this a number of times. Presently my wife appeared with a pan of bread moistened in water.

"Watch out for Suzy and Alfred," she said.

"He doesn't mind," said David of the crow, and this seemed to be true. Moreover, both cat and dog were, for the moment at least, more surprised than overtly hostile; and neither of them, probably, was able to move fast enough to catch a full-grown crow in command of his faculties. Still, I thought already that the crow's attitude to these animals was extremely casual.

"I'll feed him," David said to Peggy. "He won't trust you." Indeed, the crow, almost insolently familiar with a small human being, appeared to have reservations about large ones, and would

145

give a nervous compound hop-and-flutter backwards at our near approach, without, however, flying away.

When David sat down with the pan of wet bread, there was at first the other difficulty; the crow wasn't timid, but David was. A close view of that black, metallic beak made him tend at the last instant to throw the bread rather than give it; but this was soon overcome, and the crow was swallowing the bread, some of it permanently, along with some stones which David once in a while included in his diet. This may have been a bit thoughtless of the boy, but after all, I thought, whose crow is it? and I refrained from making speeches. Anyhow, the bird did not appear to distinguish in any absolute manner bread from stone. Sometimes he would take a piece of bread and put it carefully under a stone for future reference—he didn't generally forget these things, by the way, but was able to find them again—while sometimes he would take a stone and put that under a stone.

"His name is Joe," said David. "Joe Crow. Here, Joey, Joey."

The crow was silent, but continued to let himself be fed, and even stroked.

"He looks so bedraggled," Peggy said. "Look, the feathers on his head are almost gray. He must be starved."

"Probably yearling plumage," I said, not above introducing an authoritative note of fraudulent lore into the discussion.

"Now we have a cat and a dog and a crow," said David happily.

And so it seemed we did, for the crow began reporting daily to our house, first to be fed and then to play—with David and with the other children who turned up. It was an enchanted time, and gave us a kind of mythological status in the neighborhood. That black shape, with his black shadow, became an eerie, comic presence, walking behind the child, flying above him, perching deep in the green jungle overhead.

II

By the second day, Joey had moved on from moistened bread to pieces of salami; in keeping, said I, with the first law of the feeding of animals, that it always moves in the direction of greater expense. A grudging, unlovely remark, but I was remembering the grosbeaks who came to the feeder every winter. They would sit there, high up out of Alfred's reach, a dozen at least of them, with others resting on the clothesline when they weren't fighting for a place at the trough, and chomp away at sunflower seeds (not inexpensive) until they could barely fly. Nor did their serious gluttony prevent them from meanwhile braying and squawking and squabbling, so that they looked like a collection of Dodger fans eating peanuts in the old days at Ebbetts Field. Unlike the relatively polite nuthatch or even bluejay, these birds did not take seeds away by ones to devour in silence, but sat there crunching and munching and dropping shells on the porch along with their other droppings. When nothing was left but shells, they would bicker digestively for a while, then lurch heavily away through the air; but as soon as I replenished the supply they seemed to know it, or they had told their friends in the interim, and a large collection of grosbeaks again appeared.

It is part of the ethics of feeding birds in winter that you cannot leave off without feeling some twinges in the conscience, as though the beaked and taloned harpies of a small remorse were at you. So these grosbeaks had cost me a very fair sum, and my remark may be taken as directed at them, and not at Joey.

Besides, in return for the charm of his company, we were so obviously doing him good! In a few days, on a diet of salami, the ashen complexion of the feathers of his head deepened to its proper blue-black and rainbow shine; a few days more, and his voice began to be heard: the standard crow noise, written by humans "caw"—and yet extremely expressive, so that if you couldn't say just yet what it was expressive of, you nevertheless found yourself thinking that a few days more might make all the difference: either Joey would articulate more clearly, or you would understand better, and he would be saying something like, "In actual fact, the last place I was at they didn't feed me this good."

Or something. For if the first thing one does with a wild creature come to the door is feed it—unless it is so obviously large and threatening (lion) or otherwise noxious (skunk, king cobra) as to make this unadvisable—still, the second thing one does is form a theory or two to account for its presence.

"He must have been brought up by human beings from a fledgling," I said. "Wild birds just do not come and make up to human beings in this manner on their own."

"Probably the owners moved away," said Peggy, "and left the poor thing to starve."

Peggy's view of human behavior would make such an action about par, but I favored a less vicious image, of a kindly, white-haired old lady; she was doing the cleaning, the screen door stood open for the better beating of carpets and shaking-out of mops and rags; the clever bird (crows notoriously are) managed to open its cage and escape to a freedom it was no longer equipped to endure.

"He is a crow anthropologist," said David, "and the crows have sent him to investigate people."

"Is that what they teach you in that Social Studies book?" I asked. But this theory seemed, finally, about as good as the others. For you have theories because you are a human being, and that is what human beings do; not because the theories are likely to account for the sudden presence of a pet crow. Or rather, as I was at pains to emphasize to David, not a pet but a visiting crow.

"He doesn't belong to us," I said on several occasions in my disagreeably pedantic way. "He is a free agent, and as long as he wants to come to us that's fine, but I don't want you bringing him into the house or putting him in a cage, or anything like that. Things are exactly and beautifully right just as they are."

"He can't go back to the flock," said David. "They'll kill him for being with humans." To this remark, with its combination of sci-entific-sounding ornithology and animistic magic, I was unable to say anything except that it contradicted the crow-anthropologist theory. All the same, Joey evidently did go somewhere at night, and I rather thought it must be back among his wild fellows, who could be heard cawing mightily for an hour before dusk in the woods below the house; the wonder was that he came back.

Not that he came back exclusively to us. Several times David reported dejectedly having seen Joey breakfasting at the Durands', or hanging around Robert's lawn at lunch time.

"Well, that's the good thing about it," said I, "that he doesn't *belong* to anybody." All the same, I was ready to be a little peeved myself. There is a sneaky distinction to being selected friend and patron by a wild creature, and one tended to resent, for Joey, his making himself common.

Still, it turned out that he was with us more than with others;

maybe our salami was better. Our expectation got to the point at which Peggy said we would have to do something about him in the winter; a box, maybe, on the porch, where he could shelter from the worst of the weather.

III *Digression on Birds*

For us amateurs—what Grandma, God bless her, might have called nature-noshers—a relation of this kind with a wild creature has a marvelous charm; as though a beautiful, inaccessible world comes close and begins to open itself; an idea of edenic innocence and trust looks wildly possible, one dreams of speaking the language of birds, of understanding. . . . O Tarzan, Mowgli, Bomba, Siegfried (to grow up a bit).

My own adventures among the birds had been few and accidental; two anecdotes will sum up the range.

Once I came on a starling standing on a path. He didn't move at my approach, and soon I saw he was not so much standing as propped up stiffly on his feet and tail, like a three-legged stool. He hardly twitched as I picked him up and bore him tenderly home. Probably he had cracked his head on a branch (birds are sometimes not so bright at flying as we suppose) and was now in a catalepsy deep as Socrates'; still, I felt as proud and cherishing as could be, and hoped someone would be around to see me. All the upshot of it was, however, that I stood the starling in a safe place, sprinkled drops of water on his head as one might do with a fighter between rounds—he blinked a bit, and stood quite still, and half an hour later, when I was no longer paying him much attention, he took off, so that was that.

Then there was the yearling gull I picked up on the beach, since he too seemed unable to get out of the way as I came along. I kept him in a liquor carton for a couple of days, and tried to tempt him with cat food and even canned herring, but it was a pretty sick bird I had foolishly made myself responsible for—from his green, liquid, and foul-smelling excretions even I could understand that—and finally I had an inspiration: I would take the poor thing down to the Bird Sanctuary in the salt marshes a dozen miles away. *They* would know what to do.

I can't say, really, whether this plan succeeded or failed. My arrival with the sick gull in his carton coincided with the gathering of a group of binoculared bird-watchers who were about to be shown around the premises by a guide, and this guide, not without a touch of impatience at being interrupted, took one look at the bird and said:

"Botulism."

"I thought," said I, "you might know what to do for the poor thing."

"Oh, yes," he replied, briskly confident; and all those bird-watchers gathered round him with admiration amounting to reverence written on their faces. "Hundreds of 'em die of it every year on this coast—it's the garbage they eat. Best turn you can do him is wring his neck."

"!?" (indignation, horror).

"If you're squeamish about it, what you do is, you put him under the rear wheel and back over him."

I could see that this was a touch strong even for the bird-watchers, though if anything it probably increased their admiration they were feeling for Their Leader as a man who knew how tough things really were in this vale of tears—they would get a fine sense of inexpensive stoicism out of it. Whereas I—

"Oh dear," I said, "I don't know if I could do that."

"If you don't," said the guide, "he'll die anyhow."

And I didn't, and he did.

A painful business, though I can't see how it was my fault.

Professionals, anyhow, must necessarily be more austere about Nature, and less full of fine feelings. After all, they will point out, if Nature provided no checks, such as cats, on the robin population (for instance), in a few years the world would be so full of robins we should each of us be standing on a couple. Not an agreeable image.

My friend Thomas is a professional, member of the Society, bird-bander, trapper, writer on ornithological subjects, whom I have sometimes consulted on questions in this area. Once, when I reported to him on the phone what would have been a rarity if it happened to be what I thought it was, he ran through a list of characteristics which might reduce my find to something a good deal less spectacular, and then seemed sufficiently convinced to say:

"In this instance, I think you'd be justified in collecting a specimen."

"What?"

"Oh, yes. The Society wouldn't accept any report on this kind of thing except at the end of a gun; you'll have to have the skin."

A rather casual attitude, I thought, toward mortality; and a great price for a poor bird to pay, only for being a thousand miles out of place. In fairness to Thomas, though, I must allow his attitude toward humanity to include a similar factor of objectivity: the reduction of the race by, say, one half, seems to him a reasonable remedy for most of our troubles. As he has pointed out, if you have two major problems—overpopulation and nuclear weapons—one of them will sooner or later be viewed, not without reason, as the solution to the other.

IV *Digression on Dogs*

Practically everyone living in the countryside keeps a dog, if not more than one. I don't know what it is, there must be a myth about dogs and people. All behavior, anyhow, is a parody of behavior, so it is plain that the thoughtless automatism with which people in rural areas procure dogs for themselves or their kids must reflect some deep, unexamined presumption about How Things Are, or How They Used To Be.

These dogs are often extremely fierce, or at any rate they produce that impression. You cannot, in my part of the country, go for a walk of over two hundred feet without being barked at, growled at, sniffed up and down, and capered before. I carry a heavy stick whenever I go out. And yet I can scarcely complain, since as you have observed I too keep a dog. Suzy began life as a purebred beagle, but in the process of growth all the purity began moving to the rear, until now only her tail is purebred beagle: a very nice dog.

All the same, I do complain. And I introduce this question of dogs because of my worry about them on Joey's account. I admired our crow's calm and even gay insouciance with reference to dogs, but I could not commend his prudence. Not only would he provoke the neighboring dogs by flying along beside them as they ran, or just above their necks, and often in such a relation with the sun that they appeared to be foolishly pursuing his shadow;—not only would he dive on them and swoop past between their ears in a most unexpected and probably unsettling way, whereat even Suzy's ruff began to bristle;—but he would also, as a matter of course, walk around right behind one of them, often at a distance of no more than a foot.

The dogs chiefly concerned were, apart from Suzy, the following: Ranger, Ginger, Klaus, and Clancy.

If the perfection of a species is its beauty, Klaus was a beautiful dachshund.

Ranger and Ginger, either of whom might without injustice have been called Scrounger, went from house to house at feeding time.

Clancy had only three legs. This was the result of surgery which saved his life after he had been, doubtless through his own fault, hit by a car.

Human attitudes to Clancy reflected perhaps something of our attitudes to deformity and the deformed among ourselves, in three stages, thus: first, a deep horror, causing people to avert their eyes; second, a generous sympathy, from the perception that this brave creature got on very well on his three legs; third, the disillusioned certainty that Clancy used his deformity as a reproach and a weapon of advantage, to produce in human beings exactly the shamed embarrassment and remorse produced by the legless veteran selling pencils on the windiest corner. Altogether, about as attractive as Richard the Third.

I made as clear as I could to this crew of wretched opportunists (including Suzy) that I regarded Joe the Crow as being under my special protection; and was successful in getting from each of them a look of understanding though not of sympathy—for it is probable that our view of dogs as "nearly human," our exaggerated opinion of their intelligence, are based only on this, that by long association with ourselves dogs have developed an extreme sensitivity to guilt; conscience and remorse form the whole range to which the antennae of their supposed intelligence are tuned.

Probably all I accomplished in this way was to exacerbate in these dogs a mortal sensitivity to Joey, a sensitivity whose comparable progression in human beings may be seen to run from irritated curiosity to furtive lust to anxiety to desperate actions.

V *Digression on People*

Having a crow for family totem made us to a certain extent the envy of the neighborhood, but this view was not unanimous. It began to be said by a few that the crow terrorized very small children. All I could say to this was that they must be very silly children indeed, if they imagined that pleasant-tempered and altogether friendly and upright crow was going to do them any harm.

Then an embattled mother came to report that Joey had seized and flown away with her daughter's rattle—a silver rattle by way of being an heirloom, with (she said) the marks of her own and her mother's first teeth in it.

"Too bad," I said, "Obviously irreplaceable, isn't it?"

"Obviously," said she.

"He's not *our* crow," I said, "he only visits."

There followed some dark threats about what husbands, hers and others', had said about shooting the crow if it bothered the children. You might have thought this great *Lammergeier* of a crow was going to pick some kid up by its diaper and take off over the mountains. I assured the woman this could not happen, and even offered to show her an encyclopedia article which should put her mind at rest concerning the possible payload of any given bird relative to its own weight; but she left unappeased.

My neighbor Mr. Holsapple, a writer on philosophical subjects for ladies' magazines, also made a difficulty. A portly bearded man, Mr. Holsapple appeared one morning at breakfast, accepted a cup of coffee, and said:

"I am, to the best of my knowledge, a humane and tolerant person, without more than the normal amount of aggression—"

"Have you done something wrong?" Peggy asked.

"I am aware," he went on, "that this world has every title to be called a jungle, and that nature red in tooth and claw is everywhere around us."

"That is one view," I said, "but at the same time you must allow that recent researches have cut down very considerably on that sort of naive Darwinism—the work of Ashley Montagu, for example, would tend to stress rather the benign and even loving elements in—"

"You may say so," replied Mr. Holsapple. "You may say so. You may tell me that the man-eating shark, for instance, is largely a myth, contradicted by all the really verifiable evidence; that barracuda and piranha do not really eat human flesh, that even lion and tiger will not attack humans except when driven by extreme hunger. Still, it remains that the carnivores both large and small must eat death daily in order to exist—yourself for instance." He pointed to a leftover piece of bacon on my plate.

In the discussion following, it turned out that Mr. Holsapple was herbivorous, and had been for many years.

"Since the day," he told us, "that, doing the shopping for my wife, I walked into the supermarket and took one good look at a lamb chop, and realized all at once what it was—a piece of a beast like myself. I saw through the cellophane, I'll tell you that."

A further discussion dealt with man's place in nature, the idea of health, and possible scientific or totemic relations between meat-eating and hostility.

"So this morning," Mr. Holsapple said, "as I sat down to my work table, which I keep before the picture window giving on my lawn—as I was composing to myself to get on with this piece I am writing, a piece about Education For The Future, I was really quite disturbed to see that crow of yours—"

"He's not our crow," I said, "he only visits us."

"—that crow of yours alight on the grass before my eyes, and there proceed to dismember and devour a small mouse."

Mr. Holsapple was being to a certain extent humorous, of course. But it turned out that he was being to a certain extent serious as well.

"I wish you would tell that crow of yours," was the way he put it, "not to bring dead animals—or living ones—to my lawn and devour them in my sight. I find that sort of thing physically unsettling, as well as wrong in principle."

"I'm sorry," said I, "but I don't really see what I can do about your trouble, Mr. Holsapple. The crow is, after all, a friend, rather than a pet in any ordinary sense."

"Would you let your friends eat mice on a neighbor's lawn?"

"Just a minute!" said Peggy. "How do you know this was our crow?"

"Well," Mr Holsapple began, "I simply saw this large black bird, and I assumed—"

"I suppose," Peggy pursued, "you would be able to identify this bird by some particular markings, or characteristic individual look?"

"It seemed a reasonable presumption," Mr. Holsapple said, "that this crow was your crow."

"How many crows would you estimate lived in this neighborhood?"

"All the same," Mr. Holsapple said, as he got up, "I do wish you could convince that crow not to eat things on my lawn, at least not in the mornings.

"I've never wanted to make trouble," he added as he went out the door.

Poor Mr. Holsapple! Ah, Peggy! Ah, Portia!

VI

So, for a long and rather enchanted spell, Joey came every day, to be fed and then to play. The children, except the littlest, came, and when they ran down the lane Joey would rise and dive past them, tickling their necks with his wing, or with the black shadow of his wing. Joey would get tired faster than the children, though, and then he would sit in a tree, or on the roof, till he caught his breath and felt ready to play some more.

Sometimes in the morning or evening, after feeding, he would walk importantly around the car, inspecting his reflexion in the metal of the bumpers where they curved under. This was certainly a stage of development higher than that of dog or cat, who view a mirror as a strictly neutral and non-representational surface. What Joey saw, though, was not himself but another crow, whom he pecked at with a rather musical clang.

Now summer drew toward its close, there was a dusty silver to the still green wall of the woods, the heat began to have an indefinable feel of embers, and baseball was one day suddenly abandoned for football; which I mention only because Joey found this game more confusing than baseball, where it was easy for him to follow the runners around; and on the first day, he was hit in air by a pass. It knocked the wind out of him, he sat down suddenly in the grass, and stayed for a few minutes, but for the rest was neither damaged nor dismayed.

When school began, Joey followed David down to the village—human pride can rarely have had an occasion for soaring higher than this—and produced an educational crisis by perching outside various classrooms successively and peering in at the children in such a way as to prevent, it was said, work. On several occasions, David was told off to walk the crow back up the hill; whereon Peggy would have to drive him back to school to elude Joey.

We had by now even begun planning the crow some winter quarters on the porch, and agreeing that, in view of the severity of the winter weather, he might have to be, on some occasions, let in the house—though only if he freely decided to enter.

And then, of course, he went away, or he stayed away, or however you would put it. Suddenly—it could not have been otherwise than suddenly—he wasn't there any more. Had he gone South? Some crows did, and others didn't; there were always a few around in the winter.

David found a few black feathers in the path, over near where Clancy lived.

We did not condemn Clancy on this thin evidence. I looked at him, and he looked at me. But I looked at all the dogs, and decided their mute and universal aspect of guilt covered, concealed, and overwent the commission of any particular crime.

So that, I guess, is the mournful point, that nature returned to nature; that the wilderness, which had seemed about to speak, suddenly changed its—mind? or whatever you would call it. We were again isolated, with our dogs, in humanity, and the boundary which had been near to being dissolved at one little place was drawn again with a great firmness.

Was this the ordained result of our longing tenderness toward wild things? It looked to be so. If only, we think, if only they would come to us, they would learn how kindly we are, we humans, how generous, how loving. And here one of them had, one miserable crow, and almost without doubt died of the experiment.

Just as our dog, Suzy, at the seashore, chases wildly after the sanderlings, and when they fly looks mournful, as though to say: "I only wanted to play with them." But the sanderlings probably know better than she the extent of her wants, for she would have eaten them if she could; so with ourselves, who humanize wild nature in our thoughts, and in the reality are able only to destroy, though we do so—this is the worst of it—out of love and yearning.

There is one thought minimally happier than that, though. As between a death and a disappearance the evidence was imperfect, and not absolutely conclusive. Joey might have gone away, to return in the spring. Or some other bird-brained notion might have taken him, just to abandon us; maybe he was bored.

Anyhow, for better or worse, as my wife had suggested to Mr. Holsapple, we do not readily recognize the individuals of a wild species; bird-watching only rarely takes us that far, and we do not make those keen, subtle, unconscious discriminations of eye, ear, hair, pimple and chin which identify our human acquaintances. So, now it is spring, whenever a crow or two goes by we call out after it, "Joey," and again, "Joey," thus far without other result than a generic and rather cheerful "caw." But there seems some hapless charm in the unspoken belief that, somewhere among the anonymous many, a single crow with a name is thinking, even rather bad thoughts, about us.

III.
ESSAYS

FROM
Poetry
and Fiction:
Essays
(1963)

The Swaying Form: A Problem in Poetry

The present essay is not an attempt to solve a problem so much as an attempt to make certain that a problem of some sort exists, and, if it does, to put it clearly before you. No matter how many problems really exist—and now, as at all times, there must be plenty of them—the world is always full of people inventing problems simply as make-works for their prefabricated solutions. As a friend of mine wrote in a prize-winning poem at college, "We know the answers, but shall we be asked the questions?" He has since become a novelist.

The problem I want to try to elucidate is most often discussed as one of belief, or of value, which is prior to poetry, and the great instance of Dante's *Comedy* stands at the gate of the discussion. It is usually argued on this basis that an explicit and systematized belief is (a) intrinsically of value to the poet in his composition and (b) a means for improving his communication with the mass of mankind.

Now I shall be taking up this theme by what many people will consider to be the wrong end, and talking from the point of view of the poet. My reflections are very far from being impartial and objective, and positively invite objections, or even cries of protest.

I shall be suggesting, roughly, that the poet, if he has not attained
to a belief in the existence of God, has at any rate got so far as to
believe in the existence of the world; and that this, sadly but truly,
puts him, in the art of believing, well out in front of many of his
fellow-citizens, who sometimes look as if they believed the existence of the world to be pretty well encompassed in the sensations
they experience when they read a copy of *Time*. (These, by the
way, are the people who, adapting a metaphor of Aristotle's, think
of poetry as a gentle laxative for the emotions.)

So when I hear discussions, or see symptoms, of some *rap-
prochement* between religion and the arts—A has written a passion play in modern dress, B has composed an atonal oratorio, C
has done murals for the little church in the home town which he
left thirty years ago to become a not quite first-rate cubist with a
world reputation—my response is not one of unmixed happiness,
and I incline to see, in the characteristic imagery of this period,
religion and the arts as two great corporations, each composed of
many subsidiary companies but both in roughly the same line of
business, circling each other warily in the contemplation of a merger, wondering meanwhile where the ultimate advantage will lie,
and utterly unable to find out. To unfold a little this metaphor, I
should say that in my view the persons seated around the conference table on this occasion are not the inventors of the product—not the prophets, saints, teachers, and great masters of art—
but the usual vice-presidents, accountants, and lawyers on either
side; the bishops and grand inquisitors, the critics and epimethean
pedagogues who arbitrate these matters.

In other words, between ourselves and any clear view of the
problematic area lies the Plain of Shinar, where the usual construction work is going forward vigorously, and the serious plan-
ners exchange their watchwords: "culture," "responsibility," "values," and "communication." In this Babel, the word "religion"
may mean "weekly attendance at the church of your choice," or it
may mean the sort of thing that happened to Job—impossible to
say. Similarly, the word "art" may be applied equally to the forty-
eight preludes and fugues and to advertisements for whisky. That
these things are so says nothing against either whisky or church
attendance, but may be seriously damaging to art and religion.

Somewhere toward the beginning of things the two have a connection; as our somewhat frequently employed word "creative" will suggest. "Non merita il nome di creatore," said Tasso, "si non Iddio od il poeta." Clear enough: God and the poet alone deserve to be called creative, because they both create things. The recent history of this word is revealing: one reads, e.g., of "creative advertising," "creative packaging," and the possibility of becoming "a creative consumer." A dialect usage may be equally revealing: the mother says of her infant, "he is creating again," meaning either that the child is kicking up an awful fuss, or that he has soiled his diaper.

The relation of religion to more worldly activities is frequently characterized by extreme positions. To show what I hope I am not talking about, I shall give an example of each. Here is the extreme whereby religion, in seeking a connection with the world, becomes worldly itself:

SEES BOOM IN RELIGION, TOO

Atlantic City, June 23 (1957) AP.—President Eisenhower's pastor said tonight that Americans are living in a period of "unprecedented religious activity" caused partially by paid vacations, the eight-hour day, and modern conveniences.

"These fruits of material progress," said the Rev. Edward L. R. Elson of the National Presbyterian Church, Washington, "have provided the leisure, the energy, and the means for a level of human and spiritual values never before reached."

Despite an air of farcical silliness which will accompany any display of *hubris* which is at the same time unheroic, this statement—a kind of cartoonist's exaggeration of what one suspects is the real belief of many right-thinking persons—does fix the attention on a real question: whether it is possible for a religious attitude to exist in the acceptance of prosperity, and with its face set against suffering; a question near the heart of Christianity, and a question asked over and over, always to be answered negatively, in the Old Testament, where any statement that "the land had rest for so and so many years" is certain to be followed by the refrain, "And the children of Israel did evil *again* in the sight of the Lord, and served Baalim and Ashtaroth . . ."

The opposed extreme, wherein religion purifies itself quite out of the world, may likewise be identified by anecdote. At a conference on Elizabethan and seventeenth-century poetry, where a number of college students presented papers for discussion, the first three or four essays dealt with the lyrics of such poets as Campion and Herrick; after which a most serious young man arose, frowning, to say that his topic was George Herbert. He completed his impromptu introduction by saying, "We have heard a good deal this morning on the subject of *Love*; well, now we must turn our attention to an entirely different and more serious topic: *Religion*." This inadvertence, I am sorry to say, seemed to me the revelation of something sad and true in attitudes bearing the official institutional name of religious attitudes. We might compare a remark of Yeats, that only two subjects are of interest to a serious intelligence: sex and the dead.

But our problem may be as easily obscured from the other side, the side which professes to be that of art, as from the side of religion. If we look to that great arena of the war of words where there are no poems but only Poetry, no paintings but only Art, we find statements of similar monolithic simplicity, which affect to find nothing problematic in the matter at all.

In that arena, for example, a well-known literary journalist has written (*New York Times Book Review,* May 3, 1959): "What the arts, literature included, need more than anything else just now, is a declaration of faith—faith in man's potentialities, faith in God, however you may conceive Him."

As a citizen, I may incline to accept the vague benevolence of all this. But as a practitioner of the art of writing, I am bored and disturbed by this sort of loose talk; just as I should probably be, were I a member of some religious community, by the pseudo-liberality of that casual rider to the idea of God—"however you may conceive Him." Again we might compare the view of an artist, in the saying of Joseph Conrad that it is the object of art to render the highest kind of justice to the *visible world*: "It is above all, in the first place, to make you see."

By such exclusions I come to some definition of my theme: the elucidation of what things may be called religious in poetical works and in the professional attitude of the artist to the making of such works.

Even in this somewhat narrower definition, the problem is not easy to focus. I shall be trying to say that the artist's relation to spiritual and eternal things is comprised rather in the form of his work than in its message or its content; but that form is itself somewhat elusive, as I have indicated in titling these reflections "The Swaying Form" after the following passage in Florio's translation of Montaigne: "There is no man (if he listen to himselfe) that doth not discover in himselfe a peculiar forme of his, a swaying forme, which wrestleth against the art and the institution, and against the tempest of passions, which are contrary unto him."

Florio's somewhat dreamlike English duplicates nicely the possibilities of Montaigne's phrase, "une forme maistresse." The form, that is, is simultaneously ruling and very variable, or fickle; shifting and protean as the form of water in a stream, where it is difficult or impossible to divide what remains from what runs away. The passage, read in this way, speaks of something in us which is double in nature, on both sides of things at once or by turns. And I would identify this "forme" with the impulse to art, the energy or libido which makes works of art. It is no paradox to say that the artistic impulse fights against "the art," for anyone who persists in this business knows that a part of his struggle is precisely against "the art," that is, against the accepted and settled standards of art in his time.

So this "forme" has the following characteristics. It is (1) allied with religion, for it is against "the tempest of the passions" and thus in favor of control, discipline, *askesis,* renunciation. But it is (2) opposed to religion, for it is also against "the institution," that is, against church, state, dogma, or any fixed habit of mind. Finally, it is (3) against something in its own nature, called "the art," against, perhaps, the idea of form itself.

For a curious tension exists between poetry and belief, idea, principle, or reason. That is, while we hear a good deal about poetry's need to be based upon an explicit view of the meaning of existence, we are very often bored and exasperated by the poetry which testifies to such a view, and incline to say that it is bad poetry precisely in the degree that the poet has insisted on referring the natural world to prior religious or philosophic valuations.

Perhaps it will be illuminating now if I try to sum up the swaying form, this complicated condition of the mind, by imagining a poet at his table in the morning. He faces the blank page, the page faces his mind—which, if it is not also a blank, is a palimpsest on which fractions of world, which he receives chiefly through language, are continually being recorded and erased and coming into strange, dissolving relations to one another; these are, for the most part, not the consequential relations of thought, but rather insanely atomic instead.

To be piously in keeping with the values of the age, I imagine this poet is asking himself, "What can I afford this morning?" And going on to consider the possibilities, or impossibilities: A little *saeva indignatio?* Something smart and severe in a toga? A romantic pathos, or pathology, with wild glances *de chez* Hölderlin? The dewy freshness of an early lyricism, say about the period of Skelton and really, after all, noncommittal? And so on, since the alternatives are very numerous.

There is only one, however, which now arises to give him trouble: "How about me? Shall I be me? And who is that?" He looks doubtfully at his tweeds, his gray flannels, stares at his alert (but modern, but rootless) face in the mirror, and tries to view that crew-cut in quick succession as a Franciscan tonsure, an Augustan wig, a Romantic disorder. No good. He would like to be himself, but acknowledges that himself is poetically not what most interests him, nor what is likely to interest others very much. Sighing, he wonders if poetry, if all great effort in the world, does not involve a necessary hypocrisy (even if one calls it, more politely, not hypocrisy but drama or metaphor, a necessary approach by analogy), and now he gratefully recalls having read somewhere (it was in Castiglione, but he likes the elegant indolence of "somewhere") that Julius Caesar wore a laurel crown to disguise the fact that he was bald. Encouraged a little, he jots down a note reducing to iambic pentameter mighty Caesar—"Who hid his baldness in a laurel crown"—and adds, in prose: "Poets do this, too." Comforted, he occupies the rest of the morning contemplating the publication of a small volume of epigrams on this theme. But come lunchtime, his wife having uncanned a can of alphabet soup which seems to him the image of his condition, the problem remains: Hypocrisy. Seeming, Angelo, seeming. The truest poetry is the most feigning. But is it, really? And how shall we edify the common reader this afternoon? By being Plato? Moody and Sankey? The Pope? Alexander Pope? How shall we solve the problems of society? Affirm the eternal verities? Become rich and famous and sought-after for our opinions (the filing cabinet is full of them) on all sorts of important themes?

No, this will never do. Hypocrisy merges with cynicism. Where is that portrait of Keats?

And so the weary circle begins again. Only once in a while it opens, as something comes into his head and he suddenly commits a poem. At that time, curiously, he does not worry in the least about whether this poem faithfully represents himself, his beliefs, values, tensions, or the absence of all these. He simply writes the poem.

By this ordinary anguish, occasionally relieved in action, a great deal of literature, both good and bad, gets itself produced.

The troubles of this hypothetical or generalized poet will perhaps strike some of you as very literary, overeducated, or even positively neurasthenic, and you may be inclined to say impatiently to him, "Fool, look in thy heart and write," not caring to consider that when Sir Philip Sidney made this excellent recommendation, he was speaking, just like our poet, to himself. And, too, such is the confusion over these things, instructions to look in one's heart and write may turn out translated for practical purposes in weird ways, e.g.: "Look in thy heart and be big, free, and sloppy, like Whitman, who is now becoming fashionable again." There is no end, except for that poem once in a while, to the poet's ability at perverting sound doctrine.

If the foregoing description is even partly applicable to the poetic process, it will be plain that the world will wait a long time for "a declaration of faith" in the poems of this poet. It may also be a consequence of his problem with his identity that a good deal of modern poetry is poetry about the problem, poetry that reveals to interpretation one reflexive dimension having to do with the process of composition itself. This development, where the mind curves back upon itself, may be always a limit, not only for poetry but for every kind of thought, for that "speculation" which Shakespeare says "turns not to itself / Till it hath travell'd, and is mirror'd there / Where it may see itself," adding that "This is not strange at all." But perhaps it has become more strange in the present age, that palace of mirrors where, says Valéry, the lonely lamp is multiplied, or where, as Eliot says, we multiply variety in a wilderness of mirrors, and where the "breakthrough," so pathetically and often discussed in relation to all contemporary arts, is most faithfully imagined in Alice's adventure through the looking-glass, the last consequence of narcissism and "incest of spirit" (Allen Tate, "Last Days of Alice") being the explosion into absurdity, very frequently followed by silence.

Silence, alas, may be preferable to the demand of "educators" that the poet should affirm something (anything?) or the often iterated instruction of certain literary persons that he should *communicate* (what?). But silence, for anyone who has set out to be a poet, is an unlovely alternative, containing in itself some religious (that is, some sinful) implication of being too good for this world, so that many poets accept the disabilities of their elected condition by making many small refusals to prevent one great one. The vanities of publication, these seem to say, are better than the silences of pride. And so, for them, the weary round begins again after every poem, as they seek over and over an image of their being: hermit crabs, crawling unprotected from one deserted shell to the next, finding each time a temporary home which, though by no means a perfect fit, is better at any rate than their nakedness.

It is gratuitous, or even impertinent after all this, and surely offers no defense, to say that they sometimes write good poems in their planetary course from house to house. What can we possibly mean, now, by *a good poem*? Let that be another circle, in another hell. While the present purpose is to say something about the process itself, the kind of relation with the world which results in poetic writings and is an attempt to fix for a moment the swaying form.

When people are impatient with a work of art, they assert their feeling in this way: "What does it mean?" Their tone of voice indicates that this is the most natural question in the world, the demand which they have the most immediate and God-given right to make. So their absolute condemnation and dismissal of a work of art is given in this way: "It doesn't mean anything. It doesn't mean anything *to me*." Only in those plaintive last words does there appear a tiny and scarcely acknowledged doubt of the all-sufficiency of this idea of meaning—that there may actually be meanings, which one does not personally possess.

Now we are all forced to believe about large areas of the world's work that this is so: that all around us physicists, financiers, and pharmacists are conducting complex operations which do have meaning though we do not know what it is. While we may occasionally wonder if those emperors are in fact wearing any clothes, we more usually allow that our bewilderment belongs to ourselves and does not say anything destructive about those disciplines in themselves, even where they do not produce any overwhelmingly obvious practical result such as an atomic explosion. But about works of art we continue to ask that question, "What do they mean?" and regard the answer to it as somehow crucial.

In a realm of contemplation, the question about meaning could, though it generally does not, begin a chain reaction involving the whole universe, since the answer can be given only in terms to which the same question is again applicable. But because we are well-mannered people, or because we haven't the time, or really don't care, or because we are in fact reassured and consoled by receiving an answer—any answer—we know where to stop. So that a large part of our intellectual operations takes inevitably the following form:

A. Why is the grass green?
B. Because of the chlorophyll.
A. Oh.

So, in a realm of contemplation, meaning would itself be inexplicable. The typewriters rattle, the telephones ring, the moving finger keeps writing one triviality after another, the great gabble of the world goes incessantly on as people translate, encipher, decipher, as one set of words is transformed more or less symmetrically into another set of words—whereupon someone says, "O, now I understand. . . ."

But the question about meaning attests, wherever it is asked, the presence of civilization with all its possibilities, all its limitations; attests the presence of *language,* that vast echoing rattle and sibilance buzzing between ourselves and whatever it is we presume we are looking at, experiencing, being in, and which sometimes appears to have an independent value, if any at all, like the machine someone built a few years back, which had thousands of moving parts and no function. The semanticist to the contrary, words are things, though not always the things they say they are. The painter Delacroix expressed it by saying that Nature is a dictionary. Everything is there, but not in the order one needs. The universe itself, so far as we relate ourselves to it by the mind, may be not so much a meaning as a rhythm, a continuous articulation of question and answer, question and answer, a musical dialectic precipitating out moments of meaning which become distinct only as one wave does in a sea of waves. "You think you live under universal principles," said Montaigne, "but in fact they are municipal bylaws."

Language, then, is the marvelous mirror of the human condition, a mirror so miraculous that it can see what is invisible, that is, the relations between things. At the same time, the mirror is a limit, and as such, it is sorrowful; one wants to break it and look beyond. But unless we have the singular talent for mystical experience we do not really break the mirror, and even the mystic's experience is available to us only as reflected, inadequately, in the mirror. Most often man deals with reality by its reflection. That is the sense of Perseus' victory over the Gorgon by consenting to see her only in the mirror of his shield, and it is the sense of the saying in Corinthians that we see now as through a glass darkly—a phrase rendered by modern translators as "now we see as in a little mirror."

Civilization, mirrored in language, is the garden where relations grow; outside the garden is the wild abyss. Poetry, an art of fictions, illusions, even lies—"Homer," said Aristotle, "first taught us the art of framing lies in the right way"—poetry is the art of contemplating this situation in the mirror of language.

"Only connect . . ." is the civilized and civilizing motto of a book by E. M. Forster, wherein he speaks eloquently of meaning, art, and order in "the world of telegrams and anger," and of what exists outside that world: "panic and emptiness, panic and emptiness." W. H. Auden, also very eloquently, writes of the limiting extremes within which meaning means, between "the ocean flats where no subscription concerts are given" and "the desert plain where there is nothing for lunch."

But meaning, like religion, seeks of its own nature to monopolize experience. For example, in children's playbooks there are numbered dots to be followed in sequence by the pencil; the line so produced finally becomes recognizable as a shape. So the lines produced among stars (which can scarcely all be in the same plane) become the geometrical abstractions of a Bear, a Wagon, Orion the Hunter; and by softening or humanizing the outlines, recognizable images are produced, but in the process the stars themselves have to be omitted. So does meaning at first simplify and afterward supersede the world. Poetry, I would say, is, in its highest ranges, no mere playing with the counters of meaning, but a perpetual re-deriving of the possibility of meaning from matter, of the intelligible world from the brute recalcitrance of things. Poetry differs from thought in this respect, that thought eats up the language in which it thinks. Thought is proud, and always wants to forget its humble origin in things. In doing so, it begins to speak by means of very elevated abstractions, which quickly become emptied and impoverished. The business of poetry is to bring thought back into relation with the five wits, the five senses which Blake calls "the chief inlets of soul in this age," to show how our discontents, as Shakespeare finely says of Timon's, "are unremovably coupled to nature." So the ivory tower must always be cut from the horn of Behemoth.

The relation of poetry to religion is both intimate and antithetical, for poetry exists only by a continuing revelation in a world always incarnate of word and flesh indissolubly, a world simultaneously solid and transpicuous. At the same time, religion can never really dissociate itself from poetry and the continuing revelation; and its attempts to do so turn it into a form of literary criticism, as the scriptures and sacred books of the world, in comparison with their interminable commentaries, will sufficiently show. Poetry and institutionalized religion are in a sense the flowing and the static forms of the same substance, liquid and solid states of the same elemental energy.

This is a simple thing; it has been said many times and forgotten many times plus one. William Blake says it this way:

> The ancient Poets animated all sensible objects with Gods or Geniuses, calling them by the names and adorning them with the properties of woods, rivers, mountains, lakes, cities, nations, and whatever their enlarged and numerous senses could perceive.
> And particularly they studied the Genius of each city and country, placing it under its Mental Deity;

Till a system was formed, which some took advantage of, and
enslav'd the vulgar by attempting to realise or abstract the Mental
Deities from their objects—thus began Priesthood;
Choosing forms of worship from poetic tales.
And at length they pronounc'd that the Gods had order'd such
things.
Thus men forgot that All Deities reside in the Human Breast.

The poet's business, I would say, is to name as accurately as
possible a situation, but a situation which he himself is in. The
name he gives ought to be so close a fit with the actuality it summons into being that there remains no room between inside and
outside; the thought must be "like a beast moving in its skin"
(Dante). If he does his work properly, there won't be any other
name for the situation (and for his being in it) than the one he
invents, or, rather, his name will swallow up all the others as
Aaron's rod swallowed up the rods of Pharaoh's wizards.

Sometimes the name so given is a relatively simple one, as when
Alexander Pope gave the Prince of Wales a dog, and had inscribed
on its collar:

> I am His Highness' dog at Kew.
> Pray tell me, sir, whose dog are you?

And sometimes the name so given, the situation thus identified and
brought into being, is immensely complex, so that one has to refer
to it by a tag, an abbreviation, e.g., "King Lear."

A poem, whether of two lines or ten thousand, is therefore the
name of something, and in its ideal realm of fiction or illusion it
corresponds to what is said of the Divine Name in several significant respects:

> *It is unique.*
> *It can never be repeated.*
> *It brings into being the situation it names, and is therefore truly a*
> *creation.*
> *It is secret, even while being perfectly open and public, for it*
> *defines a thing which could not have been known without it.*

As to the poet himself, one might add this. Writing is a species
of *askesis,* a persevering devotion to the energy passing between

self and world. It is a way of living, a way of being, and, though it does produce results in the form of "works," these may come to seem of secondary importance to the person so engaged.

The young writer is always told (he was, anyhow, when I was young) that writing means first and last "having something to say." I cherish as a souvenir of boyhood that honorable and aged platitude, but would like to modify it by this addition: Writing means trying to find out what the nature of things has to say about what you think you have to say. And the process is reflective or cyclical, a matter of feedback between oneself and "it," an "it" which can gain its identity only in the course of being brought into being, come into being only in the course of finding its identity. This is a matter, as Lu Chi says, of how to hold the axe while you are cutting its handle.

I say that writing is a species of *askesis*. But as it works in an ideal or fictional, rather than a practical, realm, so it purifies not the character but the style. There is, however, a connection between the two, at least in the hope that a charity of the imagination shall be not quite the same thing as an imaginary charity.

That, then, is what I have tried to characterize as "the swaying form," a process of becoming related to nature and the nature of things (*natura naturata* and *natura naturans*). The view here taken suggests that art has some evident affinities with both religion and science on the very simple basis that all three exist in the presumption that the truth is possible to be told about existence; but these affinities themselves also define differences, distances, and intrinsic antagonisms.

As to art's relation with science. The experimental method was defined, by Galileo, I believe, as putting nature to the question, where "the question" meant the judicial process of torture. The definition seems to imply a faith that nature, so treated, will reveal the secret name for a situation; when once that situation has been isolated, treated as a situation in itself, and considered for a moment apart from the flux of all things, nature will, as it were, confess her presumably guilty secret.

Well, the artist, it seems to me, works on a not so different principle, leading from hypothesis—"what will happen to this noble nature if it can be led to believe Desdemona unfaithful?"—

through experiment—the question as put by Iago—to result, to "the tragic loading of this bed." In this sense, and not in the fashionable popular sense, art is "experimental," and its methods to a certain extent resemble those of the laboratory; art, too, produces its process under controlled and limiting conditions, cutting away irrelevancies, speeding up or slowing down the reaction under study, so that the results, whatever they may be, will stand forth with a singular purity and distinction. The instruments of science, of course, have as their aim the creation of an objectivity as nearly as possible universal in character; the poet's aim might be thought of as the same and reversed, a mirror image—to represent in the world the movement of a subjectivity as nearly as possible universal in character.

And art is akin to religion, if we will be nondenominational about it, in that the work (though not, perhaps, the artist, oddly enough) is driven by its own composition to the implication of invisible things inherent in visible ones. The subject, the content, of the art work is sorrowful, because life is sorrowful; but the work itself, by the nature of its form, dances. A beautiful passage from Proust's novel will be relevant here. Marcel is thinking of the writer Bergotte, who died of a stroke while contemplating a detail, a piece of yellow wall, in a painting by Vermeer:

> He was dead. Forever? Who can say? After all, occult experiences demonstrate no more than the dogmas of religion do about the soul's continuance. But what can be said is this, that we live our life as though we had entered it under the burden of obligations already assumed in another; there is, in the conditions of our life here, no reason which should make us believe ourselves obliged to do good, to be fastidious or even polite, nor which should make the godless painter believe himself obliged to start over twenty times a detail the praise of which will matter very little to his body eaten by worms—a detail such as the section of yellow wall painted with such skill and taste by an artist forever unknown and scarce identified under the name of Vermeer. All such obligations, which have no sanction in our present life, seem to belong to a different world based on goodness, consideration and sacrifice, a world altogether different from this one, and from which we emerge to be born on this earth, before perhaps returning there to live under the rule of those unknown laws which we have obeyed because we carry their

teaching within us though unaware who traced it there—those laws
to which every profound work of the intelligence tends to reconcile
us, and which are invisible only—and forever!—to fools.

So the work of art is religious in nature, not because it beautifies
an ugly world or pretends that a naughty world is a nice one—for
these things especially art does not do—but because it shows of its
own nature that things drawn within the sacred circle of its forms
are transfigured, illuminated by an inward radiance which amounts
to goodness because it amounts to Being itself. In the life conferred by art, Iago and Desdemona, Edmund and Cordelia, the
damned and the blessed, equally achieve immortality by their relation with the creating intelligence which sustains them. The art
work is not responsible for saying that things in reality are so, but
rather for revealing what this world says to candid vision. It is thus
that we delight in tragedies whose actions in life would merely
appall us. And it is thus that art, by its illusions, achieves a human
analogy to the resolution of that famous question of theodicy—the
relation of an Omnipotent Benevolence to evil—which the theologians, bound to the fixed forms of things, have for centuries
struggled with, intemperately and in vain. And it is thus that art,
by vision and not by dogma, patiently and repeatedly offers the
substance of things hoped for, the evidence of things unseen.

The Bread of Faithful Speech—Wallace Stevens and the Voices of Imagination

In books left by the old magician we find many things, things ill-assorted and not particularly well catalogued according to any scheme we are familiar with. It is as though a supreme identity were turning out the contents of its wallet, going through the desk, the filing cabinets, the closets, preparatory to moving elsewhere, or being other. Here are the licenses and registrations of the self, its snapshots of single raindrops in distant towns, its myths of creation, spells which worked on one occasion only, receipted bills from Guatemala and the Waldorf, inventories, formulae, annotations on unidentifiable texts; one sarcophagus containing one owl, statues of clowns, rabbis, soldiers, invocations of an uncertain someone variously called the outer captain, the inner saint, Don John, John Zeller, St. John, The Backache, turbulent Schlemihl, and so forth. A quiet and final remark, "Wisdom asks nothing more," is followed by a recipe for Parfait Martinique: "coffee mousse, rum on top, a little cream on top of that." Sometimes it seems as though toward the end he gave up doing magic in favor of meditating on its procedures, and he said: "As a man becomes familiar with his own poetry, it becomes as obsolete for himself as for anyone else." Or perhaps everything by this time had been transmuted into magical substance, so that he could say: "Life consists of propositions about life." Or a doubt would arise, so that he said: "Life is an affair of people not places. But for me life is an affair of places and that is the trouble."

Now he is gone the inheritors rummage through what is left, taking various views of their legacy. Some see only a cabinet of curiosities got together by a traveled uncle. Others, understanding they have come into the possession of a gold mine, nevertheless resent not having had the ore refined so as to be turned in at the treasury for honest paper money that anyone can understand and use immediately. A few young nephews and nieces are upset be-

cause when they say the spells nothing happens. And the earnest
amateurs of theology search the remains for the single phrase that
will transform the world. He would perhaps have said to them:

> It is to stick to the nicer knowledge of
> Belief, that what it believes in is not true.

The true inheritance, if we are able to see it, is a world already
transformed, the lucid realization of one among infinite possibilities of transformation, of projection from the shadowy presence at the center. Concerning this he quoted from Whitehead
these rather cryptic words: "In a certain sense, everything is everywhere at all times, for every location involves an aspect of itself in
every other location. Thus every spatio-temporal standpoint mirrors the world." His comment on this consists of a translation of
Whitehead's observation so that it becomes recognizably characteristic of himself and the elegantly slapdash chiaroscuro notation
which identifies his voice, his style, and with these the world they
alone express: "These words [he says] are pretty obviously words
from a level where everything is poetic, as if the statement that
every location involves an aspect of itself in every other location
produced in the imagination a universal iridescence, a dithering of
presences and, say, a complex of differences."

The voice of his poetry is that of a man thinking, a man study-
ing how I may compare this prison where I live unto the world. But
it is not philosophical poetry, though it may often adopt the air
and gesture of some myth about a philosopher philosophizing.
And if it is the poetry of man thinking, it is nevertheless not "intellectual poetry," not the poetry of "a beau language without a drop
of blood," for what the man thinks about is, at last, expressiveness
itself, the mystery of the phrase in its relation to the world. There
is a difference, which he described, for himself, as the change from
a young man to an older one:

> Like a dark rabbi, I
> Observed, when young, the nature of mankind,
> In lordly study. Every day, I found
> Man proved a gobbet in my mincing world.
> Like a rose rabbi, later, I pursued,

And still pursue, the origin and course
Of love, but until now I never knew
That fluttering things have so distinct a shade.

The fluttering things, which in that poem make such a dithering
of presences, were pigeons, and he returned to them for an image
at the close of another poem, where they have the same expressive
function of relating the light and the dark, somewhere between
things and the ambience of things, things and the thought of
things:

                   in the isolation of the sky,
       At evening, casual flocks of pigeons make
       Ambiguous undulations as they sink
       Downward to darkness, on extended wings.

In this poem, which meditates the mysteries of incarnation, of
how things come to be and cease to be, the pigeons are as thoughts,
or as the manner of our perceiving thoughts between the bright
emptiness above and the generative dark beneath, mediators
which without solving resolve. In some way, such a poem cannot
end, it can only stop at the finish of a cadence, satisfactory for the
moment but recognizably inconclusive. A dithering of presences, a
complex of differences. All is to do again.

The voice of his poems is the voice of the poet. Even in the poem
I have just been quoting from, which begins as though in the prospect of a dramatic monologue, it is the poet and not the lady who
carries the burden of meditation; she says something once in a
while, and he develops the thoughts which she might appropriately have.

This voice has a great consistency over the whole range of the
poetry: it is learned, for "poetry is the scholar's art"; it is humor-
ously eccentric, given to French phrases (for in poetry "English
and French constitute a single language"), sorrowful and somewhat fatigued, its tone and feeling much affected by the weather
and changes of season; it has a balanced gravity owing something
to many repetitions; it is a considerate voice, its altitudes of grandeur and nobility are achieved perceptibly in despite of weariness
and a leaning toward resignation. It is a poet's voice; or, you might
say, it is the voice of wisdom as this might be heard by a poet.

Nor is this so unusual. For whatever our view of the person-ative, or dramatic, element in lyric poetry, it very often happens that the poet, a middle-aged or an old man thinking of his life and the approaching end of it, of its poetry and whatever all that may mean, projects these thoughts upon the more or less mythified figure of a middle-aged or an old man thinking of his life, and so on. He not so much, that is, bespeaks for himself on the occasion a fictitious character, as he generalizes out the character he has, or thinks he has, or wants to have; often enough he will make this voice of his poem—"as of a general being or a human universe," our poet says—older than himself. For among the poet's ambi-tions is this unseemly one, to become wise by sounding wise, to be a hermit scholar in a tower first, and only after that find something to study. How odd that it should ever even seem to work.

In this process, the amount of distancing and dignifying that almost necessarily goes on may make it seem that the daily self and the self in the poem are absolutely unlike; thus Yeats and his fa-mous theory of the creation of character from the opposite: "It is perhaps because nature made me a gregarious man, going hither and thither looking for conversation, and ready to deny from fear or favour his dearest conviction, that I love proud and lonely things."

In Yeats's poetry the equivalent thought demonstrates this pro-cess of dignifying and distancing by its loftier arrogance of phrase, and by the poet's assigning to Dante what he wished to believe about himself:

> I think he fashioned from his opposite
> An image that might have been a stony face . . .

relating the austere pilgrim of the poem directly with a worldly life of lechery and cynicism.

For some poets, then, the writing of poetry may become an elucidation of character, a spiritual exercise having for its chief object the discovery or invention of one's character: Myself must I remake, Du musst dein Leben ändern, &c. Something of this sort appears in our poet also, and he said about it: "It is the explana-tions of things that we make to ourselves that disclose our char-acter; the subjects of one's poems are the symbols of one's self or of one of one's selves."

We have said so far, a little foolishly, that the poet's voice is the voice of the poet; and added that the poet hears this voice as that in which the wise might speak, the old and wise and a little foolish, an aged eagle, an old philosopher in Rome, the man in the golden breastplate under the old stone Cross, the magician opening his folio by candlelight in the lonely tower.

To view the poet as a magician is fair, if we remember that magicians do not really solve the hero's problems, but only help him to confront these; as Merlin may be said to have helped Arthur, not so much by doing magic as by being for him a presence and a voice, a way of saying which indicated a way of being. Of this relation our poet said that the soldier is poor without the poet's lines, adding this in explanation:

> How simply the fictive hero becomes the real;
> How gladly with proper words the soldier dies,
> If he must, or lives on the bread of faithful speech.

We observe here, in an aside, that some poets, ours not among them, believe, or pretend to believe, in a magic that more directly affects the world. These poets are like the Friar in the ballad, where the girl fears she will go to hell if she lets him seduce her:

> Tush, quoth the Fryer, and do not doubt,
> If you were in hell I could sing you out.

This has often been the poet's false pride about his magic; but he resembles the Friar in another way, for he too will end up in the well, without the girl.

Our proper magic is the magic of language, where the refrain of the riddling verse, "Sing ninety-nine and ninety," is simply not the same thing as singing a hundred and eighty-nine. It is also the magic of impersonation, and not without its sinister aspect, the being possessed by spirits, or by the spirit. Combining the two, it is being possessed by the word, and about this there is a certain mystery, which we are able to describe, though not to solve, as follows.

We are fond of saying that poetry is personative, hence dramatic. To say this is probably true enough, if not conspicuously helpful, for it does give at any rate our sense that the I of the poem is not quite the poet, even if we have the lingering sense also that this I is not quite not the poet either. It is a problem in style, the beginning of a problem in identities. Browning gives us an idea of Bishop Blougram, but it is an idea we cannot hold without holding at the same time an idea that the Bishop is Browningesque along with Andrea del Sarto and others. Prufrock is distinct from Tiresias, but both recognizably belong to Mr. Eliot, just as Michael Robartes and Crazy Jane sound like themselves and like Yeats; as all the dead of Spoon River sound like Masters, and so on. In the drama itself, the problem is aggravated, or dismissed: either they all sound like Shakespeare, or none of them does. Proust puts it this way, that all the sitters to one painter have a family likeness in their portraits, greater than the likeness they share with members of their own families.

So the poet's sounding like others may be his way of sounding like himself. And there is a range of possibilities here, between the impossible extremes of sounding exactly like oneself and entirely other than oneself. The limits of this range are given by Keats: the "chameleon poet," on one side, who has no character because he is constantly impersonating someone else; and on the other side the Wordsworthian, or Egotistical Sublime.

Through the other, the poet impersonates the self, his own self or one of his selves, and there are two "voices of poetry." But it doesn't stop there, for we read the poem, and then it speaks in our voice as well; this too is mysterious. When I say over some lines,

> Every thread of summer is at last unwoven.
> By one caterpillar is great Africa devoured
> And Gibraltar is dissolved like spit in the wind.

And when I go on, saying these lines that follow,

> Over all these the mighty imagination triumphs
> Like a trumpet and says, in this season of memory,
> When the leaves fall like things mournful of the past,
>
> Keep quiet in the heart, O wild bitch. O mind
> Gone wild, be what he tells you to be . . .

When I say over these things, I say them as myself and not myself, as a possibility of certain grandeurs and contempts in the self
which the poet alone has been able to release, and I ask whether
the voice that speaks at this moment is more his or mine, or
whether poetry is not in this respect the most satisfactory of many
unsatisfactory ways we have of expressing our sense that we are
members of one another. That voice, which I add by reading, or
which the poet adds to me when I read, a voice which in some way
belongs to neither of us personally, is a third voice of poetry. Our
poet, who thought of these things, said of this: "The poet seems to
confer his identity on the reader. It is easiest to recognize this when
listening to music—I mean this sort of thing: the transference."

And there is still one further voice of poetry to be considered,
though we can say little enough about it except that at certain
times it is there. That is the voice of an eternally other, the resonance that in our repetition of the poet's words seems to come
from the outside, when "the shadow of an external world draws
near"; as when our poet, calling himself for the occasion Ariel, and
speaking in the voice of this Ariel, says of Ariel's poems:

> It was not important that they survive.
> What mattered was that they should bear
> Some lineament or character,
>
> Some affluence, if only half perceived,
> In the poverty of their words,
> Of the planet of which they were part.

Our poet thought also and often about this last voice, of which
he said: "When the mind is like a hall in which thought is like a
voice speaking, the voice is always that of someone else."

His magic, ever more insistently, was a magic to open this world
and not another, but this world as an imagination of this world, a
transformation where "what is possible replaces what is not"; for that
impossible which was replaced, for "man's mind grown venerable in
the unreal," he had at most a half-friendly, half-mocking nostalgia;
and of that other, the last voice of all, and the one all poetry seeks to
hear, he said: "The mind that in heaven created the earth and the
mind that on earth created heaven were, as it happened, one."

We say it over and we feel, as it happens, better.

Composition and Fate in the Short Novel

The writer attempting for the first time a short novel must face, I should think, nothing but problems, the first, though probably the least, of which is, What are short novels? For the writer who is by habit of mind a novelist they must represent not simply a compression but a corresponding rhythmic intensification, a more refined criterion of relevance than the one he usually enjoys, an austerity and economy perhaps somewhat compulsive in the intention itself. For the writer who habitually thinks in short stories—a bad habit, by the way—the challenge is probably greater: he will have to learn as never before about the interstices of his action; he will have to think about a fairly large space which must be filled, not with everything (his complaint against the novelist), but with something definite which must be made to yield in a quite explicit way its most reserved and recondite ranges of feeling; he will have to think, for once, of design and not merely of plot. To both writers it must soon become apparent that a short novel is something in itself, neither a lengthily written short story nor the refurbished attempt at a novel sent out into the world with its hat clapped on at the eightieth page.

I am speaking, perhaps, ideally, and about the ideal; it is difficult not to. For quite apart from technical considerations, the tradition of the short novel—perhaps because for so long it was commercially useless and unacceptable—is a tradition of masterpieces; further than that, the composers of this tradition of masterpieces are almost without exception the composers of still greater works, such as *Moby-Dick, War and Peace, The Possessed, The Magic Mountain,* and so on, from which their short novels differ, in fact, by a kind of intensification of art, by a closed and resonant style of composition suggestive of the demonstrations of mathematics or chess.

The writer proposing to himself a short novel probably ought not to scare himself with the thought that he is entering that kind of competition; once he begins, of course, he will resolutely forget all about those great men and their works, and pay his exclusive attention to the business in hand. Again, though, the game is scarcely worth playing without an acknowledgment of its specific difficulties; the specific difficulties, if they can be identified, are what define the form—without them it is not a form but only so and so many thousand words—and in a discussion like this one I see no way of approaching the matter at all except by attending to the ideal so far as it can be deduced from great examples.

The material economy of the short novel, and its strict analogical style of composition, seem to be functions one of the other. The epitome of the first point, material economy, I must fetch from far away; it seems brilliantly expressed in a discussion of variety in the creation, by Thomas Aquinas, who says that although an angel is a better thing, objectively considered, than a stone, yet a universe composed of two angels is inferior to a universe composed of one angel and one stone. A variousness so strictly limited and identified as that characterizes, as though by satiric exaggeration, the universe of the short novel. As to the strict and analogical style of composition, I shall quote a somewhat extended but very rewarding anecdote from the autobiography of a most admirable novelist, Vladimir Nabokov:

> The place is . . . Abbazia, on the Adriatic. About the same time, at a cafe in nearby Fiume, my father happened to notice, just as we were being served, two Japanese officers at a table near us, and we immediately left—not without my hastily snatching a whole *bombe* of lemon sherbet, which I carried away secreted in my aching mouth. The year was 1904. I was five. Russia was fighting Japan. With hearty relish, the English illustrated weekly Miss Norcott subscribed to reproduced pictures by Japanese artists that showed how the Russian locomotives—made singularly toylike by the Japanese pictorial style—would drown if our Army tried to lay rails across the treacherous ice of Lake Baikal.
>
> But let me see. I had an even earlier association with that war. One afternoon at the beginning of the same year, in our St. Petersburg house, I was led down from the nursery into my family's study to say how-do-you-do to a friend of the family, General Kuropatkin. To amuse me, he spread out a handful of matches on the divan where he was sitting, placed ten of them end to end to make a

horizontal line and said, "This is the sea in calm weather." Then he tipped up each pair so as to turn the straight line into a zigzag—and that was "a stormy sea." He scrambled the matches and was about to do, I hoped, a better trick when we were interrupted. His aide-de-camp was shown in and said something to him. With a Russian, flustered grunt, Kuropatkin immediately rose from his seat, the loose matches jumping up on the divan as his weight left it. That day, he had been ordered to assume supreme command of the Russian Army in the Far East.

This incident had a special sequel fifteen years later, when at a certain point of my father's flight from Bolshevik-held St. Petersburg to southern Russia, he was accosted, while crossing a bridge, by an old man who looked like a grey-bearded peasant in his sheepskin coat. He asked my father for a light. The next moment each recognized the other. Whether or not old Kuropatkin, in his rustic disguise, managed to evade Soviet imprisonment, is immaterial. What pleases me is the evolution of the match theme; those magic ones he had shown me had been trifled with and mislaid, and his armies had also vanished, and everything had fallen through, like my toy trains that, in the winter of 1904–05, in Wiesbaden, I tried to run over the frozen puddles in the grounds of the Hotel Oranien. The following of such thematic designs through one's life should be, I think, the true purpose of autobiography.

A good deal that characterizes the composition of short novels is summed up and lightly demonstrated in this passage, even to a certain ruthlessness: "Whether or not old Kuropatkin . . . managed to evade Soviet imprisonment, is immaterial." And "the evolution of the match theme," with the problems attendant on it, is my proper subject here. But before going on to discuss examples I will try to suggest, without wasting time on attempts at unexceptionable definition, some of the things, other than length, which seem to set the novella apart from the short story and the novel. For the term "short novel" is descriptive only in the way that the term "Middle Ages" is descriptive—that is, not at all, except with reference to the territory on either side. And just as historians exaggerate the darkness of the Dark Ages and the brightness of the Renaissance, I shall exaggerate some elements of the short story and the novel, to make the middle term more visible.

The short story at present is a way of transacting one's fictional business which is shiny, efficient, and inexpensive; consequently it has become very attractive to non-artists. If publishers tell us despite this that collections of short stories rarely succeed, that is probably because everyone is too busy writing his own to be able to read anyone else's. To write a fine short story may be harder now than it has ever been, but there is no indication that large numbers of short story writers are aware of the fact. There are many honorable exceptions, perhaps, submerged in the flood of junk—commercial junk, high-literary junk, undergraduate junk, much of it competent and even attractive, but bearing too much the mark of the machine to give, even at the best, any deep pleasure. Short stories amount for the most part to parlor tricks, party favors with built-in snappers, gadgets for inducing recognitions and reversals: a small pump serves to build up the pressure, a tiny trigger releases it, there follow a puff and a flash as freedom and necessity combine; finally a Celluloid doll drops from the muzzle and descends by parachute to the floor. These things happen, but they happen to no one in particular.

Of many possible reasons why this fate has overtaken the short story, one must be the vast quantity of such stuff produced every day of every week and published in newspapers and magazines, on radio and television (for those "dramas" are either adapted from short stories or made up with the same requirements in mind). That so much of our experience, or the stereotype which passes for it, should be dealt with by means of the short story is perhaps the symptom, not unnoticeable elsewhere in the public domain, of an unlovely cynicism about human character, a propensity to see *individual* behavior as purely atmospheric—*colorful,* as they call it—and accordingly to require stereotyped behavior for everything having to do with the essential action. To invent an example: our hero is individual to the point of eccentricity, he is weirdly named Cyrus Pyracanth, he suffers from hemophilia, keeps pet snakes, and smokes a nargileh; but when it comes to the point, none of this has anything to do with the action his author requires him to perform, for the sake of which he might be called Mr. X and live in Bronxville on an average income and a moral equipment supplied by *Time* magazine or some other leading wholesaler. What has happened to him in the short story is not that he has lost his inwardness; only that for all practical purposes (the writer's purposes) it has ceased to matter.

It is natural that the mass production of short fiction should exert great pressure to bring the story down to its mechanically imitable elements, so that it provides solutions at the expense of problems, answers to which no one has asked the question; there is, indeed, a certain aesthetic pleasure to be gained from the contemplation of simple and pretty combinations purified, as in the detective story, of human complication and human depth; but it is a pleasure easily exhausted. The story gets its power from a whole implied drama which it does not tell aloud; its neglect of that implication reduces it to clever trickery. There is much to be said for clever trickery as a contributing means to great works, nor do great novelists often neglect this part of art which is purely artifice—but when there is little or nothing else, and when in addition all the tricks have been played so many times . . . ?

This is not simply a question of length, but much rather a question of depth; when a short story's action comprises, by brilliant symbolic reflection, the whole of life, it becomes novelistic. I think in this connection of two stories by Kay Boyle, "Keep Your Pity" and "Dear Mr. Walrus." Neither exceeds thirty pages, but those pages are written throughout with the kind of attention sometimes held to be proper only for poetry (I do not mean what is called "poetic prose," rather the reverse), whereas short stories such as I have been talking about usually betray themselves as having been written only with a view to the ending.

The word "novel" will cover a multitude of sins. I can think of an author "writing" a novella, but this simple term will not do for a novel, where I have to think of him "sitting down at his desk" and "addressing himself to the task." I think of lavish productions, casts of thousands, full technicolor, photographed against authentic backgrounds, and so on. Not all of this is accurate, or it need not be, but I emphasize it for the sake of a contrast; besides, when faced with the need for a commanding generality on this topic, I find myself to have forgotten all the novels I have ever read. The contrast I want to bring out is this: for many novelists, all but the simplest element of compositional art (the plot) is destroyed by observation, by detail work, by reality which keeps poking its head in. The leisure, the "warm earthy humanity," of the novel owes itself to this consideration: people read novellas, but they tend to live in novels, and sometimes they live there very comfortably indeed: thus you have descriptions which are nothing but descriptions, thus you have philosophical excursions, set-pieces, summaries, double plot, and full orchestration, not to mention that all the chairs are heavily upholstered and even the walls padded. Stendhal provided benches for the reader to sit down on, but many novelists erect hotels for the same laudable accommodation.

Let me try to bring this distinction back down to the ground. The master novelist is Shakespearean in combinative skill, if not in language: he handles actions which are long, complex, serious, and explicitly generalized through the social and political fabric, e.g., *The Possessed, War and Peace, The Red and the Black, Remembrance of Things Past.* The authors of such works are masters in parable and reality simultaneously. Then there are masters in parable, and I would only indicate the range of this art by mentioning together the names of Jane Austen and Franz Kafka; if I say that *Emma* and *The Trial* are, for me, like short novels in spite of their length, that will suggest my feeling that the name "short novel" does not exactly discriminate, and that some such terms as "simple" and "complex" novels might be used instead. A few lesser examples may help here: Mrs. Compton-Burnett writes short novels at whatever length, as do Graham Greene and Henry Green and Virginia Woolf. I need hardly say that the distinction is not one of quality any more than it is one of length. *The Counterfeiters* means to be a novel, so does *Point Counter Point,* so does *Nostromo,* so does *Tender Is the Night,* but I do not prefer them before *Lafcadio's Adventures, After Many a Summer Dies the Swan, The Secret Agent,* or *The Great Gatsby,* which are examples of the other kind.

I favor this distinction of the simple and complex, the Greek drama and the Shakespearean, over the other which seems to be based purely on length. Simple novels will normally be shorter than complex ones anyhow, though not always—I notice for instance that Cyril Connolly refers to *Gatsby* and *The Spoils of Poynton* together as short novels, and I, sharing his feeling or mistaken memory as to the latter, was surprised to find it just twice as long as *Gatsby.* But I shall not insist on these terms, simple and complex, and will draw my illustrations in the following discussion from novels generally allowed to be *short* ones.

We have, after all, only two ways of thinking about literary composition. In one, general ideas are illustrated by appropriate particulars; in the other, the contemplation of particulars produces general ideas. Perhaps neither of these species can ever be seen in purity and isolation in any given work, especially since the work as we read it offers no certain guide to the means of its composition, so that all literary composition appears as a combination of these extremes, possibly to be characterized by the dominance of one or the other. The pure state of the first kind, in which the author determines first upon a more or less systematic arrangement of general notions, then devises particular appearances for them, would be allegory of the most rigorously scientific sort, like an equation; literary allegories can never be quite that rigid, because every particular does more than illustrate, it modifies the general idea. The pure state of the second kind would exist only if the contemplation of particulars quite failed to produce general ideas and systematic meanings, but produced only the intense view of particulars as themselves the *irrational* demonstration of the nature of things: symbolism is a way station on this road which runs further to expressionism, surrealism, dada, and the riddles of the Zen Koan.

It is fashionably believed at present that the artist belongs finally to the irrational, that his is the ecstasy of the unique, the individual and irreducible, the opaque detail existing in and for itself; conversely, that reason, construction, architecture of general ideas, will destroy him as an artist. It is a theme which I shall not develop at large in this place, but the tradition of the short novel offers a good deal of evidence for the opposite view. The most striking element shared by almost all the great pieces in this genre is their outright concentration upon traditional problems of philosophy, the boldness of their venture into generality, the evidence they give of direct and profound moral concern. We are not entitled to suppose, of course, that such works were composed from the point of view first of general ideas and philosophic problems and paradoxes, even though sometimes—as with the *Notes from the Underground,* for example—it is tempting so to suppose. What we may insist is that these works combine with their actions a most explicit awareness of themselves as parables, as philosophic myths, and almost invariably announce and demonstrate the intention of discursive profundity—the intention, it is not too much to say, of becoming sacred books: final instances, exhaustively analyzed, of a symbolic universe of whose truth we can be persuaded only by fictions. The result for composition is that problem becomes the center of the short novel, which with a peculiar purity dramatizes conflicts of appearance and reality (*Benito Cereno*), freedom and necessity (*Notes from the Underground*), madness and sanity (*Ward Number Six*); all these are of course forms of a single problem essential and not accidental to the genre, which I shall try to illustrate by describing and giving examples of one theme which is pervasive to the point of obsession in the short novel.

The theme is broadly speaking that of *identity,* and the action deriving from it may be generalized as follows: the mutual attachment or dependency between A and B has a mortal strength; its dissolution requires a crisis fatal to one or the other party; but this dissolution is represented as salvation.

It is clear from many examples that the story of the Passion itself, with its suffering and dying Redeemer, sin-eater, scapegoat, is explicitly thought of in connection with this theme, which may be told as a religious parable, an adventure story, a fantasy, a psychological novel, often with strong homosexual or narcissistic emphasis.

1. The most literal form of this attachment occurs in the conclusion of *St. Julian the Hospitaler,* which Flaubert adapted from the *Gesta Romanorum* (though the story embodies even older materials, such as the legends of St. Hubert and St. Christopher). Julian's final penance is to lie down in the embrace of the leper, who turns into a bright angelic being and takes him to heaven.

2. In *The Private Memoirs and Confessions of a Justified Sinner,* by James Hogg, the self-righteous man is seduced and destroyed by the Prince of Darkness who appears as his double; whether his repentance speaks much for self-knowledge may be doubtful enough, but there is a redemptive note in the circumstance that he ends his life in a manger, "a byre, or cowhouse . . . where, on a divot loft, my humble bedstead stood, and the cattle grunted and puffed below me."

3. Melville's short novels, those combinations of the most baldly stated symbolism with the most mysterious ambiguousness of

resolution, explore this theme. Captain Delano in his benign un-worldliness and innocence becomes responsible for Benito Ce-reno, through whose sufferings and death he is enabled to per-ceive, beneath appearances, how things really are. The Master in Chancery becomes liable personally, morally, religiously, and at one point legally, for Bartleby. His final phrase of sorrowful com-miseration—"Ah, Bartleby! Ah, humanity!"—gains a certain force of revelation from being compared with some of his earlier state-ments, e.g., "I am a man who, from his youth upward, has been filled with a profound conviction that the easiest way of life is the best." *Billy Budd* is a somewhat more complex rendering. Billy and Claggart are represented as eternally fated to one another; beyond that it is Captain Vere who suffers the "mystery of iniquity" of this predestined encounter. Billy suffers as Adam tempted and fallen, as Cain whose brother (Claggart) is preferred before him, as the Son of God whose death redeems to order an unruly people (the mutinous Navy), but who is publicly misrepresented in history (the newspaper article) and art (the ballad). Other, less religious interpretation is possible, but enough has been said for the present purpose.

4. In Conrad's *The Secret Sharer* the story is told with a particu-lar purity as well as a rare optimism (in other examples where the disappearance of one party is allowed to do for his death, that disappearance is usually into an insane asylum). The young cap-tain, irresolute and uncertain in his first command, comes face to face with his double: "It was, in the night, as though I had been faced by my own reflection in the depths of a somber and immense mirror." By protecting Leggatt (a legate from the darkness of the sea outside and the self within), by sharing his identity, by experi-encing in homeopathic amounts the criminal element in his own nature, by at last liberating, or separating, this other self from his own at the risk of shipwreck, the young man gains a "perfect com-munion" with his first command.

Marlow says of Kurtz, "It was written I should be loyal to the nightmare of my choice," and he is loyal to the final extent of lying for him, though "there is a taint of death, a flavor of mortality, in lies." The view of Kurtz as scapegoat, as evil or fallen savior, is generalized throughout, notably in what Marlow says to his au-dience, those nameless masters of the world, the Director of Companies, the Lawyer, the Narrator: "You can't understand. How could you?—with solid pavement under your feet, surrounded by kind neighbors ready to cheer you or fall on you, stepping delicately between the butcher and the policeman, in the holy terror of scandal and gallows and lunatic asylums—how can you imagine what particular region of the first ages a man's untrammeled feet may take him into by the way of solitude—utter solitude without a policeman—by the way of silence—utter silence, where no warning voice of a kind neighbor can be heard whispering of public opinion. These little things make all the great difference." So Kurtz is an instance of absolute power corrupted absolutely, yes, but this power is further characterized as that of the impulsive, archaic life liberated, which no man can bear and live, which Marlow himself nearly died of the briefest and most homeopathic contact with, and which in some sense is the force that makes history and makes civilization.

5. The theme we are describing is of the first importance to Dostoevsky, who intensifies both the psychological penetration of the treatment and its ultimate religious or metaphysical expansions. The typical bond, between the worldly man and his sinister, underworld, epicene counterpart—his "poor relation," as the Devil is called in *The Brothers Karamazov*—occurs in the major novels in such double figures as Ivan and Smerdyakov, Ivan and the Devil, Christ and the Grand Inquisitor, Stavrogin and Pyotr Stepanovich, and, with a quite different tonality, Muishkin and Rogozhin. Two of the short novels concentrate exclusively on the development of this theme. *The Eternal Husband* ties together the seducer and the cuckold in a relation characterized as ambiguously homosexual and sadistic, a comedy agonizing enough but hardly more so than that of *The Double,* which relates how poor, stupid Mr. Golyadkin, portrayed from the outset as suffering symptoms of paranoia, comes face to face with his double, Golyadkin, Jr., who behaves insufferably, calls him "darling," pinches his cheek, embarrasses him in every way public and private, until the original Golyadkin, what remains of him, is driven off to the asylum. In this last scene several people run after the carriage, shouting, until they are left behind, and "Mr. Golyadkin's unworthy twin kept up longer than anyone . . . he ran on with a satisfied air, skipping first to one and then to the other side of the carriage

. . . poking his head in at the window, and throwing farewell kisses to Mr. Golyadkin."

6. Without giving any further examples in detail I may merely mention a few more short novels in which this theme is developed: in Chekhov's *Ward Number Six,* Andrew Ephimich and the young man Ivan Dimitrich Gronov; the young soldier and his captain in Lawrence's *The Prussian Officer*; Aschenbach and Tadzio in Mann's *Death in Venice,* Mario and Cipolla in his *Mario and the Magician*; the condemned man and the officer in *In the Penal Colony* by Kafka; Howe and Tertan in Lionel Trilling's *Of This Time, of That Place*; Wilhelm and Dr. Tamkin in Saul Bellow's *Seize the Day.*

My intention is to discuss composition in the strict sense, rather than to consider the interpretation and historical placement of this thematic insistence. Yet it is worth pausing here to observe in how many of these stories the theme is employed to show the man of the middle class, rational, worldly, either rather stupid or of a somewhat dry intelligence and limited vision, plunged into the domain of the forbidden, extravagant, and illicit, the life of the impulses beneath or the life of compulsive and punitive authority above, both of them equally regions in which every detail gains fatal significance, every perception is excruciatingly intensified, and every decision for salvation or doom: so it happens, in various ways, to Captain Delano, the Master in Chancery, Ivan Ilyich, Gustave Aschenbach, Velchaninov, Gregor Samsa, the Woman Who Rode Away, Andrew Ephimich. . . . And it is remarkable, too, how often, by the device of the double, the incubus as it were, their sufferings and perceptions seem to invade them ambiguously from the world outside and the self within. I am tempted to think that the characteristic economy of the short novel, its precisely defined space, the peculiar lucidity and simplicity of its internal forms—two or three persons, a single action, equal tension among the persons, each of whom has a fate—tends to involve the artist more overtly than usual in trying to expound by fantasies what he himself is and what he is doing in his art. Indeed, this is perhaps cryptically hinted to us by Flaubert, when he makes his Félicité suffer the lash of a coachman's whip on the road between Honfleur and Pont l'Eveque, where he himself, riding in a carriage, suffered his first attack of epilepsy, or serious hysteria. And by Melville, who sees his scrivener—unwilling to copy the writings of others—as having had the previous job of handling dead letters "and assorting them for the flames"—this in the year after a fire at the publishing house had destroyed the plates for Melville's own works. Less cryptically by Mann, who sees his artist-heroes by turns as diseased aristocrats, confidence men, and monstrous tyrants (Savonarola, Cipolla). For the fullest meaning of the theme, most minutely expounded, we should have to refer to Proust, who by the most intricately woven analogies throughout his immense work characterizes the moral isolation of the poet as, on the one hand, that of the invalid, the pervert, the criminal, the Jew, the traitor, and, on the other hand, that of the hero, aristocrat, doctor or surgeon, and commander of armies in the field.

Whether what I have tried to describe is the product of a limited historical tradition or of a tragic circumstance as near eternal as that witnessed to in Greek tragedies or in the Book of Job I am unable to say certainly and must not stop to debate here. So far as the theme results in actions typical of the short novel—actions simple and decisive, generally mortal in fact, and involving few persons—the following points of compositional interest arise.

Whereas the short story tends to rest upon action, a combination of circumstances to which the characters must very readily conform, while the novel, especially in English, goes toward the opposite pole and tends to produce "characters" as an independent value, the short novel strikes a very delicate and exact balance between motive and circumstance; its action generally speaking is the fate of the agonists, and this fate is regarded as flowing demonstrably and with some precision and in great detail from their individual natures, which accordingly are developed at considerable length. I need barely mention examples: the portraits, as distinct from the stories, of e.g., Aschenbach, Captain Delano, The Man from Underground, Gabriel Conroy, John Marcher. . . . What happens to all these persons, and ever so many other protagonists of the short novel, happens expressly to them and because they are as they are; perhaps the simplest instance is that of Captain Delano, whose innocence is represented precisely as the condition of his survival in a naughty world: "a person of a singularly undistrustful good nature, not liable, except on extraordinary and repeated excitement, and hardly then, to indulge in personal alarms, any way involving the imputation of malign evil in man. Whether, in view of what humanity is capable, such a trait implies, along with a benevolent heart, more than ordinary quickness and accuracy of intellectual perception, may be left to the wise to determine."

The same balance is maintained by the authors of these compositions, in the exact division of their attention to the inside of things and the outside, between knowledge of the ordinary, undramatic world, and imagination of the drama which takes place under its exacting conditions. How this is so may be seen most simply from *Notes from the Underground,* where the argument and its dramatic equivalent are given separately; oftener, however, the two strands are concurrent, and occasionally, in very sophisticated and elegant works, they are identical; as in *Un Coeur Simple,* which may be read as the plain product of observation, as though a "sketch of provincial life," and read again, or simultaneously, as a structure of great intricacy and density, entirely musical and contrapuntal in the laws of its being, and consequently forming a world all its own, rhythmic, resonant, symmetrical, in which every detail balances another so as to produce great riches of meaning not so much symbolically in a direct sense as by constellation and patterning, the method James called the figure in the carpet. In this connection I would mention once again Kay Boyle as possibly the foremost modern practitioner of this subtle style, especially in two short novels, *The Crazy Hunter* and *The Bridegroom's Body.*

It is this balance, so like that of the poetic drama, the balance between the appearance and the motive, the observed world and the world of law, which I conceive to be more exactly drawn and maintained in the short novel than elsewhere, that gives to works in this genre the characteristic of ruthlessness I referred to before. The ideal, that every detail should at once seem freely chosen by probable observation, and be in fact the product of a developing inner necessity, confers on these tales something of the air of demonstrations; so that, for example, when Andrew Ephimich is first drawn to visit Gronov in the asylum it is as though the chess master announced mate in twelve—we neither doubt the result nor see at all how it is to be accomplished. In this sense we sometimes feel the protagonists of short novels to be the victims not of fate or of the gods so much as of literary styles and laws of composition—

that strict style of composition discussed by Adrian Leverkühn, himself such a victim, in Mann's *Dr. Faustus*.

This again is a subject I must be content to leave implicit: whether the idea itself of the "art work" any longer has anything to do with anything; whether, being based at last on religious valuations, magical sanctions, and the sense of a universe at once "real" and "symbolic," a universe of signatures, the work of art can continue to interpret human experience. I merely note that this theme is disturbingly *there,* and pass on to safer ground.

The characteristic balance I am speaking of reflects itself very distinctively in the treatment of detail in short novels; more so, or more perspicuously so, than in long ones. A few instances will serve to conclude this discussion.

There are two kinds of relevance in literary composition, and I think they are both readily observable in principle although it is doubtful whether they can always be distinguished in the work itself. One kind has to do with the temporal succession of events, as though the single point of the idea must be viewed in an added dimension as a straight line: in order to tell how a distinguished German author dies in Venice we must get him to Venice, keep him there, and supply a disease for him to die of. He will doubtless see many things, and think many things, on his journey—what things? We need another kind of relevance, having to do with association, symbol, metaphor, as well as with probable and realistic observation; while the distinguished author is in Venice it occurs to him, waking, that his situation is like that discussed in the *Phaedrus,* and, dreaming, that his situation is like that of King Pentheus in *The Bacchae* of Euripides.

The first kind of relevance you may call external, the second internal; or, better, the first is linear, and progresses in time, while the second is radical and comes at every instant from the central conception. The difference between them, practically speaking, is that the story could be told without the contribution of the symbolic details and could not be told without the succession of events. It will be objected, perhaps, that without the symbolic details, or with other symbolic details, it would be a different story and an inferior one, and that is true enough but for compositional purposes irrelevant. What is more important is that neither kind in itself accounts for the story, what makes it worth our while to hear that the distinguished German author went to Venice and died there—for that we require something that binds both sorts together, and makes the temporal and ideal situations the subject of the same decision: in this instance the figure of the boy Tadzio, who according to the first kind of relevance is the motive for Aschenbach's remaining in Venice long enough to contract his fatal disease, and according to the second kind plays Dionysus to his Pentheus, Phaedrus to his Socrates, inspires highly relevant reflections on love and morality, beauty and disease, form and corruption, aristocratic control and chaos, and so on.

The tensions of these two criteria of choice in the short novel tend to make the selection of details extraordinarily fateful; especially it seems that everything which is symbolic, associational, metaphorically relevant, is multiply determined, as the details of a dream are said to be, and thus gains a dramatic prominence and a kind of luminous quality. I will try to illustrate by a few examples.

When Aschenbach dies, there by the shore, we are told that the weather was autumnal, the beach deserted and not even very clean; suddenly we are given this: "A camera on a tripod stood at the edge of the water, apparently abandoned; its black cloth snapped in the freshening wind." That is all, our attention is given to Tadzio, Aschenbach's death soon follows, the camera is never mentioned again.

Crudely speaking, this camera is unnecessary and no one could possibly have noticed anything missing had the author decided against its inclusion; yet in a musical, compositional sense it exquisitely touches the center of the story and creates a resonance which makes us for a moment aware of the entire inner space of the action, of all things relevant and their relations to one another.

Our sense of this is mostly beyond exposition, as symbolic things have a way of being; but some of its elements may be mentioned. About the camera by the sea there is, first, a poignant desolation, the emptiness of vast spaces, and in its pictorial quality it resembles one of the earliest images in the story, when Aschenbach, standing by the cemetery, looks away down the empty streets: "not a wagon in sight, either on the paved Ungererstrasse, with its gleaming tramlines stretching off towards Schwabing, nor on the Föhring highway." Both pictures are by Di Chirico. The camera's black cloth reminds us of the gondola, "black as nothing else on earth except a coffin," and the repeated insistence on black in that description; also of the "labor in darkness" which brings forth the work of art. For we perceive that the camera stands to the sea as, throughout this story, the artist has stood to experience, in a morally heroic yet at the same time dubious or ridiculous or even impossible relation of form to all possibility, and that at the summer's end, in the freshening wind, the camera is abandoned. It would be near forgivable, so full of Greek mysteries is this work, if we thought the tripod itself remotely Delphic.

Here is another example. At the beginning of *The Secret Sharer* Conrad gives us an image which at that time, perhaps, we cannot see as anything but pictorial: the young man, looking out across the sea, sees "lines of fishing stakes resembling a mysterious system of half-submerged bamboo fences." But when we have finished the story we may see even that image in the first sentence as compositionally resonant, as a cryptic emblem set up at the gateway of the action. This emblem suggests to us how the conscious distinctions, the property rights, of reason and society, extend also beneath the surface (of the sea, of the mind) and are in fact rooted down there: precisely what is learned by the narrator who before his adventure "rejoiced in the great security of the sea as compared with the unrest of the land, in my choice of that untempted life presenting no disquieting problems, invested with an elementary moral beauty by the absolute straightforwardness of its appeal and by the singleness of its purpose"—fine phrases, on which the story, like its opening image, comments in sympathetic, pedagogic irony.

Another example. In *The Death of Ivan Ilyich,* Tolstoy shows us the funeral service and a colleague of the dead man going in to visit the widow, who is under three several necessities which exclude one another: of showing terrible grief, of passing ashtrays to prevent the guest's spoiling the rug, of discussing the payment of her husband's pension. The visitor sits down "on a low pouffe, the springs of which yielded under his weight." The widow, however, catches her shawl on the edge of a table, so "Peter Ivanovich rose to detach it, and the springs of the pouffe, relieved of his weight, rose also and gave him a push. The widow began detaching her shawl herself, and Peter Ivanovich again sat down, suppressing the rebellious springs of the pouffe under him. But the widow had not quite freed herself, and Peter Ivanovich got up again, and again the pouffe rebelled and even creaked." A page later, as the widow approaches the subject of the pension, "Peter Ivanovich bowed, keeping control of the springs of the pouffe, which immediately began quivering under him."

This comically autonomous pouffe represents not merely the social obliquities of the interview, nor merely that inanimate objects continually mutter their comments to the detriment of human dignity and solemnity, but also how such objects may tend actively to push us where we do not wish to go, to represent some implacable hostility in the world of objects, especially those meant for our convenience. Death occurs with just the same independence of human volition, and we are emblematically informed— "As he sat down on the pouffe Peter Ivanovich recalled how Ivan Ilyich had arranged this room and had consulted him regarding this pink cretonne with green leaves"—of something we learn more explicitly later, that Ivan Ilyich's interest precisely in such things, in "decoration," caused his death: "when mounting a stepladder to show the upholsterer, who did not understand, how he wanted the hangings draped, he made a false step and slipped . . ."

This species of inner determination produces, in the short novel, not single details only but chains and clusters of iterative imagery also, such as we usually identify with the poetry of Shakespeare; and sometimes, as in *Un Coeur Simple,* it is the elegant patterning and constatation of such groups of images which alone, implicitly, supply the meaning, or meanings: an interested reader may trace on his own, for example, the provenience of the parrot-paraclete Loulou, not in the action alone, but in the far-ranging associated imagery—how it is gradually prepared for before its appearance by much talk of jungles and far places, by the geography book given the children by M. Bourais, by Félicité's childish ideas of distant places and times, by Victor's voyages and death, by Mme. Auban's dream after the death of Virginie, and so on.

I have tried to describe the short novel, according to the examples I am most familiar with, not as a compromise between novel and short story, but as something like the ideal and primary form, suggestively allied in simplicity and even in length with the tragedies of antiquity, and dealing in effect with equivalent materials.

No doubt in dealing with this subject I have slighted somewhat the complex novel and, even more, the short story; that has to do in part, as I said, with making the middle term visible, but perhaps in even greater part with my lasting delight in short novels, which I will even go so far as nearly to identify with tragic art in our fictional tradition. What is accomplished by the works I have been speaking of may be given the sanction of science as well as magic or religion in the following words of Sir D'Arcy Wentworth Thompson in the introductory chapter of his work *On Growth and Form*: "Like warp and woof, mechanism and teleology are interwoven together, and we must not cleave to the one nor despise the other; for their union is rooted in the very nature of totality. We may grow shy or weary of looking to a final cause for an explanation of our phenomena; but after we have accounted for these on the plainest principles of mechanical causation it may be useful and appropriate to see how the final cause would tally with the other, and lead towards the same conclusion." It is this double exploration which, I have contended, is undertaken in the short novel more than in other sorts of fiction. Even the matter of the length or brevity of such works ought not to be beneath discussion as "merely" mechanical; in the book I quoted from before, Vladimir Nabokov says something which I shall repeat for a conclusion to this matter. Discussing ways of seeing—the lantern slide, the microscope—he says, "There is, it would seem, in the dimensional scale of the world a kind of delicate meeting-place between imagination and knowledge, a point, arrived at by diminishing large things and enlarging small ones, that is intrinsically artistic."

The Ills from Missing Dates

Nabokov's Dozen, A Collection of Thirteen Stories. By Vladimir Nabokov. Doubleday, 1958.

In trying to fix the quality of experience dominant over these stories I thought of some famous lines by William Empson:

> It is the poems you have lost, the ills
> From missing dates, at which the heart expires.

Thus Mr. Nabokov also; where are the poets, governesses, girl friends of yesteryear? he asks over and over. More precisely, *who* were they? People like Nina ("Spring in Fialta"), Perov ("A Forgotten Poet"), or the wife of the narrator in "That in Aleppo Once" slip in and out of their stories as they slip in and out of their identities—identities for a long time nebulous, "historical," dependent upon the capriciousness of memory, then suddenly precise and unforgettable for an instant.

If that abused (and ordinarily abusive) word "experimental" may for once apply to something, these pieces exhibit Mr. Nabokov's experiments on the identities of his characters, on his relations with them, and on the questionably theatrical symbolisms, or styles of presentation, of Life, who is seen as "an assistant producer." These identities and relations are multiple, fluidly shifting; few of the persons involved are so simple as to be merely doubles, like the one in "Conversation Piece" ("a disreputable namesake of mine") or the poor, prize-winning traveler in "Cloud, Castle, Lake," who is, says the author, "one of my representatives." The result is the depiction of a world by now familiar to Mr. Nabokov's readers, a world of objects fragmentary and allusive, elusive, illusive (all three will have to do), suggesting more or less fleetingly their relation to some lost whole; a world in which the possible immanence of meaning is either a stage trick

201

on the part of the assistant producer, or else the disastrous vision-
ary madness of the perceiver. For illustration, let one story stand
for all, as by its title, "Signs and Symbols," it seems to want to do.
Here the sort of world I have ascribed to the author is compressed
into eight pages which come as near the absolute of art as anything
I have seen in the short story.

An old couple, refugees, are going to the sanitarium to take a
birthday present to their incurably deranged son; they have chosen
"a dainty and innocent trifle: a basket with ten different fruit jel-
lies in ten little jars," and this choice has cost them much thought,
since the young man's malady is such that almost any object in the
world achieves for him a frightening, hostile significance, or else is
simply meaningless and useless.

At the sanitarium they learn that their child has again attempted
to kill himself; he is all right, but a visit is out of the question.
They go home, they think about the past, they torture themselves,
and, after midnight, decide they must bring the boy home, no matter what the inconvenience, what the danger, since until they do so
life is impossible.

The decision makes them happier, and at this moment the telephone rings, frightening them; it is a wrong number, "a girl's dull
little voice" wanting to speak to "Charlie." The telephone rings
again, right away, and the old woman tells the girl "you are turning
the letter O instead of the zero." The old people sit down to "their
unexpected festive midnight tea," the man examines with pleasure
the birthday present, the ten little jars; and the telephone rings
again.

Readers who think first of "plot" will quite properly say, "but
that isn't a story"; and so, in my description, it isn't. Yet in this
simply articulated space a vast and tragic life works itself out, presenting the tension between meaning (which is madness) and the
meaningless (which is the normal, or sane, condition of present
life). The system of the young man's delusions has the high-sound-
ing name of "referential mania," and might as well be called
"Poet's Disease":

> In these very rare cases the patient imagines that everything hap-
> pening around him is a veiled reference to his personality and exis-
> tence. He excludes real people from the conspiracy—because he

considers himself to be so much more intelligent than other men. Phenomenal nature shadows him wherever he goes. Clouds in the staring sky transmit to one another, by means of slow signs, incredibly detailed information regarding him. His inmost thoughts are discussed at nightfall, in manual alphabet, by darkly gesticulating trees. Pebbles or stains or sun flecks form patterns representing in some awful way messages which he must intercept. Everything is a cipher and of everything he is the theme. Some of the spies are detached observers, such are glass surfaces and still pools; others, such as coats in store windows, are prejudiced witnesses, lynchers at heart; others again (running water, storms) are hysterical to the point of insanity, have a distorted opinion of him and grotesquely misinterpret his actions. He must be always on his guard and devote every minute and module of life to the decoding of the undulation of things. The very air he exhales is indexed and filed away. If only the interest he provokes were limited to his immediate surroundings—but alas it is not! With distance the torrents of wild scandal increase in volume and volubility. The silhouettes of his blood corpuscles, magnified a million times, flit over vast plains; and still farther, great mountains of unbearable solidity and height sum up in terms of granite and groaning firs the ultimate truth of his being.

Over against this hostile and sinister truth (the universe does mean something, and if you are able to perceive it you will go insane and die) is set the life of the old couple, displaced persons with their hopes and memories (a pack of soiled cards and old photograph albums), with the near-absolute, meaningless chaos which twenty years of history have made of their lives. And the two halves into which the universe has thus split are mediated (not put back together) by those telephone calls. Just here, where the Satevepost reader waits for his satisfaction (it will be the doctor, announcing a sudden cure by miracle drug), and the reader of rather more artsy-crafty periodicals waits for *his* satisfaction (the young man has finally done away with himself), comes the exact metaphor for the situation, as the telephone, the huge, mechanical system whose buzz relates everyone to everyone else, has the last word: "you are turning the letter O instead of the zero."

Detail for detail there's a great deal more, but that is more or less how it goes. Not all the stories are that good (which would be asking a great deal), but this is a wonderful book. It is good that the (wildly improbable) success of *Lolita* could exert enough leverage to raise its author's short stories once more over the horizon, and all Mr. Nabokov's readers, the new ones and the others who will remember much of the present volume from the New Directions edition of *Nine Stories* (long out of print and hard or impossible to come by), ought to be grateful.

FROM
Reflexions
on Poetry
and Poetics
(1972)

Bottom's Dream: The Likeness of Poems and Jokes

The poetic attempt to say the world, to name it rightly, is per-haps a matter altogether too mysterious to be talked about. When someone, behaving "poetically," looks into the landscape and tries to speak it, this mystery turns inward and takes the form of an anxious searching and striving, until (sometimes) the mind by some wild reach having an evident relation with insanity produces a phrase, and this phrase—somehow—*expresses* . . . whereupon some quiet click of accurate conjunction tells us that what has happened is somehow reasonable.

Yet this moment of expressiveness itself occurs at a crossing point, and tells us that something in language is not linguistic, that something in reason is not reasonable. It speaks of a relation be-tween inside and outside, an identity between inside and outside, but this relation, this identity, is itself unspeakable:

Suddenly, I saw the cold and rook-delighting heaven. . . .

That has no meaning, strictly, that can be expressed otherwise, or translated. How, then, to someone who for a long time entertains the phrase as a sort of empty and objectless talisman, a piece of jade turned over in the hand, does it—suddenly, as the poet says—come to identify one alone sort of weather, one alone sort of poetry, that quality the poet wanted, he said elsewhere, of "cold light and tumbling clouds"?

Echo answers. Which is not so say that nothing answers, for it may be by a species of radar that intelligence moves through the world. We might say of expressiveness itself, of the irreducible phrase, that first it is, and then it finds a meaning in the world. Or else: Whatever the mind invents, it also discovers. Or again: Whatever is revealed, in poetry, plays at being revealed.

It is that element of play that I wish to talk about as an essentially poetic quality. This quality, I think, somehow exists in all language, in language considered as an unstable fusion of practicality and dream, in language which is in so large part an instrument for repeating, but in some small part an instrument for inventing and discovering what is invented—which is only to say, perhaps, that epic poems and systems of theology are all written by people who, whatever their talents, could not have been the first to say "cat," because it had already been said for them.

Though this poetic quality exists in all language, it will most often and most easily be visible in expressions which time or custom has set free from the urgencies of exhortation and the immediate claims of life: inscriptions on tombs, the proud dominations of antiquity, Ozymandias in his desert—surely the superfluity I mean has its relations equally with the ideal and the idea of death. Yet it may as certainly be identified in the most trivial examples. If you remove, say, the headline from an advertisement and let it dry in the sun until it shrivels out of context, it will grow other and rather surprising relations:

. . . new shades of youth. . . .

Its valency, standing thus alone, is other than what it is when you put it back in its intentional place as an incitement to buy something called Ogilvie Creme Hair Color Foam. The tonality of *shades,* for instance, is more Stygian.

So in seeking to identify, if possible, something of the quality of expressiveness called "poetic" you might start, not with the sublime, but down at the humble end of the scale, with such things as that, with appearances of this quality in misprints, newspaper items, jokes . . . working your way up in Horatio Alger style to see how far your descriptions will take you (whether in the end you will marry Sophia, holy wisdom, the boss's daughter). In doing this we shall rely on the help of Freud—in some particulars on his fine joke book, "Wit and Its Relation to the Unconscious," and in general on his attempt to demonstrate systematically how mental life is continuous with itself in all its manifestations, from slips of the tongue to systems of philosophy and the visions of religion.

Also of Shakespeare, who in giving a title to these remarks gives also an instance of the quality we are trying to say something about. When Nick Bottom wakes in the forest from the true dream in which he wore an ass's head and was adored by Titania, he speaks of what has happened in language whose comic effect has much to do with its tone of reverence, its being so full of garbles from scripture, and so on; and he says:

> It shall be called Bottom's Dream, because it hath no bottom.

Probably there can be no better definition of poetry—no better definition, I am tempted to say, of anything that matters to us— though all the same it is clearly better for Bottom than for the rest of us.

Something of the quality I mean may be discovered in misprints. The mathematical probability must be quite large that any misprint, such as the omission or addition or substitution of a single letter, will produce merely a moment of nonsense in the result, and indeed that happens often enough. But given this preponderant possibility it is surprising to notice how often misprints make a curious other sense, and surprising, too, how economically such transformations may be effected. Here are a few examples:

a. The Russians are dredging what will be "the largest man-maid lake in the world." Nearly nonsense, and not quite; though not quite witty, either. Between man and lake the idea of mixed bathing has intervened to pervert the spelling by the nicest economy so that it gives another sense which hovers between the appropriate and the absurd; perhaps this secondary sense is not quite strong enough, and that may have to do with the fact that we cannot hear the difference but have to see it or spell it.

b. A reviewer of one of Kinsey's reports was made to say, "The sexual urge in females is demonstarted by". . . . Who would bother reading the rest of the sentence? Not only does "demonstarted" make sense instead of nonsense; it makes a sense which is as it were subversively appropriate to the serious discussion which was supposed to be going on.

c. A girl escaping from East Berlin "swam the icy river to be with her finance in the West." One imagines a Communist reading this with deepest satisfaction, since it confirms what he has always believed about love and money in the West. And the compositor was so taken with his invention that he used it again in the next sentence, while giving the finance's name. One observes, too, that the pertness of the criticism is enhanced by the somewhat balladlike romance of the subject.

The effect common to all three examples is that one reality gives place to another, and a tension is revealed between them: the world of information and, we might say, the symbolic world reflect one another in this tension. Moreover, the reality revealed by inadvertence is in each instance subversive of the reality intended; this is not so surprising in the first example, since we generally expect the sexual to be the hidden reality in statements, as it is in the second and third, where sexual and marital concerns themselves give way to themes of deeper mystery and deeper obsession still, theology of sorts, and money.

As to the relation of all this with the quality of the poetic, which many have called "vision," it is the first effect of Freud's demonstrations, on errors, dreams, jokes, to show that vision begins with a fault in this world's smooth façade.

The examination now of a few rather more complicated and elaborated examples will perhaps enable us to go further in our description of this quality and its mechanisms.

In "A Handbook of Arms and Armor," by Bashford Dean, I read that Japanese feudal warfare was especially rough on horses because they were not armored; there followed this sentence: "Not until the Tokugawa period, when warfare disappeared, was the horse given adequate armor."

This statement takes the mind away from arms and armor, but not entirely away. It combines with the subject another subject, of symbolic reflexions and resonances, in which the sentence bears a sadly ironic truth (everything is always too late) without in any way losing its pleasant and somehow Oriental flavor of bland paradox calmly mastered (as in the report of an English-language Japanese newspaper, that "the entire aircrew climbed out on the wing of the burning plane and parachuted safely to their death"). It would be possible, no doubt, to appreciate intellectually the wit of the proposition alone, dismissing all that was not abstract as irrelevant; but that would be to lose the nice particularity of "the Tokugawa period," the elegant coup de grâce given in "adequate," and the fine intricate play of sounds (r and w especially) and internal rimes (like that between "period" and "disappeared") which stitches the words together and gives decisive character to the entire statement.

The second example is an AP dispatch reporting that a former lawyer of Al Capone's is convicted of income tax evasion. "I have in mind that you've suffered enough," said the judge, who also said, "Ten years ago . . . you were a well-to-do man. Now you're a man without means because of the debts you incurred in paying off the taxes. You've lost your law practice. This is a strong reminder that the power to tax is the power to destroy."

Something here, maybe the biblical austerity of the last sentence especially, strikes me as bearing the quality of expressiveness I am after; something both tragic and funny, featured by the judge's deadpan style—is he aware, right there, of the comparison implied between gangsters and governments?—and the whole rather complicated situation of the feelings wants only a touch of arrangement, a little bit of pointing, to be brought out. I imagine the former lawyer brooding on what has been said to him:

> Ten years ago, I was a well-to-do man,
> Now I am a man without means.
> I have received
> The strong reminder.
> The power to tax is the power to destroy.
>
> The lesson of the State's Do What You Can,
> That is what the law means

Though we are deceived,
O strong reminder
Of Alcatraz, my master, my joy.

Out here beyond the average life span
The end no longer means
What it did. Reprieved
By the strong reminder,
I get up the ante and go to destroy.

My last example is also a news item, reporting that a jet plane
was shot down by its own gunfire. It is probably interesting
enough to know that we live in a world in which this has become
possible, but the thing sticks in the mind as well as the throat. An
admiral and what the *Times* called "other Navy experts" explain:
"The shells left the cannon traveling 1,500 feet a second faster
than the airplane. After entering their trajectory they immediately
began to slow down and fall because of air resistance and gravity.
Meanwhile, (the pilot), going into a steeper dive, began a short
cut across the shells' curved course. About two or three miles from
the point at which the shells were fired, they reached the same
point the plane had achieved. . . ."

This may already be a poem, finished and impossible to meddle
with, though the newspaper's account is a little dispersed on the
page for my entire satisfaction, and stuffed with irrelevant details.
All the same, the relations expressed between murder and suicide
are splendidly and as it were secretly there: "a short cut across the
shells' curved course" is in itself a fine piece of virtuosity, giving
the truth of the human situation with a decisiveness not so easily
matched in poetry, though surpassed in this of John Webster: "Like
diamonds we are cut with our own dust."

So it seems that this episode of the jet shot down by its own
gunfire may be only the last playable variation on a theme poets
have constantly handled; the particular comparison which comes
to mind is with Hardy's "The Convergence of the Twain (Lines on
the loss of the 'Titanic')" where the likeness and prospective identity of ship with iceberg are guaranteed at last by their literally
coming together: the point of the joke, which Hardy calls "con-
summation."

Not trying for the moment to demonstrate the relation of such things to poetry, I shall say instead what characteristics my examples have in common.

Each is a thing in itself, a something decisive which the mind easily recognizes and detaches from the context in which it occurs. To say almost the same thing in another way, each example has the intention of giving information, but is received by the mind as giving something else; the statement, as it is made, crosses over from the practical realm into another, the realm of the superfluous and ideal, where it becomes a focus for meditations on the human condition under the figure of armored horses, aged lawyers, jet pilots who shoot themselves down.

This crossing over, this relation between two realms and the process of moving between them, is perhaps comparable with the relation, in poetry, between letter and allegory, between the picturesque and the symbolic.

The examples have, though in varying degrees, a reflexive character or one in which contradictions resolve; they are, again in varying degrees, increasingly from first to last, about retributive justice, and it may be this which gives them their quality of decisiveness and finish. This reflexive character could be put another way, as a principle of economy: they use their materials twice. And they all three, rather unexpectedly, exhibit the pathos of the obsolete, or obsolescent; they are all about something's being caught up with, something's being over.

Our next step will be to see if the mechanism of a joke in any way illuminates that of a lyric poem; we shall limit ourselves to brief examples.

One critical resemblance between the two will be clear to anyone who has ever tried to make up either—(by the way, how do jokes get made? I do not know that anyone has seriously studied this question)—and this is the problem of the ending. Anyone can begin a poem, anyone can begin a joke (the pointlessness of doing that is very clear, it seems, but many people begin poems). As Plato says in the Laws, "The beginning is like a god, who while he lives among men redeems all." There is a grand feeling of liberty about beginning anything, for it looks as though any gesture in the whole world will do. But, in the difficult world of forms, the gesture you elect will entail consequences good and bad, seen and unseen. Sooner or later, you have to ask yourself how to stop, what it means to stop, what it is that has finished. This is the question we will now examine, first with reference to a few jokes.

a. A riddle. How do you catch the lions in the desert? Answer: you strain off the sand, and the remainder will be lions.

b. From Shipley, "Dictionary of Word Origins," s.v. Strategy. A Chinese general sent his advance guard up to the edge of a forest. To find out if the enemy were in ambush there, he ordered each man to throw a stone into the forest, and if birds flew up there were no men there, so that it would be safe to advance. All this was done, birds flew, the army marched forward—and was captured. For the opposing general, also as it happened Chinese, had said to *his* soldiers: Men, I want each of you to grab a bird, and let it go when they throw those stones.

These instances are perhaps directed against the intellect's characteristic wish to simplify situations so as reductively to bring out logical structure at the expense of everything else in experience, the wit being that this same essentializing structure is employed to bring out the absurdity of logic in this world. Both jokes make use of the same almost absolute economy, using as much as possible in the response what was given in the stimulus, merely revising the elements of the relation in an "impossible" way.

The pleasure we get must come from the fulfillment of an expectation that the resolution in both instances will make use very purely, indeed exclusively, of the given materials, plus our surprise at the use made, which as straight men for the occasion we should not have thought of. But note that although we should not have thought of the reply, the very fact of its employing *only* terms already used gave us a not quite explicit sense that we might have thought of it in another instant; that though we did not in fact think of it, our minds were playing with the possibilities of lions-deserts, stones-birds, so that the answer, as a matter of timing, seemed "right" or "inevitable," responsive to a wish on our part for symmetry and economy together with a certain shock, the compounded fulfillment of fairly definite formal expectations with a material surprise. We might compare what happens with what happens in music, eighteenth-century music, say, where to a strict and relatively narrow canon of harmonic possibility, including certain clichés of cadence, is added the composer's originality at handling his materials within the convention.

c. From Freud, "Thoughts for the Times on War and Death" (1915). A husband to his wife, "If one of us should die, I would go and live in Paris."

Here we observe, as with so many jokes, and especially those bearing on sex and marriage, that the sentiment itself is about as unfunny as it could be, setting the death of one partner against the pleasure of the other and leaving no doubt of the choice that would be made. The wit, we suppose, the element which allows us to laugh, comes from two circumstances: first, that the wish expressed is one very widely entertained but usually concealed; second, that it breaks from its concealment so economically, using as its means a very slight grammatical displacement of the solemn, "objective" statement, with its air of entertaining the worst contingencies, which the husband must have consciously intended.

Thus, like our misprints earlier, this remark makes a revelation of sorts. A revelation can be only of that which is hidden, what is hidden is secret, what is secret is so because it is, or is thought to be, evil, shameful, taboo (sacred); finally, this evil represents something we believe to be true. So that the revelation is subversive of the usual order of appearances, beneath which it shows another order, one that gains its reality from the comparison of the two.

d. A last example, not a joke, but from Freud's analysis of one of his own dreams. He dreamt of a place called Mödling. No amount of personal association gave any reason for its presence in the dream, until he went through the following process of dream etymology or even archeology: Mödling, from earlier Mödelitz, from the Latin Mea Delicia (my joy) = mein Freud.

Though not strictly a joke, this instance purely illuminates a vital quality of wit, which takes the longest way round only as the shortest way home, whose beginnings and endings seem to be disposed upon a circle, not a straight line. This quality has to do with that economy we mentioned earlier in connection with our first two examples, to which it adds, however, the further consideration that this economy may tend to be reflexive, to turn back on itself and use itself again in a new sense (here quite literally a translation into another language and back). This is in itself a very poetical idea about the nature of forms, that they are like human beings who in seeking the world find themselves, like Odysseus who encompassed a vast world simply by trying to get home (this aspect of the journey is finely brought out in a beautiful poem by Cavafy, "Ithaka"). So also Donne, "Thy firmnesse makes my circle just, And makes me end where I begunne." (The example suggests another and more recondite possibility, that dreamer, poet, and wit are somehow endeavoring to say the world as a form of their own name. "When Thou hast done, Thou hast not Donne." This would only rarely, if ever, be demonstrable, though I have observed my own name, only slightly concealed, in my contention that the poet is a "namer of" the world. But it is in this sense that Shakespeare, with a "profound" or "abysmal" pun, has Bottom say of his night in the enchanted wood, "It shall be called Bottom's Dream, because it hath no Bottom.")

Summing up what we have so far: our examples tell us about the effect and mechanism of jokes that they depend on a strictly limited material, which they resolve surprisingly in terms of itself. Freud would remark that this economy is itself a source of our pleasure, and adduce such terms as remembering, recognition, recurrence, as analogous; and would add, what we discovered from one of our examples, that hostility may also be a pleasure-bearing part of wit. For, after all, a smile, physiologically speaking, is a step on the road to a snarl and a bite (cf. "sarcasm," a "biting remark").

So we have: economy of materials
            sudden reversal of the relations of the
               elements.
            introduction of absurdity, but
            the apparent absurdity, introduced into the
               context of the former sense, makes a new
               and deeper sense;
            the hidden is revealed.

We may suspect that makers of jokes and smart remarks resemble poets at least in this, that they too would be excluded from Plato's Republic; for it is of the nature of Utopia and the Crystal

Palace, as Dostoevsky said, that you can't stick your tongue out at it. A joke expresses tension, which it releases in laughter; it is a sort of permissible rebellion against things as they are—permissible, perhaps, because this rebellion is at the same time stoically resigned, it acknowledges that things are as they are, and that they will, after the moment of laughter, continue to be that way. That is why jokes concentrate on the most sensitive areas of human concern: sex, death, religion, and the most powerful institutions of society; and poems do the same. We might consider in this connection how grave a business civilization must be, to require professional comedians. Or, as Empson said (in a poem), "The safety valve alone knows the worst truth about the engine."

In general, to succeed at joking or at poetry, you have to be serious; the least hint that you think you are being funny will cancel the effect, and there is probably no lower human enterprise than "humorous writing." Still, there are poems which clearly also are jokes, yet by no means light verse, and one of these may serve for a bridge between the two realms; the inscription on the collar of a dog which Alexander Pope gave the Prince of Wales:

> I am His Highness' dog at Kew.
> Pray tell me, sir, whose dog are you?

This couplet possesses fully the characteristics we have distinguished in jokes: the sentiment itself is tendentious, might even come near to being savage were it not spoken by a dog with an air of doggy innocence; by cleverness it gets away with the sort of revelation of how societies exist which might at various times and in various realms cost a man his life or liberty; it works economically, by transformation of the given material. Probably, to be pedantic, the wit consists in getting us to accept the literal meaning of "dog" in the first line, so that we receive the metaphorical "dog" of the second line with surprise, but a surprise conditioned by expectation, for it is after all the same word.

The example raises another point, that one mechanism of economy in joking is the pun, either in the use of one word in two senses, as here, or in the use of two words of similar sound which mean different things but still somehow establish a resemblance beyond that of the sound. Notice that in the archaic economy of poetry it frequently happens that a resemblance in sound is, though cryptically, a resemblance in sense, as in the kind of logical connection hinted by a rime, or in these examples:

> For ruin hath taught me thus to ruminate (Shakespeare)

> O Attic shape! Fair attitude! (Keats)

We may add this as well. The "purely formal" arrangements of poetry, such as measure, rime, stanza, which it appears not at all to share with the joke, are in fact intensifications of a characteristic we have already noticed in jokes: the compound of expectation with a fulfillment which is simultaneously exact and surprising, giving to the result that quality sometimes thought of as inevitability, or rightness. Observe, too, that many jokes show a rudimentary form of stanzaic progression, by being arranged in a series of three, with similar grammatical structure, so that the hearer correctly anticipates the punch line as coming the third time a character says something, does something, and so forth.

Here is an example in which the humor is overtly savage, and any responsive smile might be accompanied by some gnashing of teeth; it is from Swift's "Satirical Elegy on the Death of a Late Famous General"; he means the Duke of Marlborough:

> Behold his funeral appears,
> Nor widow's sighs, nor orphan's tears,
> Wont at such times each heart to pierce,
> Attend the progress of his herse.
> But what of that, his friends may say,
> He had those honours in his day.
> True to his profit and his pride,
> He made them weep before he dy'd. . . .

What is possibly the oldest joke in the world says, "With friends like that you don't need enemies." Its present form seems to be Jewish, but I have found it in Tacitus, who remarks on the persecutions under Nero, "Those who had no enemies were betrayed by their friends."

And now, to climax this sequence, an example from whose grim strength all the laughter has fallen away; and yet it seems that the mechanism of the joke remains unchanged. It is Housman's "Epitaph on an Army of Mercenaries."

> These, in the day when heaven was falling,
>   The hour when earth's foundations fled,
> Followed their mercenary calling
>   And took their wages and are dead.
>
> Their shoulders held the sky suspended;
>   They stood, and earth's foundations stay;
> What God abandoned, these defended,
>   And saved the sum of things for pay.

Among so many fine things here, we single out the splendid economy of wit which remembers "and took their wages" from the first stanza to bring it back in a savage reversal as "the sum of things."

But by now you may have the serious objection that I am being unduly free with the idea of a joke. Engrossed in my pedantries, I seem to have forgotten that the first thing to see about a joke is that it makes us laugh; whatever doesn't do that cannot really be likened to a joke.

I should reply as follows. There is a great range of jokes whose intent is indeed to make us laugh. But can you really distinguish these as absolutely separate from and in no way resembling the range, at least as great, of such artifacts of speech as: riddles, proverbs, aphorisms, epigrams, gnomic sayings, anecdotes, parables . . . ? Jokes, it is reasonable to claim, have often been the instruments of moral teaching, and even religious revelation. Their humor may be far indeed from laughter (consider the other meaning of "funny": strange, wrong), or may be close to it without invoking it, as in the riddles of the Zen Koan or those Tales of the Hasidim collected by Martin Buber. To take one example only, with what sort of laughter does one respond to this joke by Nietzsche: "The last Christian died on the Cross"?

I think I may continue to claim that poems and jokes resemble one another, laughter or no; and that the essential characteristic, in virtue of which the resemblance obtains, is not the laughter but, far rather, the quality of decisiveness and finish, of absolute completion to which nothing need be added nor could be added: not laughter, but the silence with which we greet the thing absolutely done.

You may go on with examples from a more ambiguous realm, where the quality of the response may be hovering and doubtful. Here is Herrick, on Julia weeping:

> She by the River sate, and sitting there,
> She wept, and made it deeper by a teare.

Its delicacy, its reticence, are not without humor; probably its miniature aspect asks for a smile. And yet, to even a moment's contemplation, it grows very large and the thin, molecular film of that tear spreading over the river is enough to express the world's sorrow; just exactly as in that saddest joke of all, where one rabbi comes to another who is weeping for the death of his son.

> "Why do you weep," asks the one, "seeing it does no good?"
> "That is the reason," says the other, "I weep because it does no good."
> And the first rabbi sat beside the other, and wept with him.

There are poems by William Blake in which the feeling seems to be resolved actually by ambiguity, or by the maintaining a tension (a balance?) between two possibilities of feeling. This is difficult to explain, but less difficult to demonstrate. In "The Chimney Sweeper," a boy is the speaker; he tells of his and his friend Tom's wretched life, and of Tom's beautiful dream, in which an Angel opens the coffins of all the chimney sweeps and sets them free; then the poem ends:

> And so Tom awoke and we rose in the dark
> And got with our bags & our brushes to work.
> Tho' the morning was cold, Tom was happy & warm,
> So if all do their duty, they need not fear harm.

My point is this: one first reads the last line as spoken by the child, and spoken straight. Yet one cannot fail to catch, I believe, another voice, that of William Blake, who is also speaking the same line at the same time, in a tone of righteous indignation, in a snarl of woe against Church and State. And the same thing happens in "Holy Thursday," where, after describing the poor children being walked to church by beadles, and how their songs were "like harmonious thunderings the seats of heaven among," he finishes with the moral: "Then cherish pity, lest you drive an angel from your door." Again, you can read it straight: pity the poor children, for their angelic prayers really are powerful in heaven; or it is possible to sneer it, as if it meant to say: what sort of pity is it, that allows children to be poor? If you try reading the poems aloud, I think you will see that this tension is there. It is a tension which Blake expresses explicitly in one of his jokes, one of those quatrains which read like nursery rimes until they explode in your face, taking most of the moral world with them:

> Pity would be no more,
> If we did not make somebody Poor;
> And Mercy no more could be,
> If all were as happy as we.

The course of an argument will normally be thus, that many matters from the roots come together in a single trunk, a thought which can for a certain time be sustained; but inevitably, at last, the trunk divides in branches, the branches in twigs, the twigs bear leaves, and the leaves fall. Perhaps we are just now arriving at the place where the trunk divides and becomes several instead of one, and I ought to say here that I am not trying to show that jokes and poems are one and the same thing throughout the range. We have the same problem with metaphor generally, where the assertion that A is like B implies that A is also other than B, and not the same thing at all. "To thee the reed is as the oak." The poet meant, not that there was no difference, nor that both reed and oak are plants, but that the differences, to Imogen as dead, were a matter of indifference.

Or else you might say that at a certain point in an argument the thought, which had seemed identifiably one, begins to become indistinguishable from a good many other thoughts—as though we had gone a long way round only to discover ourselves back in quite familiar territory. Here are some of the landmarks of that territory, which perhaps our journey at best has but allowed us to see for a moment as though they were new.

The real resemblance, the illuminating one, is that poems and jokes to succeed must do something decisive; which may seem to mean that their endings are somehow contained in their beginnings. This of course is precisely the magical, illusionist, or religious character of art, which has customarily rested on the assumption that God in creating the world did something coherent although mysterious, and that therefore history, at the last great day, would be seen as "like" a drama. So that poetic art has concerned itself characteristically with doubleness, and with what oneness can possibly or impossibly be made out of doubleness: with freedom and necessity, with changelings, with going out and coming back, with echo, mirror, radar, with serious parody; here we approach Aristotle's notions of recognition and reversal, and may see them operant not only in the major forms of tragic poetry, but also and equally in the minute particulars of the poet's art, e.g.,

> With eager feeding food doth choke the feeder.

> Property was thus appalled,
> That the self was not the same;
> Single nature's double name
> Neither two nor one was called.

We see also that the mechanism we have attempted to describe is like that of the plot in a story, also a magical device for dealing with time as though it were eternity, a way of doing two things—at least two!—at once, a way of handling appearance and reality as mirror images of one another. As Rebecca West says, "I am never sure of the reality of a thing until I have seen it twice." The mechanism we mean is what gives us this power of seeing a thing twice: it is like those striking moves in chess, called generally double attack—the pin, the fork, double check, disclosed check—which show the contrapuntal effect of getting two moves for one and thus, as it were, making time stand still.

Our examples thus far have been chiefly epigrammatic in nature anyhow, and so the resemblance to jokes has been clear enough. But a poem is, for one thing, more ambitious than a joke; literally, it takes more world into its ambit. So for a conclusion let us look at two somewhat larger instances.

Pied Beauty

Glory be to God for dappled things,
For skies of couple-colour as a brindled cow;
For rose-moles all in stipple upon trout that swim;
Fresh firecoal chestnut-falls; finches' wings;
Landscape plotted and pieced—fold, fallow and plough;
And all trades, their gear and tackle and trim.

All things counter, original, spare, strange;
Whatever is fickle, freckled (who knows how?)
With swift, slow; sweet, sour; adazzle, dim;
He fathers forth whose beauty is past change:
    Praise Him.

This poem of Hopkins' seems not only to illustrate the relation
we have been discussing, but also to take this relation for its subject: it gives a religious guarantee, which is perhaps the only guarantee available, for the real resemblance between particular and
generality, between detail and meaning; it so relates the unique
with the universal as to show them the same and not the same; its
transaction seems to define metaphor for us as: the exception
caught becoming the rule.

And a last example:

The Collar-Bone of a Hare

Would I could cast a sail on the water
Where many a king has gone
And many a king's daughter,
And alight at the comely trees and the lawn,
The playing upon pipes and the dancing,
And learn that the best thing is
To change my loves while dancing
And pay but a kiss for a kiss.

I would find by the edge of that water
The collar-bone of a hare
Worn thin by the lapping of water,
And pierce it through with a gimlet, and stare
At the old bitter world where they marry in churches,
And laugh over the untroubled water
At all who marry in churches,
Through the white, thin bone of a hare.

By the romance of the beginning we are drawn into one sort of world, a belief in one sort of world; of which the decisive emblem at the end offers a sudden and absolute vision. The change could not be more abrupt, but neither could the harmony be more convincing, and one is a function of the other, and both are mysterious. As though to say once more, "It shall be called Bottom's Dream, because it hath no bottom." But now the leaves begin to fall.

On Metaphor

While I am thinking about metaphor, a flock of purple finches arrives on the lawn. Since I haven't seen these birds for some years, I am only fairly sure of their being in fact purple finches, so I get down Peterson's *Field Guide* and read his description: "Male: About size of House Sparrow, rosy-red, brightest on head and rump." That checks quite well, but his next remark—"a sparrow dipped in raspberry juice"—is decisive: it fits. I look out the window again, and now I *know* that I am seeing purple finches.

That's very simple. So simple, indeed, that I hesitate to look any further into the matter, for as soon as I do I shall see that its simplicity is not altogether canny. Why should I be made certain of what a purple finch is by being led to contemplate a sparrow dipped in raspberry juice? Have I ever dipped a sparrow in raspberry juice? Has anyone? And yet there it is, quite certain and quite right. Peterson and I and the finches are in agreement.

It is like being told: If you really want to see something, look at something else. If you want to say what something is, inspect something that it isn't. It might go further, and worse, than that: if you want to see the invisible world, look at the visible one. If you want to know what East really is, look North. If you have a question concerning the sea, look at the mountains. And so on.

I say that is a simple example in part because the finches were visibly there. Even so, the matter is complicated by the presence of language. It is not alone a matter of seeing, but of saying as well, of the power of the word whether in Scripture or Dictionary. I might paraphrase Hamlet's observation: "Nothing is but saying makes it so." Seeing and saying, the dictionary tells me, were perhaps originally related; and "a saw" is still "a saying." As to this power of the word, whose limits are unknown, Erich Heller gives this wise instruction as from teacher to students: "Be careful how you interpret the world, it *is* like that."

In speaking of metaphor, I wish to be free to develop the term as

223

far as I am able, as well as to place it with reference to other words in the series of which it is a part, of which it is perhaps the middle term, standing between the utmost expansion and the utmost compression, between the story or fable at the expanded and the symbol or name at the compressed end.

For this very reason of a proposed freedom, however, it will be well if I apply now to the dictionary to ask about the strict construction of the term metaphor: in Rhetoric, metaphor is one of the four tropes, the others being synecdoche, metonymy, and irony, and is described as "Use of a word or phrase literally denoting one kind of object or idea in place of another by way of suggesting a likeness or analogy between them." Examples: "the ship *plows* the sea; a *volley* of oaths." The examples are suspiciously like those that Pope, in "Peri Bathous," collects under the head of catachresis, or "The Variegating, Confounding, or Reversing Tropes and Figures": Mow the Beard, Shave the Grass, Pin the Plank, Nail my Sleeve. Which is worth remarking only for this reason, that as metaphor depends upon a compound of likeness and difference not always stable in the fashions of thought one man's metaphor may be another man's foolishness. The dictionary, for instance, illustrates catachresis with a rather famous example: "To take arms against a sea of troubles," which some have tried to justify by the example of Cuchullain among many other heroes of fable who tried to fight the sea; if that is fair pleading one may see by it how the metaphor is a highly compressed and allusive rendering of a dramatic episode.

The dictionary goes on about metaphor with a useful distinction: "A metaphor may be regarded as a compressed simile, the comparison implied in the former (a marble brow) being explicit in the latter (a brow white like marble)."

I found that most helpful, for somehow at school I had regularly been taught that the difference between the two terms was that simile used "like" or "as" and metaphor did not, but seemed rather to assert something like identity. I had never been able to understand that distinction very well; to say, as some do, that "he is a lion" is more ferocious or leonine than "he is like a lion" did not impress itself upon my mind as making a real difference. But the dictionary distinction is useful as leading to a further thought: the simile isolates for you the likeness in virtue of which the comparison is made; the metaphor leaves it up to you to isolate the likeness or for that matter not to isolate it. In the given example, I didn't think of "white like marble" at all; the expression "a marble brow" brought into my mind fleeting thoughts of heaviness, coldness, hardness, pallor, a monumental quality associated with the tomb.

Even under the strict construction of a dictionary definition, therefore, the metaphor reveals rather mysterious properties. As though—and these are metaphors—it were a nucleus that held to itself an indeterminate number of particles, a tone to which a not quite random series of overtones responded, a sound that echoed from some surfaces but not from others. Compared with the simile, the metaphor is both more implicit and less selective, less abstract, and more multivalent. It doesn't give itself away, but awaits, if it doesn't indeed demand, the reader's participation for its fulfillment. In this sense, it belongs to leisure, philosophy, and contemplation, rather than action.

Here is an instance, possibly a foolish, and certainly a trivial, instance. If we are at dinner and I say "Please pass the salt," the entire sense of the communication is absorbed at once; you pass the salt, and that finishes our business together. But if we are not at dinner, and neither table nor salt is available, you will think me extremely silly for saying "Please pass the salt." Let us suppose, though, that for some reason you value my good opinion, and that I insist on repeating my silly request. What happens? I think what happens is that your mind begins to play with such symbolic or metaphorical possibilities as learning has acquainted it with on the subject of salt—such things as being the salt of the earth, taking things with a grain of salt, sitting below or above the salt—and that these resonances will come to seem to you expressive of something not necessarily simple about the relations between us: I may be acknowledging our equality, doubting or pretending to doubt something you have just said, or accepting you into my tribe.

But here is, I hope, a better example. At the entrance to the Zoo in Washington, D.C., I read the following notice:

> All persons are forbidden to cut, break, injure, remove, or pluck branches, flowers, or plants of any kind, or to have in their possession while in the park any tree, shrub, plant, or any part thereof.

I suppose this message must have a practical use, or it wouldn't be there. All the same, without the message the thought of doing any or all those things would probably not have crossed my mind at all, and I stood there a little amazed, first at the somewhat pedantic detail of the commandment (imagine the dialogue: "I didn't cut it." "Well, you broke it." "No, I did not break it." "Anyhow, you injured it"), but beyond that at the poetical depths and ranges to which the sign invited, or even compelled, anyone who stopped to consider it. The Garden of Eden and man's first disobedience. The wood at Nemi where the challenger plucked the golden bough. Aeneas finding his way to the underworld. Dante in the Wood of the Suicides, where the torn branches screeched at him, "Perchè mi schianti, perchè mi sterpi?" What would happen if one had the temerity to cut, break, injure, remove, or pluck . . . ?

So far the relation is not quite metaphorical, merely a parade of harmless educated commonplaces. But that the sign should be at the entrance to a Zoo seemed to add the necessary deepening to the complex of resemblance. For surely the Zoo, or Zoological Garden, expresses in imagery something of our feeling for the Earthly Paradise, where Adam gave the beasts their names, where we had nothing to fear from the gorgeous or powerful or merely odd emanations of our as yet undivided nature; even while by its bars and cages and other enclosures it expresses that this feeling is conditioned by the Fall, and that the animal kingdom with its gruntings and brayings and howlings and hissings is a presentation to us of the divisions of our nature, a kind of natural hell externalized.

That leads to something else I want to suggest about metaphor, though quite uncertain of being able to demonstrate it as a law: that one resemblance, insufficient in itself, reveals another. Not that the second is *deeper*, as they say, for one human thought is perhaps no deeper than another; but that there is a gradient between them, shallow or steep, and the revelation of its existence is surprising but somehow just. Another silly example: the words "prenatal" and "parental" are anagrammatic arrangements of one another. That isn't much by itself, but it expresses something of the operation of metaphor to see the mechanical resemblance as it were warranted by another, that the two words belong to the same cluster and have to do with a single subject matter.

One more example here may help. In E. O. James's book *Pre-historic Religion,* I read that with certain exceptions the people of Ancient Mexico "were destined to pass at death to the dreary subterranean region, Mictlan, 'a most obscure land where light cometh not and whence none can ever return.' There they were sunk in deep sleep, but class distinctions were maintained, the lords and nobles being separated from the commoners in the nine divisions into which it was divided. At the end of the fourth year of residence in this cheerless abode the ninth division was reached, and in this its denizens were annihilated."

If I am reading this for information only, to pass a test, say, in a course on the subject of Primitive Religion, I shall probably absorb the "facts" and read on. But if I stop for only a moment, certain mechanical resemblances will very likely make me think of a college or university, and I may try rereading the passage to see how it works when that way regarded. The major mechanical resemblances are, of course, the four years and the class distinctions; the latter might have to do with fraternities, athletic achievement, popularity, or any other way of becoming a lord instead of remaining a commoner.

But there it will stop, *unless* I happen to be in a mood either viciously critical or sadly despairing of what goes on in universities and colleges. If I am in either condition, I shall go on to develop the allegory suggested by the obvious and mechanical resemblances, and read the passage with the other reference as far as I am able to: "Yes, it's true, there is no light here and once the students arrive they can never go back. They are indeed sunk in deep sleep with reference to the intellect, and aroused only by a perpetual snobbery or squabble over 'class distinctions.' But no matter, when they pass through the eight divisions (corresponding to semesters in four years) they will all be annihilated, they will become alumni—which by a foolish etymology would be derived from a (privative) + lumen (light), out of the light."

And so the factual passage has become a metaphor, and far removed from the author's intentions. But for this to happen, I repeat, the factual, mechanical, numerical likenesses were not enough; they had to be reinforced by an attitude, which in this instance I brought to the material. In poetry, most likely, this attitude would in great part be supplied by the context, which would specify the field of application as well as something of the tone of voice.

Resuming what has been said so far about metaphor, I have ascribed to it the following characteristics. 1. The instance of the
purple finches suggested there was something uncanny about metaphor, a sleight-of-hand sort of thing wherein the word is quicker
than the eye. 2. A metaphor may be a compressed story— much as
a joke that appeals to a group of friends need not be told in full
whenever some application of it turns up in talk: the last line, or
even a single catch-word, will be plenty. 3. The metaphor leaves
implicit a complex of resemblances, where the simile will isolate
one and make it overt. 4. Metaphor works on a relation of resemblances; one resemblance draws another, or others, after it. 5. Exag-
gerating, one might say that any piece of language is capable of becoming metaphorical if regarded with other than a literal attention.

The last point most likely has to do also with the circumstance
that language is, or seems to be, as Owen Barfield says, nothing
but "an unconscionable tissue of dead, or petrified, metaphors."
That these metaphors may be not dead but only sleeping, or that
they may arise from the grave and walk in our sentences, is something that has troubled everyone who has ever tried to write plain
expository prose wherein purely mental relations have to be discussed as though they were physical ones. When I read long ago in
college, for example, that Descartes believed the pineal gland to be
"the seat of the soul," I heard nothing literal in "seat." Only years
later I found out that he supported the belief by identifying two
little dents in this gland as the marks of the soul's behind.

Student writing, not unexpectedly, is particularly productive of
examples, I suppose because the student is confronting for the first
time consciously the fact that mental relations may be quite complex, and because he is often not conscious of the dormant metaphorical life in words that look harmlessly abstract, or safely dead.
Thus, "Richard III is impervious to the pitfalls of disappointment
because he has no honor to prevent his stooping to find another
way out. His wits, sharpened to deadliness on his hump. . . ."
This was a hump, indeed, that another writer could not get him
over: His hump is an insurmountable burden. Once in a great
while, though, such things become great treasures, they confirm
Blake's idea that if a fool persists in his folly he becomes wise, and
the plain foolishness of the fact becomes the mysterious truth of
metaphor: "Man is descended from the man-eating ape."

It goes with this, and with the complexly associative nature of metaphor, that you cannot reason by means of metaphor or similitude for any length of time without running into trouble. A metaphor in a discourse ought to be like the sudden bursting of a flare, so that you see for an instant not only the road ahead but also its situation in the terrain around. Maybe that is why the best imagist poems are so very short; if the poet puts himself under the deliberate limitation of never specifying applications, never moralizing or drawing the general conclusion, but proceeds only by giving illustrations and leaving his auditors the option of saying, if they can, what the illustrations illustrate, he will do best to stop at that mysterious place where perception shows signs of turning into thought. Even in the more traditional discourse of poetry, where argument is not excluded, there is the danger that if you plant your metaphors too thick none of them will grow. Dante seems to have been aware of this, by his way of clearing a space to either side of his formal and extended figures. But once again the difficulty may be identified by anecdote; this one is said to have been Einstein's reply to a request for a simple explanation of relativity:

A blind man was walking with a friend on a hot day; the friend said, "O, for a nice drink of milk." "Drink I know," said the blind man, "but what is milk?" "A white liquid." "Liquid I know, but what is white?" "White is the color of a swan's feathers." "Feathers I know, but what is a swan?" "A bird with a crooked neck." "Neck I know, but what is crooked?" The friend took hold of the blind man's arm and stretched it out. "That is straight," he said, and then, bending the arm, "That is crooked." "Aha!" cried the blind man. "Now I understand what milk is!"

II

In what follows I should like to develop the idea of metaphor with a more particular reference to poetry, saying what I am able to of its uncanniness on the one hand, and of its relations with meaning on the other. If I find it next to impossible to talk about what metaphor is and does except in metaphors, I hope you will take that as a difficulty of the theme itself, and not as my mere wilfulness; the word itself, after all, is a metaphor, as you can see

from its odd but exact survival in our word "ferry." And when you
look into the derivation of Greek φέρειν and Latin *ferre* you find
them associated with our verb "bear," arousing the wildly metaphorical suspicion that what is hidden within the word is not only
the notion of "carrying across" or "transferring" something from
one place to another, but the idea of being born, of how thoughts,
like children, come out of the nowhere into the here: an ancient
and traditional idea concerning the production of thoughts, such
as may be seen from Socrates' considering the philosopher's business as that of the midwife, or from this Shakespeare's Richard II:

> My brain I'll prove the female to my soul;
> My soul the father: and these two beget
> A generation of still-breeding thoughts,
> And these same thoughts people this little world
> In humours like the people of this world. . . .

I suppose we shall never be able to distinguish absolutely and
with a hard edge the image from the metaphor, any more than
anyone has so distinguished prose from poetry or perception from
thought (these are instances, not necessarily parallels). We shall
very often be able to tell, just as we can very often tell the difference between snow and rain; but there are some weathers which
are either-neither, and so here there is an area where our differences will mingle. If the poet says, simply, "The red bird," we shall
probably take that as an image. But as soon as we read the rest of
the line—"The red bird flies across the golden floor"—there arise
obscure thoughts of relationships that lead in the direction of parable: the line alone is not, strictly, a metaphor, but its resonances
take it prospectively beyond a pure perception, if perception could
ever be quite that. Metaphor stands somewhat as a mediating term
squarely between a thing and a thought, which may be why it is so
likely to compose itself about a word of sense and a word of
thought, as in this example of a common Shakespearean formula:
"Even to the teeth and forehead of my fault."

So I assert that the procedures of metaphor resemble the procedures of magic. And if the physical sciences have a relation to
magic with respect to the material world, so that men can on their
account now do many things that before could only be thought, or
dreamed, so I should say that poetry has a relation to magic with

respect to the ideal world. Poetry has of course always been associated with magic, though latterly the idea appears as merely sentimental; as people do not "believe" in magic, it may be no more than an honorific way of saying that poetry no longer matters. Yet I wonder if there may not be a more specifiable sense to this metaphor about metaphor.

Speech and light have most commonly been the vehicles of magic art, and it is easy to see why: both share the capacity to act across distances and through an invisible medium. The idea of comparison is like that. And the rhythmical character of poetry, that cosmic and physiologic piety whereby things change while the form remains, is also characteristic of ritual incantations for magical purposes. But it is possible, I think, to go further than this.

In *The Golden Bough* Fraser tells us that magic is based on two principles: "first, that like produces like, or that an effect resembles its cause; and, second, that things which have once been in contact with each other continue to act on each other at a distance after the physical contact has been severed." The first sort he calls Homeopathic, or Imitative, Magic; the second, Contagious Magic. Here is a Malay example that combines both principles: "Take parings of nails, hair, eyebrows, spittle, and so forth of your intended victim, enough to represent every part of his person, and then make them up into his likeness with wax from a deserted bees' comb. Scorch the figure slowly by holding it over a lamp every night for seven nights. . . . After the seventh time burn the figure and the victim will die." The likeness of the victim draws upon the Homeopathic principle, the materials drawn from his body on the Contagious principle.

Transferred to poetry, I imagine that the first principle, of likeness, appears at first glance easy and probable, while the second appears neither easy nor probable. Yet let us try to follow the comparison for a little; if we do, I think we may see mysteries, not merely problems, emerge.

Here is a metaphor from *The Divine Comedy*:

> Noi siam vermi, nati a formar
> L'angelica farfalla.

> We are caterpillars, born to become
> The angelic butterfly.

Specified in its context, simple in its statement, this figure allows
of little if any doubt as to its meaning, though that it should have a
meaning doesn't in the least clear up its mysteriousness, which is
as much inherent in the metamorphosis of caterpillar into butterfly as it is in the parallel relation of body to soul, or of this life to
the next.

Here is a modern example, however, of the same relation: a
caterpillar looks at a butterfly and says, "Waal, you'll never catch
me in one of those durn things" (Marshall McLuhan, "Understanding Media"). Though the relation is constant, the applications may be several, though all of them on the lines of Ophelia's
"We know what we are, but not what we may become." The figure
parodies an old joke about flying machines, the caterpillar's locu-
tions make him out to be a country bumpkin, the story behind the
figure may be about growing up, about technological change, or
still about the relation of body and soul. In fact, in its context it is
used to illustrate "the principle that during the stages of their development all things appear under forms opposite to those that
they finally present."

Now both examples are metaphorical: the metamorphosis of an
insect illustrates a proposition about human beings. But equally in
both the metaphorical relation takes place between two symbols,
and at least in the example from Dante the relation is so ancient
and widespread in tradition that the symbol of the butterfly alone,
in an appropriate context, would carry the sense. So, once again, a
metaphor is a kind of condensed myth, and the symbol is its emblem, which conveys sufficient knowledge to those familiar with
the story behind it. In the same way, the early Athenians are said to
have worn as a badge or totem the golden image of a cicada in sign
of their having been autochthonous and self-begotten just as they
supposed the cicada to be. So there you have the contagious principle at work: the likeness between an Athenian and a cicada is not
self-evident, but requires the knowledge of a tradition behind it, a
tradition which must have said that the original Athenians *were*
cicadae before the symbol said that Athenians resembled cicadae
in virtue of a particular trait held in common.

A metaphor may show signs of being the compact, allusive form
of a story or fable; and the symbol, in turn, may be the even more
compact precipitate of a metaphor. We might extend these rela-

tions in either direction, though I suspect we should come round in a circle by doing so: from story, to metaphor, to symbol, to the name itself. This is not an historical account, for you have to have names for things before you can tell stories about them, and surely the process may work both ways; so that name, or image, might stand equally at either end of the series. The everyday working of such a process of expansion and reduction may be seen in the fact that we have for our convenience *names,* which stand for immensely complex sets of events: your name, my name, the names of Hamlet and Lear, such names as DNA, The Age of Reason, the universe. So do great trees grow from little seeds with the apparent purpose of producing little seeds, and it may be, as I think Samuel Butler was the first to say, that a chicken is but an egg's way of producing another egg.

Something of this may be seen by contemplating for a few moments the mystery of names and naming.

What sort of word is a name? I remember being told in school that a name was a proper noun; an answer chiefly valuable for discouraging a further question. But in later years that word "proper" became a little less empty, and I was able to see that in its curious equivocations lies the traditional answer to my question. A name is a *proper* or correct noun because it belongs to, or is the property of, what it names. The two senses attest to a capitalistically profound respect for possessions (and for being possessed, too, perhaps), and run almost indistinguishably close together: as in the Latin *proprie,* which means both "each for himself, singly," and "correctly, or strictly speaking"; the difference being perhaps no more and no less than that between our verb "appropriate" and our adjective "appropriate."

A name, then, is supposed to be *peculiar* to the thing named (peculiar being also a word of property, *pecunia,* referring to the calculation of wealth in cattle); it is no mere arbitrary label but is felt to bear within itself some real distinguishing essence. If that is so, then naming things will have been the privilege of a very great, even magical, insight or power, such as seems to be ascribed to Adam at the creation: "And out of the ground the Lord God formed every beast of the field, and every fowl of the air; and brought them to Adam to see what he would call them; and whatsoever Adam called every living creature that was the name there of" (Genesis, 2:19). Nor were these names given by Adam merely arbitrary; on the contrary, it was believed at least as late as the eighteenth century that Adam "came into the world a philosopher, which sufficiently appeared by his writing the nature of things upon their names; he could view essences in themselves, and read forms without the comment of their respective properties" (Robert South, *Sermons Preached Upon Several Occasions*).

So it seems to have been thought that names were essences, that things would reveal their names, which is to say, metaphors about their natures, to the discriminating eye, thereby revealing also, according to the Doctrine of Signatures, their usefulness or menace to man; as the heart-shaped leaves of the fox-glove make apparent that the extract of this plant will be the specific for angina pectoris; concerning which Scott Buchanan observes: "This is a classic illustration and it is usually cited to show the primitive imagination correlating shapes of organs and shapes of herbs by magical impulse. Actually it is the mnemonic distillate of what must have been considerable experience. . . . Two things should be noted about it: its truth value is not zero: its truth value can be increased by more knowledge" (*Doctrine of Signatures*).

One further consideration will lead us back to metaphor, magic, and our Homeopathic and Contagious principles.

Rabelais tells us, in a passage of most learned fooling with derivations (*Le Tiers Livre*, Chapitre L), that plants get their names in one or another of eight ways:

1. from their first finder, or cultivator, as "panacea, de Panace, fille d'Aesculapius."
2. from their country of origin.
3. by ironic antithesis ("antiphrase et contrariété"), "comme absynthe, au contraire de pynthe, car il est fascheux à boire."
4. from their powers or functions, "comme aristolochia, qui ayde les femmes en mal d'enfant."
5. by their distinctive qualities, like heliotrope.
6. after people metamorphosed into them, "comme daphné, c'est laurier, de Daphné."
7. metaphorically, "par similitude," as "iris, à l'arc en ciel, en ses fleurs" (and men reciprocally take their names from plants, as Cicero from "des poys chices," or chick-peas).
8. morphologically, "de leurs formes," "comme trefeuil, qui ha trois feuilles."

From that chapter, which is one of the lessons in the great un-compiled handbook of the poetic art, we may learn something of the primacy of the contagious principle of metaphor over the homeopathic principle which at first seemed so much more obvious. In only a very small number of Rabelais' categories do names "make sense," without further knowledge, to present observation and rational reflexion. We can see why a plant with three leaves might be called a trefoil, but no amount of unaided thought will tell us why a plant is called artemisia. In most of the categories, even those based, like antithesis and contrariety, upon formal relations, we cannot understand a name until we understand something else; and that something else is most often a unique and particular something else, something that happened, or is said to have happened, only once, and which therefore does not enter language as a generality; it has to be remembered to be understood, and if it is not remembered it cannot be derived by reason and cannot be known; it is a part of history, or tradition.

Hence, whether names are or are not in the first instance arbitrary, they bring something arbitrary into discourse, something obstinately unyielding: bringing in the individual, they bring in history, or tradition, and the stern idea of a world in which things happen once and for all.

So names are compressed fables, or histories.

And the evocative power of names, whether or not they are recognizable as distorted, combined, or corrupted words, depends upon the strange relation they make between the real world of happening and the ideal world of reason. Names relate to language as human beings relate to possibility, or as, for Dante, Beatrice related to Virgil, and the realm in which Beatrice was the guide related to the realm in which Virgil was the guide.

In general, and without even touching upon, much less trying to solve, the mystery of which came first, we may divide the matter this way, that the Homeopathic principle reflects nature, while the Contagious principle reflects history. And as to what in all this matter of the metaphorical expansion of names or condensation of fables is magical, only this, that although many metaphors propose a relation verifiable to the reader, a relation between objects whose natures are known (the legs of a table, the shoulder of a mountain) another sort of metaphor proposes a relation not verifiable by any living person, between two objects only one of which is known, as for example in "Care-charmer sleep, son of the sable night, Brother to death," and so on, or in the verse of Dante quoted before. There what is known is proposed as a presumptive demonstration of what is not known, what can be seen as a reflexion of what cannot be seen.

Poetry in the hands of the great masters constantly tends to a preoccupation with the second sort of figure, making statements about invisible mysteries by means of things visible; and poems, far from resting in nature as their end, use nature as a point from which they extrapolate darkly the nature of all things not visible or mediately knowable by the reason—the soul, society, the gods or god, the mind—to which visible nature is equivocally the reflexion and the mask. Such poetry is magical, then, because it treats the world as a signature, in which all things intimate to us by their sensible properties what and in what way we are. Poetry is an art of naming, and this naming is done by story-telling and by metaphorical approximations and refinements, according to the two principles of magic I have described.

James Dickey

James Dickey, *Drowning with Others*.

Coming to know an unfamiliar poetry is an odd and not so simple experience. Reviewing it—conducting one's education in public, as usual—helps, by concentrating the attention; perhaps, though it is a gloomy thought, we understand nothing, respond to nothing, until we are forced to return it actively in teaching or writing. It is so fatally easy to have opinions, and if we stop there we never reach the more problematic, hence more interesting, point of examining our sensations in the presence of the new object.

The following notes have to do with coming to know, with the parallel development of sympathy and knowledge. Undoubtedly they raise more questions than they can answer; and they may strike the reader not only as tentative but as fumbling and disorganized also, for the intention is to record not only what happened but something as well of how such things happen.

The situation of reviewing is a special case, narrower than merely reading, and nastier, certainly at first, where one's response is automatically that of a jealous cruelty. Hmm, one says, and again, Hmm. The meaning of that is: How dare anyone else have a vision! One picks out odds and ends, with the object of making remarks that will guarantee one is A Critic. Little hairs rise on the back of the neck. One is nothing if not critical. For instance:

> I spooned out light
> Upon a candle thread . . .

Triumphant sneer. Surely this it too ingenious by far? Has he no self-control?

But already I have suspicions of my behavior. I am afraid that a great deal of literary criticism amounts to saying that mobled queen is good, or bad.

Despite myself, I observe that I quite like Mr. Dickey's characteristic way of going: a line usually of three beats, the unaccented
syllables not reckoned, or not very closely reckoned; it offers an
order definite but not rigidly coercive, allowing an easy flexibility
and variation. Although the line so measured will tend to the ana-
pest often, it doesn't lollop along as that measure usually does,
maybe because the poet is shrewd enough not to insist on it by
riming:

> The beast in the water, in love
> With the palest and gentlest of children,
> Whom the years have turned deadly with knowledge . . .

All the same—give a little, take a little—an indulgence in riming
makes hash of this procedure. Mr. Dickey once indulges, in (mostly) couplets:

> With the sun on their faces through sand
> And the polyps a-building the land . . .

And so on. Awful. Enough about that.

II

At a second stage, perhaps a trifle less superficial, I find myself
thinking how very strange is the poetry of meditation musing on
inwardness, where the images of the world are spells whose repetition designs to invoke—sometimes, alas, only in the poet—a state
of extraordinary perceptions, of dreaming lucidities sometimes
too relaxed. This poetry has not much to do with the clean-cut,
muscular, metaphysical way of coming to conclusions; probably
in English Wordsworth is the inventor of those landscapes most
closely corresponding to certain withdrawn states of the mind,
reveries, day-dreams—the style that Keats, with sarcasm in which
there seems all the same a proper respect, calls the Wordsworthian, or Egotistical Sublime.

One of the qualities of such a poetry—or of Mr. Dickey's poetry, to come off the high horse—is a slight over-insistence on the
mysteriousness of everything, especially itself:

> A *perfect, irrelevant* music
> In which we *profoundly* moved,
> I in the *innermost* shining
> Of my blazing, *invented* eyes,
> And he in the *total* of dark . . . .

This is the language of a willed mysticism, and it is hard to see any of the words I have italicized as performing a more than atmospheric function—the poet wants the experience to be like profound, perfect, innermost, &c., and incants accordingly.

Another quality, which I take to be related also to the tonal intention of a grave continuousness, is the often proceeding by participles, as though nothing in the world of the poem ever quite happened but just went on happening, e.g. (from the same poem):

> With my claws growing deep into wood
> And my sight going slowly out
> Inch by inch, as into a stone,
> Disclosing the rabbits running
> Beneath my bent, growing throne,
> And the foxes lighting their hair,
> And the serpent taking the shape
> Of the stream of life as it slept.

The objections of this stage have a perfectly reasonable air of being right: you describe a characteristic, and present evidence to show that this characteristic *is* in the poetry. Surely this is How To Do Literary Criticism? All the same, I am still suspicious, and even beginning to get annoyed, because by this time, in order to say what I have said, I have had to read many of the poems a number of times, and have realized that I care for some of them a good deal. In particular, "The Owl King," from which I have quoted the two passages, looks to me like a moving and thoroughly accomplished performance. Even more in particular, the two passages themselves, when read in their places, look appropriate to what is going forward. I have a residual feeling of being cantankerously right in my objection to the first passage quoted, but would incline to say now that the passage is a weak place in the poet's process, but not destructive of the poem.

III

There does come a further stage, where one begins to understand something of the poet's individuality and what it decrees for him in the way of necessities, his own way of putting together the bones and oceans of this world.

Mr. Dickey's materials have a noble simplicity, a constancy extending through many poems. Merely to catalogue them is no use; to project in a single relation their somewhat delicate developments is perhaps impossible, but I shall have to make some more or less compromised try at it.

My impression of the process of his poetry is that it runs something like this: water—stone—the life of animals—of children—of the hunter, who is also the poet. It is rarely or never so simple as this, yet the intention seems often enough this, a feeling one's way down the chain of being, a becoming the voice which shall make dumb things respond, sometimes to their hurt or death, a sensing of alien modes of experience, mostly in darkness or in an unfamiliar light; reason accepting its animality; a poetry whose transcendences come of its reconciliations. Salvation is this: apprehending the continuousness of forms, the flowing of one energy through everything. There is one other persistently dramatized relation, that of the child to his father; and one that is more autobiographical, that of the poet to a brother who died before he was born. And now to particularize this matter.

These are poems of darkness, darkness and a specialized light. Practically everything in them happens at night, by moonlight, starlight, firelight; or else in other conditions that will make ordinary daytime perception impossible: underwater, in thick fog, in a dream—I note especially a dream of being in a suit of armor—inside a tent, in a salt marsh where because of the height of the grass you "no longer know where you are."

Another term for this situation is blindness: the blind child whose totem, or other, is the owl king who cannot see by day but for whom, at night, "the still wood glowed like a brain." In another poem the owl's gaze "most slowly begins to create / Its sight from the death of the sun." For this power of creation from within, and for being a hunter, the owl is the magician-poet of an intellectual and "holy" song; in "The Owl King" it is he who for the lost,

blind child incarnates the mighty powers of sight, growth, belief,
resulting in reconciliation and understanding:

> Far off, the owl king
> Sings like my father, growing
> In power. Father, I touch
> Your face. I have not seen
> My own, but it is yours.
> I come, I advance,
> I believe everything, I am here.

The power of poetry, which is to perceive all the facts of the
world as relation, belongs in these poems equally to both parties:
to the hunter and his victim; to the child and the father he is trying
to become; to the father and the child he was, whom he has lost
and is trying to find again. The paradoxical continuousness of all
disparate forms one with another, in this generated world, is what
Mr. Dickey's poems concentrate on representing, often by the traditional lore of the four elements, as in "Facing Africa," where the
speaker and his son look out over the ocean from stone jetties
(hence "the buttressed water"), where

> The harbor mouth opens
> Much as you might believe
> A human mouth would open
> To say that all things are a darkness.

Thence they look toward an Africa imagined to "bloom," to be
"like a lamp" glowing with flashes "like glimpses of lightning,"
giving off through the darkness "a green and glowing light." In the
crisis of the poem this serial relation of the elements is fused in the
imagined perception of the other continent, the alien life:

> What life have we entered by this?
> Here, where our bodies are,
> With a green and gold light on his face,
> My staring child's hand is in mine,
> And in the stone
> Fear like a dancing of peoples.

Perhaps it is central to Mr. Dickey's vision that stone and water are one, the reflected form of one another.

Possible to continue for a long time describing these complex articulations of simple things. Very little use, though, to a reader who has not the poems to hand. Besides, it must be about time for someone to ask, "Well, is it great poetry or isn't it?" and someone else to ask, "What about objective, universal standards for judging poetry?"

About all that I shall say to the reader: If you believe you care for poetry you should read these poems with a deep attention. They may not work for you, probably they cannot work for you in just the way that they do for me, but I quite fail to see how you are going to find out by listening to me.

Probably the reviewer's job goes no further than that. Not to be thought of as malingering, though, I shall make a couple of other remarks.

I have attended to Mr. Dickey's poems, and they have brought me round from the normal resentment of any new experience, through a stage of high-literary snippishness with all its fiddle about "technique," to a condition of sympathetic interest and, largely, assent. There are some brilliant accomplishments here: among them, apart from the ones I have partly described, "Armor," "The Lifeguard," "The Summons." There are also some that sound dead, or (what is effectively the same thing) that I do not much respond to, including some that I don't understand. Where his poems fail for me, it is most often because he rises, reconciles, transcends, a touch too easily, so that his conclusions fail of being altogether decisive; that near irresistibly beautiful gesture, "I believe everything, I am here," may represent a species of resolution that comes to his aid more often than it should. Perhaps he is so much at home among the figures I sort out with such difficulty that he now and then assumes the effect is made when it isn't, quite.

There is this major virtue in Mr. Dickey's poetry, that it responds to attention; the trying to understand does actually produce harmonious resonances from the poems; it seems as though his voyage of exploration is actually going somewhere not yet filled with tourists: may he prosper on the way.

Everything, Preferably All at Once: Coming to Terms with Kenneth Burke

In one perhaps accidental symbolic act, Burke expressed his essence: he had some of his early books reissued by *Hermes* Publications. Hermes, originally a boundary stone, presently grew a face and a beard and went on to become the Roman god of boundaries, Terminus. Rising still further, he became Hermes Trismegistus, "the fabled author of a large number of works (called Hermetic books) most of which embody Neo-Platonic, Judaic, and Cabalistic ideas, as well as magical, astrological, and alchemical doctrines." In other words, everything, and preferably all at once.

The dictionary from which I drew this description of Burke in his aspect as Hermes identifies him with the Egyptian scribe Thoth, who above all "created by means of words," and "appears sometimes . . . as exercising this function on his own initiative, at other times as acting as the instrument of his creator." That is a doubt one may properly have about any scribe whose *oeuvre* is imposing enough to make one wonder whether he is representing the world or proposing to replace it; Milton, for instance, invoking his heavenly muse, claims to merit the instruction by reason of his "upright heart and pure"; and yet through the intended humility I have always heard a certain obstinacy in "upright," and thought of it as comparable with another Miltonic epithet, "erected." But the doubt may be peculiarly appropriate to Burke, who "above all creates by means of words" in the special sense that he creates words, terms, terminologies—the business of Hermes. And when you ask whether he does this on his own initiative or as the instrument of his creator, you get the somewhat cryptic though certainly comprehensive reply from his address to the Logos:

> For us
> Thy name a Great Synecdoche,
> Thy works a Grand Tautology.

243

Schopenhauer once called the world a vast dream dreamed by a simple being, but in such a way that all the people in the dream are dreaming too. A lovely figure, and in its logological translation it might do for Burke's world as well: a vast dream dreamed by a single Word, but in such a way that all the words in the dream are dreaming too.

But I have just remembered that part of my title, "preferably all at once," is about Burke intensively: it comes from him. (Somewhat as when you make what seems a good pun you can never be certain it isn't waiting for you in *Finnegans Wake*.) There is a passage late in *A Rhetoric of Motives* that I had been meaning to cite somehow, as an instance of Burke's excessiveness about terms and of one's appreciation of his rightness if one would only think about it (as I. A. Richards said, a book is a machine for thinking with).

The passage is called "Rhetorical Names for God," and after some introductory talk a page-and-a-bit goes to a listing of terms you might use when appealing to the Deity. The range is indeed extensive, as is proper to the All in All, going from "ground of all possibility" around to "nothing" and taking in *en route* such things as real estate, money, sleep, excrement, and death. But now I especially note: "Center, circumference, apex, base (preferably all at once)."

By this example I mean only that when you speak of the writers you care most for, you not only speak about them—you also speak them.

Here is a sort of monkish metaphor for what Burke does: he illuminates texts. In its application to criticism the figure tells us one of the things we most expect from critics, that they should offer us particular enlightenment about particular works, showing us things we had not seen and that, once seen, compel us to acknowledge their truth and significance. In its more medieval aspect the figure suggests an independent activity integral to the other and, in Burke's criticism, identical with it: as in the illuminations of the *Book of Kells*, Burke is using the text while weaving up his own designs.

Most simply put, he can get more thoughts out of a book than anyone else can, evoking in his reader time after time a mixed attitude of surprise, gratitude, and chagrin—"yes, of course, why couldn't I have seen it for myself?"—while at the same time, in the same gestures, often in the very same sentences, he is developing a method and a terminology which the reader, if he will, can master for application elsewhere.

For this reason, there is very little in Burke's writing of what Whitehead stigmatized as "inert knowledge." Everything is in movement, in development; everything is always being used for all it's worth, and sometimes maybe more.

There is an enthusiasm in all this that sometimes comes near enough to madness: criticism as rhapsody, or *furor poeticus*. Nor do I mean that in disparagement, though aware that some writers would; for among the most appealing things about Burke, to my mind, is the sense he has, the sense I get from reading him, that thought, if it is to matter at all, must be both obsessive and obsessively thorough, that thinking, if it is to salvage anything worth having from chaos, must adventure into the midst of madness and build its city there. Also that this action never really ends until the thinker does; everything is always to be done again. Also this: that system begins in inspiration, order in improvisation, method in heuristic. Here is one of Burke's own and somewhat breathless descriptions:

> So we must keep trying anything and everything, improvising, borrowing from others, developing from others, dialectically using one text to comment upon another, schematizing; using the incentive to new wanderings, returning from these excursions to schematize again, being oversubtle where the straining seems to promise some further glimpse, and making amends by reduction to very simple anecdotes.

That seems characteristic, even to "we must"—for Burke makes many and difficult demands upon his readers—and even to "make amends"—for he is as magnanimous as he is demanding.

Back in the days when such things mattered more to the literary community at large than perhaps they do just now, there was much debate upon a question, raised I believe by T. S. Eliot, as to whether criticism could be, or should be, "autotelic." Much debate, but relatively little illumination, probably because that forbidding word "autotelic" implied the expected answer, that criticism had better humbly confine itself to the ancillary task of digging nuggets of wisdom, or pure form, or whatever, out of the superior materials provided by the poets and novelists, and not set up in business on its own. And indeed there was much local and practical justification for the expected answer, inasmuch as when criticism did its thing, usually under the formidable name of aesthetics, the results were often of a dullness far beyond the call of duty.

But all the same, the very fact that the question was raised indicated some anxiety about the expected answer; and the massive development of criticism as both an art and an industry around that time suggested the perhaps horrifying thought that if the critics went on as they were going there was some remote chance that some one among them might one day actually learn something about literature *in principle,* and not only about this work and that work in snips and snaps and *aperçus.*

Well, in Burke and some others (among whom I should name especially I. A. Richards and William Empson), I conceive that there began to appear ways in which criticism could be "autotelic" in such a style as not in the least to prevent its traditionally imputed function of praising and damning and qualifying the work of "creative" writers; and it appeared indeed that by its new independence criticism was able to perform its traditional function not merely better than before, producing "insights" at such a rate as for a few years almost made people believe in progress once again, but also at depths and over ranges not previously suspected to exist. Having begun with the usual critical attempt to winkle "meanings" out of literary works, Burke and others (and a good few more than I have mentioned) were led on into quite new questions—at least for the tradition of criticism in English, and in modern times—about meaning in general, what it is and how it arises and in what ways it relates to language. In fact, the same question that had been asked about criticism now appeared about language: was it ancillary to meaning, instrumental to thoughts that somehow had an independent existence? Or was it autotelic, and capable of generating worlds, or the world, primarily by reason of its own internal arrangements, as the language of mathematics, or, more darkly, of music, seemed to suggest?

Kenneth Burke's researches in this area seem to me venturesome, enchanting, and productive. And I have sometimes thought of them as contributing to the development of a new species of epic poetry, a poetry containing its own criticism much as a dream sometimes contains its own interpretation more or less explicitly; this poetry might be that intellectual comedy which Valéry, himself an anticipator of it, said he would value more highly than either the divine or the human. (The question whether such a poetry would have to come in verse seems entirely secondary; from the "creative" side one might cite *The Magic Mountain, Finnegans Wake,* and *Remembrance of Things Past* as works containing their own critique.) In what follows, rather than trying to describe Burke's "system" or "doctrine," which anyhow is always evolving out of and dissolving into method, I shall try a species of rhapsodic impressionism and imitation.

Putting first things first, in accordance with Burke's principle of "the temporizing of essence," the mind's first move upon the world is to assert something, to be active. The assertion will probably be suggested by the world, yet it will also have in it something both arbitrary and peremptory, and at least prospectively insane. This is what writers commonly call "having an idea," a phrase usually treated as ultimate and unquestionable, but which with Burke's help we may see a bit further into.

The essence of "having an idea" is "giving a name." Its effect is always to say to the phenomenon, "Be other than thou art." It is both prayerful and commanding, it both asks and asserts. It challenges, and upon the challenge it moves into a combat with "the world" which at its best it both wins and loses. Wins, in that a more or less large range of particular appearances is brought into patterned clarity, simultaneously articulated and integrated, by coming under the sway of the idea. Loses, in that the victory is only for a time, and more especially in that the idea of its own nature overextends itself and like a tragic hero perishes in its pride, in its triumph, in the *hubris* brought on by success. This happens from two considerations in particular: every One, in becoming many, attempts to become All and falls abroad into chaos, nothingness, the abyss. Or else: every idea, at the end of the line, loses all content and meaning other than itself; it reaches redundancy, tautology, pleonasm, and at last says, uninformatively enough: I am that I am. These two ways of losing may be regarded as the damned and redeemed forms of one single but unsayable thing.

These two ways, moreover, have to do with simple figurations that may stand for the base of all thought: the line and the circle. Nor is it accidental, I think, that line and circle, and the spiral compounded of their motion, make up our ways of thinking about time—bringing us again to the "temporizing of essence."

We do not ordinarily believe we make progress by going 'round in circles; and yet in a round world we may have no other course. Consider how it is precisely, though mysteriously, the circling of the heavens that creates time, whose even progress along a straight line is among the blandest of our metaphysical assumptions, though possibly surpassed in this respect by the one that claims we don't have metaphysics any more. Or a homelier example: almost any literary critic will affirm, if only as costing him nothing, the assertion that "Finally, what the poem means is what the poem says," a pure yet somehow heartening tautology in that he will as readily affirm from experience that our circular course from what the poem says at first to what it says at last, or as near last as we ever get, improves our knowledge in reckonable ways.

Perhaps both line and circle have damned and redeemed forms, or ways of being thought about. The circle, from antiquity a "perfect" and sacred figure, is complete, hence eternal, simple, and rounding upon itself: the mind of God, in a phrase I've heard attributed to half a dozen writers from Bonaventura to Pascal, is a circle whose center is everywhere and whose circumference is nowhere. Alternatively, the circle may stand for futility and unending repetition and the boredom of a bad eternity. In the same way, the line in its optimistic leaping forth suggests progress; but as the progress is from an unknown (or nonexistent) past to an unknown (or nonexistent or endless) future, it may likewise engender feelings of hopelessness.

Otherwise put: If a storyteller says to us, in effect, "This happened, and then that happened, and then something else happened . . ." we are bored; no matter how many things happen, we "keep waiting for something to happen." Whereas if a story were limited to the recital of its *idea,* there could be no story; for stories have to be one thing after another. So that a story *is* the compound of line and circle, as Burke indicates in a simple figure:

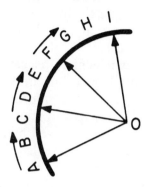

upon which he comments:

> Any narrative form . . . in its necessary progression from one episode to the next is like the stages from A to I along the arc. But as regards the principle of internal consistency, *any* point along the arc is as though generated from center O. And the various steps from A to I can be considered as *radiating* from generative principle O, regardless of their *particular* position along the arc of the narrative sequence.

What is said of stories holds also for philosophies, which arose out of stories and which retain, using terms for persons, the "dramatistic" cooperations and conflicts, mergers and divisions, of stories. It may hold true in a peculiarly poignant way of Burke's philosophy, a corpus of mythology relating how certain heroes or demigods, called by the family name of *terms,* incarnated themselves in the world of action where they overcame the old dragon of chaos, established order, gave laws, and so on, until at last defeated by the dragon's mother, once named by Burke as "material recalcitrance." But, happily, new generations of terms arose . . . and the story is always beginning just as it is always ending.

Burke's mind must be a fascinating but terrifying place to live in. So it would seem, anyhow, from the homeopathic experience of it in small doses that one gets from his books. Despite the order imposed by narrative, despite a grand friendliness of manner and a most beguiling disposition to admit mistakes, to begin again, to reveal not only the result of thought but much of its process as well, the chief thing I note about his mind is that it cannot stop exploding. In the early books the footnotes, like large dogs leashed to dwarfish masters, often marched along for pages under a few homeless-looking lines of text; in the later books this habit has been overcome by the expedient of relegating the footnotes into appendices (the dogs get bigger, but are kept in their own kennels); while after *A Grammar of Motives* and *A Rhetoric of Motives* (1945 and 1950 respectively) the completion of the proposed grand design has been deferred by a huge volume called *Language as Symbolic Action,* a smaller though still substantial one called *The Rhetoric of Religion,* and an unpublished though mimeographed *Poetics* of three hundred pages, not to mention numerous uncollected articles, unpublished notes, etc. (the dogs are beginning to wag their kennels?).

Once, when asked to make suggestions about a Burke essay in manuscript, I indicated a few places where it might be cut. Some weeks later a letter announced earnestly that after thoroughly considering my remarks he had rewritten the whole thing and cut it from sixty-five pages to seventy-six. And during the question period after a recent lecture in which he had been talking about the cycle of terms and the generative power of any dialectical term to spawn a terminology, I heard Burke tell the class: "Any term will lead you to the others. There's no place to start." Ah, I thought, that means there's no place to stop, either. And I wondered: which half of Burke's mind will win? The linear, progressive, orderly half that proposes to itself systematic philosophy and sequential argument from beginning to end? or the radical, explosive half, the lyric and rhapsodic philosopher whose entire effort is to make every poor part contain the glorious, impossible whole, as in the Ptolemaic cosmology the Primum Mobile goes racing 'round at enormous speeds only in order that every place may catch up with every place and be at rest in the peace of the Empyrean? For, certainly and a little remarkably, I still have scarcely any idea of what the proposed third canticle, *A Symbolic of Motives,* may contain, no matter what anticipations of it must inevitably have come up in the story so far. Surely a place where any writer might beseech

Apollo for both peaks of Parnassus, where either one had served before.

I mention this because it belongs to the figures of line and circle which I seem to have got stuck with, and because it is at the heart of that cooperative conflict between narrative and essence, image and concept, myth and philosophy, that Burke calls "the temporizing of essence."

Language, for Burke, not merely mirrors the world it seems to see, but also generates it. This is the sticking point at which over and over he divides from all philosophies proposing to base on scientific models; and not only divides from, but undercuts and gets beyond, seeing the human hope precisely in the rich polyvalence of terms, the Shakespearean equivocations, which those philosophies propose to exclude.

That language in any sense makes the world is a thought intolerable to those who view the world, implicitly or otherwise, as a solid existent (like Descartes's *res extensa*) which the mind passively records as a camera does in univocal concepts which it may then manipulate as a computer does.

For Burke, language is literally making, constitutive, or *poetic* of "reality." To the extent that its terms are not only positive ones, such as "house," but dialectic ones, such as "good" or "high" or "sinful," capable of division into and merger with other terms, it is language itself that makes the symbolic world. This is the distinctively human world in which we struggle along on the guidance of phantasy, the world of human action as over against the world of sheerly physical motion described by physics according to models that positivist philosophers constantly claim to emulate by various "reductionist" schemes according to which human motives are viewed as mechanisms, and according to which "God," "soul," and "spirit" are progressively read out of the act until at last, by a miracle comparable with the stomach's digesting itself and emitting a satisfied belch, "mind" too is read out of the act by the very mind that claims to be doing the reading.

Yet there is an important way in which Burke, while at odds with "scientistic" philosophers if not with science itself, is adventured on somewhat the same quest as that of physics: he would bring the world of human action, as it would the world of physical motion, under the dominion of few, simple, and elegant laws. It is

tempting to wonder what would happen if his discoveries in this
line educed the kind of cooperation among the learned that routinely goes on in physics; but they do not. And besides, this kind of
thought may be peculiarly related to its thinker; as I have heard it
observed of another original and self-made philosopher, Rudolf
Steiner, that he was everywhere and his disciples nowhere.

The sense in which the internal resources of language themselves generate views of the world formed the subject of *A Grammar of Motives*; whereas *A Rhetoric of Motives* studied the ways in
which these same resources might be wilfully manipulated for
conflicting purposes. Between the two there was already noticeable a considerable area of overlap, which will perhaps extend
also to *A Symbolic of Motives* in its presumable "transcendence"
of the area of competitive identifications—the marketplace, the
human barnyard, as Burke says—by considering the forms and
methods of literature as "timeless" patterns.

So we have a triad, and the progression through it, something
like Inferno-Purgatorio-Paradiso, and something like the equally
celebrated id-ego-superego. Something like, at least, in the important respect that the outer terms are represented as eternal fixities
while the middle one is the scene of conflict, development, and
playing-out in time and history of the patterns beneath and above.
As if, to adapt one of Burke's analogies, the grammar is a chord
which the rhetoric breaks into linear form as an arpeggio, while
the symbolic, the chord again and newly understood in relation to
its constituent notes, will be but a moment in time, the ear of corn
reaped in silence before the initiates at Eleusis, whose trials had
brought them to that wordless understanding upon which even
Plato and Aristotle agree.

That seems a good place to stop, a high note to sustain so that
we know this particular aria is over. Of the much more that might
be said, I will bring us down to the ground by only one further
reflection.

It was during the normal confusions of sophomore year that a
friend gave me a copy of *Attitudes toward History*—"two mouse-
gray volumes," he said, "containing all knowledge." And I could
see what he meant. The two things in especial that Burke said to a
young man of eighteen were "Everything is interesting" and "Everything is a language." The sense in which those two things are one

might well take thirty years or more to put together, but I'll try to put my results into a small anecdote and an emblem.

Most of one's education in those days was not only liberal education but self-education, and permissive extremely. The Great Books were the ones we thought our teachers had never read; at least, they were never mentioned in lectures. Still, I once confided in an admired professor that I'd been reading Kenneth Burke. "Ah," he said, and there came upon his face an expression of solemnity which ever since I've identified with Harvard Square—when you meet it elsewhere it's derivative—as he said: "Brilliant; brilliant, yes. But hardly solid."

I have sometimes unworthily thought—for that professor was admirable at teaching—that some people found solidity so universal a value they even wanted it between the ears. But thirty years later I found my emblem in an invention that was new when the world—the symbolic real one, of course—was new:

> Rounding upon itself, it became a perfect sphere when closed. It was made mostly of nothing, its critics pointed out that it was full of holes; besides, they said, it obviously leaks. Philosophers added that it was vain to suppose you could encompass the Void with bits of string, and as a final blow they said it was a tautology.

All the same, it caught fish.

Randall Jarrell (A Myth about Poetry)

Randall Jarrell, *The Complete Poems*.

Language is a great magic. The young poet turns it on and it begins to tell him wonderful things, so many wonderful things he can scarcely believe, at times, that this instrument that the mouth of man has been playing the tunes of for hundreds of years and for thousands of years should yet have reserved to himself so many fresh inventions, marvelous cadences, new sayings of oldest thoughts, and all done by sending out on the indefinitely accommodating carrier wave of the sentence the huge and fathomless words of power: night, cold, sky, life, love, water, bread, grief, fire, death. . . . It is the world over again, the world made new. His favorite poet has said it: "*Im dunkeln Dichter wiederholt sich still / ein jedes Ding: ein Stern, ein Haus, ein Wald.*"

A star, a house, a wood, that's how it goes, simple and miraculous. And to be a poet, a *dark* poet, in whom as in his favorite poet's favorite figure of pool or lake the world reflects itself again, how fine that is!

The poet works, of course he works; he scribbles and revises and thinks: There! that's a bit better. But it is not so much like work as it is like watching; he has to be there to watch—that is the condition of its doing itself under his hand, under his eye; but he has no doubt that it does itself. He is only the sorcerer's apprentice, who has turned on the broomstick; a fateful comparison, which we should prefer not to have made, did it not force itself upon us. For great magic is always dangerous to the magicker.

The language that tells the poet wonderful things is in this way an embarrassment and then a danger, that it won't stop telling him wonderful things. More than that, as the wonderful things accumulate they also tend to integrate and form coherencies willynilly; they bind up into a story that the poet is not only telling but also being told; they may even insist, finally, on telling him the

254

truth, which is no less true and no less perilous for being true not of some merely objective world but of that peculiar universal, the world with himself in it, or, as literary people like to say, *his* world.

That is something he need not consider at first, for at first what he hears is not *a* story, it is many stories, each one different from the others, and they well up in all their rich particularity and self-ness as from a source that ever supplies itself again. Only after many years, maybe, does the outline of the poet's own and unique story begin to emerge among the multitude of stories he has told; a very mysterious course of development in which his preoccupations, or even his obsessions, go out into the world and shape it slowly in their own image, until by an unreckonable reversal that world returns upon him to flood his consciousness with his own obsessions. It is perhaps this that makes poets, as they grow old, fall silent or else repeat themselves: having made their reality, they have to lie in it.

Something else happens, too. The world goes on, and the poet's life outside the poems goes on, in the inextricably double and mutually concealing motion of its history and his biography, so that change in the one and change in the other, recognition and reversal, increase of anguish in the world and increased consciousness of anguish in the self, can never be quite distinguished one from the other, much less kept separate. And the marvelous sayings that language has said? Language goes on saying them, with an undiminished energy in which there is something impersonal, overpowering, indifferent. Moreover, without the poet's being able to do anything to stop them, the sayings begin to appear as true in application to the world outside the poems that earlier had encompassed them and kept them in their fictive world, the only world in which such sayings may be safely said. The poet had always wanted to reach reality, hadn't he? His elders had always said reality was the object. And there he is at last. His story phases with the world and becomes the world; with its great power of patterning and formulating and recasting every material in its own image, it cannot do otherwise.

In some such ways do poets come into the desolation of reality, or wither into truth. There are many expressions for this condition; many modern artists rather rashly seek it out, optimistically calling it "the breakthrough." Fashionable people a few years ago called it "The Existential Level," unconsciously and not wrongly suggesting it was more like falling through than breaking through. Blake thought of it as dumb Despair always existing beneath "the rough basement" of language. A semanticist called it "the objective unspeakable level," and our poet, in that novel of his where the characters' clichés are wittier than most writers' epigrams, named it "definition by ostentation." How do you do it? "You simply point." And he seems to define it, a few lines later, as the condition in which one sees the world as "one of those stupid riddles whose only point is that they have no point."

That is one side of it, of which Wordsworth said: "We poets in our youth begin in gladness, / But thereof come in the end despondency and madness." And Eliot said:

That is the way things happen.
Everything is true in a different sense,
A sense that would have seemed meaningless before. . . .

And in the end
That is the completion which at the beginning
Would have seemed the ruin.

And the other side? The other side is, I think, more personally the poet's own, and to it belong the wit, the charm, the gaiety, the energy, and the courage that for many years and many poems sustain the life, sustain the work, above the gulf—demonic, divine, or void—where all things lose their names.

The foregoing is a myth about poets and poetry. I do not know whether it is true, or whether it is applicable. It came to mind from reading Randall Jarrell's *Complete Poems,* and from reading over also much else that he wrote, and from reading much that was written of him by friends, colleagues, acquaintances, and by his wife in the collection bearing his name edited by Robert Lowell, Peter Taylor, and Robert Penn Warren (1967).

A myth is not a review. Randall Jarrell and I reviewed one another amply during his life—perhaps as many as three times each; we said, both of us, some harsh things, some funny things, some kindly things, and altogether were nothing if not critical. I should feel sorry to write, from ignoble security, literary criticism that is unable to evoke, indeed provoke, his answering voice.

Attentiveness and Obedience

When I agreed to act as editor of a collection of essays by some American poets on their art, I proposed to the contributors several questions that seemed to me of some interest, with the idea that these might form a sort of thematic center for the book. But because a poet's view of his own work is necessarily personal, I left it to the contributors to decide whether they would be stimulated by the questions, provoked by the questions, or so unaffected by the questions as to pay them no mind. As might have been anticipated, some of the contributors responded to the questions and others did not.

At that time, I did not contemplate being a contributor myself; but now that I find I am one, it seems only just that I thrash around for a while in this labyrinth of my own devising and try to describe my work with reference to those questions I so glibly asked without a thought of ever having to answer up myself.

I

Do you see your work as having essentially changed in character or style since you began?

In style, I hope and in part believe it has, for I began and for a long time remained imitative, and poems in my first books, not to mention the undergraduate work that preceded publication, show more than traces of admired modern masters—Eliot, Auden, Stevens, Cummings, Yeats. I think these reminiscences largely dropped away in later work; though as a corollary to that it should be said that I never consciously sought for what people call "one's own voice," originality, a uniquely recognizable style; so far as anything like all that happened—I am uncertain how far that is—it happened more or less of itself, while I concentrated on writing this or that poem.

Stylistically, I began under the aegis of notions drawn, I suppose, chiefly from T. S. Eliot. Along with many other beginners, I learned to value irony, difficulty, erudition, and the Metaphysical style of composition after the example of John Donne. Again along with many others I learned from William Empson to value ambiguity; it was part of our purposeful labor, in those days, to fill our poems with somewhat studied puns which could be said to "work on several different levels," though often they did not work even on one. I think the direction of my development was away from all these things considered as technical devices; I now regard simplicity and the appearance of ease in the measure as primary values, and the detachment of a single thought from its ambiguous surroundings as a worthier object than the deliberate cultivation of ambiguity.

Yet more than a trick of the old rage remains; as, for example, coming across an abandoned railroad waiting room in which there was a clock with no hands, I came to see that clock somehow as the serpent himself, who initiated human time, and said of "the still mainspring, / Behind the even and the odd," that it "Hides in its coiled continuing / A venomous tense past tense." The difference in meaning, depending on whether you read the first "tense" as adjective or noun, seems to me to belong quite properly to the "tensions" developed by the poem as it reaches that conclusion.

So if character or attitude can be distinguished from style in a technical sense, there has perhaps been not so much change. Brought up to a poetry of irony, paradox, and wit as primary means of imagination, brought up to a view that did not always sharply divide the funny from the serious and even the sorrowful, I continue so, and have sometimes found it a strain to suffer critics gladly upon this issue in particular.

Given so much, however, of consistency in development, I think there have gradually appeared two marked changes in my poetry. The first has to do with the natural world, which I came to rather late, having been born and raised in the city. During the war and since, I have lived in the country, chiefly in Vermont, and while my relation to the landscape has been contemplative rather than practical, the landscape nevertheless has in large part taken over my poetry.

The second change is harder to speak of; it involves a growing consciousness of nature as responsive to language or, to put it the

other way, of imagination as the agent of reality. This is a magical
idea and not very much heard of these days even among poets—
practically never among critics—but I am stuck with it. Trying to
say this somewhat difficult idea, I come upon this: I do not now, if
I ever did, consent to the common modern view of language as a
system of conventional signs for the passive reception of experience, but tend ever more to see language as making an unknowa-
bly large part of a material world whose independent existence
might be likened to that of the human unconscious, a sleep of
causes, a chaos of the possible-impossible, responsive only to the
wakening touch of desire and fear—that is, to spirit; that is, to the
word.

To put this another way: having a dominantly aural imagination, I not so much look at nature as I listen to what it says. This is
a mystery, at least in the sense that I cannot explain it—why
should a phrase come to you out of the ground and seem to be
exactly right? But the mystery appears to me as a poet's proper
relation with things, a relation in which language, that accumulated wisdom and folly in which the living and the dead speak
simultaneously, is a full partner and not merely a stenographer.

I once tried to say something of this more or less directly in a
poem called "A Spell before Winter." It is about Vermont in late
fall, when the conventional glory of the leaves is over and the tourists have gone home, and the land not only reveals itself in its true
colors but also, in the figure of the poem, speaks:

A Spell before Winter

After the red leaf and the gold have gone,
Brought down by the wind, then by hammering rain
Bruised and discolored, when October's flame
Goes blue to guttering in the cusp, this land
Sinks deeper into silence, darker into shade.
There is a knowledge in the look of things,
The old hills hunch before the north wind blows.

Now I can see certain simplicities
In the darkening rust and tarnish of the time,
And say over the certain simplicities,
The running water and the standing stone,
The yellow haze of the willow and the black

Smoke of the elm, the silver, silent light
Where suddenly, readying toward nightfall,
The sumac's candelabrum darkly flames.
And I speak to you now with the land's voice,
It is the cold, wild land that says to you
A knowledge glimmers in the sleep of things:
The old hills hunch before the north wind blows.

To see certain simplicities and to say over the certain simplicities—they are in a sense the same thing; a philosopher of language tells us that see and say come from the same root, "for to 'say' is to make someone else 'see' vicariously that which you have 'seen.'"

II

Is there, has there been, was there ever, a "revolution" in poetry, or is all that a matter of a few sleazy technical tricks? What is the relation of your work to this question, if there is a relation? Otherwise put: do you respond to such notions as The New Poetry, An American Language Distinct from English, The Collapse of Prosody, No Thoughts but in Things, the Battle between Academics and—What?—Others (A Fair Field Full of Mostly Corpses)?

Because I was the one to phrase this question, a certain surly sarcasm in the asking probably betrays at least the tone of my response and the somewhat distant attitude I take toward the theater in which these war games go on in what looks like continuous performances. But I shall elaborate a little.

I think there was a revolution in poetry, associated chiefly with Eliot and Pound; but maybe it is of the nature of revolutions or of the nature of history that their innovations should later come to look trivial or undistinguishable from technical tricks. I remain grateful to Eliot and Pound and the others, for winning for poets the freedom to do anything that seems to them necessary. Nowadays, if you want to write in free verse, or "cadenced verse," or no particular verse at all, you can do it and no one will object so long as you don't write a manifesto proclaiming your courage and wits to (or against) the world. In fact it is also probable that no one will even notice what you are doing unless you write a manifesto, for if the "revolution" won freedom for poetry it also won for large parts of the world freedom from poetry. And why poets should still be found, fifty years later, fighting for that "freedom to experiment" as though they did not have it, is a mystery, but maybe one of the sillier mysteries.

It is also possible that the revolution produced, as revolutions will, some bad effects from which poetry can only with difficulty recover; introducing, among many other things, an extreme insistence on qualities rightly thought to be virtues in the then-obtaining situation—urbanity, consciousness, control, a certain dryness—its example may have cut poets off from great ranges of experience that begin and end in places deeper than consciousness can be happy in. So many people now concerned with the poetic art are obsessed with technique, even if the obsession is avowedly directed toward "liberation," that poetry sometimes appears as a technology, as though the "new idioms," announced with the regularity of new hair styles, were going to make obsolete everything that preceded them; which for a short, bad time they appear to do. One might put the point as a riddle: if poems are written by poets, idioms are written by guess who?

I tried to say something of this in a poem, "Lion & Honeycomb," whose title alludes to the riddle wherein Samson asked how from strength shall come forth sweetness. The speaker in this poem is a poet, discontented and somewhat angry with himself and with the other poets, too. It seems he has come to a place where he knows he has lost the way; all his art appears to him merely as skill, or technical virtuosity; he feels especially that he has lost the vital truth of poetry, the great wonder that first beckoned him into its enchanted realm. The process of the poem is the finding his way back to first things and if the poem succeeds, which isn't for me to say, the strength of his angry rejection at the beginning should resolve in the sweetness of the images he comes to at the end, the remembrance from childhood of two instances in particular, soap bubbles and skipping stones, where a certain gaiety, marvelousness, energy, maintained itself against gravity, even against possibility, in a hard world.

Lion & Honeycomb

He didn't want to do it with skill,
He'd had enough of skill. If he never saw

Another villanelle, it would be too soon;
And the same went for sonnets. If it had been
Hard work learning to rime, it would be much
Harder learning not to. The time came
He had to ask himself, what did he want?
What did he want when he began
That idiot fiddling with the sounds of things?

He asked himself, poor moron, because he had
Nobody else to ask. The others went right on
Talking about form, talking about myth
And the (so help us) need for a modern idiom;
The verseballs among them kept counting syllables.

So there he was, this forty-year-old teen-ager
Dreaming preposterous mergers and divisions
Of vowels like water, consonants like rock
(While everybody kept discussing values
And the need for values), for words that would
Enter the silence and be there as a light.
So much coffee and so many cigarettes
Gone down the drain, gone up in smoke,
Just for the sake of getting something right
Once in a while, something that could stand
On its own flat feet to keep out windy time
And the worm, something that might simply be,
Not as the monument in the smokey rain
Grimly endures, but that would be
Only a moment's inviolable presence,
The moment before disaster, before the storm,
In its peculiar silence, an integer
Fixed in the middle of the fall of things,
Perfected and casual as to a child's eye
Soap bubbles are, and skipping stones.

It goes with all this that I have not much sympathy for either side
of the perennial squabble about, most generally, form and content; as a great master said, when you look at a cow, do you see the
form or the content of the cow? No ideas but in things is a slogan
having considerable pathos, a brave challenge. But people who try
to follow it will find themselves either smuggling thoughts back in,
or writing Imagist poetry over again. As for An American Lan-

guage Distinct from English, if people want to write poems in that
language, fine. But if they want to argue with you about it and the
room hasn't got a door, you listen to what they have to say as
patiently as possible and then ask them to say it over in American.
Mostly these slogans amount to edicts decreeing that from now on
you should walk on one foot only; when you have got that much of
the message you needn't wait around to find out whether they
mean the right or the left. The same master I quoted from a moment ago also said, perhaps to artists,

> Great things are done when Men & Mountains meet;
> This is not done by Jostling in the Street.

III

*Does the question whether the world has changed during this
century preoccupy you in poetry? Does your work appear to you to
envision the appearance of a new human nature, for better or
worse, or does it view the many and obvious changes as essentially
technological?*

This is by all odds the hardest of the questions, for me. I am not
even certain now what I meant by it, and perhaps would not have
asked had I known a response would be demanded from myself.
Probably my secret thought was that the other poets, by their answers, would somewhat illuminate the depths of the question. But
I shall have a go.

It sometimes seems to me as though our relations with the Devil
have reached that place, so near the end, where paradox appears
immediately in all phenomena, so that, for example, the increase
of life is the fated increase of mortal suffering, the multiplication
of the means of communication is the multiplication of meaninglessness, and so on. At the obsequies for the late President of the
United States the "eternal flame" was extinguished by holy water in
the hands of children; in the material world that may have been an
unfortunate accident, but in the poetic world, where one is compelled to listen to symbolic things, it appears as possibly a final
warning, a witty and indeed diabolical underlining of the dire
assassination itself.

So if paradox and accenting the hidden side of the paradoxical has always played such a part in my poetry, perhaps the seriousness of that view of life, its necessity even, may now begin to appear. The charge typically raised against my work by literary critics has been that my poems are jokes, even bad jokes. I incline to agree, insisting however that they are bad jokes, and even terrible jokes, emerging from the nature of things as well as from my propensity for coming at things a touch subversively and from the blind side, or the dark side, the side everyone concerned with "values" would just as soon forget. And a commitment to paradox, I think, is liable to be as serious as a commitment to anything whatever else. I shall try to put this in a plain relation with my work in poetry.

In the first poem, "A Spell before Winter," I spoke of "the running water and the standing stone." This distinction of imagery goes far and deep in my poetry and has assumed, over the past seven years, the nature of an antithesis. Long before writing that poem, I had observed in my work a growing preoccupation with statues, with heroic monuments, as representing the rigid domination of the past over present and future; stillness, death, power, compacted into giant forms; the standing stone that looks over the landscape assumes early in history a human face, a frown, even a smile; becomes a god.

The thought of statues as representing a false, historical immortality seems clearly related to the scriptural prohibition against the making of graven images; and the category in which the statues finally come, which I generalized out as "effigies," may include also photographs, mythological figures such as Santa Claus, even mannequins in shop windows, or anything that tends to confirm the mind in a habitual way of regarding the world, which habitual way is, to be short with it, idolatry. There are many examples in my work, and I have chosen one which represents newspapers, by a slight extension of the thought, as a sort of verbal effigy, idolatrously confirming human beings day after day in the habit of a mean delusion and compelling them to regard this mean delusion as their sole reality. I say this halfway as a joke with the name of a newspaper, *The Daily Globe*.

> *The Daily Globe*
>
> Each day another installment of the old
> Romance of Order brings to the breakfast table

The paper flowers of catastrophe.
One has this recurrent dream about the world.

Headlines declare the ambiguous oracles,
The comfortable old prophets mutter doom.
Man's greatest intellectual pleasure is
To repeat himself, yet somehow the daily globe

Rolls on, while the characters in comic strips
Prolong their slow, interminable lives
Beyond the segregated photographs
Of the girls that marry and the men that die.

(I might mention for the benefit of foreign audiences that in American newspapers the pictures on the obituary pages are almost exclusively of men, those on the matrimonial pages exclusively of girls.)

It is the contention of my poetry very often that the world is increasingly, and with an increasing acceleration, dominated by habitual idolatry, by images for which my first representation was that of statues. The extension of the argument to television, for instance, is not difficult. So that, if my poetry does envision the appearance of a new human nature, it does so chiefly in sarcastic outrage, for that new human nature appears in the poetry merely as a totalitarian fixing of the old human nature, whose principal products have been anguish, war, and history.

As to the opposite attitude, and the image opposed. Well, if you do not take your notions of this world from newspapers you take your notions of this world from looking at this world and listening to what it seems to say. A great novelist, Thomas Mann, characterized the religious attitude as "attentiveness and obedience." His illustration of all that is not attentiveness and obedience is given in his story of Joseph, where he portrays the mean-spirited businessman Laban as having buried, according to ancient custom, his first born beneath the foundation of his house; unaware, so to speak, that the human spirit, with the divine spirit, had moved on from that old-fashioned idea of security. The image that has seemed to me most appropriate for this notion of "attentiveness and obedience" is the image—so dialectical, so subtle, so strange, and yet so evidently an emblem for human life and the life of the imagination—of a stream, a river, a waterfall, a fountain, or else of a still and deep reflecting pool. This image, of the form continuing in the changing material, belongs also to cloud and fire, and I once gave it a somewhat political shape in a despairing epigram: God loves (I said) the liberal thrice better than the conservative, for at the beginning he gave to the liberal the three realms of water, air, and fire, while to the conservative he gave only the earth.

Of the many appearances of this figure of water in my work, I have chosen one that seeks to set the nature of water in relation to human perception and human imagination.

Painting a Mountain Stream

Running and standing still at once
is the whole truth. Raveled or combed,
wrinkled or clear, it gets its force
from losing force. Going it stays.

Pulse beats, and planets echo this,
the running down, the standing still,
all thunder of the one thought.
The mind that thinks it is unfounded.

I speak of what is running down.
Of sun, of thunder bearing the rain
I do not speak, of the rising flame
or the slow towering of the elm.

A comb was found in a girl's grave
(ah heartsblood raveled like a rope).
The visible way is always down
but there is no floor to the world.

Study this rhythm, not this thing.
The brush's tip streams from the wrist
of a living man, a dying man.
The running water is the wrist.

In the confluence of the wrist
things and ideas ripple together,
as in the clear lake of the eye,
unfathomable, running remains.

The eye travels on running water,
out to the sky, if you let it go.

However often you call it back
it travels again, out to the sky.

The water that seemed to stand is gone.
The water that seemed to run is here.
Steady the wrist, steady the eye;
paint this rhythm, not this thing.

In this brief account I have stressed the liberal virtues and neglected the conservative ones, scorning the solids of this world to
praise its liquids. That is not the whole truth, for how could you
tell the stream but by its rocky bed, the rocks directing the water
how to flow, the water—much more slowly—shaping the rocks
according to its flow: But maybe I put the accent where I do
against this world which so consistently in politics, religion, even
in art, even in science, worships the rocky monument achieved and
scorns the spring, the rain cloud, and the spark fallen among the
leaves.

IV

*What is the proper function of criticism? Is there a species of it
that you admire (are able to get along with)?*

Perhaps my views of the present posture of literary criticism are
clear enough already. If I say of that whole area, where busy fellows run about praising this and damning that, that it could do
with more patience, more scrupulous attention, and above all
more charity, I probably mean "to me," and who needs that?

FROM
*Figures of
Thought*
(1978)

Figures of Thought

Thought is the strangest game of all. The players are the Nominalists vs. the Realists. Realists wear colorless jerseys and are numbered One, Many, & All. Nominalists wear crazy quilts instead of
uniforms, and their numerals tend to be such things as the square
root of minus one. This figure conceals two important circumstances: that there are not in truth Nominalists and Realists, but
only the nominalism and realism of each player, who happens to
be alone on the field where he plays himself; and that by the tacit
pregame move of dividing into Nominalist and Realist he has
made it impossible to win or even finish the game, although—and
it is not a little—he has made it possible to play.

Thought proceeds to create the world by dividing it—what? the
world, of course—into opposites, as in the initial Yin and Yang of
the *Tao Te Ching,* the series of divisions in the first chapter of
Genesis, the Love and Strife that Yeats took from Empedocles to
be the base for the sequent complications of *A Vision,* and so on.
Once there are the opposites, a mere two tricks make game. The
first is that the opposites will have to bear on one and the other
hand the whole weight of the much and many of the world as
experienced: every leaf and every star must join one team or the
other. The second is that, as a world of opposites is impossible,

intolerable, the opposites must be mediated and shown to be one; because, of course, in the world as experienced they *are* one. That was where we began.

A productive model for the enterprise is map-making. Projecting a spherical world on a plane surface involves the cartographer in several distortions for every accuracy, beginning with the creative and mythological decree that there shall be two opposites named East and West; not quite truth, not quite fiction, this prevents any absolute or metaphysical arrivals, or even destinations; on the other hand, it makes—and nor is this a little—navigation possible.

The opposites at first embody themselves in stories. How stories got started is as unknown and like to remain so as how language did (they got together and talked it over among themselves?). With interpretation, whether exegesis or eisegesis, we are in a little better case: Edwin Honig tells us in his lovely book *Dark Conceit* that the behavior of the gods in Homer and in Hesiod was so scandalous it couldn't possibly mean what it plainly said it meant and had to be allegorized; hence scholiast, who begat rhapsode (like Ion) who begat exegete who begat theologian who begat literary critic who so far has begat nothing but more literary critic; an entire and respectable industry raised upon the strange mythological ordinance that things, in addition to being themselves, hence uninformative enough, had to mean something . . . else.

A splendid instance of how all this works except when it doesn't is Lord Bacon's procedure in dealing with the Wisdom of the Ancients. Having first decreed that the figures of Greek myth *meant* something esoteric and wise and open only to initiates but dark to all the rest of the world, and having then decided, or decreed, that the Sphinx *meant,* of all things, Science, he goes about with equal enthusiasm and ingenuity to translate term for term out of story and into thought, and is able to tell you why Science should have talons, why Science should appropriately be thought of as carried to Thebes on the back of an ass, and so on and so on, not at all indefinitely.

A main consideration to emerge is this: there is a plenty of ways to be wrong in our interpretations, and no way at all to be sure of being right. It is in this respect that the story—the novel, play, poem—is, as Northrop Frye said, silent; and it is in this respect that the story resembles Nature. That is, I may identify a certain tree by as many characteristics as the handbook affords me, but it will never up and say 'You guessed it. I am indeed a box elder.' What we know is never the object, but only our knowledge. Though Milton might well have wanted to condemn Dr. Johnson and approve John Crowe Ransom for what they wrote about *Lycidas,* the poem itself will never do either. What we know is not it, but only our knowledge of it. That may be sad, but it does, as beforesaid, make navigation possible.

How then do we, even tentatively and provisionally, approve one interpretation above another? One possible answer, a humble one concealing, as so often happens, titanic pride: We just like one interpretation better than another, and as soon as we do that we find reasons plentiful as blackberries, just as Lord Bacon did in demonstrating that the Sphinx was, or meant, or represented, Science. We may, and often do, try to recommend ourselves, our interpretations, and the reasons for them to some not quite identifiable community of our fellows, involving ourselves in some risk of tautology, not to mention snobbery—this is the sort of thing you'll like if you're the sort that likes things of this sort, as I do—and an infinite regress, which will probably, however, be put a stop to by a change in Fashion, that last and most pervasive and secret of mythologies.

Harold Bloom's *The Anxiety of Influence* is offered as A Theory of Poetry. It is praised by no less sufficient an authority than Morris Dickstein, as "The most provocative and original piece of literary theory in English since Frye's *Anatomy of Criticism.*" I can agree to provocative; I was provoked. And to original as well, but only in the sense of Dr. Johnson's saying that when the cow ran dry you could always milk the bull. But my trouble with the book may merely have been that it was too difficult for me, as I am afraid my brief description of its contents must inevitably show.

Bloom begins with the beguiling simplicity—but it is the last one we are to meet—of his premise: poets are influenced by the poets who have gone before them. His figurative way of describing the situation also looks simple at first: the problems of poets in dealing with the influence of past poets, or with the anxiety attendant upon it, are comparable with the problems people have in growing up, or dealing with the influence of the parents (though to Bloom the Father alone seems important), so that the model in both instances is what Freud called, "with grandly desperate wit," the family romance. Upon this base the author quickly erects a large rhapsodic apparatus of specialized terms and perhaps somewhat too many characters.

The ways in which the new poet (ephebe) copes with the old poet (precursor) are six in number, and their names are: Clinamen, Tessera, Kenosis, Daemonization, Askesis, and Apophrades. These Six Revisionary Ratios, as Bloom calls them, are summarized in an Introduction. One example will be fair to give, and as it must stand for all I rolled a die and came up with:

> 5. *Askesis,* or a movement of self-purgation which intends the attainment of a state of solitude; I take the term, general as it is, particularly from the practice of pre-Socratic shamans like Empedocles. The later poet does not, as in *Kenosis,* undergo a revisionary movement of emptying, but of curtailing; he yields up part of his own human and imaginative endowment, so as to separate himself from others, including the precursor, and he does this in his poem by so stationing it in regard to the parent-poem as to make that poem undergo an *askesis* too; the precursor's endowment is also truncated. (*The Anxiety of Influence,* Introduction)

Rating the above for difficulty, I should say it is harder than Clinamen, much easier than Apophrades, and about the same as the other three.

These titles head up the six main chapters, to which are added a Prologue, an Interchapter called A Manifesto for Antithetical Criticism, and an Epilogue. Prologue and Epilogue are about the Fullness, the Father, the Path, and sound enough like a statement of faith that I may excuse myself from dealing with them; the Manifesto, however, is criticism, and I cite a few provocative and original sayings from it:

> Every poem is a misinterpretation of a parent poem.
> There are no interpretations, but only misinterpretations, and so all criticism is prose poetry.
> The best critics of our time remain Empson and Wilson Knight, for

they have misinterpreted more antithetically than all others.
Criticism is the discourse of the deep tautology . . . the art of
knowing the hidden roads that go from poem to poem.

Alas, I do not know whether these things are so or no. If I too
admire Empson and Wilson Knight I have evidently been doing so
for thirty years for the wrong reasons. Bloom is unflinching about
accepting the consequences of his axioms: he really does believe
that his book is a poem, "A theory of poetry that presents itself as
a severe poem . . ." It doesn't *look* like a poem. And it doesn't
sound like a poem. But if he says it's a poem? He ought to know,
he wrote it, didn't he?

While he limits himself to assertion, Bloom is on privileged
ground. But the two brief appearances of reasoned argument in
what I have quoted—"and so" in the second sentence and "for" in
the third—don't at all appear to me to connect, and I am tempted
to think of Bloom that his form is logic but his essence is confusion. Nor is it at all easy to improve one's opinion as to whether
these things are so or no by applying to the six main chapters, for
Bloom's explanations routinely seem to make things worse, as in,
e.g., a paragraph about "Binswangerian *Versteigenheit* (or 'Extravagance,' as Jacob Needleman wittily translates it)," about
which my bewilderment is not resolved by being told that "Binswanger's summary is useful if we read it backwards." Maybe my
problems with Bloom's thoughts are problems merely of style; but
what's so mere about that?

One minor nuisance. Bloom improves his quotations from the
masters by adding their intentions, tones of voice, and even probable facial expressions, as in "Freud, with grandly desperate wit,"
above, and "Kierkegaard . . . announces, with magnificently but
absurdly apocalyptic confidence. . . ." And he can go further
along this line, not only reading Binswanger backwards but telling
us what Nietzsche might have thought had he lived to read Freud.
But there are greater difficulties than that.

Bloom writes a literary and allusive shorthand which is, moreover, almost entirely associative; one thing reminds him of another
and he can't stop, so that he is sometimes nothing but ellipsis, all
beads and no string. On a single page he names, not merely in a
catalogue but in what is proposed as a series of related relations,

Goethe, Nietzsche, Mann, Emerson, Thoreau, Blake, Lawrence, Pascal, Rousseau, Hugo, Montaigne, Johnson, Aristotle, Homer, Arnold, Keats, Kierkegaard, several of them more than once. Not counting the repetitions, this amounts to one name every two lines, and is very hard to understand. No doubt that to the formidably learned author each use of each of these names stands for something he could identify far more precisely; but to the reader the game becomes merely bewildering in a short while. Finally I thought to recognize the source of this idiom as the graduate seminar; just to have done the required reading is not enough, you have to have done it in the last twenty minutes.

Bloom has too many hypostases, too many nonce characters, more terms than he has work for them to do. The principal ones are the Six Revisionary Ratios, which are held to be *the* ways in which poets may handle—or fail to—the anxiety of influence. After being summarily described, these terms are treated throughout as unquestionably distinct clinical entities, as real as if each one had been abstracted from hundreds or thousands of cases, when in fact the whole field of observation contains not many more than half a dozen major instances from Milton on, and maybe a dozen more fleetingly alluded to.

In addition to the six principal terms and the anxiety of influence itself there are ephebe and precursor (he doesn't always capitalize his characters), The Covering Cherub (by Blake out of Genesis and Ezekiel), The Idiot Questioner (Blake, in *Milton*), a bald gnome called Error and his two little cousins, Swerve and Completion (the feeling of having strayed into a comic book grows stronger here), and as many more as you can or care to identify by the mode of their generation and decay, of which the following gives an instance:

> Chomsky remarks that when one speaks a language, one knows a great deal that was never learned. The effort of criticism is to teach a language, for what is never learned but comes as the gift of a language is a poetry already written—an insight I derive from Shelley's remark that every language is the relic of an abandoned cyclic poem. I mean that criticism teaches not a language of criticism (a formalist view still held in common by archetypalists, structuralists, and phenomenologists) but a language in which poetry is already written, the language of influence, of the dialectic that gov-

erns the relations between poets *as poets.* The poet *in every reader* does not experience the same disjunction from what he reads that the critic in every reader necessarily feels. What gives pleasure to the critic in a reader may give anxiety to the poet in him, an anxiety we have learned, as readers, to neglect, to our own loss and peril. This anxiety, this mode of melancholy, is the anxiety of influence, the dark and daemonic ground upon which we now enter. (italics in original)

Chomsky's remark *is* an illuminating one; indeed, it is a key to his work. But what save rhapsodic association governs its relation with the ensuing sentences? Unless Bloom has some other source of Shelley's remark than the celebrated place in the *Defence,* the remark is really quite different: "Every original language near to its source is in itself the chaos of a cyclic poem." I don't know that the difference makes much difference to the argument, for I'm not at all certain what the argument is, though Bloom's misremembering suits his theme of melancholy declension, influence, and anxiety, better than Shelley's Romantic fervor about origin and source. Further, I am aware that there are these three ways of reading, as reader, as poet, as critic. But the hypostasis of them as three distinct persons together with the permutations mentioned—and those not mentioned but which the reader trying to negotiate the sentence to its end may already be fearfully anticipating—makes hash of what sense may be intended.

If you took the key sentence beginning with what he means ("I mean . . .") and removed that parenthesis during which you spent three weeks in the stacks, you would still not be quite out of the woods:

> I mean that criticism teaches not a language of criticism . . . but a language in which poetry is already written, the language of influence . . .

Reader, this statement is made by the same fellow who has just handed out his half-dozen Revisionist Ratios, Kenosis . . . Apophrades, holding them to be the nub of the matter, and now declares that criticism does not teach a language of criticism. My ho head halls. What criticism teaches, he says, is a language in which poetry is already written, e.g., finding the Emerson in Stevens, the

Milton in practically everyone? No doubt this is a rich territory for scholarship; but criticism? When I dreamed long ago about an art critic who went to the museum to measure the distance between paintings I thought it was hyperbole, but now it turns out to be Bloom.

He does admit at least once to a doubt about the enterprise, ascribing it to his own Idiot Questioner: "What is the use of such a principle, whether the argument it informs be true or not?"

> Is it useful to be told that poets are not common readers, and particularly are not critics, in the true sense of critics, common readers raised to the highest power? And what *is* Poetic Influence anyway? Can the study of it really be anything more than the wearisome industry of source-hunting, of allusion-counting . . . ?

And he develops the doubt for another ten lines citing Eliot, Emerson, Frye, and Arnold. But he overcomes it.

Such doubts as may occur to a reader, however, or as did occur to a poet, Wallace Stevens, get the usual short Freudian shrift. There are two devices which may be appropriate to the analytic session, as from doctor to patient, but which, when used in discourse between supposed equals, turn brutal and vulgar. One is to say that if the reader is not conscious of the problem then he must be *unconscious* of it. Bloom's example is Stevens. The other is to say that if the reader thinks an idea inapplicable, inaccurate, or plain not true, he has a *resistance* to it. Bloom's example is Stevens. And the final flip is to say that one's denial is an example of what one is denying; thus Bloom, after quoting Stevens (including "I am not conscious of having been influenced by anybody"):

> This view, that poetic influence scarcely exists, except in furiously active pedants, is itself an illustration of one way in which poetic influence is a variety of melancholy or anxiety-principle.

As for the Six Revisionary Ratios themselves, I cannot tell the reader whether they are so or no, whether they exist or not. Kenneth Burke once quoted C. S. Peirce on the usefulness of "words so unattractive that loose thinkers are not tempted to use them," with this sequel:

It is vital for science that he who introduces a new conception should be held to have a *duty* imposed upon him to invent a sufficiently disagreeable series of words to express it.

Peirce called this "the moral aspect of terminology," and surely Bloom has done his moral duty. But though the terms are sufficiently disagreeable, are they science? These ways of being influenced, or of showing it, exist only for so long as enough of us agree with Bloom that they do; built into the nature of things they are not. Even in science, alas, if the new conception you introduced happened to be phlogiston or dormitive virtue or the luminiferous ether, you would no doubt do well to distinguish a half-dozen varieties of each by wonderful names.

I've a good few more quarrels with Bloom, both style and substance. But sufficient unto the day. I guess the main one is that though I agree to influence as a fact, and agree that the project of Coriolanus ("as if a man were author of himself, and knew no other kin") is unlikely to work for any of us, I hold to the belief that you do at last grow up and stand there on your own, as what Philip Rieff called "the healthy hypochondriac who rightly expects to survive all interpretation." When you begin, you write: "The grass is green," and everyone says "Aha! Wallace Stevens." Twenty years later you write: "The grass is green," and it sounds just like you. This is a mystery, with which relation durst never meddle. But Bloom, as far as I make him out, doesn't believe it. Even his "strong poets" (he's very high on poets being *strong*), the ones whose poems "most move me"—the only statement made independently of apparatus that I found in the whole book, a touching moment indeed—even those poets, A. R. Ammons and John Ashbery, are much diminished in comparison of the former times:

> And as in lasting, so in length is man
> Contracted to an inch, who was a span. . . .
> (John Donne, *The First Anniversary*)

The world just is degenerate from Milton's day, that's all. The myth latent in Bloom's book is perhaps the oldest one of all, an inheritance already aeons old in the Hindu tradition when the anxiety of its influence affected Daniel and Hesiod, Ovid, Dante,

Peacock . . . and Bloom. It is the Myth of the Four Ages, of which the first three range from paradisal to endurable but happen to be mythological, while the fourth miserable one is perfectly real and happens to be home to us. Bloom doesn't appear to notice this, but he states the sequence plainly enough. Shakespeare is out of it; he "belongs to the giant age before the flood" (and Marlowe his precursor just wasn't big enough to matter). So the four ages are: Milton, the Enlightenment, Romanticism, and "a further decline in its Modernist and post-Modernist heirs."

From Bloom's book I derive three melancholy lessons, or laws.

1. That the life of the institutionalized intelligence, as by its own sort of entropy, grows ever more difficult and never less so.

2. That intelligence itself, which is responsible for so much of the small freedom we have or can use, is intrinsically committed to determinism. That is one way of expressing the curse on knowledge.

3. That the effort to render English unintelligible is proceeding vigorously at the highest levels of learning.

It is the more reassuring, then, to have Denis Donoghue's *Thieves of Fire* as a moving demonstration that none of the three is necessarily true.

There are a few ways in which the two books are alike, and the comparison is illuminating as to the differences as well. Both are short, both are about interpretation, the principle of action in both is the application of a myth to several writers, Milton being the one they have in common and the one they begin with in principle as well as in time. Beyond this, though, they resemble one another mainly as opposites might be thought to do; in the terms of Pascal's famous antithesis Bloom is geometry and Donoghue is finesse.

Donoghue's myth is that of Prometheus, and because his book began as the T. S. Eliot Memorial Lectures for 1972 at the University of Kent the author must have faced a pretty problem in manners right at the start, for not only was Eliot himself the least Promethean of poets, he also had the most serious and grave reservations, however now and again qualified, about all Donoghue's Prometheans: Milton, Blake, Melville, Lawrence. I am glad to say Donoghue's solution is as elegantly courteous as his problem may have been shrewd, as time after time Eliot is brought in to have his say from the shades, reminding the author and his readers that the Promethean is not the only kind of literature, and certainly not the only one worth having.

Thieves of Fire seems to me a beautiful example of thought at its work of creating by dividing; of the use of myth as an instrument or figure of thought: "The myth of Prometheus begins as a story, an anecdote of transgression, but because many generations have found it significant it has become a category, one of the available forms of feeling." In Donoghue's deep and sensitive reading, the story of the theft of fire, with the associated stories of cheating Zeus out of the sacrifice and of Epimetheus and Pandora, becomes the story of the Fall which is also the Rise: the fire is not only what broils the flesh and forges the sword, it is also thought, consciousness, conscience, guilt; our first benefactor being also the first great thief, and we ourselves uneasy with the gift because we are connivers and receivers of stolen goods. "Prometheus provided men with consciousness as the transformational grammar of experience."

From the story, too, comes the figure and character of Prometheus as an identifiable type of mind, or imagination:

There is no evidence that Zeus thought any the better of men for their new skills. The imagination has always been a contentious power, as a result, so far as men are concerned in their relations with the gods. A typology of the imagination would be an explication of the several ways in which men have risen above themselves by the possession of consciousness. The Promethean imagination is only the most extreme gesture in that account, and it is not alone in featuring arbitrary defiance in men, a show of force in the gods answered by a show of blasphemy in men. The predicament remains: imagination, the divine power in men, falsely acquired, stolen from the gods in the first of many similar outrages. Since then, the Promethean imagination has always been defiant: it starts with an incorrigible sense of its own power, and seeks in nature only the means of its fulfilment.

Thought of this kind delights me by its clarity and serviceableness; and an integral part of the delight is Donoghue's modesty, tact, and sense of limits: simplification is a necessity of thought, but all simplification is oversimplification: "There is no thought which embraces all our thought," he says, quoting Merleau-Ponty and going on to his own equally engaging formula for the tragedy of mind: "One of the deficiencies of anything is that it is not also something else."

Out of this balanced good sense emerges not only the Promethean imagination with its titanic powers and devastations, its sense of destiny's being, as Rilke said, *always against,* but its antitype, the imagination receptive and obedient; "content with ready procedures and with the range of feeling which they allow . . . he hands his feeling over to the language, and is happy to abide by its determination." That is said in description of Herbert's "Decay" as over against Milton's sonnet "On the Late Massacre in Piedmont," and a similar balance obtains between Wordsworth and Blake.

Donoghue is especially convincing about the consistency of his related relations as to their characterizing presence in attitudes to language, nature, and God or the gods: his poets are compared as "prescriptive" or "descriptive," as modelers imposing their own thought upon the material and even upon its recalcitrance, or as carvers concerned to release from the material significance felt to be already present in it.

The feeling I got over and over from *Thieves of Fire* is that its author is making his cuts through reality just at the joints, and that is why it looks so easy. I am sadly conscious of having given much more time to saying why I don't like Harold Bloom's book than I am able to give to saying why I do like Denis Donoghue's book; a matter of the squeaky axle getting the grease. And I suppose it may be said that my likes and dislikes are, after all, arbitrary. But I would add one criterion for "liking" that may be thought to relieve it at least somewhat of its absolute subjectivity, willfulness, or capriciousness, though it too must, I suppose, depend ultimately on my feeling that it is so. That criterion is the production of insight, the power conferred on the author by his metaphor, or myth, of producing one after another observation about literary works and about the imagination that impress his reader as fresh, useful, true (remembering always that interpretation *is* misinterpretation, or, as Augustine put it, "What I am telling you is true in a way *because* it is false in a way.") I think Donoghue has had great and merited good luck in this respect; time after time I find him

making remarks, whether he is interpreting the story of Prometheus itself or using it to illuminate certain traits in his authors and
their books, that arouse my warmest admiration—together with,
of course, that bare edge of envy that alone guarantees my feeling
that he is getting things right: "Yes, of course, why couldn't I have
thought of that myself?" Donoghue's interpretations, in detail as in
the large, bring conviction because they illuminate. I can't bring
the two sides of criticism's tautological equation any closer together than that, and had best stop right there.

Poetry and Meaning

What I have to say to you is very simple; so simple that I find it hard to say. It is that poetry is getting something right in language, that this idea of rightness in language is in the first place a feeling, which does not in the least prevent it from existing; if it is subjective, which I doubt, it is not "merely subjective" (as students say, and o dear how often they say it); that this feeling of rightness has largely been lost, if not eagerly assaulted with destructive intent, by people who if they ever wake up are going to find it extremely hard to recapture or even to remember what that feeling was.

One possible, and to me likely, consequence of these simplicities will have to be contemplated; it is that poetry in English is coming to an end. I have hesitated fearfully for a long time before that statement, realizing that coming from a middle-aged poet it will helplessly be heard as one more variant of the common cry of middle-aged poets, "I had talent once, where did it go?" And yet it seems as though the evidence is massive that not poetry alone but a great deal to do with language in relation to mind is fast approaching an end where it will be transformed into something unrecognizably other. To some of this evidence I shall return later on; meanwhile I can at least show that the thought of such an end or such a transformation is not one I hold all by myself.

To show that the question has been seriously entertained I may cite the instance of H. G. Wells and his last work, a little pamphlet called *Mind at the End of Its Tether*. It was written just after the Second World War and in the last year of the author's life, and in it this great progressive, humanitarian, scientifically-minded, and positivist intelligence—who had predicted in one work after another so much that has come literally true—turned right round to the opposite and declared that intelligence and world, which had for the length of history run on parallel courses, were now separating, like two ships whose paths diverge in the night, or like two celestial bodies that approach one another only to fall away into illimitable dark. Admitted that Wells was old, tired, mortally ill, we have still to inquire whether he was saying something true, or at least probable enough to be given the steadiest consideration, or whether he was merely expressing one more symptom of his malady.

A. M. Turing once said that the question "Can machines think?" was too meaningless to deserve discussion, and suggested that the proper short answer was "Can people?" But he added this: "Nevertheless, I believe that at the end of the century the use of words and general opinion will have altered so much that one will be able to speak of machines thinking without expecting to be contradicted." You will observe that to this scientist the point is not that superior machines will be invented, though they almost undoubtedly will be; it is that we will have changed our ways of using words, so that thinking will no longer mean what it did. Indeed, this change may in large measure already have taken place. Hannah Arendt says of this, "If we compare the modern world with that of the past, the loss of human experience . . . is extraordinarily striking. It is not only and not even primarily contemplation which has become an entirely meaningless experience. Thought itself, when it became 'reckoning with consequences,' became a function of the brain, with the result that electronic instruments are found to fulfill these functions much better than we ever could."

And Owen Barfield, possibly the clearest and most searching thinker of the present time, says—though he calls it a provocative heterodoxy—"I have been coming to feel for some time that imagination, *as an end in itself,* is a vein that has been, or very soon will be, worked out. I am in doubt whether much more that is really significant can be done with it" (*The Rediscovery of Meaning*).

There is at least a funnier way of viewing the matter. Otto Rank says somewhere that it took long ages for soul, or spirit, or what we call mind, to work its way up into the head. In some cultures this vital principle inhabited the soles of the feet—the Buddha's footprint is holy—and in others the genitals, the stomach, bowels, heart, liver, and solar plexus were its abode. But among us for a couple of centuries or more thought is commonly believed to be something done in the head, and its sacred function is protected from contamination by the lower parts of the body by collar and tie; compare the expression "white-collar worker" for someone whose business is mental.

Considering this progression we might reasonably ask by way of extrapolation where this principle of life has left to go. And the student of such matters might look long and hard at the sudden efflorescence of hair styles, including beards and wigs, among the young in late years. It suggests sadly enough people's coming to the dismayed realization that the only thing about yourself you have the power to change, until you go bald, is hair; and it irresistibly reminds me of that species of scientific thought, becoming every day more common, which observes that hair grows out of the head and goes on to infer that the head is full of hair. We are already assured by science that the head does not contain thoughts or words, but only neurons—to which I suppose the teacherly response would be, "Which of you neurons said that?"

Turning from this topic for the present, I remark that the spectacle, now some centuries long, of western man patiently endeavoring to reason himself out of thought and read himself out of the universe, would be as fit a subject for a comic poet as for a tragic one, were its consequences not so brutal and so lamentable.

I return now to my first assertion: poetry is a way of getting something right in language, poetry is language doing itself right. This idea came first, as ideas have a way of doing, as a thoughtless phrase. I am a most inefficient teacher of verse-writing—but imagine what a monster an efficient one would be!—and term after term, no matter what resolutions of patience and goodwill I began with, three weeks later I found myself saying to the students about their productions such things as: But it's not right, it just simply isn't right . . . and even more cruelly on occasion: if there's nothing right what's the use of trying to say what's wrong with it? And sometimes I would rhapsodize to my poor class about how poetry was simply language doing itself right, language as it ought to be, language as it was in the few hours between Adam's naming the creation and his fall. The whole art of poetry, I would say, consists in getting back that paradisal condition of the understanding, the condition that says simply "yes" and "I see" and "it is so." Naturally enough, it doesn't happen often. But it does happen.

My students, accustomed to classes in which their instructors explained themselves, explained literature, and in fact left nothing unexplained that could possibly be explained, and now confronting a teacher who apparently couldn't or wouldn't explain one blessed thing, and especially not the one blessed thing they were there to have explained to them, were understandably puzzled. All the same, they behaved very kindly about it. At most, the ones inclined to philosophize would point out to me that my criterion of rightness could never be defined and in any event was merely subjective.

Meaning I could never *prove* anything was right.

I do have a reply to that objection, though unfortunately it is a rather unwieldy one because it has to include some consideration of our intellectual habits with respect to subjects and objects, or, as Coleridge used to say when drinking, sumjects and omjects.

It was Coleridge, I am told, who introduced the words subjective and objective into our language. Ruskin, who was very funny on the theme, hated the words and said they were foisted on us by a combination of German dullness and English affectation. However that may be, I call it to your attention as significant that whole populations which had formerly been able to express their thoughts without resort to the words subjective and objective—whole populations, by the way, including Chaucer and Shakespeare and Milton—now, less than two centuries after their entrance into the language, can scarcely get through a classroom hour without leaning heavily on them. Students, in particular, appear to experience from their use some kind of magical resolution of any difficulty of thought.

I am not trying to take away these terms, which seem to stand to our intellectual astronauts as spacecraft and space respectively. But I would point out first that though Coleridge introduced the words into philosophizing in English he was far indeed from denigrating thought, feeling, or belief by calling them "merely" subjective. In fact I came by chance on a place where he does just the opposite and refers to the natural world as "all that is merely objective."

The great dictionary is pretty funny, as well as illuminating, on *subjective* as a philosophic word, now obsolete, "Pertaining to the real or essential being of that which supports qualities, attributes, or relations; substantial; real," for it adds, after what might be a thoughtful pause, "objective in the modern sense." Funny, as the sight of great learning trapped in its words may often be, and illuminating about the great change in the mind of the world from a time when true subjectivity could strictly be attributed only to God, to the present, when saying that something or someone is being subjective means a considerable variety of things, all pejorative, e.g., you think it's so but it's not; maybe, but it's not important; you're being emotional when you ought to be reasonable.

It is by some such process as is represented in the changed meaning of such a word as *subjective* that the mind has reached its present most familiar predicament, ludicrous and pathetic by turns, whereby a learned discipline begins its course of studies by excluding as far as possible all feeling, including especially the feeling of interest, curiosity, pleasure, delight that prompted the study itself, and winds up several years and thousands of pages later plaintively asking itself about human values and wondering where they are to be found. The entire development is of the greatest historical interest, but in the result, it is rather like the man found by a policeman searching under a streetlight for his lost watch. Did you lose it here? asks the policeman, one would have thought unnecessarily. No, I lost it over there, but I'm looking here because the light's better.

This distinction of the whole world into subjective and objective probably began with Galileo's, and then Locke's, division of the qualities into primary and secondary. The dictionary gives the former as bulk, figure, number, situation, and motion or rest, "which are in the object as in our perception of it," while the secondary qualities, tastes, sounds, colors, and so on, "are modes of our perception induced by some character in the object which does not coincide with the perception itself." One notices immediately that the primary qualities have the air already of being what are called "hard facts," while the secondary ones are already a touch sentimental and unmanly. And the scientific way of developing this distinction had the effect of progressively reducing even the primary qualities to quantity, or number, alone, so that only what is enumerable is effectively regarded as real. With this fateful distinction, which indeed did not rest as a distinction but became a division, much else separated that had formerly been one and the object of a single attention; poetry, for example, in the eyes of most of the world, became "only poetry." I shan't pause to drop a tear for "only poetry," but would suggest that poetry, and literature generally, may be the last remaining place where that about subjective and objective does not apply; and that an appropriate emblem for this characteristic of literature is the situation you have in *Hamlet,* where the Ghost is neither subjective, for the soldiers can see it just as well as Hamlet, nor objective, for when it next appears Hamlet alone can see it, while his mother can see "Nothing at all; yet all that is I see." I've a sense that we all incline by training and study to be like Gertrude about our ghosts. Wallace Stevens poignantly varies Gertrude's line, speaking of "a mind of winter" and of

> the listener, who listens in the snow,
> And, nothing himself, beholds
> Nothing that is not there and the nothing that is.
> ("The Snow Man")

Now there is one great trouble with the intellectual and learned school of approach to the art of poetry; it is a trouble that secretly afflicts, I am convinced, a great part of our thoughts about a good many things, and it is this: we are much too concerned to turn our experience into a result, something tangible, and in the course of doing this we forget what the experience felt like in the first place, and, still more important, how through all our studies we remain related to time in two ways, biographical and historical. This is a simple enough thought, and that may be why it is almost always forgotten, though sometimes I've the feeling of its being deliberately excluded. But it bears importantly on this business of poetry as getting things right in language. For the lover of poetry would never have become a lover of poetry, much less a student of poetry, had he not at first had this feeling of rightness and certainty about some piece of language. That came before all question of study, of English courses, of why it was so; enough that it simply was so. James Dickey writes in an essay that he remembers what first attracted him to poetry; it was the rightness of the expression "to sweat it out," in relation to the soldier's experience of war.

That brings me to another point about the experience of the rightness of language, and to another thing that is dreadfully wrong about the idea of poetry as a subject to be studied in schools.

It is most important to any inquiry into this idea of rightness in poetry that we be as candid as possible about our actual relation, of feeling and thought, to the phenomena; and with respect to this problem I begin by observing that neither teaching nor criticism is very often quite candid about this relation. For there is always present a temptation, which we almost always yield to, to make our experience of poetry both more intellectual and more pretentious than it is or ought to be. There is a somewhat comic, somewhat vulgar and mercantile, aspect to our serious and no doubt well-meaning endeavors to convince others and even possibly ourselves that the experience we are getting from poetry is certifiably profound, lofty, sublime, organic, harmonious . . . even pleasurable. You may supply other adjectives, from whatever schools of criticism, as you care to.

Without denying that our experience of poetry is sometimes one or more of those things, I think it proper to acknowledge that it is not always like that, and may not often be like that. A primary pleasure in poetry is surely something low enough to be beneath the notice of teacher or critic—the pleasure of saying something over for its own sweet sake and because it sounds just right. For myself, certainly, and for you if you will remember how it truly was, the thing said over will not necessarily be A Great Thought, though great thoughts are not necessarily excluded either; it may be as near as not to meaningless, especially if one says it without much attention to its context. For instance, a riddling song has the refrain: Sing ninety-nine and ninety. I can remember being charmed enough with that to say it over and over to myself for days, without ever having a single thought about its meaning except for a certain bemused wonder about how different it was from singing a hundred and eighty-nine.

Or else it may be something proverbially helpful, that you say to yourself when things are going wrong: "Time and the hour runs through the roughest day." Perhaps this would not have meant so much to me without the little grammatical oddity of "runs" instead of "run." And here are a couple of lines from the *Comedy* that delight me as much now as they did when I first came across them so many years ago:

> Cosi di ponte in ponte, altro parlando
> Che la mia commedia cantar non cura
> (*Inferno*, XXI, 1–2)

No deep insight here, nor lofty wisdom; he is talking in effect about what he is not going to talk about, and though it is wonderfully appealing to be told that Dante and Virgil said things to one another in Hell that we are never going to know, that is not the whole charm of the lines:

> So from bridge to bridge, talking of other things
> That my comedy cares not to sing.
> (my translation)

It loses much of its delightsomeness in English; loses that lovely, off-handed strolling lilt that makes the Italian, especially of the second line, so wonderful to say. There's a clue in that, maybe, in that *ambulando* rhythm that imitates the two poets walking along; for Paul Valéry gave perhaps the shortest definition of poetry recorded: it is what it says.

One more example. I sang to my children a nursery rhyme I must have missed in childhood:

> Fiddle dee dee, fiddle dee dee,
> The fly has married the bumble bee.
>
> Said the fly said he, will you marry me
> And live with me sweet bumble bee?
> Said the bumble bee, I'll laugh and sing
> And you'll never know I carry a sting.
>
> Fiddle dee dee, fiddle dee dee,
> The fly has married the bumble bee.

I don't know in the least what there is about this that made me so happy I went about the house chanting it for days on end, in all sorts of situations . . . until I observed that when I did my wife was beginning to look sideways at me, as though this little verse was turning into A Dark Thought About Marriage.

Which suggests a further step. It is part of the power of a poem to generate meanings from what may originally be meaningless. Perhaps what I am thinking of as rightness in language is this abstract power, or power gained from being very abstract (as Stevens said a supreme fiction had to be)—the power to handle a great many situations at once, the power of poetry to be somewhat more like a mind than a thought. These apparently trivial examples of things that one repeats to oneself rather as though they were talismans, are they not after all the stuff and substance itself of poetry, and more visibly so for not being so cluttered with meanings that we can't see the things themselves? After all, delight itself may mean nothing. Love may mean nothing. The world appears to have every prospect of never meaning anything again. But love and delight and, so far, the world, remain.

In an earlier essay I made a detailed comparison between the mechanisms visible in certain sorts of poetry and the mechanisms of jokes. I found the comparison illuminating even if it would not hold equally for all kinds of poetry (I never claimed it would). But in connection with the question of rightness in language as over against the claim that such rightness is "merely subjective" it is appropriate to draw on that earlier essay for a moment, in order to say as follows.

1. When you understand a joke, you laugh. In fact, your laughter quite simply *is* your understanding, which doesn't express itself in a separate verbal form.

2. When you fail to understand a joke, in a company where every one else seems to understand it and laughs, you either say "I don't get it," or you give one of those fake and feeble laughs which you know everyone else will see through at once. What do you not do?

3. I submit that what you never do in this situation is say that the joke is subjective or merely subjective.

4. If someone explains or interprets the joke to you, your difficulty will perhaps be cleared up, but too late; you won't laugh as hard as you would have, had you understood immediately, that is, without the mediation of more words.

5. Therefore a joke is a way of getting something right in language.

6. A poem too is a way of getting something right in language, save that the proper response will be not laughter but silence, or the acknowledgment that it is so, it is as it is; that the miracle has happened once again: "something understood," as Herbert says finally and ever so quietly about prayer.

7. It is in this sense that poems ought to be approached as sacred objects. One expects not so much to learn them as to learn from them. They give a certain definition to experience, and it may be

that it is to experience we should refer them, rather than to exegesis. By contrast, definitions given in dictionaries break up experiences into units in order to make them—the units, unhappily,
not the experiences—easier to understand; but dictionary definitions will at last be found to be circular, hence not definitive, while
a poem is "the burning bow that once could shoot an arrow out of
the up and down" (Yeats).

You will no doubt have been thinking for some time that this is
all very well, but when are we to have an example? other than, of
course, those agreeable trivialities he quoted a few minutes back.
But I have deliberately withheld examples because I want the idea
of rightness to be as open, contentless, empty if you like, as may
be. For I am not at all certain it is so important for each of us to
have the same ideas about the same things, even if it is that particular species of what Lovejoy called "metaphysical pathos" that more
than anything else informs and sustains the university and the
culture. What is important to each of us is to have the idea of
rightness, to grasp it feelingly. If we do not have it, perhaps poetry
is not for us; music goes on though many are tone-deaf and few
have absolute pitch; absolute pitch has never been accused of being subjective on that account. If you are in the presence of a
greater vision than your own—Shakespeare's for instance—and
do not see what he is talking about, you don't say he sees nothing,
for that would be like telling a microscope that it exaggerated.

In keeping with a somewhat oriental style of going at a subject,
a style that abstains from saying what the subject is directly, but
hopes to produce an immediate vision of it by indirect means and
dark hints—this negative approach is usually translated as "no-
knowledge," and commentators warn us not to confuse it with "no
knowledge"—I shall present, instead of examples of rightness in
poetry, a couple of examples in which, as far as I am able to see,
nothing went right at all.

The first is by a student, who has generously allowed me to make
use of his effort. In fact it was this student who kindly put me straight
by telling me that my idea of rightness was purely subjective.

OPUS 125

The hall of deafness still had heaped
a confusion of memories,

a pile awaiting craftsman's wit;
but he wished he could hear his sobs
when pain forced and hacked into tears,
or, the huge laugh like a giant's
that knew that after all it was
hard work setting sounds in order. . . .

I forbear to quote the remainder. I don't want to make fun of it
either. It's sad. You can see it's about Beethoven writing the Ninth
Symphony, and you can feel that it is very sincere, but it's awful. I
said to the student, who by the way is a very intelligent one, "Here
you are, you've read and probably understood half the literature of
the past four hundred years—but you've never heard anything."
Maybe the motto of the English Department could be this line
varied from Eliot:

We missed the experience, but we had the meaning.

My second example of getting it wrong is professional work, so
far as poets may be said to be professionals. Anyhow, it appeared
in *Poetry Magazine,* a title in which, I have often thought, the
word *poetry* has exactly the force that the word *beauty* does in the
title "beauty shoppe." Beyond that, not wishing to be invidious, I
shall not identify the author; the following is how he begins a piece
of some sixty lines:

A small voice is fretting my house in the night
A small heart is there . . . Listen,
I who have dwelt at the root of a scream forever,
I who have read my heart like a man with no hands
reading a book whose pages turn in the wind,
I say listen, listen, hear me
in our dreamless dark, my dear.

If I read that in a sufficiently sonorous and reverential tone,
some of you will doubtless have thought it beautiful, but you are
wrong. (It is best, I think, for me to say such things plainly and
without qualification.) That is one of the unmentioned and possibly unmentionable dangers to poetry recitations, that any old garbage will go down all right if it's read with conviction.

About that passage I shall comment briefly. For if silence is the appropriate response to rightness, it may be that the real use of talk is about wrongness.

To read the book of the heart is an ancient, conventional expression, hence not good enough for our poet, who wishes to be simultaneously intense, complex, rhapsodic, and desperate, not to mention modern. Still, he is unable to resist this honorable old figure, the heart as a book to be read. So he fancies it up a bit. The speaker is reading the book of the heart? well, chop off his hands at the wrists to show that this is no easy matter; now, to clinch the point home, spring up a wind and start the pages of the book flapping; compared to the speaker's problems here, it would be a cinch for him to dwell at the root of a scream forever. This poetry is intense, indeed, with the grim intensity of someone trying to masturbate too soon after having masturbated.

Maybe from examples such as these we can see the beauty even of wrongness, that from it we infer that a right way of doing things does exist, even that many right ways of doing things must exist, even as from the idea of getting lost we infer the existence of roads and destinations.

I began by saying that I thought this idea of rightness had largely been lost, or destroyed, and that on that account we might have to contemplate the end of poetry as we have known it. And I promised to return to that thought and the evidence for it, knowing that everyone likes a bit of an apocalypse to finish on.

It is a sound maxim for a prophet to hold before him, that when he is about to peer into the future and say that something awful is going to happen, he might well turn around and ask himself if it hasn't happened already. Blake said of this, that prophecy meant simply, If you go on doing thus, the result will be thus. And I add that my favorite prophet is Jonah both for being short-winded and for being wrong about the destruction of Nineveh, that great city wherein, says the Lord in one of his infrequent jokes, are more than sixscore thousand persons that cannot discern between their right hand and their left hand; and also much cattle. Which a poet once brought up to date as follows:

> The Lord might have spared us the harsh joke;
> Many that live in Nineveh these days

Cannot discern their ass from a hot rock.
Maybe the word 'cattle' refers to these.

I hope that I, like Jonah, am wrong; though if I should be I too
might be displeased exceedingly.

There is a sense, utterly true but not very helpful, in which everything is always ending and always beginning. The fabric of the generations simply is woven that way, seamlessly, and only the work of
the historical intellect divides it up. Imagine someone living through
the fall of the Roman Empire in a provincial town, in Marseille say,
or London; he would live his life day by day, as we all do, and never
know that he had lived through the fall of the Roman Empire. He
would notice, perhaps, certain signs of neglect; the garrison might
go slovenly and unshaven, the roads might not be so well kept up,
proclamations would be fewer than they used to be . . . and when
people began to notice the absence of something called The Roman
Empire they nostalgically replaced it with a Holy Roman Empire
and pretended it was the same thing, sort of. So it may be with my
subject. I will present my evidence as best I can.

For one thing, the posture of the literary mind seems these days
to be dry, angry, smart, jeering, cynical; as though once people
had discovered the sneaky joys of irreverence they were quite unable to stop. This is one typical process of Shakespeare's tragedies, where the intelligent and crafty young destroy the stupid old
and, with them, the sacred something that these complacent dodos
by some accident had in their charge, and the intelligent and crafty
young at last, as Ulysses says, eat up themselves.

This symptom in itself is perhaps not much. Literary quarrels
have usually been acrimonious, indeed are less personally spiteful
now than in the Age of Pope. The world has always been as full of
people plugging their friends as of people unplugging their enemies. Yet the public discussion, the criticism, that attends on
poetry, has appeared to me as coming close to the point at which a
smart shallowness and verbal facility will jettison meaning altogether; the same thing has been happening in poetry itself. I shall
not now give examples, but I ask you to consider whether it is not
as I have said. Not only the terms of abuse, but more importantly
the terms of praise, appear in a language whose vagueness of sense
is closely related to the extravagance of its claims.

This kind of shrillness may be the sign of considerable unacknowledged anguish of spirit. As though everyone felt some big thing was breaking up, and made bigger and louder noises to pretend that all is as it was. For it ought now to be possible to turn and look back over the modern period, as it foolishly goes on being called, and see how some one thing—I should date it perhaps from the middle of the last century, from Baudelaire and Swinburne, say—was gathering momentum in a direction and was assembling armies of adherents, but that not so long ago this momentum, giant as it was, divided itself among the members of the armies, diminished, and may now be flickering out in brief contingencies.

I don't know just what name would be right for this momentum. It had to do with a slow collapse in the idea of meaning which progressed simultaneously with an imposing acceleration of the rate at which knowledge was accumulated. Everyone who thinks much about poetry will have observed how in the early years of this century it abruptly became much harder to understand. Not all of it, by any means, but I need mention only Eliot, Pound, Hart Crane, as instances. By heroical efforts of criticism and exegesis Eliot's poems, which seem to have impressed many of their first readers as being written in Linear B, were made part of the common language, so that even ball games now may end not with a bang but a whimper. The same process has not happened to the Cantos of Ezra Pound, and I incline to doubt it will happen.

What I am calling the slow collapse in the idea of meaning, which made poetry so very hard to understand and consequently conferred on English Departments a large part of both their real and spurious importance, evidently did not happen in poetry alone. It happened even more conspicuously and at about the same time in physics, in painting, in music; the whole world suddenly became frightfully hard to understand. And there is a corollary to this that I find most interesting: the mind responded magnificently to the challenge of all this difficulty in ever so many ways . . . and from asking concerning the meaning of this poem or that went on to ask concerning meaning itself. Again, I need mention only a few names: Kenneth Burke, William Empson, I. A. Richards, all seem to have begun by inquiring about the meaning of poems and then to have felt themselves irresistibly drawn to the question beyond: what is meaning, and how does it happen to arise? And the new

science of linguistics here enters the picture. Men are now beginning to understand, doubtless as yet in a fumbling and vague sort
of way compared to what may be coming, what sort of entity a
language is and what relations, of possibility and of limitation, it
has to thought. Realizing that language is an abstract and utterly
arbitrary but totally articulated system of relations, men now begin to see that they may invent other languages for other purposes—indeed, they do so already.

Anthropology too, with its close relations, folklore and comparative religion and mythology, gets into the act, and for the first
time men begin to have a clear and coherent understanding of how
literature arose, and what it is, and even a little what it does.

Now these are very real and reckonable advances. I am not
antiscience, though I do think that our ways of thinking about
what science does and is doing are inadequate and even stupid,
and I am not against the accumulation and coordination of knowledge. But I think it is clear that to understand a given matter will
have its effect on doing. Students of what is called nowadays The
Creative Process do not observably turn into artists. And when the
depths of things are exposed to the dry light of reasoned explanation, they may well dry up. For it is paradoxical, and therefore in a
round world true, that a great deal of knowledge may come to
resemble a great insanity. That may be why I am forced to contend
that a vast increase in knowledge was simultaneous with a slow
collapse in the idea of meaning.

It is commonplace to observe that we today are the beneficiaries
and victims of more language than any people has ever been subjected to in the history of the world. Even going for a walk or drive
in the country, we see that the landscape more and more carries
written messages—signs. Two strange and related consequences
come from this circumstance.

For one, the public language of press and the other media imposes upon us a public dream, a phantasy written in a language
that is neither right nor wrong but, say, serviceable. Not so much
that it tells us what to think, though it tries to do that as well, but it
makes of no avail our freedom of thought by telling us what we
must have these thoughts about, and by progressively and insensi-
bly filling us with a low, dull language for thinking them.

The second consequence seems to be that the languages of art and of learning grow ever more recondite, as if they were the distorted mirror images of the public language, which they relate to, more or less as a dream relates to a newspaper.

Yet here too the opposites coincide, for the public dream that is the daily dream of all appears as no less insane, and no less under the threat of an ultimate meaninglessness, than the private dream that is the nightly dream of each alone. And if the languages of the arts and sciences grow progressively harder to understand, the matching phenomenon on the other side is that in the public language it is getting progressively harder to say anything that refers to reality.

I think I can now give a name to the period that is over. I shall assert that it lasted from the middle of the last century to the middle of this one, and I shall call it The Age of Art, or The Aesthetic Age. Its dominant characteristic was the claim that salvation was by art alone. What that salvation would be, or would be like, was specified in ever so many different ways by different artists, but it scarcely ever failed to be asserted that the way and the truth and the life was by art.

Matthew Arnold has often been rebuked for suggesting that art would be the religion of the future, but if you take his statement not as a slogan to wave but as a statement of what was going to happen, it would seem that he was historically accurate, or prophetic.

And if you ask why I hazard a guess that the great period of art may now be over, I can but suggest that, while holding that idea firmly in mind, you look around you. And I would remind you that even if I am somewhat right about what is happening, it may not be altogether a disaster. The world is a very deep place, no matter how much of it we explain, and explain away, and the end of a particular form of experience does not mean the end of experience. Forms are there to be transformed, and of all this something kind and good may come one day. Or so I hope.

FROM
New and
Selected
Essays
(1985)

Some Minute Particulars

On this otherwise happy occasion of the *Post-Dispatch*'s making its century—and long may its pages flap—the editor's mandate
to his contributors is formidable, severe, and forbidding: we are to
"search for ways to identify a new set of ideals and principles
shared by most Americans to form the fabric of a firm social
order, while retaining the underpinnings essential in the struggle
for democracy and the fullest possible realization of freedom for
the individual." The premise for our mission is the agreement of
many observers "that the American Dream has been shattered,
that many Americans have discarded the old structure but have yet
to agree on a new one to guide this country in the future." My
own part in all this is indicated by two questions: "Are new directions needed in what our writers are saying or how society receives
what they have to say? Does the structure by which the arts are
organized and supported need to be changed?"

This is a mighty big order. We are being positively invited, if not
indeed firmly instructed, to do some Viewing With Alarm before
winding up with positive, practicable recommendations such as
"Go thou and do otherwise." As a respectable minor poet not
accustomed to seeing a whole civilization change its ways at his

bidding, I am a touch bemused as well as bewildered, grateful for
being invited to join so distinguished a company but uncertain
how to behave in its midst. Sort of typical of poets, I think, not to
begin with "What do I think about all this?" but with the more
technical question of "What sort of style, tone, voice, is best for
dealing with these great and vital, but also vague and general,
issues of the time?" But then, as one of my teachers was fond of
saying, "How do I know what I think till I see what I say?"

The premise that things is bad all over, that the country is going
to hell in a bucket, is very hard to beat, ancient, traditional, honorable as it is. For one thing, if a contributor to a symposium of single
voices in individual broom closets were to say, "Well, taking a quick
view of western civilization since, say, Easter Week of 1300, which
Dante spent in hell, purgatory and heaven, and taking no bets on
what may be going to happen tomorrow, I'd say we weren't getting
on badly, no, not badly at all," he would surely lay himself open to
accusations of wilful blindness, optimism, and above all hardheart-
edness. For look at all the suffering, the misery, starvation, unem-
ployment, anxiety, inflation, taxes, illness . . . the list could be endless. It would be no defense, either, for such a contributor to point
out that, just at the moment at any rate, we are not in The Black
Death, the Thirty Years War, that ever so many maladies formerly
fatal have been overcome, that our lives, those of ordinary citizens,
are comfortable in ways and to a degree beyond what the Sun-King
Louis the Fourteenth could have imagined or commanded had he
had the imagination. No, all this would not do, and quite properly
not. The trouble about evil, whether natural or humanly contrived,
is that a very little of it goes such a long way, and the answers to our
many and difficult problems will differ extremely depending on
whether they are given by people who are going on to dinner at the
Ritz or by people who are kept in tiger cages and fed on catfood
when fed at all. Nor would it avail for such a contributor to point
out that for all the many predictions of doom unless we mend our
ways, much wickedness, great tribulations, and maybe even greater
inadequacies, are still with us; Chicken-Licken would continue patiently pointing out that the heavens, after all, were really falling
this time, and would probably adduce incomprehensible statistical
curves to prove it. Alas, it is not only our sins that resulted from the
Fall, so did their remedies; so do our virtues.

The first rule for taking an exam is not, as some pupils seem to believe, "Bullshit your way through," which rarely works. It is, "When you don't know the answer, dispute the question." Question the question, argue about its legitimacy, criticize every term in which it is phrased, and finally deny the questioner's right to ask it *in those terms*. It'll get you a C+ almost every time. As I certainly don't know the answers to the editor's questions, that is what I shall have to do, or at any rate try to do.

For one thing, do I know what this American Dream that has been shattered is, or was? Three martinis in every lunchbox? That the rich should be able to lie down on the poor in perfect safety as well as comfort? Liberty and justice for all, and now leave me alone while I go pursue some happiness the way the Declaration says? These do not strike me as responsive, yet they have the minimal virtue of acknowledging my ignorance of what this Dream may really be.

Another of my questions has to do with "a new set of ideals and principles," which comes very close to being a contradiction. Ideals and principles are of all things the ones most firmly identified with the past, the archaic, the springtime of a people. The mere mention of them is almost bound to be followed by reference to Socrates, Jesus, the Buddha, Confucius, followed by a glance at the Hebrew prophets, Magna Carta, the Declaration, and the Constitution; even the beginning of all things, in Genesis, is given in the Vulgate as "In principio," meaning that not only in the beginning but also in principle God created the heaven and earth. The sole exception I know of to the above list of venerable notables is Lao-Tse, who was too funny to be included, his view being that wickedness entered the world with the advent of benevolence and right thinking. No, ideals and principles are not all that easy to fashion anew, they are difficult or impossible even by definition: like inventing a new platitude (difficult), or girlwatching in the Men's Room (can't be done).

There follows the appalling question of our adherence in conduct and thought to whatever ideals we do now have or profess. For it does seem as though, while the religious rebuke us for our failure to live up to our ideals, writers, beginning with perhaps Blake and continuing through Ibsen, say, and Shaw, and growing in fervor if not in diagnostic power through the present, have rebuked us for the ideals themselves as containing vast and secret capacities not only for cruelty and injustice but for justifying cruelty and injustice as the greatest virtues, without which civilization must inevitably go to pieces; a sort of moral equivalent of the Second Thermodynamical Law, according to which without a steep gradient between rich and poor, powerful and feeble, no work could get done. The argument, too long to take up here, might best be expressed in a sorry aphorism attributable, say, to a team of anthropologists looking at our lives: "We thought they were sinning against their religion, but no, they were only practicing it."

My last and hardest question is, how do you get a clear overview of something so vast as a civilization? How do you get a handle on so complex a set of variations in order to find their theme? After all, we use in a single day more printed-upon paper than all Europe used during the whole of the eighteenth century (I made up that statistic some years ago, to sound impressive, and no one has ever contradicted it; it must be true), so that any opinion whatsoever can count on massive and flabbergasting support from pictures, charts, graphs, percentages of persons polled, and so on. About this, the poet William Blake instructs us with characteristic vigor and certainty:—

> He who would do good to another must do it in Minute
>   Particulars:
> General good is the plea of the scoundrel, hypocrite and
>   flatterer,
> For Art & Science cannot exist but in minutely organized
>   Particulars
> And not in generalizing Demonstrations of the Rational Power.
>   —*Jerusalem*, plate 55, lines 60–63

Oliver Wendell Holmes took a slightly different slant on the same question when he announced that the whole business of man upon the earth is the framing of general propositions, and no general proposition was ever worth a damn.

But here we touch on some pretty high matters having to do with the power of language to talk about itself, and therefore to contradict itself, questions associated with mathematics and with such names as Gödel, Tarski and Russell; all of whom I so perfectly don't understand that I should get right away from the subject after only one instance: The Barber of Seville says he shaves every man who does not shave himself. Does he shave himself?

Retreating from all that in fair order, here is a particular sufficiently minute drawn from my own business of fooling around with language to see what turns up; it is an old New England rime ascribed by Barlett's *Familiar Quotations* to that prolific poet Anon:—

> Use it up
> Wear it out
> Make it do
> Do without

I have long liked it for its terseness. But the reason for bringing it up in this discussion is that it does seem to offer some kind of handle to the national character with its ideals and principles. Its intention is evidently to recommend to us as a model for conduct the Puritan virtues of thrift, frugality, industry, as exemplified in the lives of our forefathers and their moremothers in building up the country out of their stern and rockbound souls as well as shores; and the tight-lipped, give-nothing-away quality of its diction excellently illustrates the moral instruction offered. Of course, a moment's reflection upon humankind will tell us that our forebears (and moremeres?) must have had among them as many lazy, profligate, lecherous slobs per thousand head of the population as we have among ourselves, so that the little rime reflects not the truth, but only what people a bit later on would like to believe was the truth. Once again, ideals and principles are invariably referred to the past, and the past referred to is always a mythical past.

Now it's a funny thing that if you look again at that little rime, thinking about the present instead of the past, and apply it not to individual behavior but to the nation and the world, you can see a quite different, indeed opposite, reading from what we suppose was its original intention. If you were concerned about ecology and pollution, you might say that far from being a moral instruction to thrift, &c., it is a devastatingly accurate pithy description of what advanced technological civilizations are in fact doing to the earth and its resources, its last line being a plain prophecy of the probable result:—

> Use it up
> Wear it out
> Make it do
> Do without

Drawing on William Blake again, we may use his notion that any honest man is a prophet, because prophecy is nothing but saying, "If you go on thus, the result will be thus." And on Bertrand Russell, who said that for us to have an entirely unambiguous language would be extremely inconvenient, and therefore, thank God, we do not have one. Just imagine, I add, what would happen if we all took a Stop sign to mean unambiguously and exclusively what it said.

One way or another, I was enough taken with the old New England maxim that while driving through Massachusetts and seeing how many towns ended in "ham" (pronounced "em" and meaning a pasture beside water), I answered up as follows:—

> If you can't Wareham
> And don't Needham
> Stoneham
> And Dedham

which I imagine to be another aspect of the national character, as real and as mythological as the first.

Now viewing with alarm and looking into the future are more than national pastimes, they are huge industries appealing to our fears and to our desire for spectacle. Because we all are fated to die, apocalyptic scenarios have a considerable power to thrill and chill at once, and consequently we have a large class of apocalypticians paid handsomely enough for imagining alternative disasters; not only in movies, where burning buildings, sinking ships, and giant sharks are presented as allegories of our predicament, but also in think tanks where serious scholars are said to consider for our good the relative probabilities of (a) nuclear annihilation, (b) overpopulation so severe we shall have to sleep in shifts, and (c) our extinction by boredom owing to immensely increased leisure. On those terms, you not only can't win, you also wouldn't want to.

There is even a new art, with pretensions to science, called Futurism, or Futurology, and I have on my desk (and have but briefly looked into) one of its latest manifestations, called *Hand-book of Futures Research,* edited by Jib Fowles, from which I learn, first, that the whole business has come into being only during the last decade (which might have mightily surprised the Roman augurs and haruspices, had they been around to know it), and, second, that one chapter, called "The Optimistic Outlook," is followed by another called "The Pessimistic Outlook," offering us a choice of futures to suit—what? our temperaments, perhaps? being in this way like the Letters to the Editor column, often the best and the worst written parts of a newspaper on the same day, where we are offered a balanced sample showing that what is good is bad, and vice versa, and leaving us hopelessly confused in the middle, or muddle.

Of all this looking into the future—which may be what "new ideals and principles" come down to—I imagine a large part to be composed of serious thought and study, another and unfortunately large part to be seriously intended but based on pseudo-scientific or at least inapplicable and misunderstood scientific methodology—ever so often the idea appears to be that if you quantify your doubts, uncertainties, or plain ignorance, they will magically turn into knowledge—and a third large part, composed of nuts. We may wish them all well, these thinkers, while keeping to ourselves a little irreverent skepticism just short of the cynical.

For ever since I became conscious, a little, of this great country and this great world, we have been hit by about one major catastrophe a decade (at least), and I should like to look at a couple of these in order to wonder what Futurologists might have had to say about them, had Futurologists—in their present quasi-scientistical form—been among us, which they surely should have predicted being.

The Great Depression, which happened when I was nine. We are told that some savants saw it coming, and that others—not savants, but smart—made their money out of it; nevertheless, it may fairly be allowed to have been a surprise to many, including my parents.

World War II was, or should have been, fairly predictable, not only from the Depression and the German inflation, not only from the establishment of Fascism in Italy in 1922 and in Germany in 1933, but from coming attractions shown all over the world from China, Ethiopia and Spain in the middle to late thirties; yet it was not predictable to Neville Chamberlain and his government in

1938, and although it was foreseen by many in our country it was
also unforeseen by many in our country, and the mode of our
entry into it two years after it started was totally a surprise.

The Drug Culture. All during our youth, the most noticeable
sign on any Main Street after dark was, after the movie marquee,
one saying DRUGS. Written in letters of light a foot high, and
stating its import as plainly as possible, this might have been, and
ought to have been, a pillar of fire by night to our soothsayers. But
as far as I am aware, no one ever took it in its prophetic sense.

So also with Korea, Vietnam, the rebellion of the youth (probably not over, only sleeping), Watergate, and the derivative Korea-
gate (which doesn't seem to have the same box-office appeal,
maybe too comic).

Atomic fission and fusion inspired so many prophets of what
had happened that by now it is hard to remember what they said,
save that things was bad all over. We are so delightedly appalled
and thrilled with announcements of The End by our sages that
we—and they—fail to notice how many great things *have* ended,
with cities destroyed, nations going down, torture reinstituted as a
matter of course, great empires collapsing in war or revolution or
both; as if these things were not sufficiently universal to suit our
apocalypticians, who went right on wrongly predicting the next
nonevent.

Some time ago I found two simple rules to cover all this sort of
thing, and I offer them for the edification of whoever will be edi-
fied by them. One was the statement of a general from the Pen-
tagon addressing the Congress: The period of greatest danger, he
told the legislators, lies ahead. One imagines everyone nodding
solemnly. The other is a fine remark attributed to President Eisenhower: Things are more like they are now than they ever were
before.

Armed with those two laws we can't go wrong, can we? But I've
just remembered a third, that a friend quoted in our youth as a
family proverb: The future is in the lap of the gods, and they're
standing up to see what's going to happen.

O yes, and while I was writing this I happened to see a headline
on the sports page: MERCY ENDS LOSING STREAK. I surely
do hope so. And you never know what sort of statement is going to
be prophecy.

FROM
The Oak
in the Acorn
(1987)

Preface

These lectures were given before my class in The Modern Novel at Brandeis University in the winter and spring of 1968. Their being written out in more or less full was owing in the first place to fear. Bennington College had accustomed me for nearly two decades to classes of not more than twenty pupils, often fewer than that, who could be talked with instead of at, and here at Brandeis I now was to face an audience of over a hundred; plainly a situation where works, more than grace, were to be relied on.

My notions of teaching, homemade for the most part, and received by precept and example from such colleagues as Kenneth Burke and Stanley Edgar Hyman, were (and are) simple and but two in number: 1) if you know the work to be taught pretty thoroughly, and only if you do, 2) the Lord may put the words in your mouth; though I would now add a cautionary 3), but there is no guarantee He will.

So every week during that hard and happy semester I reread Proust's book. And every weekend, like the parson of some odd faith whose sabbath falls on Tuesday, I composed my sermon, and so was able to face my century of students with nervous eagerness instead of abysmal anxiety. I was helped in composition by the circumstance that I write in just about the style I talk, and at trailing distance of the same speed; as I told this class and others over many years, if you get the knack of keeping the sentence in your head while varying its possible orders till it sounds about the way it should, you will save a great deal of paper, not to mention some vexation of spirit. I should add that this was my fourth or fifth reading of *Remembrance of Things Past,* not my first.

I first read through this immense novel not at Harvard as might have been expected, but under the less likely auspices of the Royal Canadian Air Force, at Nr. 2 Service Flying Training School in Uplands outside of Ottawa, where I was being taught to fly an aircraft oddly named the Harvard II (the reader of Proust learns to delight in connections, however trivial).

This was in the winter of 1942/1943, a severe one even for that part of the world, when the streetcars froze in their tracks and my (moderately Proustian) moustache froze white with instant age, as if for that famous last Guermantes' party, on the dawn walk down from barracks to flight line. There was little temptation, and less opportunity save for the odd weekend pass, to go into Ottawa for its metropolitan delights; and besides, one was always so tired.

The life of the cadet at Nr. 2 SFTS curiously combined military savagery (lacking only the enemy, who came later) with the coddling environment of a moderately nice nursing home. After a day of flying, waiting, ground school classes, waiting, flying, waiting, one was given supper about five, a little after dark, and in effect put to bed at six, with the freedom simply to be until lights out at nine.

Three pieces of good fortune helped me here. First, four years of college had taught me to read. Second, my beautiful boozy Aunt Ruth had given me Proust's book in English for a graduation present. And third, I was assigned an upper bunk just under one of perhaps only half a dozen ceiling lights. Had I been put in a lower bunk, I couldn't possibly have read for two or three hours a night without ruining the eyesight indispensable for flying, and my life twenty and forty years later on would have been other than it has been, and poorer.

So after a day of the military life and the life of learning to fly which made things much more bearable than the military life alone would have been, I retired most every evening to Combray, Balbec, Paris, to the continuing company of such persons as Swann, Odette,

M. de Charlus, Saint-Loup, and most of all Marcel, to a whole other world built of the enchantments of language, a world which in *this* world would have been, even supposing it ever to have existed outside Proust's imagination and now mine, as inaccessible as the Grail Castle, or Kafka's. Quite apart from its power over my later life, this was a saving experience and a sacred and solitary refuge from a milieu not notable for eloquence or subtlety, a milieu linguistically so barren that one would now and then show up for Church Parade on a Sunday, just to hear a little music, a little speech not limited to (though not always other in intention than) *shit* and *fuck you*. It seemed then, and seems now, a way of redeeming time. But it did not occur to me for a long time, for many years indeed, that there was a curious coincidence in a boy (for I wasn't much more) lying in bed reading a book about a boy lying in bed. . . .

So passed away two decades and more, and I wrote these lectures, which I put away after they were delivered, and thought little more of for the twenty more years till now. I taught a course in Proust again, at Washington University, but because I had got back to my proper and preferred class size of fifteen to twenty pupils, I had no need of formal lectures, for which I substituted my usual style of ramble and bumble.

But I am happy that owing to the kindness of the dedicatee in asking for them the lectures of long ago about long ago are now being published. It marks, for good and ill, the end of forty years at teaching, and the beginning of the forty-first. I hope my readers may have help and delight of what I have done, and be sometimes reminded of the happiness of learning.

The lectures have been left as much as possible in their original form, mostly in complete sentences though not always so, and with their warts unremoved.

Ezra Pound defined a teacher as someone "who must talk for an hour." Fine. But I add my own, in the form of a brief but characteristic conversation with a friend:

"Did I tell you my definition of a teacher?"

"No, I don't believe you did."

"A teacher is a person who never says anything once."

"O yes, I remember now, you told me that last week."

In Conclusion

The instructor who discourages his pupils from beginning the endings of their essays with "And so we see that . . . ," especially when no one has seen anything of the kind, or indeed anything much, had better forbid himself the same way out. But all the same there is something to be said, and he should try to say it.

"What has concluded, that we should conclude something about it?" was attributed by my teacher I. A. Richards to Benjamin Paul Blood, whom I have never seen quoted or cited by anyone else, ever. I did not conclude about Benjamin Paul Blood, however, that he never existed, only that after uttering his one luminous un-illuminating sentence he retired to a hillside with other sages, I. A. Richards among them, and for all I know may be sitting there still. Looking unsuccessfully for that quotation, I was reading again in Richards' *Principles of Literary Criticism* and thought as I had a few times before that if the theory there advanced was not a good theory, nor likely to be furthered by whatever tremendous advances in the neural sciences, the book was nevertheless the book of a wise and gentle and good man; may something the same be worthily said of the rest of us.

I too had said, unconsciously following Benjamin Paul Blood, that teaching "was a process trying to look like a result." As a careful and consequential thinker, or teacher, I was only twelve years or so in producing the corollary: "yes, but isn't everything?" like history, I meant, and life and the world entire.

Freud had kindly enrolled teaching among his three impossible tasks: to rule, to heal, to teach. I continue to think it decent to be up there among the other impossibles. I got into the art, or trade, long before I had heard that or much of anything else, and also by accident and without advanced degrees. For in 1946, by the exemplary generosity of our government in establishing the G.I. Bill and so inducing colleges and universities to find warm bodies to put up against the veterans (twenty of them, and still in combat

boots), I became a teacher, or anyhow a kind of dogsbody responsible for The Bible and Shakespeare and The Modern Novel and
Modern Poetry (with my first book coming out, I was presumed to
know something of that) and whatever else needed doing. It was
the beginning of my education, and I remain grateful for it.
Teacher and pupils were of an age, about twenty-six, and generally either friends or friendly, if only on the ground of deep and
base suspicions of what we had got ourselves into.

This small book has been about teaching as well as about Proust,
as any of you getting this far will have noticed. Many wonderful
things have been said about teaching, and I will reproduce two
while warning you that in spite of my admiration I can't afford
either.

Plato comes first, as he should, and in the Seventh Letter (341
c–d) says of his own teaching, "There is no way of putting it in
words like other studies. Acquaintance with it must come rather
after a long period of instruction in the subject itself and of close
companionship, when, suddenly, like a blaze kindled by a leaping
spark, it is generated in the soul and at once becomes self-sus-
taining."

And Henry Adams, after two and a half millennia, adds: "Even
to him education was a serious thing. A parent gives life, but as
parent, gives no more. A murderer takes life, but his deed stops
there. A teacher affects eternity; he can never tell where his influence stops."

How happy I am not to believe any of all that; but I think
Adams more on the mark when he adds immediately after: "A
teacher is expected to teach truth, and may perhaps flatter himself
that he does so, if he stops with the alphabet and the multiplication
table, as a mother teaches truth by making a child eat with a
spoon; but morals are quite another truth and philosophy is more
complex still." Teachers of Plato's kind may still exist. Some of
Kenneth Burke's students at Bennington witness to the sort of illumination they experienced after months of bewilderment, when,
about the end of April, the simplicity of Kenneth's teaching at last
came through. And I once heard Stanley Edgar Hyman's last class
in Myth & Ritual compared to "the reaping of the ear of corn, in
silence, before the initiates at Eleusis"; though I think to remem-

ber it was Stanley himself who did the comparing, in a tone compounded inextricably of pride and self-mockery.

Altogether, though, it is a deficiency of teaching as an art form that it stops, without ending. And that it is all to do again. The common teacherly complaint that the students keep getting younger amply testifies to it. Mostly we teachers must finish, like surrogates for Henry Adams' mom, by reminding our pupils of the order of the alphabet and advising them to continue using a spoon on the soup. Philip Rieff's splendid book *Fellow Teachers* is a harangue so bracing—damn braces, says Blake, bless relaxes—that I read it every other year; but who could live up to it save its author alone? Our betters constantly admonished us, in our earlier years, that we must teach literature As Literature, not as an adjunct to history, psychology, philosophy, or (beneath all) the sociable sciences; but when I asked in meeting how I was supposed to do this, the subject changed.

There's a Buddhist anecdote I prefer even to Plato. A man in danger of being drowned in a flood grabbed hold of a raft that providentially came by, and was drifted to safety. In gratitude he strapped the raft to his back and carried it for the rest of his life. I couldn't have predicted the moral, Reader, and nor I think could you: So do all they that live by the doctrine.

But my favorite epitome of teaching and learning, one that works, I now see, in substance, form, and context, is one by Proust. It is remarkable how in old age, after following as best we could every fashion in history, psychology, aesthetics, and so on, we return to the moral; or maybe it isn't so remarkable, for M. H. Abrams holds it is the most persistent and recurring idea of the function of letters in life from antiquity through the eighteenth century, and indeed it keeps showing through even the most sorbonnical refinements of the present moment.

The scene before us is this. Marcel, now adolescent, has made the acquaintance of the great painter Elstir, and is walking with him to Elstir's summer place at Balbec, when it suddenly occurs to him that this man of genius, this lonely sage and philosopher with his marvelous talk, master of all wisdom, may have been in his youth the silly and corrupt painter once taken up by the Verdurins and known as M. Biche. Marcel, remarkable as ever for his superb tact and social refinement, asks Elstir about this, and is answered.

Elstir says that yes, he was indeed that man: "and as we were now already almost at his house, a man less distinguished of intelligence and spirit might perhaps have simply and a bit drily bade me farewell and afterward taken care never to see me again. But that was not how Elstir dealt with me." And now there enters another voice for a moment, that of the aged Marcel or that of Marcel Proust himself, another wise and deep master who had also been a silly and corrupt young man, and knew it: "In the style of a true master—and this was perhaps, from the point of view of pure artistry, the only way in which Elstir fell short of the true sense of mastery, for an artist, in order to live altogether in the truth of the life of the spirit, ought to be alone, and not spread himself around, even among disciples—in every situation involving himself or others, he sought to draw out, for the better instruction of the young, the element of truth contained therein. So he now chose, in preference to words that might have avenged his pride, words that might teach me something." The brief sermon follows:

"There is no one, however wise he may be," he said to me, "who has not at some time in his youth said things, or for that matter done things, which he hates to remember and would wish to have erased. But he ought not to regret them absolutely for he could not be certain of having become wise (in the degree to which that can happen at all), unless he had gone through all the foolish or hateful forms that had led up to that last of forms. I know that there are young men, the sons and grandsons of remarkable men, whose tutors have instructed them since their schooldays in nobility of spirit and moral refinement. Perhaps they have nothing in their lives they need wish away, they might publish and sign everything they ever said, but they are pathetic persons, characterless children of pedants, whose wisdom is a nothingness and without issue. Wisdom is not had as a gift, one has to find it for oneself after a journey that no one can take for us nor spare us, for it is a point of view about experience. The lives you admire, the attitudes you find noble, were not arranged by parent or preceptor, they come from beginnings altogether different, being influenced by whatever fashion of wickedness or stupidity reigned around them. They stand for fight and victory. I can see that the portrait of what we were in early days is no longer recognizable to us, and would in any event be unpleasant to look at. But it ought not to be denied, for it is a witness that we have really lived, that out of the common elements of life, the life of the studio and artistic cliques (if we are talking about a painter), we have drawn something that goes beyond them."

It was for the substance that I first admired and loved that passage, and still do. But as I copied it out I saw that in context it represented also the formal situation of teacher and pupil, for while Elstir has been talking Marcel has thought of little else but possibly seeing the little group of girls appear on his horizon, and of his disappointment at their failing to appear.

So there is teacher, handing out the platitudes—this is the order of the alphabet, eat your soup with a spoon—reveling in what a friend of my youth, now many years dead, called in his autobiography "the yes-they-are-Eternal Verities," while Marcel, or Lucretius' Memmius, or anyone in any class, is dreaming of love.

And so we see that.

IV.
NOVEL

Federigo Or, the Power of Love (1954)

For speculation
turns not to itself

Till it hath
travell'd and is
mirror'd there

Where it may see
itself. This is not
strange at all.

—Shakespeare

for my
Mother
and
Father

BOOK ONE

As silent as a
mirror is believed

Realities plunge
in silence by . . .

—Hart Crane

Chapter One

YOUNG men in our country are brought up to believe that they have a destiny, a guiding idea shaped like a star; most of them pass their lives in unawareness that this destiny is gradually becoming the sum of everything that has happened to them, and need not have been represented by a star in the first place, being perhaps more like the false beacon set up by smugglers to direct a vessel toward a convenient disaster. Disaster, *dés*, from, *astre*, a star.

Of those who become aware, most do nothing; they thankfully accept a life which offers the safety of indistinction, and have a grateful but erroneous impression that they might have been summoned to the impossible and were not. A few others of this class, however, take upon themselves the obligation of ruin. It is not a matter of responding to the summons of destiny, though, for the obligation of ruin is like any other human destiny in that it has first to be invented.

Julian Ghent was thirty-six years old, no longer such a young man, before he had more than an obscure and distorted awareness of these simple things. It came to him in a bad moment of revelation while he was standing alone in the midst of a cocktail party. He looked down into his martini, saw the pearl onion at the bottom of the glass, and said aloud in a voice of naïve amazement: "I am exactly like all these others, if you come right down to it."

One of these others, a small round old gentleman, happened to be passing. "Has it just struck you?" he inquired. "Die early and avoid the rush." He winked rapidly twice in a row, and before Julian could say anything squirmed away between the nearly touching behinds of two tall ladies, one of whom was Julian's wife Sylvia.

On another occasion, turning away for a moment from the person with whom he was speaking, he saw down a long, gloomy corridor off the room a woman bending to a mirror flanked by two electric candles which gave a reddish, dull illumination. The woman was perhaps applying lipstick, or searching through a handbag on the table before her, and all he could see was her back. This image, so religiously staged in the frame of the hall, so quiet and remote from the noisy room in which he stood, was like a door opened upon some secret world, like a strange reproach. It captivated Julian's mind, and in an instant he imagined himself in love with this woman, having a hidden understanding with her, an apartment perhaps near Gramercy Park, a separate life in which love alone would form the reason of existence. In the moment of his fancy he had already reached the point at which this relation too must begin to cool, when the woman turned away from the mirror and advanced up the corridor into the room; even before her face entered the light he recognized his wife. This little incident, which he could not altogether forget, began to seem the epitome of his mode of existence at this time, and the place from which might begin either self-examination or the examination of others.

He took to watching his own face earnestly in the mirror while he shaved, and in consequence cut himself badly a number of times. So long as he regarded this face of his as no more than an irregularly contoured knob which periodically presented itself for shaving he had run into no such trouble, but the moment he began *watching* the face it seemed to become another being, whose hostile glance was making his hand nervous. "You are your own worst enemy," he said to it across the impenetrable glass. But beyond this remote index of an attitude—that the sight of his own face wrought him to accidental violence—or that the sight of him worked on this face in the same way—the face told him nothing much. Perhaps he had carried it about in too many sorts of weather, adjusted its expression to meet too many people, for it ever to tell him anything again, a face which would never again be caught, as people used horribly to say, with its bare face hanging out.

"And it is with this that for over thirty years I have deceived the world."

He considered this assertion, and its object, in communion over the bathroom sink one morning. The face which returned his stare was shaven down one side and lathered down the other, like a drawing by Picasso, or like the wartime poster showing one half a cheery English gent in tweeds and one half a German officer with a sinister fraction of mouth. Julian had been for some reason mightily taken with that poster (which advertised by this means the need for security), and dated from his first view of it the habit—compulsion, he would have agreed, not seriously, to calling it—of shaving in exact halves, from which he never departed. Another thing he always remembered while shaving was something which had been told him by a friend, say rather a good acquaintance, named Marius Rathlin, a person of a psychoanalytic or otherwise devious predilection of thought, that "the lather is the white beard which we put on in symbolic expiation of the black beard which under its cover we furtively remove—we take the curse off the shaving away our manhood." Marius had probably been making an elaborate joke—it was hard to tell about Marius's jokes, and shaving was surely not so complicated as all that— but Julian had been unable to rid himself of that statement, which ritually traversed his mind at the midpoint of the morning shave.

The face did not, to an objective view, look able to deceive a world; but that would be, of course, the prime requisite in any face able to deceive a world—just as your true Machiavel begins his career by writing a tract against Machiavelli. Not that Julian's face proclaimed innocence so very extravagantly, but a keen observer might think to detect there a certain want, not of experience, perhaps, but of penetrative experience. A good face, still quite young, with a strong, broad brow (not high) balanced by a strong but not outrageously strong chin. A nose slightly hooked, large, yet of relatively delicate structure, somewhat a beak but not a prow. His eyes were set quite deep, adding shadow to their own darkness; people had estimated them variously (in Julian's presence) as *honest* and as *intense*. He had dark brown hair, which since the war he had got in the habit of having crew-cut, following in this the fashion which made advertising men and interior decorators resemble nice eagles and lost athletes. His mouth was evenly shaped and moderately though not ascetically thin of lip; he had, however, bad teeth which had given him—as they would continue to do—a good deal of trouble not to mention expense, and his by now unconscious wish to conceal this fact made his smile a trifle more grim and sardonic than it generally intended to be. This was the face with which, as he had just observed, he had deceived the world for more than thirty years; whether the round number was merely a convenience or referred to some five or six years during which he had not, or felt that he had not, deceived the world, would be hard to say.

The question now came up as to what he had deceived the world into doing, or not doing. No answer immediately returned from the mirrored face, both halves of which regarded him with an inscrutable cold honesty that committed neither of them to anything.

In one way, Julian acknowledged, the mere being alive was answer enough—alive and of a fortunate fate so far. A dangerous acknowledgment, as many tragic examples tend to show; call no man happy till he dies. But Julian was unprovided by religion with any apotropaic gesture such as crossing oneself or spitting back over the left shoulder or walking widdershins three times around the house; and as a private citizen he had surely no more private place for such a thought than his own bathroom, the inner and anonymous temple, no doubt, of many a modern home, with its altar and its holy ikon (reflecting the deity in the devout) and its facilities for purgation, baptism, regeneration. What he meant, anyhow, or in earnest, incredulous humility thought that he meant, was that he had not been born, in this century, a German or Polish Jew, a Negro in Florida, a faithful Nazi, or any of a number of things which if one at all believed in fate, and he vaguely did, might just as easily have been his fate. He had not even been killed in the war, and that could quite well have happened on a few occasions he knew about, by a difference of a few centimeters, and probably on a number of occasions he knew nothing about.

Moreover, he made his way in the world. That, perhaps, was the answer; that the outward Julian, the one to be observed (by others) as in a mirror, was getting on quite comfortably, making a go of what commonly represented itself as life, lived well, appeared successful, was married to a handsome and charming woman, had a number of good friends; while the other Julian, who did the observing, who looked out of the deep eyes but could never, by any arrangement of mirrors, look into them, did not quite believe in the truth, the solidity, the reality (if that word must enter the discussion) of what was going on. This Julian, the one under the lather, so to say (for so he said, as he had resumed his shaving), the German officer behind the bluff and tweedy gent, felt, had always felt without ever having been able to make out a good reason for it, like a spy, a secret agent. If people knew, they would destroy him, and it was this alone, doubtless, which gave success in the world a slight but dangerous charm, allowing to a dull respectability something of energy and *élan*. Did others, he wondered, feel this in themselves, the secret subversion mining away at everything they stood for? He supposed they must, and at the same time could not see how they could. "I alone, I am the man" (and the arms outstretched waiting for someone to bring the cross).

The razor nicked him bitterly at the Adam's apple, and he watched in the surprise of slight shock the blood begin to spread in the white lather. It was a quite extreme cut, to judge by the rapid flow of blood; Julian bemusedly wondered just where one drew the line between "I cut myself shaving" and lonely farcical death in the bathroom. Nevertheless he continued shaving, and when he had finished entered the shower.

If the bathroom could be compared to a place of worship (undenominational), probably the shower was its confessional. For Julian at any rate it briefly became every morning the warm, liquid medium in which thought was born again out of the night, and the personality assembled once more by means of the missing fragments which somehow the shower returned to him, often enough as occasions of contrition and remorse. If he had been drunk the previous night it would be in the shower that suddenly and without consciously willing it he recalled as by revelation what he had said, what he had done; often, too, dreams of the night before were held in abeyance until with the rushing water they came flooding back, bearing on wave after wave their odd assortments of junk and people he had not seen for years, and dead people. Julian did not "know too much" (as people say nowadays when they mean they know nothing at all) about psychoanalysis, but because Sylvia his wife was under a species of such treatment, at some expense to himself, he maintained even to himself a kind of faith in it as "letting all these things come to the surface" or "not keeping things all locked up in there." Besides, the images from his dreams were frequently attractive or amusing; and as neither friend nor analyst nor even the remarks of his wife had convinced him he was responsible for his dreams along with everything else in the world, these images may have been the only pure pleasure in his life. So he stood in the shower and let them run as they would, with a charming inconsequence.

Julian put his fingers to his throat, which hurt. It was impossible to see, with water flying everywhere, if the bleeding had stopped. Doubtless it had not, for in entering the shower he was behaving exactly, though on what he hoped was a smaller scale, as suicides did who slashed their wrists and held them in warm water.

"Creature of habit," he said to himself. "You might be bleeding to death." But he thought that was probably not the fact.

But did the world know it was being deceived? Did it care? *Mundus vult decipi,* a view formerly held in much esteem among learned and superior people, who had very likely, however, not meant it exactly as Julian did. And did, or would (if it knew) the world wish to be deceived by Julian Ghent, of all people? It seemed doubtful. More likely, they—not a lapse in grammar but meaning of course the bureaucracy and cartel of everyone, anyone and no one, who are (is?) all-powerful in this world, its trinity in fact— most likely that They were watching, had always been watching, just as They (or He, or It) had always been said to watch the fall of every sparrow, the progress of Julian Ghent through time, space, kindergarten to college, the war, the marriage, work and pleasure; watching his growing fondness for scotch instead of bourbon, his aversion from pipes and increasing affection for an after-dinner cigar; watching his dreams, his varying preferences in movies, women, games and subjects of conversation; watching his wishes to be someone else, to begin a new life far away under another name, to be unfaithful to his wife with this one that one and the other one; watching his vanity and remorse, his only slightly ex- panded waistline and few gray hairs, his admiration for the harpsi- chord, discomfort among small children and most secret feeling that he ought to have been a monk or priest.

They, then, watched all these things—and the Lord alone knew what, if anything, They said. But it seemed to Julian certain, just now, that what he regarded as his good fortune, what socially speaking he could regard in no other way (though he might won- der what, exactly, he was going to do with it), consisted not in Their approbation but at the very most in Their noncommittal silence. Quite possibly They were giving him enough rope, with which he would one day, in the most natural way in the world, hang himself. Or, as he had once heard it said, "The future is in the lap of the gods, and they are standing up to see what is going to happen."

Under the hot shower Julian tried to produce the image of his liberty. He found himself unable to achieve any satisfactory representation of his robbing a bank, smoking opium habitually (though he might try it once) or even arguing with a policeman. Nor could he convincingly sign on as a deckhand for a long voyage (or any voyage). A vision of his losing everything he owned at cards produced a better result; he could see quite clearly the gray dawn outside the window, but the faces around the table remained vague. Now he had an affair with Alma Alter, the wife—though nearly divorced at this time—of his best friend Hugo (she had recently, it seemed, had a nervous breakdown; which might mean, for all Julian knew, that she had gone insane), and all at once the two of them were found dead in a hotel room as the result of a suicide pact. Even this had a reality of only a rather remote sort; mostly Julian imagined Hugo and Sylvia talking the matter over in quiet, earnest tones, so quiet in fact that he could hear nothing they said. He would have liked a greater display of feeling after his death by his own hand, but could not bring them to it. So much for doing as one pleased.

He turned the shower abruptly off, for to have finished with cold water would have seemed sacrilegious—that absurd dancing about—and at the same time too transparently moral for what was after all, as the world goes, his rigorously moral nature. The bathroom was hot and steamy, the mirror clouded over so that he could no longer see himself in it. No religion, probably, could have done more for a man, but Julian must needs wipe at least one spot clear, in which he perceived that the wound at his throat continued to bleed, not so much as at first but quite steadily. In spite of remedies—the styptic pencil hurt a good deal and did not quite stop the flow, the wound must have been deeper than that; and the patch of toilet paper he applied curiosity forced him to remove too soon—a little blood fell on the collar of his clean white shirt, which he therefore changed. Then, when he had dressed and readied himself for the world, pulling his black knit tie to a mean, hard knot like a midget fist at his throat, he joined his wife in the dining room for coffee.

2

Julian himself seldom had more than toast and coffee for breakfast, and he experienced this morning the usual slight twinge of indignation on seeing that his wife had already finished a plate of what seemed to have been fried eggs; moreover, in the corner next the kitchen door the two dogs were noisily eating large portions of horse meat, the mere idea of which nearly turned his stomach.

These two dogs, handsome afghan hounds of a *café au lait* color, had been given to Julian and Sylvia for a wedding present by Hugo Alter; there had always seemed something ironical in the gift, but as Hugo was not an ironical sort of person Julian concluded that these hounds merely typified his wealthy friend's propensity for doing people favors which were not only imposing but also something of an imposition. Neither Julian nor Sylvia had ever cared much for dogs, but in the first enthusiasm over these two, whom they had incautiously named Troilus and Cressida, they seemed to have made a commitment which they could not go back on even after, as a matter of domestic policy, Troilus and Cressida had been properly gelded and spayed. So the dogs remained, an emblem of something in their master and mistress which was at once aristocratic and faintly ridiculous, to eat quantities of horse meat, to be taken for walks twice daily, to spend the nights locked in the hall bathroom with the light on (they whimpered in the dark) and to form a subject of reproach among acquaintances who said, "It is wrong to keep such large dogs in an apartment in the city." Julian thought it probably was wrong, yet the elegance of these animals satisfied his pride enough so that he submitted to the inconvenience of their keep as to a just penance; while Sylvia, since she had undertaken psychoanalysis, believed that they were a "surrogate" for having children.

Julian kissed his wife, who smiled a bit absently and reminded him that Hugo's party would be that same evening; then he sat down and conspicuously straightened the newspaper which she had slightly disarranged. The stream of communication between them, even at its best not a torrent, dried up at breakfast to the thinnest trickle of news items and the arrangement of schedules and occasional ill-humored remarks. They did not quarrel, being reasonable people, but there would be usually, in the morning, an air of ill-temper and sullen constraint somewhere in the space between them. At the same time, life had to go on, which it did by means of observations like these following.

"You've cut yourself shaving again."

"Yes. I was thinking about something else."

"Shall I get some Mercurochrome?"

"No, I don't think so, thanks."

Sylvia, who would have felt better for being allowed to put Mercurochrome, or even iodine, in her husband's wound, poured him his coffee. As she leaned over him to do so, she kissed him very lightly on the forehead and he looked up at her with an ambiguous grimace rapidly turning into a small smile.

"Do you have a headache?" she asked, as she sat down.

"No, I don't, thank you," he replied (it was his habit to add "thank you" at this time of morning to any phrase of hers which had a rising inflection). "I just haven't quite woke up." He spread the newspaper out over his toast and coffee, and scanned in a cursory way, as if making sure of the world's continued existence, its columns of orderly violence: the ships gone down, the gangsters shot to death, the young men who jumped from high buildings.

"I wish you would not do that," Sylvia said. "Rest the newspaper on the toast, I mean. It gets in the butter."

"There is nothing of any use on the last page," Julian answered, but nevertheless folded the paper to one side.

"You don't feel very well, do you, poor thing?" she continued. "I thought you were drinking a great deal, even for you."

"You believe I drink too much?" Julian inquired, in a tone that was meant to be quietly dangerous but in fact sounded merely petulant. Still, Sylvia withdrew before even this approach to a direct challenge.

"It's entirely your business," she said. "I'm sorry you don't feel better."

"I feel perfectly all right, I guess," he said, torn between resentment and the wish to be pitied. The newspaper, which he continued to scan, served to generalize his thoughts just now, so that he was wondering in how many apartments through the city this same scene, or one recognizably like it, was being enacted. Is this the only way in which it is possible for human beings to live? he asked himself silently, and rattled the newspaper in slight, involuntary emphasis, whereat the dogs turned to look at him as though about to ask intelligent questions, then went back to their horse meat.

"The mail should be in by now," Sylvia offered. "I'll go down and get it."

Julian was just about to say that he did not wish his wife to walk through the front hall of the building in her bathrobe or housecoat or whatever, but he recollected just in time that a most important letter would almost certainly arrive in this mail. So he said nothing, and in this way was enabled to enjoy the mail and his resentment both at the same time.

As it was the first of May, there appeared a large stack of bills, and these he leafed through quickly without opening any of them, only permitting himself an ironical smile as he passed the one from his wife's psychiatrist, Dr. Mirabeau. When he came to the letter he had expected, he opened it decisively, after having noted with approval the cheap quality of the envelope—"such as might have been procured from any one of a hundred stores"—and the indistinctive typing of the name and address. Inside, on paper of the same sort as the envelope, was a message composed of letters snipped from magazines and pasted together. Julian read:

> SIR—
> A word to the wise. Your wife, sir,
> is too much alone. And not always alone.
>   Your friend,
>   FEDERIGO

The calm with which Julian received this sinister communication was owing entirely to his having composed it himself, in his office, the afternoon before, and posted it on his way home. The full range of his intentions in doing so was obscure even to himself, and in fact the entire idea, which yesterday had aroused him to enthusiastic assent, this morning appeared very dubious, the product of a mind not at all points touching reality.

Briefly said, what he wanted to do was to give the nature of things, with which he was extremely bored, a slight push. The plan, of which his imagination had not at all taken in the cruelty, was to allow his wife to see this letter as if by accident, the effect being the same as if he should have said to her, as he could not have done nor would in any case have dared to do, "You see, if in future I should be unfaithful to you, there is an excellent reason for it— turnabout is fair play," or at least, "You can see that I was honestly misled by this dreadful letter" or "those dreadful letters" (for there were to be more).

Julian's problem, as he himself suspected, was that morally speaking he was a coward. It is the essence of cowardice not simply to be afraid, but to shilly-shally and willy-nilly, not to be wholehearted in either desires or aversions; cowardice, which thus relates to irony, urbanity, sophistication and a whole host of civil virtues, is in love with the might-have-been, the between-state, the long, long chance of having everything both ways, or twenty ways at once. We might go on: cowardice is reasonable, and temporizes; cowardice is long-suffering; cowardice is perhaps everything the apostle claimed for charity, except charitable.

To a more courageous man, several courses of action would have been open. He might simply have gone ahead with an infidelity, trusting to discretion, luck and the outlay of considerable sums of money that his wife would never get to know, or would not get to know for a long time. He might have announced to his wife that he no longer loved her and would not any longer live with her (he might have finished by saying dramatically but not altogether wildly that marriage under these circumstances was a sin) and they would have arranged for a divorce or a separation according to her response—a certain quantity of stark emotion, of ugliness, would have to be faced up to. Or he might simply have said to himself: Very well, this is what marriage is, love is replaced after a number of years by boredom. We have made our bed, let us continue to lie in it, like the rest of the world—which we did not make. And he would take up tennis or golf instead, or do chess problems in the evening.

There is one more solution, which is found, probably, by very few: to discover again in one's wife that essential strangeness which was the beginning of love, and which is never lost but only gets forgotten, not replaced but overlaid by a number of dangerously familiar details. But, for this, courage, though still necessary, is probably not sufficient by itself; a certain ingeniousness, perhaps a certain perversity, would also be required.

Julian, regrettably, did not possess the requisite clarity of soul for any of these actions, some of which, while quite possibly vicious in the eyes of the public morality, are nevertheless erotically, or *charitably,* virtuous. It must be allowed, though, that he felt in himself this want of purpose, and characteristically had become more devious than ever in seeking to provoke some direct action. The anonymous or pseudonymous letter was the improbable yet perfectly exact resultant of a number of opposed forces within his soul, which was full of that mysterious, romantic fever which does not die, as it is said to do, after adolescence (which does not really die either), but merely sleeps until it is once again aroused by boredom.

The most dangerous thing about his state of mind, in the first place, was that his present ambitions to infidelity began in a negative and entirely theoretical manner, not with the image of a particular other woman whom he desired, but with the idea only of being unfaithful. This idea, which is inductively the concomitant of marriage after perhaps the first year, had fastened on Julian's thoughts with ferocity and persistence; as is usual with abstract notions, it had spread throughout his thought like a contagion, affecting everything; just as, according to the philosophers, jaundice makes us see everything in the world as a mere function of jaundice, so the idea of infidelity cast its somewhat lurid light over the entire contents of Julian's mind, and possibly by now its meaning had no longer very much to do with sex *per se,* if sex can ever be said to be *per se.*

A situation of trust had always obtained, and so far as he was aware still obtained, up to this very moment—he was thoughtfully replacing the letter in its envelope—between Julian and Sylvia. They had trusted each other first out of love and later out of indifference and forgetfulness. Of course, there had been theoretical discussions between them on this subject. Flirtations at parties, a quite common thing in the class with which they were associated, were perfectly all right, they could agree on that—beyond, if not beneath, notice. But there would not, there must not, be anything *serious.*

"If you ever did," Sylvia once said in the course of such a theoretical conversation, "I should kill her. And perhaps you as well," she added, while Julian sat there wondering: With what? Sometimes, alone, he would take this remark out and examine it for minutes at a time. Detached from the earnest, rather humorous tone of her voice, it seemed melodramatic and improbable; Julian could not believe she really felt that way. More likely, he thought, she employed this fiction as a means of supporting the emptiness she too must feel—for after all, the world was full of people being compelled to accept it, however grudgingly, on stingy terms, and doing, or refraining from doing, this thing that thing and the other thing for no better reason than that it was or was not done; how should they not dramatize as strikingly as they could this sorry condition?

But this situation of trust existed, and to break that trust, of course, was more attractive by far to Julian than any merely sexual motive: to do evil, as though just to show that one could. For it was evil, that was his opinion, his final opinion against all those who would have said deprecatingly that it was merely natural. It was evil, darkness, corruption, Julian believed that about the sexual act itself, he shared to this negative and repressive extent in religion, that although pleasure was to be derived from sleeping with a woman, that pleasure was itself bitter, angry, committed beyond its means—as marriage itself would witness. In this he resembled those early Christians, some of them martyrs and saints, who engaged in all manner of whoredom and beastliness for the reason that after the initial unchastity of marriage nothing else remained to matter.

The major motive behind all this was nothing more ardent or in itself erotic than curiosity, a trait which killed the cat, invented arts and sciences, and belonged in the first instance to woman.

Out of this complex of circumstances came the inspiration for the letter, which satisfied a deep moral necessity for Julian by that device which psychologists, like the alchemists of old, call *projection*. It afforded, or seemed to, pretext and justification; above all, it had the indispensable appearance of coming from outside, of being a message from the world and thus of making an objective situation which was, however, perfectly fictional.

The composition had cost him a couple of hours and a good

deal of trouble, brief as it was. How were these things done? The form of the phrases—that second "sir" in particular, and the sneering repetition of "alone"—now seemed to Julian transparently theatrical, and in such a way, moreover, that anyone who knew him at all well must immediately also know him for the author. Imaginative persons suffer in committing a crime for just this reason, that they are compelled to witness their action from inside and outside simultaneously, and cannot understand how others can possibly overlook their practically candid and exposed guilt. So it is, perhaps, that imaginative persons can commit their crimes only under some special, sustaining inspiration which has the appearance of entering the head altogether from the outside, from the world, with no inward complicity at all. The letter, for Julian, had been such an inspiration, which came to him with an immediacy, wholeness and unexpectedness that prevented him altogether from being horrified at the time. Now, at breakfast, he was in truth a little horrified.

As for the name Federigo: that was a special inspiration, too. Twice during the past few months Julian had been mistaken for a person called Federigo; once on the street, once at a party. This in itself would not have been so striking, such mistakes are made all the time. But the strange thing was that on each occasion the other person had clearly refused to believe Julian's disclaimer. The haggard young man on the street had sneered disagreeably, saying as he turned away, "I don't want to force myself on you, you know. There's no need to *lie*." And the quite charming girl at the party had smiled at him archly as she said, "I won't tell anyone if you don't want me to." On this occasion Julian was quick enough to ask, before she could get away, "Who is this Federigo?"

"Don't be ridiculous," the girl had replied, "I've promised not to tell anyone."

From these circumstances Julian had gathered that there must be an extraordinary resemblance between this Federigo and himself; also that Federigo was a man accustomed to going about incognito—in this day and age!—and in a position to make his acquaintances respect the fact. This last seemed to Julian almighty impressive, and he began privately to call himself Federigo. The name had a charming, operatic flavor which fitted very well with the secret identity Julian often wished he could have. So, when he was pasting together the anonymous letter—which he did very clumsily—and about to subscribe it simply and tritely "A Friend," he all at once remembered Federigo, which seemed to him at the time to be the final deep and witty touch to the whole affair. Right now, as I say, he was a little horrified, not least because he was wondering if possibly he had not used this pet name for himself thoughtlessly in Sylvia's hearing, or perhaps even said it in his sleep. In that case . . .

"What has happened?" she asked. "You are looking very strange."

Julian realized he had been holding the envelope rigidly before him for perhaps a minute. This would have fitted in splendidly with his plan, which made it necessary to arouse by some such means his wife's attention, for ordinarily, so far as he knew, she did not read his mail; but now he hesitated, for a number of reasons, to go through with the scheme. Several disagreeable possibilities, unforeseen in his first infatuation with the idea, rapidly presented themselves. Suppose she confronted him boldly with the fact of her innocence and demanded to know what he was going to do? Suppose she said to him (as Julian thought she very well might): You did this yourself? It also occurred to him that, according to a certain still widely accepted scheme of morality, a husband, on receipt of such a message, would be expected to kill his wife. Would Sylvia expect that? And what would she do? Kill him instead?

"It is nothing," he said, absently achieving just the right tone, the tone in which Othello replies to Iago's "I see, this hath a little dash'd your spirits." Characteristically, his suppositions at this moment did not at all include one which ought perhaps to have come first: that husbands who provoke reality by asking questions about the honesty of their wives may receive replies which they do not altogether like.

If I don't go on now I have got this far, he thought, I shall never get so far again. Also I will always have to reproach myself for losing my nerve.

He placed the letter on the table and covered it with the newspaper which Sylvia would pick up as soon as he had gone.

"I'll just walk the dogs now," he said, as he did every morning. "Back in ten-fifteen minutes." She responded vaguely and habitually, by a slight lift of her chin, to his kiss.

Viewed from the outside, there was something handsome and

prosperous about the spectacle of Julian, an upright man in the prime of life, walking two such aristocratic, long-nosed animals, each attached to him by an elegant silver chain and choker with very small links. Troilus and Cressida were admired, and their owner slightly envied, by the few persons whose business led them to that block so early in the morning: a street cleaner, two doormen on Fifth Avenue, a number of people waiting for the bus on Madison. It was a fine, fresh day, which the sight of what seemed to be a member of the leisured classes, of American aristocracy, intensified in the eyes even of such as felt the slight envy. Even if it was May Day, they had no wish to destroy Julian or his world or the society which had produced him, though they would rather have liked to be him, that is, to replace him in his life with that superior version of himself which they could so easily have supplied simply by taking thought. No doubt one or two concluded their brief reflections on this subject with the idea that he, poor fellow, probably had troubles of his own; for, as everyone knows, money is not happiness.

Julian as a matter of fact was not a person of leisure, and as these things go he did not even have a great deal of money. But appearances impress. They impressed even him, as he coyly passed his image in shop windows on Madison Avenue, to the extent that for a few moments he forgot the situation into which he had busily projected himself.

When he returned to the apartment with the dogs, however, he found his wife reading the paper. The letter remained more or less where it had been; perhaps accidentally moved when she had picked up the paper? Perhaps not moved at all? Julian was unable to decide, and he stood thoughtfully at the edge of the table for a long moment.

"Is there something you wanted to say?" Sylvia asked in a neutral voice. Julian hesitated over the interpretations it was possible to put on this question.

"I thought so," he said at last, being cryptic in his turn, "but I guess I've forgotten what it was. Anyhow, I've got to be off to work now."

He walked casually past the table and picked up the letter. In the involutions of his plot he was already uncertain whether he wanted this action to be noticed or missed by his wife. Such are the problems for the amateur in the realms of darkness.

3

Sylvia, who had not failed to notice her husband's preoccupation, opened the letter as soon as he left the house with the dogs. Her first response was a kind of sinking horror such as she might have experienced had a rather expensive shop sent her a bill with the decimal point accidentally moved one place to the right. She very nearly opened the window in order to shout down to her husband on the street below; she was prevented from doing so not only because it would have been ridiculous, but also because she could not think what she would shout.

"It is some sort of joke," she said. "Someone is being funny." She poured herself more coffee, sat down at Julian's place, and began to inspect the letter more closely.

> SIR—
> A word to the wise. Your wife, sir,
> is too much alone. And not always alone.
> Your friend,
> FEDERIGO

For a few moments the impulse to play detective altogether overcame her more serious considerations, sentiments of indignation and bewilderment. A passion for mystery stories enabled her to go rapidly through all those characteristics of an anonymous letter which tell the detective nothing: she saw quite well that the message was composed of letters cut from magazines and newspapers and pasted together; that the address was typed; that the paper and envelope were "such as might have been procured from any one of a hundred stores"—beyond this she saw nothing of any use.

Then she became angry. The sneering theatricality of "a word to the wise"—she saw it as accompanied by a wink—and that nasty foreign name Federigo—by association of sounds she saw a small man in a green *fedora*, he wore dark glasses and a little mustache, Sylvia wanted to squash his face right in—made her tremble with anger, and she was brought up short before her own absolute helplessness. This was the most frightening thing about the anonymous letter; it came from the wide outside, out of the everywhere into the here. Who was Federigo? and where? and what was he talking about? But perhaps, and most likely, in fact, there was no such person, the name came out of the plays of Shakespeare, or the telephone book, or the racing page of the *Daily Mirror.* Not only was she helpless in her rage; even worse, her curiosity was balked in its very beginning. You cannot reason with the anonymous letter, you cannot ask it to elucidate obscure points, fill in details, be less elliptical. Sylvia could nearly have danced around the room crying "Come out and fight." But there was no way of convincing the anonymous letter of her entire innocence. Moreover, no one is ever entirely innocent, and, as political trials in various countries show quite clearly, particular and present accusations have a way of picking up reinforcements from remote, all but forgotten sins; while broad and general accusations, like this of the letter, are, for sensitive persons, blank checks on a vast accumulated capital of guilt.

"Could it mean my having lunch now and then with Marius?" she wondered. "But, of course, there is nothing in the least wrong with that. Why shouldn't I have lunch with him? Marius, it's true, would be quite pleased to make love to me, but that is all foolishness and I have never encouraged it. Beyond a joke, that is. And besides, who could know about that? I even tell Julian about it, most of the time—'I had lunch with Marius today'—and he says 'how nice.' No, there's nothing there."

She thought for a few minutes more.

"It is Hugo," she decided. "It is Hugo, who wants to make trouble. But why?"

Sylvia, who was several years younger than her husband, had met him early in the war, and by the time he went overseas they had a quite definite understanding, known to their families and friends though not published as an engagement. This understanding, however, had not prevented Sylvia from being seduced and got with child by another person, though the child had been aborted with the knowledge and pained co-operation of her parents, who had been most kind. Sylvia had very nearly died at that time, and there was some doubt if she could again bear children.

Without her confession of this incident it is doubtful whether Julian, whose knowledge of the world had considerably expanded though it had not deepened during the war years, would ever have married her. But that episode gave her, in his eyes, exactly the flavor of sad experience, of tragic possibility, which he would most have wanted to be affected by; she had had, in those days, a dark unhappiness, which had since given way to a kind of severe complacency (she was no longer quite so thin, either). She wore her premarital experience like an unobtrusive talisman, ready to be drawn forth and prayed to in emergencies, believed that the object of marriage (already achieved) was a quiet happiness, occasionally wondered whether or not she was as happy as she believed proper, and used her earlier life as a living witness that happiness consisted in their being always honest with one another. "If I had not told you, I don't think I could have lived," she had sometimes said to him. What she had never told him—and it seems characteristic of this kind of honesty in action—was that her seducer (if that is not too strong a word; but in her confession the whole affair had become more nearly like a rape) had been Julian's good friend and roommate at college, Hugo Alter, who was still, or again, a member of their circle of acquaintance. Sylvia had said, in response to Julian's somewhat hesitant probing of this point, that the man, a stranger and an officer in the Navy, had died in the war: "In the Coral Sea," she said, actually filling her mind at that moment with the pathos of this translucent coral image. In saying this she was moved, perhaps, by a real delicacy of feeling: to have given her fiancé that knowledge in its entirety would have been to give him a difficult and highly ambiguous responsibility; and her having to bear that one piece of information herself, alone, in a lifetime of silence, also appealed to her morally passionate nature as a punishment hardly short of the tragic. Thus she was enabled to entertain privately the most romantic notion of her life without ever running the risk of *having something happen.* Though there was one point about which she remained in doubt; she had never exactly spoken to Hugo Alter about his anonymity to her husband. She had instead, at an early meeting after the war and after her marriage, given him a long, flashing and intently imperious look which she hoped and believed had clearly enjoined silence (a silence which he would have no motive for breaking, would he?) and a silence, moreover, unmarred by any giggle or smirk of recognition. She had been, so far as concerned her own mind, beyond those rapids and on a calm water; at least that was what she firmly maintained in her one glance to that man, her first lover and, so far as first things really come first, her only one.

And now Hugo had broken the silence? Had he? Only one other person knew the whole story of this incident (to which Sylvia now began to give more importance than it really need have had after so many years), and that was Dr. Mirabeau; it had been one of the first things she had told him, last year, when Hugo's wife Alma had persuaded her to undertake psychiatric treatment. Sylvia, however, firmly rejected the notion that Dr. Mirabeau could be Federigo; though she had heard terrible things about crooked alienists, she did not believe them about this very reputable and good man, to whom she had said so much. That was the awful thing about the anonymous letter, it led one to suspicion everywhere.

But no, it must be, it had to be, Hugo Alter. Though she could not in the least think of a good reason why. Yet, even going back as far as the first boy who had kissed her, as a crush on another girl in her freshman year at college, she could think of no other possible occasion for the anonymous letter.

By the time her husband came back with the dogs, Sylvia was full of honest pity for him, though she also felt indignant at the idea of his taking that contemptible letter with any seriousness whatever. She decided against speaking of it to him at this time, in the first place possibly because she never read mail addressed to him. She would first speak to Hugo; or she would tell Mirabeau first, and see what he said. Meanwhile, both her pity for Julian and her indignation against him suggested to her that it would do him good, poor thing, to suffer for a bit. One good thing about this wretched letter, it would make him keenly interested in herself, with an interest she had felt the want of for some time.

It characteristically never crossed her mind that Julian might feel impelled to kill her on the basis of the anonymous letter; she never even reached the point of having to say to herself that "people don't behave that way any more." The amusing possibility of Julian's shooting her in consequence of an honest misapprehension could not have occurred to her, and had it been mentioned by someone else Sylvia would have said: "Shooting me? With what?"

So that on Julian's return the letter was back on the table, where the paper had been before she picked it up. She saw him retrieve the letter and slip it into his pocket in a quick, gliding motion as he walked past the place; and she wondered whether she had been supposed to notice or not to notice this action.

Chapter Two

JULIAN arrived at the office a few minutes before nine, but his employer Mr. Ballou was already closeted with a client; he had left with Miss Duddon, at the switchboard, a note of instruction: Julian was to see, at ten o'clock, a Dr. Thybold, and at twelve-thirty to lunch with a Mr. Archer More at a club called the Round Table. The names of both clients were new to Julian, though he believed he had heard something somewhere about an Archer More, and Mr. Ballou had appended to his message a couple of curt and cryptic orders:

> Dr. Thybold. Treat this little bore politely, but with contempt; He must *want* us. Small change, may come to something. Don't repeat DON'T let him know about Olympics.

Olympics was the brand name of a new, king-size cigarette, an account which Mr. Ballou handled personally, and which he was pushing toward the big money on the basis of a complex imagery associating the product not merely with good health but with athletic vigor as well; Julian wondered why this was not to be mentioned to Dr. Thybold, and decided that the doctor might be the purveyor of some small (not king-size) brand of medicated cigarette.

> Mr. Archer More. This will sound a silliness, but treat it seriously. Always treat this much money seriously. This is a big chance for you.

With this information, and nearly an hour in which to think it over—but there was very little to think about—Julian went into his office and smoked several cigarettes.

342

The entire suite of offices was very small—he could even hear Mr. Ballou's voice next door when it rose to some sort of climax, though he could not make the words out—but extremely ornate, with gold wallpaper, indirect lighting, and thick, fitted carpets throughout. "I am being impressive," Mr. Ballou had said when they moved in two years before. "My office has always been under my hat, but now I am being impressive." Indeed, up to that point he had trained Julian, whom he treated not as an employee but as an apprentice and future partner, to do business largely in restaurants and bars, to sketch out schemes rapidly and persuasively on the backs of menus, and above all to give the impression of a large and complicated organization full of underlings, busily working away in an office building elsewhere. Such an organization had never existed except in the imagination of clients, the only place, according to Mr. Ballou, where such an organization had any right or reason to exist. "I pray you to remember," Mr. Ballou said to Julian on taking him in, "that our interest here is only in money. It is as simple as that, and if you remember it you will not go far wrong." He added, "That you are here at all comes from my affection for your parents, which will not, however, serve to keep you here unless you give promise of being, in office hours at least, as single-mindedly avaricious, and as efficiently so, as your humble servant." Mr. Ballou frequently and without visible irony referred to himself as "your humble servant." He was a tall, fat, powerfully built man of over fifty, with curly gray hair and features which, in moments of anger or other emotion, emerged decisively and arrogantly from their recesses of folded fat. Particularly since the death of his parents Julian had admired Mr. Ballou and intensely respected him as a father; even better, liked him as he had never been able to like his father. What he cared for most in the older man was perhaps what he himself was most deficient in, a capacity for the forthright, even blatant, expression of feeling, particularly on themes concerning which Julian's own upbringing would have taught him to rejoice or sorrow in silence. Money was one of these themes. Woman was the other. Julian had seen Mr. Ballou kiss a large check, weep over it, then send him out to the bank to have it magically transformed into one-dollar bills which made a stack large enough to cover his bulk to the shoulders as, still weeping, he sat on the floor in his office. And Miss Duddon, whether or not she knew it, was but one in a long sequence of switchboard operators, all of whom, on being interviewed, had been turned around for Julian's inspection by Mr. Ballou, who would pinch their cheeks and slap their behinds, saying: "Look at this, isn't it marvelous? It's marvelous!" Girls who did not take kindly to this treatment, which was for Mr. Ballou not a sexual approach but an innocent and honest admiration for the flesh, were not hired. Julian's sensitive soul had at first been embarrassed and irritated by this behavior; he was incapable at that time of seeing anything innocent about it. Later he came to marvel at, and envy, his employer's ease at this kind of behavior, seeing to his surprise how friendly and pleasant those rather stiff, nervous and absurdly dignified girls became at being treated so. At the same time he became convinced that all this depended, for Mr. Ballou, on a life of the utmost personal probity in such matters; in his naïveté, however, he decided it must be because the old gentleman was "past the age for such things."

There was a peculiar, cryptic joke which Mr. Ballou had taken to using on Miss Duddon almost every morning. He would come in, kiss her on top of her lovely blonde head, and make some such remark as: "The virgin and the sack of gold! The virgin even without the sack of gold! How do you do it, day after day?" to which he would somberly add, "It must be the police force."

The explanation of this performance, which Julian got at the request of Miss Duddon, who was embarrassed to ask for the meaning of a joke at which she had so often laughed, turned out to be proverbial: in the Empire of Genghis Khan, Mr. Ballou explained, it was said that a virgin carrying a sack of gold could walk in perfect safety across the whole of Asia.

"Imagine it," he said, spreading his hands to show this vast extent, "across all Asia. In New York she's lucky to get once around the block."

For no fathomable reason the story struck Julian as an epitome of life in Mr. Ballou's office, where he was on the whole very happy. He and Miss Duddon spoke about their employer behind his back but affectionately as Genghis Khan.

Julian had also, on several occasions, seen Mr. Ballou in his anger, and found it a most disturbing sight. He had not known the literal equivalent for the expression "to dance with rage." The walls shook, pictures came down.

Mr. Ballou had lately several times spoken to Julian about the latter's carrying on the firm's operations "after your humble servant passes on." "Passes on" was the only euphemism Julian had ever heard Mr. Ballou use for any fact of life, and he would not have been surprised to see tears of prospective mourning flow from those shrewd, friendly eyes, which however on such occasions merely glittered at him gaily. He realized, however, that Genghis Khan considered him as a son, and he was touched by it.

As to what were the firm's operations, or more particularly his own part in them—Julian's job at this time was a strange one. He had been removed by Mr. Ballou from commercial advertising, where for some years he had dutifully helped to sell whiskey, cigarettes, brassieres, girdles ("foundation garments," as he had learned to call them), soap flakes, perfumes and automobiles, and he had been put to work on a new, experimental project with the general title (for window-dressing) of Private Policy Advertisement, or, as he personally thought of it, in terms picked up during the war, The Line Shooting and Chewing Out Division.

A new development had been creeping up on the advertising world for many years; in simplest form, the idea behind it amounted to this, that in order to advertise you did not need to make anything or distribute anything of a tangible nature that you wished to place before the buying public, you did not need to be, even, in business; it was enough that you had an opinion about something, were unable by talent to publish this opinion in the usual manner, and had money to pay for having your opinion in print. A vast, new market opened up by means of this simple device (or better mousetrap), which, far from having been the original inspiration of American know-how and get-ahead, spread from Mexico, where it had for some time been extremely popular as a means of airing grievances, telling the world what was wrong with the world, putting pressure on government, et cetera. In this country the same practice had been followed in a relatively primitive way at election time, when a citizen or body of citizens might buy space to plug their candidate of choice; but it was now seen that more could be made of the idea than that, much more; it had, without doubt, a great future, and could advertise itself as democracy in action, on the ground of its demonstration that in our country one opinion was just as good as another, if not better.

As a matter of fact, the experiment was working splendidly; only Julian sometimes felt as though he had entered a new, insane world, which was, however, extremely interesting. People came to him out of nowhere, bringing thousands of dollars, because they personally did not like communism, creeping socialism or low necklines; they took advertisements protesting against foreign policy, domestic policy, labor, business, the American Medical Association; or they attacked, within the limits of the laws of libel, such persons as columnists, authors, labor leaders and famous actresses. The idea was beautifully taking hold, it required of the advertiser not one blessed thing more than money and an opinion (if he had no opinion he could buy one of those, too); he did not have to manufacture anything, distribute anything, or even be able to write—Julian's department would produce whatever he needed, in appropriate tones of wrath, plain common sense, honest indignation, pathos, even humor when necessary, on subjects ranging from birth-control to "the ever-increasing death toll on our highways" (Julian had only a few months before brought forth a charming tribute to the one-millionth victim of the automobile, a kind of valedictory and congratulation speech).

The thing in all this which struck Julian as particularly insane was its open and evident altruism. The people who came to him on these errands came straight from the world of profit and loss, of hard cash, the open market and an eye on the main chance—usually the reason for their having this money to (as he thought) *throw away* was that they had bitterly gouged it out of the world in the fierce competition of the market place; yet when they appeared in his office he saw something else about these hard, strong people, not only their narrowness of mind, bitter animus and surpassing belief in their own absolute and utter righteousness, but also and at the same time—without, it seemed, any contradiction *they* were aware of—a kind of not unattractive shyness. In some way, he dimly perceived, they had something to sell, and a prospective customer for it, too; they were purveying their own good opinion of themselves, and trying (by the only means they knew, advertising) to make themselves buy it; there was perhaps something a little sinister in the circuitous objectivity with which they went about this thankless and no doubt frequently impossible task.

"Dr. Thybold," said Julian cordially, rising to his feet as the doctor was introduced by Miss Duddon.

"Thybold," said the doctor. "As in 'thy,' not as in 'thigh.' Please."

"Dr. Thybold," Julian corrected himself. The two men shook hands and sat down. The doctor put a briefcase on the table between them. Julian waited.

"Nice place you have here," the doctor began. "Kind of small, though." Julian remembered Mr. Ballou's instruction.

"We find it suitable," he said.

"I thought there was more to your kind of work," Dr. Thybold continued. "Writers, artists, models, photographers . . ." He looked around as though possibly these services might be concealed in the walls.

"That is all done elsewhere," Julian said with a spacious wave of the hand.

"Yes, of course," said the doctor doubtfully. Decisively hitching forward his chair he began to come to the point.

"I represent," he said, "I represent a small, independent—you're rather young, aren't you, for so responsible a position?"

"No," Julian said, "as a matter of fact, I'm not."

"Oh," said Dr. Thybold, visibly embarrassed. "No offense."

"None at all." The doctor, a thin, middle-aged man of somewhat gray complexion, appeared to Julian to be extremely nervous; in an ecstasy of unexpressed self-importance his hands kept playing with the latch and handle of the briefcase which lay before him.

"My associates and I," he began again, "that is, we have decided to place in your hands—" he broke off once more. "You must realize," he said, "that I am a scientist, I am not used to—the noise and bustle of the business world."

"It is not noisy here," Julian said.

"No, it is not, is it?"

"And no one is bustling." Julian was becoming bored with this performance, however, and thinking to put the doctor at his ease extended a pack of cigarettes.

"Smoke?"

Dr. Thybold drew himself up and glared indignantly at Julian.

"No!" he cried, with a forbidding gesture of the hand, and

added, as Julian began to take a cigarette himself, "young man, if you knew what you were doing, you would throw that wicked, wicked package out the window."

"The window?" Julian stopped in the act of striking a match; the unlighted cigarette dangled from his mouth.

"If I could show you," Dr. Thybold went on, "if you could only see a photograph, a color photograph, of the tissues of your lungs at this moment, you would throw that cigarette away and swear off as of now." Whatever difficulty the doctor had experienced in getting started was at an end. He quickly unlocked the briefcase and rummaged in it. "Wait," he cried, "perhaps I have a photograph with me, yes—no, that's not it—here it is!" He pushed across the desk a large, glossy print showing a circular area generally red and yellow in color, spotted heavily with black.

"That is the portrait," he said impressively, "of what you can expect your own lungs to be like in twenty years."

Julian had a moment's horrified vision of himself in twenty years. He would be fifty-six. This vision did not, however, include the state of his lungs.

"And the person," he said, "from whom this picture was taken—?"

"Dead," said Dr. Thybold, not without a trace of satisfaction. "A hale, hearty man—"

"But dead."

"A hale, hearty man of little more than fifty summers, sir," Dr. Thybold swept imperturbably on. "Dead, you might say, in the prime. And all for what, do you suppose?"

"For smoking?"

"Naturally for smoking. Lung cancer, young man. Wait, let me show you some diagrams and charts which my associates and I have prepared from our researches." The doctor plunged back into the briefcase. Julian would very much have liked to light his cigarette just then, but thought it best to wait until the first fury of the attack had expended itself.

For fifteen minutes, more or less, the doctor explained to Julian a number of graphs and statistical summaries which he laid in a row across the desk like a solitaire. So far as Julian could take it all in, it appeared that the incidence of cancer of the lungs, which was greater anyhow in men than in women, rose quite steeply, past the age of forty, for a group of people who smoked more than twenty-five cigarettes a day; a comparable group of nonsmokers at the same age remained relatively, though not entirely, free of this particular disease.

"Very interesting," Julian observed when the doctor seemed about at the end of his demonstration. "Of course, there are so many things one might die of in the meantime. . . ."

"Please," said the doctor, "this is not a joke."

"If you don't mind," Julian said, "I think I will light my cigarette."

"That," said Dr. Thybold sharply, "is merely the voice of despair. It is not too late, young man. Take my case, for instance, or that of my associates. Why, as soon as we even suspected where our researches were tending, what conclusions we should be forced to come to, why, we simply gave it up, all of us together. It is not so hard to do, really. Let me tell you how we did it."

At this moment Julian lit his cigarette. The doctor glared at him, and continued.

"What we did was, each of us brought a fresh carton of his favorite brand. We got together right there in the laboratory, we made a little ritual of it, you see, and we burned every last one of those cartons. If you do it all together, like that, say with a Bunsen burner, it's much easier, you see."

"I see," Julian said.

"Besides," added Dr. Thybold, "it helps more than you'd believe to put a little investment of money, like that, into giving it up. Once you've burned a carton of cigarettes you paid out your good money for, why, you've a real stake in not smoking. And another thing—" he smiled thinly in reminiscence—"what an orgy it was, tobacco fumes everywhere for weeks."

"And this incident took place," Julian inquired, "how long ago?"

"Four or five weeks," said Dr. Thybold with a marked decrease in enthusiasm. "I feel like a new man already, you wouldn't believe it."

"Well, no," Julian said. "At least, I wouldn't have thought of it by myself." He blew a large cloud of smoke across the desk.

"Please," said Dr. Thybold, blowing and ineffectually pushing the cloud away.

"Sorry," said Julian.

"One must expect to suffer for what one believes," said Dr. Thybold.

"Yes, I suppose so," Julian said. The two men sat in silence for a moment or so, the one elaborately blowing smoke away from the other.

"Perhaps you can tell me now," said Julian, "what you had in mind to do about all this?"

"It was our idea," answered Dr. Thybold, "to enlist your aid in putting our message across the—across to the public. We haven't a great deal of money, of course, only what was left over from the research grant made by the Hobugger Foundation. But we want to use that money in the most effective way possible."

"You know, I suppose," said Julian, "that the Hobugger Foundation comes from a fortune originally made in Cellophane packaging, and that it is allied by marriage to one of our largest cigarette families?"

"I know," said Dr. Thybold.

"It may not have occurred to you that under the circumstances—"

"Poetic justice," said the doctor.

"Oh," said Julian. Then he asked, "Just what do you hope to achieve by this plan?"

"Very simply," Dr. Thybold replied, "to stop people from smoking cigarettes." Delivered of their message at last, his large, nervous hands folded themselves respectfully on the briefcase.

Julian was taken aback by the enormity of the idea.

"We want to scare 'em half to death," said the doctor. "That's where we need your help."

"I don't know if you've got any very good selling points here," said Julian doubtfully, indicating the graphs, charts, etc. "Or, rather, unselling points." He tried to smile. "After all, you can't expect people to give up cigarettes just because they are going to die."

"Young man," Dr. Thybold said earnestly, "your cynicism doesn't convince me at all, not at all. I suppose it is a mask you find useful in your business, but deep down, believe me, I know and you know right from wrong. Understand," he added, "it is not my generation, or even your generation, that concerns us, my associates and myself. It is already too late for us, probably too late for you. We live in a world of blackened lungs. But it is the children, my friend, the children. Do we want them to make the same mistake we made, do you want them blindly to pursue the course of action which is killing their fathers? I don't see how any man in his right senses could sit there and tell me he was willing to see his children destroyed by cigarette smoke."

Julian, with contemptible bravado, lit a fresh cigarette from the one he had finished.

"If we can't shame the parents into swearing off," said Dr. Thybold, "we want to shame them into stopping their children from ever contracting the filthy habit."

"Just there," Julian said, "you may have a possible line of attack; that might have a tremendous appeal. I have noticed frequently that the more people smoke the more anxious they are for their children not to. You might work up some sort of direct mail campaign, possibly form clubs, a national society—"

"Exactly so," Dr. Thybold interrupted. "That's the sort of thing we have in mind. Since all we can do on our own, with relatively little money, is initiate the drive, we must recruit people to help, they themselves must—" he hesitated—"pick up the ball and carry it across the goal line. For let me tell you," he went on in a rather hushed voice, "the end we envision, what we are working toward, is the passage of legislation, federal legislation—"

"To prevent smoking?"

"More than that. To make it a crime to grow, cure, or be in possession of tobacco. Public health officers will be sent out to burn this weed just as they would do now if it were marijuana."

"One question, doctor," said Julian. "What do you get out of all this? What is your motive?"

The doctor assumed a weary smile only very faintly tinged with indignation.

"Is there nothing in your world but money and self-interest?" he asked. "Will you, can you possibly, understand me if I say that my friends and I are motivated by an altruism which is both morally and scientifically as pure as can be? by the simple and sufficient idea of playing our part in building a healthier America? Look: it is as simple as this: cigarette smoking is an evil, science tells us so. Very well, we will stamp out cigarette smoking just as we would communism, prostitution, syphilis, or any one of a host of evils."

"Well," said Julian, "perhaps we can work something out. But we're going to have to scare people plenty."

"Nothing vulgar, of course," said Dr. Thybold, "but no shilly-shallying, either. Just—you know—back the hearse up to the front door."

Julian and Dr. Thybold spent the next hour or so in drawing up a budget and the major lines of the proposed campaign. They became quite friendly once the principle of the thing had been made clear, and toward the end of the interview Julian scored one minor triumph. He had been smoking continuously, and in an absent-minded moment he extended the pack to Dr. Thybold, who with equal absence of mind accepted a cigarette and a light. When Julian called this to his notice he first got angry, but then smiled.

"It just shows you how a habit gets under your skin," he said. "Still, I guess one more won't hurt."

Julian had never dined at the Round Table, which he had heard of as extremely expensive and really rather a club than a restaurant. Arrived there, he was looked at with some suspicion until he mentioned the name of Archer More, after which everyone was at once smiling respectfully. A clerical-looking man in black, who took reservations, led him through the dining room to a small table in the corner. On the way, they passed the Round Table from which the establishment took its name. There were a dozen or so seats, about half of them occupied by gentlemen of middle age who were, it was evident, drunk.

After a few moments Mr. Archer More turned up. He seemed not in good health, and was piloted across the room by a young waiter, on whose arm he leaned heavily; he stopped nevertheless to exchange greetings with the gentlemen at the Round Table, who seemed from what Julian could hear to be making jokes at his expense. For the rest, Mr. More was a very small man, wearing a neat gray suit; his starched collar was drawn up tightly enough to make the chin and jowls bulge over it, and there flowered from this focus a broad, stiff bow tie of blue with white dots. He was smiling as though automatically, and to Julian he resembled a frog in a fairy story. The waiter assisted him into place on the banquette along the wall, and brought pillows which he arranged with what amounted to medical attention under the arms on both sides. Thus propped, Mr. More turned to Julian with an intensified smile, and introduced himself.

"Though I'm afraid you must have heard of me already," he added, and giggled.

Julian, embarrassed, was about to deny this, when suddenly he recalled that he had indeed heard of Mr. Archer More; the process of his thoughts must have been clearly visible on his face, for Mr. More giggled with added vigor, saying: "Yes, I am *that* Archie More." Then, with a kind of collapse into the seriousness of an aged schoolboy, "I realize it is nothing to be proud of."

A waiter just now brought them, without any consultation, two large martinis; Mr. More took his glass, with which he made a sort of perfunctory duellist's salute to Julian, and drank off his drink as though he had come in from the desert. Julian, drinking more slowly, thought that he could literally observe the gin coursing through the myriad small veins of Mr. Archer More's face, restoring its character, firming its texture, tinging it to a healthier color—doing, in fact, all that embalming fluid would have done had Mr. More been dead.

This somewhat haughty and holier-than-thou similitude crossed Julian's mind because he had just identified this man as the Archer More who had become something of a culture hero to his generation by reason of his having married, legally and in succession, some ten, possibly eleven, women, to all but the latest of whom, after divorces attended by scandalous publicity, he doled out fractions of an enormous, inherited fortune. He was a man, in other words, very easy to be holier-than or haughty about; perhaps, in fact, too easy, as Julian now began to believe. For, after all, the stern moralist may compare himself favorably to a man once or twice divorced and not everyone, at any rate, will laugh; but when it came to a man with ten divorces to his credit, or under his belt, or however you put it—a man who, had these been enemy aircraft instead of women, would be an ace twice over—the comparison simply fell over on its face, the moralist began to seem petty and niggling before this huge demonstration of what morality was and what it might be. So Julian, after his first impulsive reaction of distaste, looked at Mr. More—who had already been served a second martini—with admiration and incredulity; thinking, just as he might have thought on meeting a celebrated artist or statesman, "Why, he is only a man, and not even a very big one."

"Well, you know my history, no need to go into that," Mr. More

was saying. "You'll want to know why I called you in." He beamed
at Julian over the top of his glass. "I have already discussed it with
Mr. Ballou; in principle, that is. He is a very *good* person, Mr.
Ballou, don't you think so? I have experience, and I can always tell
real goodness in a human being—if he doesn't happen to be a
woman, that is. And I can tell you this much, too, my boy—that
Mr. Ballou has a deep respect and affection for you. Never you let
him down, young fellow, for he holds you in very high esteem
indeed. I might tell you a number of things he said to me about
your work, your character—don't want to swell your head, though.
Just remember one thing: goodness in human beings is not something you meet up with very often, and that Ballou has goodness."
Archer More looked Julian straight in the eyes; Julian, speechless
as a child, could only nod his assent to all this. "And so have you,"
Mr. More concluded. "I can size people up *like that*." He snapped
his fingers unsuccessfully, giggled again, and once again became
owlishly serious.

The waiter brought more martinis, Julian's second and Mr.
More's third.

"As you've probably read in the papers," began Mr. More with a
great air of getting down to business, "I'm breaking up camp
again. Lois is the eleventh try for me, and as God is my witness"—
he raised his right hand solemnly, with the martini glass—"all I
ever wanted out of those eleven girls was *love*. Did I want money?
Did I want power?" He glared at Julian.

"No," Julian said.

"No," said Mr. More. "I wanted love, that's all. When I saw
romance, I went after it. The fountain of youth, that's what I was
looking for, and each time I thought I'd found it at last. I really
mean that. Perfect sincerity at all times, that's my rule."

Julian nodded as though his head were on a string.

"So when the romance faded out—you know how it happens,
my boy—are you married?"

"Yes," Julian said.

"How many?"

"One," said Julian, rightly taking it that Mr. More meant wives
and not children.

"Marvelous," said Archer More, pressing Julian's hand in a gesture of dignified affection. "I respect you for it, son. You stick with

the little woman and you'll never go through the hell I've gone through. I'd envy you, if it weren't against my principles.

"But to get back to business," he went on, releasing Julian's hand, "when I saw that Lois was going just where the others went, I finally started to do some thinking. Archie, I said, maybe you've been looking for happiness the wrong way—you've been trusting in the strange woman all this time, she with the attire of a harlot and subtle of heart, as it says in the Book. You couldn't take it, I said, that Adam learned the lesson for all of us, once and for all— oh, no, you had to go ahead and learn it eleven times, like the dumbest kid in the school."

The waiter, without being asked, brought another round of martinis. Julian wondered when they would order lunch.

"Even then, you know," Mr. More continued, "I was fooling with the idea of trying just once again. I said to myself, Archie, why not make it a round dozen and then stop? After all, you've got a reputation for it now, wouldn't it sort of be letting people down? Sometimes, you know, you have to do what people expect, in this world," he added, emphasizing this general point by prodding Julian in the ribs. "But I saw through that," he went on. "That business of *just one more,* that's what the Devil always says. Besides, if I had yielded just for the sake of reputation and made it a round dozen—only for the world record, say—what would that have been?"

Julian, prodded again in the ribs, did not know what that would have been.

"Pride, spiritual pride," said Mr. More. "Just like taking another drink when you don't need one and don't really even want one." The making of this somewhat obscure connection caused him to look at and then empty his glass. After a moment the waiter replaced it with a full one. Julian began to perceive that they were not going to order lunch, but that this in fact was lunch.

"Well, I don't want to bore you by making a long story of it," said Mr. More, "but I can tell you this, in strictest confidence—I don't want it to break in the papers until I'm ready for it—once I've finished with Lois, I'm finished, for good, no more, *finis,* period. Now, of course, you're asking yourself, 'What will the poor old bugger do instead?'"

Julian, who had by no means been asking himself anything of the sort, nodded seriously.

"Well, I'll tell you, son," Mr. More said slowly and solemnly, "the Lord God has come back into my life, and blessed glad I am to be able to say it. When you're my age, young fellow, I hope you'll know that light which shines from above and says it's never too late to mend. I know I've lived badly, I know I stopped going to church many years ago—and I can see now it was because I'd have been ashamed to be seen in the house of God, being the man I was. But that's all over now, and I'm going to make it up to Him the best way I can. Son, I know that my Redeemer liveth, and my heart overfloweth with gladness." Mr. More put down his glass and seized himself with both hands in the region of the heart; for a moment Julian feared he was actually having an attack.

"Give up all that you have and follow Me," said Mr. More earnestly. "That was the word that did it for me, Give up all that you have and follow Me. I said to myself, you old potbellied drunk, you lecher, I said, what have you got that you can give up? You haven't got happiness, you haven't got friends, you haven't got honor, all you've got is money. Well, you're going to give up that money, lad, and be happy in the Lord."

Mr. More giggled, hiccuped, and motioned to the waiter, who was already bringing him another martini.

"Don't you think if we ordered now—?" Julian began to ask with desperate diffidence.

"Time for just one more," declared Mr. More, "till I finish what I've got to say." He leaned closer to Julian. "What I'm going to do is, I'm going to advertise the love of God." Dramatically settling back, he allowed a silence to descend upon this statement.

Julian nodded with an air of dazed thoughtfulness.

"Full page ads, *Times, Tribune, Life,* the whole works, as long as the money holds out," said Mr. More with a gambler's gesture of hurling his chips on the table.

"And then?" Julian asked.

"Consider the lilies of the field, son," said Mr. More. He raised his glass. "To the lilies of the field," he said, and they both drank.

"What I want, to start with," he continued, "is simplicity, simplicity and size. I want people to know what I know. It could start this way: I AM THE LIGHT OF THE WORLD, in block caps maybe two three inches high, and under that in little letters the place in the Book that comes from. Then, son, you go on from there. Just go to the Book for your inspiration, you're a writer, you know what I mean, you can phrase it better than I could. Just tell people straight, without any fancy verbiage, how they can save themselves and make this world a better place for all of us to live in, if they'll only believe on the Lord. You might even just scare 'em a little," he added reflectively. "Hell, and all that. But not much, go easy on the brimstone and so forth.

"I tell you what," he concluded, "I want you to sketch out, say, about half a dozen full-page spreads like that. I don't want to begin and then just peter out, you know; there's got to be enough for a real series without scraping the bottom of the barrel. And I want it to rise, you see what I mean? A crescendo. I want it to be a work of art."

"A crescendo," Julian said, "beginning with I AM THE LIGHT OF THE WORLD."

"Don't worry, son," said Mr. More, "you'll figure something out, you've got a head on your shoulders. Consider the lilies of the field. Waiter!"

The waiter brought another round of martinis, and Archer More made Julian solemnly drink with him to the success of this odd enterprise. A silence followed. Julian was horrified and impressed, also somewhat drunk, and his stomach ached with hunger. It was hard to believe the little man could be serious, except that he patently was so; and Julian recalled Mr. Ballou's injunction: always take this much money seriously. There was no doubt about the money's really being there, and Julian supposed no one could prevent a man from hurling his own wealth in whatever direction he chose. Practically speaking, a steady course in the Casino at Monte Carlo (or across the river in New Jersey, for that matter) would very likely have the same result, and who could say that Mr. More's chosen course was not the more satisfactory of the two just as it was quite possibly the more amusing?

Julian realized that the silence had continued for an unduly long time. He turned to Mr. More with the idea of saying something about ordering food, and saw that his host had quietly and without making a disturbance relapsed into unconsciousness. Owing to the pillows, whose meaning now became clear, he had not fallen over; Julian was once again reminded of the embalmer's art.

Lunch was over.

2

Sylvia's relation with Dr. Mirabeau began perhaps more as a matter of fashion than anything else. Hugo Alter's wife Alma was going to him at that time, and Alma spoke very convincingly about psychotherapy, of which the value, she said, was preventive. "Besides, it is the most fascinating thing in the world. You learn so much about yourself." Sylvia, who occasionally suffered from asthmatic attacks which Alma declared were the result of a want of affection in childhood, allowed herself to be convinced because she was bored and, at the same time, curious. This step had been easy, like the famous descent into Avernus; Dr. Mirabeau was charming, courteous, intelligent, though it is true that he was also expensive. The proposition that all illness—and everything else, health included—was psychical in origin Sylvia found extremely attractive; she quickly learned a certain quantity of the profession's cant-terms, which she discovered helped her never very exciting or witty conversation a good deal; she and Alma, in particular, were able to carry on brief critical exchanges in public about almost everything that was said, with the double assurance of being always listened to and seldom understood.

On the other hand, one did not so readily get out of Dr. Mirabeau's softly tenacious grasp when once one had got in. After the first few meetings, when Sylvia had become established as a patient, the doctor formed the disconcerting habit of treating whatever she said rather as evidence than as rational discourse. After six months, for example, Sylvia became bored, and said to him several times that, after all, there was nothing *really* wrong with her, and that she thought (in a casual voice, referring to it just in passing) she might just as well stop. Dr. Mirabeau, to her bewilderment and, presently, indignation, did not seem to hear these remarks, which at first Sylvia would simply interpolate in the course of her reminiscences and associations as she lay back on the quite comfortable couch which was the doctor's operating table. Finally, though, she faced him across the desk as she was leaving after a session, and said straight out that she had had enough. The doctor folded his hands and smiled gently at her. He was personally, by the way, a most comforting and comfortable person, fat, somewhat soft, with large, liquid brown eyes which were imitated, lower down, in the pattern of beautiful foulard ties he had made for him to his own design.

"Of course," he said, "you are a mature, rational being, you must make your own choices, I quite understand that. And I quite understand, moreover, the sense of desperation which makes it necessary for you, particularly at this moment, to be decisive. You have been feeling as though too much depended on me, as though your own will were somehow being betrayed. That is quite natural—at this stage."

Though she was frightened by the words "at this stage" Sylvia would nevertheless have left for good. But the doctor simply and quietly went on talking.

"As a mature, rational being," he said, "you naturally want to have a full understanding of the causes underlying your decision. You believe, of course, that this is a free decision, rationally arrived at. . . ."

As Sylvia did not leave at this point, the result was that she did not leave at all. Dr. Mirabeau with admirable logic convinced her in a few minutes that it was not Sylvia, that free and rational being, who wished to discontinue the treatment, but Sylvia's illness which like an independent entity—"like one of those demons which primitive psychology, under the guise of religion, saw as taking possession of the soul and speaking through it"—thus realized its own deepest wish to hide from the dry, rational light of diagnosis.

The demon, or illness, had a particularly good excuse *at this stage,* the doctor continued, because *at this stage* certain superficial and symptomatic anxieties appeared to have vanished, or at least abated: no asthmatic attacks during the past several weeks, fewer worries in general, a better *tone* (tone was one of his favorite words, which he accompanied by an expressive gesture of the hand). Sylvia might of course take her chance, these symptoms *might* never return, they *might* not even be replaced by others. He, Dr. Mirabeau, could not exactly say that he was satisfied; he hoped that she would not, even with the best intentions, even to praise him, tell others that she had really—*seriously*—been a patient of his; but of course he could not prevent her from quitting if that was what she felt compelled to do.

Six months after that, it was a question of money, the consequence of an argument with Julian, who had demanded to know how long "all this" was to go on. "It is not doing much for you so far as I can see," he had said. "You behave exactly the same as always."

"Yes," Dr. Mirabeau had said, giving her a smile of friendly complicity. "We often have this trouble with the family, with friends—people on the outside, in general. Their want of comprehension is troublesome, but one can understand it. On the other hand"—and he looked at Sylvia keenly—"we very frequently also find the patient hiding behind these so-rational, so-sensible complaints about money, which we may sometimes suspect the patient has even led his family on to make, not so?"

Sylvia objected that she had certainly not made her husband say what he had said.

"Not consciously," the doctor continued. "Of course not. But you are willing enough, are you not, to use such a complaint as a way out? The demon speaks again.

"Let us look at it this way. The therapy is expensive, that is perfectly true. Why? Well, you will say, because the doctor must be highly and expensively trained, he can take but a few patients at a time, he must make a living. . . . That is all part of it, certainly, but not by any means the most important part.

"It is expensive because it is good for the patient, it is necessary for the patient, that it be expensive. You see, my dear Sylvia, if I treated this objection to the cost as rational I should have to agree with you. I do agree, it is abominably expensive. But money, after all, is one of the deepest motives of the mind, the strongest resistances are intimately connected with spending money—which is after all but a surrogate image for *giving oneself,* and therefore admirably fitted for expressing sexual tensions—so that we know, when in the course of our analysis we reach this typical argument about how much it all costs, we *know* then that we are reaching the heart of the matter, where the strongest psychical repugnances have set up their defenses. You can see, then, that the therapy must cost a substantial sum, because it must cost a sum which shall be meaningful to the patient, which shall represent a real investment in health. Otherwise, the larger investment remains on the side of the illness and nothing can really be accomplished, it would be like gambling with stakes too small to bother the players."

The fact that the cost of the therapy must, under the circumstances, be more meaningful to Julian than to his wife was evaded by both parties to this discussion. But just lately a far more horrifying thing had come up, which was Alma Alter's going mad, insane, or, if not mad or insane, then something rather shockingly close to it. Sylvia could not help the feeling that the analysis itself was the disease, or induced it, and that it would have been better, had it not now been too late, to bear those evils that we have than fly to others that we know not of. But, concerning this, it was difficult to get Dr. Mirabeau to speak at all, much less commit himself to any unequivocal statement. "Madness," he said, "a frightening word, true. But after all, what is normal? It is a matter of degree."

This matter of degree had put Alma into what was called a *rest home,* an expression of which Sylvia had her doubts, and which seemed to her to conceal nameless and terrible excesses under the guise of treatment.

Nevertheless, perhaps as a matter of necessity, she trusted Dr. Mirabeau, with whom her relation at this time was, in every respect but the carnal, more intimate than what she had with her husband; and this morning she arrived at his office full of excited indignation over the anonymous letter. It was typical of Dr. Mirabeau, however, that he would not let her discuss this matter across the desk in a friendly and sensible way, but insisted on her first lying down as usual.

"Calm yourself," he said, "and collect your thoughts. There is plenty of time. Take a few deep breaths, try to relax. Feel yourself relaxing. There. And now?"

It was very difficult for Sylvia, lying down, to put the proper passion into her recital; even to herself, she sounded as though she were describing what there had been for breakfast.

"How interesting this is," Dr. Mirabeau said. "Again, please." He frequently made her repeat things, and Sylvia told the story, which after all was not long, a second time.

"You have a copy of this letter with you?"

"No," she replied. "I told you—he came back and put it in his pocket."

"I see," said Dr. Mirabeau, and was silent for a few moments. "Then you had this letter in your possession," he said, "for how long?"

"A few minutes, maybe ten minutes," Sylvia said.

"But you remember the contents exactly?"

"Yes, of course. Just as I told you."

"And there is, now, no reality whatever to the accusation?"

"None at all that I can think of."

"'None at all that I can think of'—does that not imply some reservation? That if you thought for a moment more—?"

"No," said Sylvia quite sharply.

"Don't be indignant," the doctor said. "You know you have nothing to fear from me. In this office the ordinary rules of morality do not exist. Let us try in our usual way; associate to this letter, please."

"But this is a perfectly real letter," Sylvia rather plaintively said. "It is not a dream, it came in the morning mail."

"Of course," the doctor said. "I don't say you are wrong, but please realize that it would in any case seem so to you. From where I sit," he added, "you can see that it does not look altogether convincing."

Sylvia became speechless with indignation. She sputtered for a moment, and sat up.

"Please," said Dr. Mirabeau, waving her back. "Let us look at it rationally for a moment, you and I together.

"It is early morning, you have very recently come from the world of sleep, you have only just emerged from that great ocean, or even not quite emerged altogether. You have made coffee, you are sitting there over a hot cup of coffee, thinking—about what were you thinking?"

Sylvia did not remember. Perhaps, she said finally, she had been thinking what she would find to say to the doctor himself, later in the morning. It had rather embarrassed her, she now recalled, that she did not remember any dream from the previous night.

"Ah," said Dr. Mirabeau. "Now your husband comes in, he sits down, he too has coffee, you do not talk much."

"No, not very much."

"You do not break the mood of revery, of quiet, diffused feeling. Your husband has breakfast, he goes out to walk the dogs, all is as usual. While he is gone you continue to sit at the table."

"I moved over to his place and picked up the paper."

"Exactly. And you saw this letter on the table."

"Which I had seen my husband was concerned about."

"Yes. And you read the letter, and of course experienced a certain number of thoughts about its contents: first it was a joke, then you became indignant, then a little frightened, et cetera."

"Yes."

"Then you determined that your husband must not know you had read the letter, so you put it back where it had been."

"Yes."

"He returns. His entrance, with the dogs, breaks the mood abruptly. And when he leaves for the second time, there is no more letter." Sylvia felt rather than saw that the doctor, above and behind her head, spread wide his hands in the magician's gesture which says *quod erat demonstrandum*.

"But I saw him pick up the letter and put it in his pocket," she insisted.

"Of course. Secondary elaboration, which the dream supplied to terminate itself in a satisfactory and coherent manner."

"The dream!" Sylvia sat up once again. "But I saw it happen, this all took place not in bed but at breakfast. It was broad daylight."

"Sylvia," said Dr. Mirabeau, with a soothing sternness, "you may be right. Please remember that I have no means of judging except on the evidence as you present it. The thing may have happened exactly as you say. But try for a moment to look at it objectively, and at least admit to yourself the strength of the evidence against it.

"First, it was early in the morning, you acknowledge that you were still sleepy. Second, the letter exists within a closed circle of evidence, there is no objective witness to its being there at all—unless, of course, your husband should confirm your story by producing the letter; but until or unless he does we have only your version to go by. Then, third, the extreme unlikeliness of the letter; you yourself say that its charge has no basis in fact—and, really, Sylvia, in this day and age, and especially in your class of society, people very seldom send such communications, they have many vices but anonymity is not one of them. Then, finally, and most convincing, at any rate to me, there is the extreme vividness of the text of the letter as against the relative vagueness of everything else in the story; in short, not only does a critical look at the circumstances suggest you dreamed it, but the letter itself, in addition, has all the appearance of being a product of dream. And, as you confess, you had just been wishing you had a dream to present to me this morning."

Sylvia could say nothing, at first. She felt trapped. But at the same time she began to feel that Dr. Mirabeau was right, though her reasoning differed somewhat from his: in the first place, she argued, it would be so much nicer if the anonymous letter did not exist. As a matter of fact, she could not recapture the reality of the situation; it did have, undeniably, a dreamlike air, and she admitted as much to Dr. Mirabeau.

"Possibly you are right. I would certainly prefer to believe that horrible letter was unreal. But it all seemed so vivid—"

"Ah ah," interrupted Dr. Mirabeau warningly. "Not unreal, my dear. What you mean is, if I may be a little pedantic, that the letter did not have the kind of *waking reality* which we are accustomed to dignify by calling it, exclusively, 'real.'"

"But it did," Sylvia faintly pleaded. "That was what was so horrifying about it, that it seemed so real."

"We know by now, you and I, what a character actor the dreamwork can be," said Dr. Mirabeau cheerfully. "The thing we have now to discover is, just what *is* the reality in this anonymous communication from the realms of night."

"Do you think," Sylvia nervously asked, "that it means I want to be unfaithful to my husband, and that in the note I punish myself for this wish?"

"Ah, now," said Dr. Mirabeau with the air of a connoisseur, "that's just a trifle glib, don't you think? Remember always that the note is part of the dreamwork, and the dreamwork in itself means nothing, it certainly never means what it says. Let us start instead in our usual manner, not with the whole but with its elements. Now, just what, in the whole experience, strikes you immediately as having the most significance, as standing out from the rest?"

"Federigo," Sylvia unhesitatingly replied. "I remember thinking there was something extra loathsome about that name."

"Yes," said the doctor. "Go on."

"I don't think I dislike foreigners," Sylvia said. "Not consciously, that is."

"I think you will find," the doctor said with a certain jovial coyness, "that there lurks behind the name no foreigner but someone very close to home, very close indeed."

"My husband?" asked Sylvia doubtfully.

"No, no, think again," said Dr. Mirabeau gently. "Think slowly and carefully. Associate to the name Federigo, please."

"A fedora hat," Sylvia said, "and dark glasses. There's some idea of disguise, I think . . ."

"Yes, yes, go on."

A moment later it came to her.

"Ego!" she cried, almost gaily. "Myself! It is right in the name, plain as day."

"Of course," said Dr. Mirabeau in a kind voice. "Now we begin to get somewhere. Continue, please."

Sylvia lay back and shut her eyes. It was quite plain, she deeply hated herself. For the first time that morning she found she was able to relax.

When Sylvia emerged from the darkness of Dr. Mirabeau's office, she was always refreshed by the brilliant reality of the daylight; sometimes she even ascribed this intense feeling for the beauty of the world to the therapy itself, like the man who hit himself on the head with a hammer because it felt so good when he stopped. But perhaps the cycle of her days was more complicated than that. Dr. Mirabeau canceled out her anxieties of the previous days and nights, then the bright sunlight canceled out Dr. Mirabeau and the anxieties generated by the analytic session itself; life seemed to begin again, and had for the first few hours at least a feeling of buoyant freedom. It ought to be allowed, though, that perhaps a part of this feeling was caused by Mr. Marius Rathlin, who had formed the habit of meeting her once or twice a week for lunch; this morning he awaited her on the sidewalk when she came up the steps of the brownstone building in the basement of which Dr. Mirabeau had his office.

"You look splendid," said Marius, "like Aphrodite emerging from her first communion."

Sylvia smiled graciously to this; she felt splendid too. The fine May weather, the hard, keen visibility of the buildings in this quiet side street, and her own appearance, all seemed to go brilliantly together, like a page in *Vogue*; she wished she had brought the dogs along.

"Where shall we go?" she asked, with perhaps a greater display of spirit than absolutely necessary.

"I thought that if you were not altogether starved," said Marius, "we might walk in the Park. Then to Mme. Modera, where the sole is said to be quite fair. You, of course, may prefer something else." Marius's references to his being a Catholic were frequent, but usually rather remotely allusive than direct; it was as though he had taken this means of reminding Sylvia not of his religion but of the fact that it was Friday.

As they began to walk Sylvia took his arm, as she usually did, for no better reason than that he seemed to expect it; in such things Marius was very much a gentleman, so much more so than people whom Sylvia really believed were gentlemen as to be somewhat embarrassing. The elegance of his small manners, his extreme formality in dress, his witty but somewhat oratorical conversation which had so much a way of being a monologue—all these things were at once pleasant and disturbing. A walk in the Park with Marius went like the recitative to a first-rate musical comedy, probably more learned and exclusively witty than anything one would see on Broadway, but having about the same connection with common reality. Even his poverty, and Sylvia believed it was perfectly true, what she had often heard said, that he was the poorest person of their acquaintance—even his poverty seemed disguised in such a way as to make sure of shining through his elegance; as in a theatre, again, where the audience is supposed to know at once that the young man is poor, and, a moment later, that he is bravely concealing the fact. After they had lunched together a few times Marius had gravely, with the air of admitting her to a new stage in friendship, asked her advice about the proper way of turning his shirt-collar, which was frayed; Sylvia, who took a motherly but amateurish interest in his problem, could not conceal that he knew far more about how it was done than she did, since Julian, of course, would simply have bought another shirt.

Even now she had no idea what Marius did, if he did anything. He referred to himself as a scholar, or as a student, a title he could very reasonably claim from a large if somewhat disordered store of knowledge relating mainly to customs and manners, but he discouraged very bluntly Sylvia's inference from this that he was writing a book. "I am a dilettante," he told her. "The fact that, nowadays, all dilettanti write books should not be taken for a definition of the species in its true, primitive state. I like knowledge, therefore I study; I respect knowledge, therefore I write no book." And again: "To know something, and then not to write it down in a book—that is original virtue. And in the fullness of time, at the last great Book-Burning, I may perhaps have the privilege of standing with the elect, and joining in their blessed laughter." All this simply confirmed Sylvia in the belief that Marius was writing a book, and inspired her to think that this book, when finished, would be a wonderful achievement. She sometimes secretly thought that he might dedicate this work to herself; their friendship, of a young man for an older woman—she was some four or five years older than he—was of exactly the sort to make such a thing possible, it was romantic, light, *spirituel* (a word she had taken from Marius himself), and, above all, perfectly honest. Sylvia was a woman who could permit herself the most intense spiritual excesses in what she believed was utter innocence, simply on the ground that "nothing really happened." The troubadorlike courtship of the young man flattered her intelligence, and her age (which for this purpose she slightly exaggerated, as if she had been his aunt), with no peril to her chastity—an object which she unconsciously regarded as equivalent to her self-respect, her position in the world, her comfortable apartment and, objectively considered, excellent husband. It also seemed to her that she was preserved from danger in this regard by Marius's religion, which he took so seriously—this too was unfashionable and exotic in him—that he must certainly impose upon himself the most rigorous prohibitions with respect to love. The fact that his conversation, while always polite, and unmarred by those four-letter words which men and women used so frequently in each other's presence these days, was extraordinarily free, seemed to her a paradoxical guarantee of the same security. The immodest proposals which he frequently put to her were, in her opinion, part of the tender and witty joke which formed their friendship and permitted their freedom: "At half-past five this evening," he would say, "you will desert your husband and steal his car. We will drive to a small motel on the shore of Lake Erie, and there pass a week of delicious indulgence. Then you will return as if nothing whatever had happened." "Can't we find something less plebeian than Lake Erie?" Sylvia would ask, joining a trifle heavily in the fun.

This morning, however, Sylvia found difficulty in keying herself to Marius's mood. The anonymous letter, now Dr. Mirabeau had convinced her it was a dream, began to trouble her again, as much as or more than it did when it had been a reality. Now that she was out of the doctor's office, out of that comfortable darkness, so like that of a movie theatre, where one projected one's private vision into a kind of temporary and provisional being, she began once again to doubt. The letter had seemed so real. . . . But of course that effect could be duplicated by the dream, people constantly said of their dreams that they were more real than reality. The letter was unlikely, and if it had been real it remained unlikely that Hugo would have done such a thing; what profit would there be for Hugo, what did he stand to gain? Hugo had trouble enough right now, with Alma, with preparations for the divorce, with this new girl he wanted to marry.

While they walked along, while Marius was amusing about the grass, the trees, the children, Sylvia tried to tabulate the consequences of the anonymous letter considered first as a dream, then as a reality. No matter which it was, she now saw, Marius was the point at issue. Supposing there really had been a letter, well, it was very likely that some *friend* (how horrifying!) had seen them at lunch together and put this nasty interpretation on it and felt impelled to stick his nose into other people's business by writing to Julian. But if it should have been a dream, that was nearly as bad; she saw now how her friendship with Marius was open to misconstruction—how open it must be, in fact, if she herself had so misconstrued it in a dream which had the air of being a prophecy and a secret warning. Perfectly true, after all, though she had not until now paid it much attention—perhaps even tried to conceal it from herself—that Marius had a certain reputation for being dangerous to women. It was very unlikely, she admitted to herself with some bitterness, that she was the only one upon whom he exercised his charm; no doubt there were others, even at the same time, with whom the rewards were at least more immediately satisfying. Sylvia experienced that shadowy disillusion which comes over people when they barely begin to suspect they have been foolish.

"What can he see in me?" she asked herself. "I am older than he is, he must know so many more attractive girls. . . . And he knows, of course, that I would never really sleep with him."

"You are a bit subdued," said Marius. "Has your shaman read disaster from your dreams? a coffin among the tea leaves? Or perhaps you are merely depressed with Central Park, which would be understandable: it brings back the most disagreeable recollections of one's grubby childhood."

"It is nothing," Sylvia said. "I was only thinking."

"That is a certain sign of dejection in beautiful women," said Marius. "It probably means you are hungry." And he led her out of the Park by the nearest exit, where he got a taxi.

At the Café Modera they both had the sole, Sylvia perhaps because to do something so specifically Catholic had about it a romantic and very nearly a sinful atmosphere. She was not altogether happy, even so, and during the meal kept looking about to see if they were being observed by anyone she knew, but saw no one. The coffee was strong, black and bitter, with a slice of lemon in it; over the second cup she said:

"I don't think we ought to meet again like this." At once, but too late, she regretted this statement, which seemed to commit her to a more serious view of having lunch with Marius than she would have believed proper.

"What a very charming thing to say," said Marius, smiling. "I don't know if you realize how I will cherish that remark."

"Please," she protested, "I really do mean it. I mean, we know, don't we, that we are not going any further with this? I've enjoyed it, I've enjoyed it a great deal. But I can't believe, Marius, that you can be serious about it, and if you were it would be my duty to stop you. It simply would not be fair to you."

"The last refuge of the wounded ego," he observed, "is altruism."

"Please be serious for a moment," said Sylvia with a light asperity, out of her deep belief that it was impossible to be serious while being intelligent.

"I merely meant," he replied, "that I might be allowed to judge what is fair to me."

"My dear," she said, with an intention of keeping the tone light, as Marius did seem slightly offended, "kindly remember that I am an old married woman."

"You've no cause to say I haven't kept it steadily in mind."

"Don't be angry, Marius, you know that's not what I meant."

"You meant, then, what?"

Sylvia paused, and, to give a kind of dramatic countenance to this pause, put her hand gently on his. She felt very ashamed of having to say next, and truthfully, that she was afraid of what people might say, so she did not say this but instead let herself be led to a new concession which she believed to be harmless because she did not mean it.

"I'm afraid this might become too important," she said in a low voice, not looking at him, "to me."

"Dear Sylvia," Marius said, "I have hoped it would."

"So we must stop, that's all," she said with a new energy, disengaging her hand. "It has been fun, Marius, a great deal of fun. But there are limits."

"So it seems," he said, with some bitterness. "No, don't go just yet, there is something I must say to you."

Sylvia, who had been putting on her gloves merely out of nervousness, and not because she had been ready to leave, settled back in her chair with a slight sigh to indicate unwillingness. She was governed in this, as she hoped he was too, by the conventions of a final interview, which imposed on the parties concerned not only certain appropriate emotions but also a quality of rounded and dramatic finish; because there would be no second chance, everything must be said as well and beautifully as possible right here and now. It is perhaps for this reason that such final interviews are so seldom final. Few people have the strength to resist explaining themselves just once more.

Marius had the waiter bring a fresh pot of coffee.

"I don't flatter myself that I can change your mind," he began. "You are a very strong sort of person, Sylvia. Our friendship has meant a good deal to me, and I hoped it had to you as well."

"It has, it has," she earnestly put in, being not so displeased at the idea that she was a strong sort of person. "But don't make it sound so final, darling. We'll meet again. Why, we'll all be at Hugo's house tonight, won't we?"

"I suppose so," Marius replied. "But that's not the same thing. You were the one, you know, who said there were limits—we may draw them at different places. If I can't see you alone like this, it would be better not to see you at all."

"Marius, you are being very childish now."

"That may be," he said. "Sylvia, didn't you ever think I might be in love with you?"

"Please don't talk like that, it's not fair," she said.

"*Not fair*," he repeated, somewhat disagreeably. "Organized games."

"It is not fair to Julian, in the first place," Sylvia said. "There are some things one simply doesn't say. And besides, dear, marriage *is* an organized game."

"Sylvia—do you love Julian?"

"I do," she said, with something of the tone of altar or court-room.

"Are you still in love with him?"

"Marius," she said gravely, "for all your intelligence, you don't really understand much about marriage, do you? Or about life itself, for that matter. Things can't always be in that first pink flush of romance. People quiet down after a number of years, and become more, well, more sensible about living."

"They do?"

"Yes, they do. Julian and I have a very nice life together, which is something you don't understand. If you did, you couldn't even think of trying to break it up in this way."

Sylvia put into this speech more fervor than necessary, perhaps out of a feeling that she was saying more than necessary; she was somewhat chagrined, then, to hear Marius laugh at her with a kind of superior sympathy.

"Poor Sylvia," he said. "I wouldn't have believed you'd thought about infidelity as much as all that. Marriage must be a frightful institution. It is, after all, hardly recommended in the Scriptures— 'better to marry than burn' is not exactly what you would call a testimonial, is it? Here you are, after seven years of it, burning merrily—though in a theoretical way, admitted—and at the least question, up you come like a clerk of canon law, ready to give the reasons why and the reasons why not. Tell me, my dear, supposing I were Olympian Zeus, and could spread a cloud about our love so that no man could see, or spread fear about it so that no man who saw would speak, would you then—notice that even under those circumstances I am not asking you to come to my bed—but would you then, in a whisper, acknowledge what you truly felt for me?"

"That would be very different," Sylvia said, feeling that she retreated with dignity. "You are not Olympian Zeus. This is the real world, remember." She herself remembered at this moment the question of the anonymous letter, and wondered whether it was or was not the real world that she was at this moment sitting in.

"What you call the real world," Marius said, "is continually being manufactured out of dreams like these. Sylvia, I am advising you, now, that I love you."

"I don't hear you," she said, actually putting her fingers in her ears so that it was as from quite far away that she heard him repeat, "I love you." She turned to him decisively.

"Marius, this is becoming a frightening conversation. We've had such good times together, why couldn't you let it finish that way? I'd never have stayed here to listen to you, if it hadn't been that this was the last time."

"Exactly," Marius replied. "If you had not insisted this was the last time I'd not have had the courage to say what I have said."

"Well, then."

"Well, then, if you will promise that this is not the last time, that we can continue to be good friends—Sylvia, all I ask is to be allowed to love you, which is something I can't help."

Just now the waiter presented the check, and remained hovering a few feet away; Sylvia looked around to see that the dining room was nearly empty.

"We really must go now," she said. One of the things which disturbed her was that it had become customary for her to pay for the lunch on these occasions—and it sometimes crossed her mind that a good meal might be, for Marius, at least a strong secondary motive in his friendship—and this way of using her husband's money occasioned her perhaps more anxiety than had anything else, until now, about these luncheon dates; money, as Dr. Mirabeau that very morning had so sagely observed, being a surrogate image for *giving oneself,* and therefore admirably fitted for expressing sexual tensions. At this moment, with the waiter hanging about, Sylvia thought she saw a means of solving this difficulty of conscience and perhaps indirectly discouraging Marius at the same time.

"You must promise to be good, then," she whispered to him, again putting her hand on his, "and if you really mean it, you should begin by paying for my lunch."

Chapter Three

Hungry, and somewhat stupefied, Julian returned to his office and had Miss Duddon send out to the drugstore for sandwiches and a copy of the Bible, which he would need in order to think about Mr. More's campaign. He wished he might discuss this matter with Mr. Ballou, but it was a custom in the office, precisely on account of such luncheon engagements, that from three to five in the afternoon was a period set aside for *thinking*. Julian frequently took a nap at this time, and would have done so today but that some small worry kept nagging at him; he finally remembered that what he absolutely must do before returning home was to compose the second anonymous letter. He sighed, and pulled a sketch pad toward him.

One of the unanticipated difficulties in his scheme, he now began to see, would be a certain lack of content; he sat there like a schoolboy unprepared for his exam. Really, he thought, he did not know very much about Sylvia's way of passing the time, and these anonymous letters could not go on for very long being merely sinister and vague; finally they would have to make some identifiable suggestions. But as soon as they did, once they at all committed themselves to a particular line of attack, they would, would they not, become ridiculous? She would begin to laugh at them; she would, and this would be fatal, discuss them openly with Julian. He wondered whether she had actually read the first one, that morning, and, if so, what she had thought. He tried to imagine himself in her place, receiving such an accusation made in such a manner, but this made him feel acutely what a bad thing it was he had undertaken, his guilt came on him in a physical form like nausea—what a terrible thing to do to anyone! He resolved not to go on with it, and, pushing away the pad, took up the Bible instead.

On the other hand . . .

On the other hand, assuming she had read it—and she must have, for otherwise why would she have asked him, in that curiously neutral tone of voice, whether there was anything he wanted to say?—why did she not speak up at once, why not say something right out instead of simply sitting there? Why had she not proclaimed her innocence and said in a straightforward manner that the letter was ridiculous?

Because she was not innocent?

The appearance of this thought in Julian's head, being as it was sudden, unexpected and, above all, not a product of his own scheme, compelled respect if not immediate belief. With very mixed feelings he began to see himself as the victim of some fatally destructive irony deep in the nature of things.

"Federigo, my friend," he said to himself, "we've done it now."

He did not, at this moment, fully believe in the truth of his new discovery, but its possibility, even its likelihood from certain points of view, dismayed him; there was, however, a quality of amusement even in his dismay.

This quality of amusement, this slight gift for sensing absurdity everywhere, had affected Julian's view of life for as long as he could recall; in college, for example, he had had the ambition of becoming a saint, or, undenominationally, some sort of holy man; and sometimes even now he thought how much easier that would have been than the life which was actually his. This ambition had come less, perhaps, from a sense of sympathy with the sufferings of the world than from a dreamlike sense of the silliness of the world. There had been about him then, what was perfectly proper for an undergraduate, a certain want of commitment to a real world, a world really and intransigently existing, and this slight imperfection, this little hollowness where there should have been belief, still formed, negatively, a part of his character, a kind of abscess. For all his scarcely expressed ambitions to sainthood he had not in his adult life ever quite believed in God, and now and then he put it to himself that that was his trouble; but in reality his trouble was simpler than that—he did not quite believe in the world.

So when Julian began to perceive on his horizon this cloud no bigger than another man, his reaction was to be amused, which he was able to be even while he was being troubled. To put the matter exactly, he did not *really* believe his wife Sylvia had been unfaithful to him, but he began for the first time to imagine how easily possible it was that she might be. He could not be angry, either, for he had no image to be angry about, but he also began to perceive how angry he might, in theory, become. Experimentally, more or less like a chemist, he made in his mind a couple of theoretically possible combinations: Sylvia and Marius, Sylvia and Hugo Alter; and for one instant he achieved the real and painful sense of being laughed at by other people, the sudden appreciation of a world baseless, unstable, fluid, in which all one had thought of as one's *position* turned out instead to be merely motion. But after a moment the energy required to sustain these imaginings proved insufficient; a vision of Hugo's mouth, smiling, simply faded out on him; and he was left once more with the hypothetical notion, the platonic idea, of his wife's possible infidelity, in which, again, he did not *really* believe.

There remained the matter of the anonymous letters, which perfectly expressed Julian's relation with a real world. In this new light, it scarcely mattered, for the moment, what the next letter would say, but there must be a next letter, since, as he now began to perceive, the ultimate object of the game he had begun—far beyond providing him with an excuse for adultery—was to get the real world to commit itself, which it had already begun to do. One put to the world a hypothetical question; one received, it would appear, a real answer; it was with some exhilarated yet anxious sense of this situation that Julian once again took the pad, and composed the following message:

> SIR—
> Who is Sylvia, what is she? etc.
>   FEDERIGO

That this "etc." seemed to set no limit to his wife's activities Julian noted in passing but Federigo made no bones about.

With considerable labor he cut the appropriate letters out of a copy of *Harper's Bazaar* and assembled them on a page rather dirtily, getting glue all over his fingers; he waited till Miss Duddon had gone home, and typed the envelope on her machine. Then, after washing his hands—but the glue clung very tenaciously—he rolled up the copy of *Harper's Bazaar* and left the office, posting the letter in the chute outside while waiting for the elevator. He thought, seeing the envelope fall rapidly and irrevocably away, that it would be wiser to mail these communications from some other postal district; also that this was probably using the mails to defraud—but who was being defrauded, and of what, he could not just now decide. The magazine he took along and disposed of in a street-corner garbage can several blocks away.

For some reason, perhaps as a free expression of his newfound criminal character, Julian was unwilling to walk home by his usual route; instead he decided to go through Central Park, where he had not walked since his boyhood—already, he noted with surprise, a considerable distance away. It occurred to him, for the first time bringing with it a sense of discomfort, that he was growing older and would one day die, and all for what? He would have lived a life after the model of the city itself, regular, rectangular, numbered, any place in which might be readily located by a simple system of coordinates, and as readily forgotten. It might be true also that he had grown up as the city had, and that his parallels and perpendiculars had developed from a crooked maze of random growth, far downtown, but it seemed that little of that remained; people of his sort, people whom he knew, did not go there unless they happened to be artists, or brokers with a seat on the Exchange, whose work for some reason had remained in that weird tangle of streets while the rest of the city spread steadily north. Even the business of the anonymous letters, the stirring of some complicated viciousness against regularity and order, now seemed to him to be a freedom of much the sort suggested by Central Park itself, a limited and provisional disorder frowned upon on four sides by the structures of order, a small oblong of chaos set down in the midst of cosmos; even the chaos gave subtle hints of control, the paths wound and meandered lazily but with purpose, here was a zoo, here a playing field, policemen walked their beats here as elsewhere; uptown, in the mid-region of this chaos, the two museums monumentally confronted one another like emblems of the days of creation, irrevocably dividing the city into Art on the east and Nature on the west.

His slight thought of death and of the implacable passing of time evoked in him bitter, rebellious feelings, and, at the same time, a poignant sense of the beauty and ugliness in things; he looked outside himself as with new eyes.

The weather was excellent, though a trifle too hot. Julian entered the Park at Sixtieth Street and Fifth Avenue, where more than at any other place the walk is lined with benches, and the benches, in such weather as this, crammed with people, making of this section, which leads to the Zoo, a kind of social promenade. Though the occupants of the benches were of many different sorts, it seemed to Julian that there was nevertheless something generally the same about them; the same air of sullen, listless freedom, of open-throated uneasiness in which the idea of being *dégagé* and informal had produced a result rather shameful and slovenly. There seemed to be among them a large proportion of insane persons; several times Julian avoided the glance of a man or a woman talking vociferously, often in what seemed a foreign tongue, to no one, or to the pigeons which in this place fluttered and clattered impudently around all heads and hats. The behavior of these birds filled Julian with disgust; their constant nearness to human beings had completely destroyed their natural wild timidity and made them, in his opinion, insolent. The ways they went, their flights between two people sitting together, for example, seemed to him estimated on a nice calculation of human baseness, servility and docile indifference. For his own part, he several times had to duck to keep from being flapped in the face with a wing, and it did not improve his view of the matter that he thought the habitués of this sector must be laughing at the sight. He imagined also that if he lashed out at any pigeon which came too close, and broke (for example) its wing, all these people would rise up in one mob and give him a terrible beating, simply out of human feeling and kindness to animals.

As he looked, rather furtively, at the faces that he passed—furtively, so as not to be challenged as having issued any invitations (for even the slightest glance at man or woman was likely to get in return an exceedingly bold, questioning look)—it struck him how completely, under circumstances of the slightest informality, people went to pieces in their dress and personal appearance, how their flesh, feeling the least permissive liberation from cloth or strap, began at once to bulge yearningly toward the great openness and horrible freedom of nature. The men who had taken off their hats proved to be shining bald with sweat; when they opened their coats their bellies tended to push aside contemptuously the flimsy sport shirts and peer forth in hairy boldness. With the women it was even worse: straps fell from shoulders, jabots crumpled, skirts rode high over knees spread wide apart, garters like instruments of constricting torture were disclosed cutting deep into the fat which rolled up on either side of them. The still air reeked with smoke as though it were a poolroom, and the walk was thick with cigarette butts, cigar butts, mashed bits of unidentifiable goo (some of it like chocolate, some like blood) and mashed bits of quite identifiable turds, presumably of dog. There were also, chiefly on the grass behind the benches, great quantities of tired-looking newspaper, some of it yellow. The white excrements of the pigeons fell everywhere, stippling the sidewalk, the benches, possibly now and then the people; and through all this ran the confused burble, marked by transient passages of clarity, of what seemed one vast conversation.

Julian was disturbed less by the scene, however, than by his attitude toward it, which appeared to him to be precious and undemocratic. "Would you want people to do without a park altogether?" he asked himself, and saw at once the danger of falling into the opposite heresy, that of pitying people because of their appearance, their behavior, et cetera.

Nevertheless, it was a relief to reach, after two blocks, the Zoo. The animals, comparatively neat and orderly, each had individual cages, or there would be two or three in a cage, all members of the one family; this effect of decency, and the comparative coolness of the houses, some of which however smelled bad, made a pleasant impression on Julian, who philosophically compared the calm demeanor of the lions and tigers with the frenzied rushing about of the humans, particularly the children.

"The powerful, the splendid and the cruel," he thought, "are locked up; that is what this world is."

Looking up, he saw a number of balloons, gas-inflated, which had escaped their owners' grubby hands and were now sailing aloft and becoming smaller and vanishing into the hot yellow haze of the sky; a few of these balloons had become lodged in the branches of trees, where they hung like moons over a garden party, and this sight for some reason struck Julian as terribly sad, a real emblem of loss and loneliness, yellow balloons, and green, and orange.

"It is love," he told himself, "which does all this."

The thought came to him as an inexpensive sort of revelation while he stood in the crowd which pressed to the bars of the pool where the sea lions played. The sight of these beasts in the water, and even their disappearance in the water, entranced Julian. Here, he thought, was power and freedom, he could even imagine from this small pool how smoothly, silently, and at what great speed they would travel under the waters of the wild, arctic sea, themselves mysterious, tranquil and assured. Their behavior on land, however, displeased him; when they hauled themselves up into the concrete house that had been built for them, or stretched out on its roof, they seemed domestic and ridiculous; they amused the crowd, he thought disgustedly, by *being human.*

But the thought of love, just now, disturbed him a good deal, mainly, in fact, by its absence in himself; he did not seem to love anyone. Whatever it was he felt for his wife Sylvia bore no resemblance to those pale, passionate dreams of adolescence which he did not just now feel for anyone else either, and which he remembered at this moment only to wonder where they might have gone. It was true—though scarcely interesting—he was getting older, he would one day die. There came into his head the faces of women adored, caressed, some of them in reality, long ago; he had no desire to caress these women at present, some of them must be, in fact, well along in years, married, with children of their own who would now, or in a few years at most, be going through the same novelty of passion themselves, wondering why no one in the world had ever experienced the same before. Most frightening of all, one could do nothing to stop this terrible passage of time, which cut down and down on the limitless variety of life until, finally, nothing remained but the narrow grave. Was it now, already, too late? A few, trivial years, and he would be dead; many of these people standing near him would be dead, some of the children, even, would be dead. The thought was like a secret intimacy.

He was standing next to two young men, one black and the other white. The fact that they were companions pleased him; it was democratic, like a poster in the subway. Just in front of them stood a young girl—a young woman, say—whose age he would put about twenty or so; she was blonde, her profile as she intently watched the sea lions seemed to Julian very delicate and pure, also somewhat withdrawn, as though no crowd existed about her at all. He wondered if she were with the two young men, and decided that even if she were not they would soon try to pick her up; he envied them.

As though she felt his eyes on her, the girl turned and looked at him without disapproval, with a neutral sort of curiosity that finished, as she turned away again, in a demure, rather secretive smile. She seemed to be merely watching the sea lions again, but Julian felt the tension her glance had caused in him; and felt it, too, as though they both had the same senses, so that what he was feeling clearly must be felt by the girl. The strangeness, anonymity, of this relation—for it was already a relation—its secrecy in public, attracted him, and he tried to get up courage to go on, but was prevented by his uncertainty concerning the two lads behind her, who, even if they were not her companions, would surely see what he was up to. The fear that a rejection would make him ridiculous in their eyes made Julian highly conscious of his own appearance, his being well-dressed, and, for this place and this season, very formally dressed. Nevertheless, while he half watched the seals, he affected a vague smile, so that if she turned round again she would see him smiling and yet not irretrievably smiling at herself; the expression might be interpreted just as she chose.

She did turn, she smiled more openly. Then by a piece of luck the two young men moved away, out of the crowd, so that no one remained between them. Julian edged forward and to one side in such a random and apparently unconscious manner as to suggest that the people behind were pushing him forward to the railing at which she stood. His hand, on this railing, was touching hers, which she moved slightly away; but at the same time she smiled once again.

"Hello," he said.

"Hello," said she.

They stood and watched the sea lions for a few moments; the ease with which this had been accomplished somewhat frightened Julian even while it attracted him; his mind, racing on with the flickering speed of an old film, saw this girl already his mistress, saw the guilt, the inevitable discovery, shame, ruin. . . .

"Do you come here often?" she asked him, and, when he replied, "I thought I hadn't seen you here. I come to watch the seals, they look so cool. You must be very warm in that heavy jacket," she added.

"Would you like something to drink?" Julian politely asked, and she took his arm as they left. Julian was embarrassed, however, to see those two young men, the black and white, standing a little distance away, and hoped they had not noticed. "Though, after all," he asked himself, not without a certain pride, "what difference would that make?"

At the café on the terrace Julian had a beer and the girl, who said she did not drink, a coke. This dispelled somewhat the strangeness of their meeting, and Julian began to be a little bored. The girl was very pretty, however, though coarser of feature in full face than in profile.

"What is your name?" she asked, and he replied: "Federigo."

"Mine is Bianca," she offered in return. Evidently the convention belonging to such meetings was to be satisfied with first names. "What a lovely ring," she said, taking his hand for a closer look. "Is it your family crest?"

"Well," said Federigo, embarrassed, "it used to be, long ago."

"My family is very poor," she said. "Both my parents are dead."

He could not think of anything to say to this, and so they were silent for a moment; then he asked, "Do you usually let strangers speak to you like this?"

"If I think they're nice," Bianca said. "I do pretty much as I please."

"Don't you have to work?" he asked.

"Sometimes I do modeling," she replied, and added, "I live with my uncle and aunt. If they ever knew I spoke to strange men—oh, lordie." She looked at him boldly, with a keen curiosity.

"You're married, aren't you?" she rather announced than asked. "Oh, it's not hard to tell, you have that heavy sort of look about you."

"Are you married?" asked Federigo.

"Lord, no," Bianca said gaily. "I was, once, but my uncle had it annulled. My uncle is very strict."

After their drink, they walked; at first she took his arm, later they went along hand in hand. It occurred to Federigo, horrifyingly, that they might meet some acquaintance of his; but he decided it was unlikely, in the midst of the Park, and made it a point of honor to keep hold of her hand.

Bianca was fairly tall, and slender; she walked in a free, rather dawdling manner which allowed her body now and then to lean for a moment against his. She wore a perfume which he thought crudely alluring; there was about it a pathos of poverty which set a kind of debased and romantic tone to their being together. So far as Federigo was concerned, they were getting on splendidly; Julian also, for his part, felt a sweet, wild, yet strangely innocent pleasure in all this, as though Central Park were a kind of Eden within whose bounds nothing that happened could really be wrong. They did not talk much, finally; before parting, they sat together on a bench in a relatively lonely walk among trees, and smoked a cigarette.

"I like you, Bianca," he said, savoring the bittersweet of duplicity in the aroma of her hair.

"I like you, Federigo," she replied.

"We might meet again," he suggested, "we might go out together some evening."

"This is so sudden," she said, with a little laugh. "What about your wife?"

"Never mind about her," he said, feeling the most delicate twinge in the conscience. "Let me call you up."

"Oh, I couldn't do that," she said. "If my uncle ever got to know . . ."

"Let's meet somewhere, then. We can arrange it now."

"You are persistent, aren't you?" Bianca laughed again.

"Sometimes, not every night, but sometimes, I go for a walk in the Park. I like to go into the Zoo at night and look at the seals."

"Tonight, then?"

"It could be," she replied. "About eleven?"

"You couldn't make it midnight, could you?" He had remembered Hugo's party. "Just at the stroke of midnight, by the seals?"

"It would be awfully late," she said, considering gravely, "but I could try."

She got up, shook his hand rather formally, leaned close to him for a moment in the mere sketch of an embrace, then walked away down the path.

"Midnight, then," he called after her, but she did not look back.

2

Sylvia and Marius did not part after lunch. As they stood on the sidewalk outside Mme. Modera's, and seemed to have, at least from Marius's end, some trouble in at last saying good-by, Sylvia looked at her watch with a show of efficiency and announced that she must drive out to the rest home and pay a visit to Alma.

"I haven't been to see her *once* since this latest trouble," she said. "It's shameful, the way we neglect people when something goes wrong for them. We're afraid of catching it ourselves, I guess."

"You know, I ought to go, too," Marius said. "I'll drive out there with you."

This was not precisely the response Sylvia anticipated, since she had introduced the subject of Alma only in order to make the farewell less lingering; in fact she had not, in her own mind, finally decided whether to visit Alma that afternoon or no. It was such an extremely nice day, she feared that the sight of her friend in doleful circumstances (Sylvia imagined Alma lying naked on straw, in a cell) would depress her dreadfully—and then, what would there be to talk about? On the other hand, though, it would mean a drive into the country, Marius would be pleasant company on the way, and above all he would share the burden of finding something to say to Alma.

"We'll take the dogs along," she said, as though on sudden inspiration. "They need the air, poor things."

They stopped in the apartment to get the dogs, and waited there while the car was brought around from the garage. In the ten minutes or so that this took, Marius attempted to make love to Sylvia, who permitted him to kiss her, not very convincingly, once, then made herself out to be very busy tidying things in the kitchen. Marius followed her about from refrigerator to sink and so forth, but Troilus and Cressida, liberated from their captivity in the bathroom, kept frisking about their mistress so that they got in his way.

"Visit Alma another time," he said, not altogether serious and not altogether as a joke either. "Lock up the dogs and we'll spend the afternoon here."

"Please," Sylvia said, "you're not being funny in the least."

The car was a convertible, they had the top down. With the

dogs in the back seat, sitting up with their noses in the air, the entire group looking quite aristocratic, they drove across the Triborough Bridge and out on Long Island toward the sea. Once they got on the parkway, Sylvia drove very fast, and Marius, glancing at her face in profile, with the long hair blown back, admired her more than ever and thought of her as Artemis; at the same time the speed made him nervous, and, though he forbade himself to say anything on this point, he sat very tensely and kept pressing with both feet on the floorboard as if it were one large brake.

When Marius said to Sylvia, at lunch, that he loved her, he had not meant it in the least, but was consciously, with the tact of a dramatist, responding to the situation which was forming itself between them. Such dramas had no author, they were the common property of the agonists, a *commedia dell'arte;* there were, however, certain conventional lines of plot and even of dialogue laid down to guide people in their improvisations. It had seemed to him that "the girl" (so he called her now, in his thoughts) wished to crystallize a certain romantic and critical element in their relation, and that she wished to do this, in the first place, for reasons that scarcely had any personal connection with himself at all. He wondered why, and decided—not for the first time—that she must be unhappy; unhappy, probably, in her marriage, but without any guarantee that she would be otherwise without her marriage. He regarded such qualities as, finally, built into people—he himself, for example, was unhappy—and without much prospect of change no matter how they might delude themselves by making local and particular changes in either their circumstances or their habits; as a matter of course, however, he rebuked himself for this somewhat Calvinist tendency in his thought. But at the same time, because he was unhappy, unhappiness powerfully attracted him, and though he did not love Sylvia when he had announced to her that he did, he recognized at least in theory the force of that maxim which would have it that we do not run away because we are afraid, but are afraid because we run away. Almost invariably, in so rational a mind as his, the formulation preceded the sentiment; the mind was spontaneous but the feelings had to be coached.

Among their friends, Sylvia and Julian were considered to have a *very good marriage;* they were supposed, that is, to be happy, and much admired on this account by numbers of people who regarded them as a kind of model which might be proposed for the ideal but which it would therefore be hopeless to try to imitate. Marius alone, it might be, saw this ideal as the last hypocrisy of all; he saw this at first simply out of a gift for paradox, but it seemed now to be demonstrating itself before his eyes. He asked himself, sitting there in the car, how far he was prepared to follow this situation, and correspond in it to the role which Sylvia, no doubt, would devise for him; and he replied that his interest in the situation itself, to say nothing of the attractiveness of the girl, would take him very far indeed; only he doubted that he would be very often prepared to pay for lunch.

Sylvia, meanwhile, was wondering whether she ought to tell Marius about the anonymous letter, and, if she did, whether she had best treat it as a dream or as a real event. Marius was intelligent, and for this reason she doubted he would be helpful. Probably he would laugh, especially if she presented her trouble as having been caused by a dream; his knowledge of psychiatry was, intellectually at least, superior to her own, and allowed him to take, sometimes, a very cynical line about her views of the subject; to which she would insist that all his knowledge, since it was not the product of real experience, did not enable him to understand the first thing about the matter; nevertheless, he would very likely laugh at her.

She had sense enough not to take Marius's declaration of love with any great seriousness; people did that sort of thing, it was a kind of game, the charm one discovered in one's acquaintances depended, in a way, on their doing that sort of thing with the right, the light, emphasis. Being admired was pleasant, of course; but tenable only in connection with the utmost honesty. Sylvia's view of marriage, in this respect, made it out to be an up-to-date zoo, where there are no cages but only moats and deep trenches which from most angles of vision let the animals appear to move in perfect freedom and even to approach the spectators; it was an ideal illusion of nature, the animals seemed to stay where they were out of freedom and a sense of duty which had led them to choose their environment, but the trenches were very wide and deep.

Nevertheless, the letter, whether as dream or reality, had produced in her feelings today a critical moment; not that she had not already, many times, entertained the idea of having an affair (only to dismiss it because she did not really believe such things were done by other women she knew well), but that the letter extended the range of her imagination by suggesting not only that she was already having an affair but also that it was, on the whole, as much amusing as reprehensible. Federigo, whoever he was, was right; she did get left too much alone, and if it happened one day that she took a lover, Julian would be as much to blame as herself. Perhaps not quite so much.

Still, what was virtue, and what did one expect of it? If one were well brought up, and had virtue drilled into one in all sorts of subtle and crude ways for so many years, so that by the time one married one simply *was* virtuous—had taken the iron into one's own soul, so that there need never be any prompting from outside again—one began implicitly, she supposed, to expect some kind of reward for it. One went on for years being virtuous—a negative thing to be, by the way—and slowly began to come to the consciousness that *this*, whatever it was, the way one actually happened to be living, was the sole reward and all the reward one was going to get. One became convinced—or did one?—that *this* must be happiness, if only in contrast to the dreadful unhappiness that lay the other way; an unhappiness of which occasional examples came to her notice, one of which they were at this moment going to visit. There were casualties, undeniably; being married to a man like Hugo Alter, for example. You might even say Alma should be happy to be rid of him, but madness (if that was what it was) would be a considerable price to pay for so dubious a freedom, and even so, it was not the full price, it did not take into account a dozen or so years of marriage, a dozen or so years wasted on an unsuccessful experiment. Wasted? It seemed a sweeping judgment.

"It is dreadful about Alma, isn't it?" she said at this point to Marius, and added, primly, "One hates to see even a bad marriage break up. People should stick together."

"*Pour encourager les autres*," Marius put in.

"There's that, of course," she said. "But doesn't it seem to you that Hugo is being pretty despicable? I mean, this unseemly rush to get the divorce through while she is in this condition?"

"It seems that if she got much worse there could not be a divorce," Marius said. "And then, too, they had arranged it before she absolutely collapsed."

"I suspect—it's a dreadful thing to say—but I suspect he bribed the doctors to say she was sane. I don't know," she added hastily, "it sounds very melodrama when you say it right out—but I really believe people behave that way sometimes, you know. We don't see them doing it, we only see the results, but there must be terrible cruelty in so many places."

"I've never had the least doubt of it," Marius replied, "but I don't really believe he bribed the doctors. I should think that was not easy to do, really."

"Hugo is extremely rich," she reminded him. "That is probably why everyone goes along with whatever he does. He always was conspicuously and publicly unfaithful to her, for years."

With me, among others, she added to herself; for it was perfectly true that at the time of his brief affair with Sylvia Hugo had been already married to Alma, though it was true also (for what it was worth) that Sylvia and Alma had not yet become acquainted. Sylvia found it disturbing to have to recall this circumstance exactly as she was taking such a stern moral line. She had always thought of herself as the victim in that episode, but it now began to seem as though her resistance had been not altogether what it ought to have been. At any rate, whether so or no, she had nevertheless played some little part in developing the situation for which she had just denounced Hugo.

"I don't excuse any of us," she therefore added. "The way we behave, it looks as though we don't care—as if nobody believed in marriage any more. Just as soon as the divorce comes through, you know, he will marry that girl Louisa—everyone is quite aware he has been keeping her for at least one whole year, anyhow. She lived this winter in that old house of his, somewhere out here on Long Island, by the ocean."

"It must have been cold," Marius said.

"And the odd thing was," Sylvia continued, "her mother and younger sister were there with her, all perfectly at home, knowing the whole situation—he used to visit her weekends. It must have been funny," she suddenly added, "with mother sitting out on the porch in the snow."

"Hugo and Alma were as good as separated at that time," Marius said.

"Oh, no. It was when she found out about Louisa and the house on Long Island," Sylvia insisted, "that she broke down, finally. She tried to kill herself, you know."

"No, I hadn't heard that," said Marius, without surprise. "Are you sure?"

"She did. It was really rather ridiculous—how awful of me to laugh!—but it seems she hung herself from the chandelier by her bathrobe string, but it wouldn't hold her weight, she's rather heavy, you know—it pulled out all the plaster in the ceiling and came down on her head. She was quite badly hurt, just physically. Then, when they had her in the hospital, when she seemed to be almost well again, she broke this interne's nose, she kicked him, I believe, and rushed out through the corridors in her nightgown. I hear she got as far as the reception desk before they overpowered her. And now she is in this *rest home,* as they call it"—Sylvia wrinkled up her nose to show she was not deceived about rest homes—"and the doctors, if you please, say she is perfectly sane, only a little depressed." She laughed shortly. "She might well be depressed."

Sylvia turned to Marius, causing the car to swerve violently for a second, and said: "The cynicism of it is what bothers me." Seeing the expression of alarm on his face, she got the car back under control before continuing with: "At least, when people get divorced like that, they oughtn't to be allowed to marry again."

"Maybe they still believe love is possible," said Marius.

"For better or worse, in sickness and health, till death do us part," Sylvia said. "What a mockery!"

"Well, it is an institution," he observed, "and like all institutions it requires an occasional human sacrifice."

Compared with Sylvia's drastic expectations, their visit to Alma was at once a relief and a disappointment. The rest home, in the first place, was a pleasant-looking establishment consisting of a large, old-fashioned country house surrounded at a little distance by white cottages, all tastefully landscaped with trees and shrubbery and flower borders, more or less like an extension of the parkway itself and evidently very expensive. They saw one or two nurses, it is true; otherwise, they might have been in a hotel.

Alma was not even alone, much less in bed (or locked away, as Sylvia had darkly imagined, in a dungeon); she was already entertaining half a dozen men and women whom Sylvia and Marius did not know, and whom she introduced as her friends. She seemed poised, quite pretty, though thin and pale, and unenthusiastically pleased to see the newcomers; she said it was sweet of them to come, and made a nurse bring martinis in a beaker, with medicine glasses. She herself did not drink anything, but kept rolling about on the palm of her hand a little pink pellet.

The room, a glass-enclosed porch on the south side of the main building, was filled with conversation and smoke, like a cocktail party, which Sylvia uncomfortably supposed was just what this was. She felt a little ashamed, but also a little angry at Alma.

"What is your little pink pill there?" she asked in a quiet moment, just to have something to say to her friend.

"Darling," said Alma, "that is my escape. A marvelous idea, I wonder why it hasn't become more fashionable than it is. When all you delightful, normal people begin to bore me, when your charm ever so slightly shows signs of failing, I shall pop it in my mouth and take a swallow of water. Then, in ten minutes, no matter how clever you believe you are being, I'll be asleep. One has just to remember to lie down with the limbs decently disposed and clothed, before it takes effect."

They stayed for half an hour; when they left, the party was still going on. Alma thanked them for coming, but did not seem particularly interested in having them do it again.

"You expected, perhaps, a padded cell?" asked Marius, as they drove away.

"No," Sylvia replied, "but I should have expected illness to be treated with more seriousness, more—I don't know—decency, I guess."

"Such as having Alma chained to a wall?"

"Don't be silly, you know what I mean. It seems as though nothing is serious any more."

"You mean," Marius said, "that one's strong feeling about the marriage vows demands a certain demonstrative unhappiness among the ruins. My dear, you would make a good Catholic, of a certain sort, but I am not sure it would be Christian."

"It is damn difficult to sympathize with people, sometimes," she said after a while.

"To pity them, you mean," he said. "Sometimes they just won't be pitied, more power to them. Listen, Sylvia, while you drive I'll tell you a story I read the other day; it will afford you," he added sententiously, "moral satisfaction."

"Yes?"

"Here it is. You know, don't you, that many primitive people have curious beliefs about the power of the dead? There's one tribe I recall, in the South Seas, where the people are very gentle and loving with one another—no wars, no violence—but when they die, the belief is that they become bitter enemies of the living. There's a parable, too, but that's not the story I mean to tell. This story is about the tribe of the Halmahera, very fierce and brave in battle because they have strong spiritual help. The way they get this strong spiritual help is, they capture a young boy from an enemy tribe and bury him up to his neck in the earth; then they torture him dreadfully, all the time telling him that the torture will stop as soon as he swears an oath to be forever on their side in battle, and always be loyal to them, the Halmahera, until now his enemies. Finally the boy can't stand the torture, and he swears the oath. At that moment, a man behind him, who has been stirring molten lead in a caldron, pulls his head back by the hair, forces open his mouth, and pours the molten lead down his throat."

"How frightful," Sylvia said.

"They regard it," said Marius, "as a certain guarantee he will not break his vow."

Chapter Four

FEW things, perhaps, have so little formality and stiffness about them as a modern party, where people appear to be blown together by a cyclone for a few hours of arduous merriment which most of them will later think of as having been a mistake; nevertheless, ancient and ceremonial purposes occasionally show through. The party at Hugo Alter's house would be in effect, though implicitly and without any announcements, the celebration of his engagement to Louisa Leonard; also, in a sense, her formal introduction to his society, the people with whom he habitually associated; thus, by remote parody, her debut. The old, traditionary forms, by which were asserted the solidarity of the tribe, persisted, although the tribe itself, now called *society,* no longer had any easily discoverable identity or meaning, and although the forms themselves, because Hugo was not yet as a matter of fact divorced, had to express themselves more by intention than by ceremony. Still, it was a public acknowledgment, as everyone concerned was assumed by everyone else concerned to know and recognize; that this was so afforded great satisfaction particularly to Mrs. Leonard, Louisa's mother and Elaine's, who felt that she had brought her troops through a long, difficult campaign to a victory which was honorable because it was victorious, and which would retrospectively supply, therefore, any loss of honor possibly sustained during the conflict.

Mrs. Leonard was a gaunt, austere lady of very old family, with manners and a tone which gave to a mere want of money the appearance of colonial simplicity. The idea that in allowing her daughter to receive the attentions of a married man she had behaved substantially like a madam would have been received by her—had anyone dared to present it—rather with surprise than indignation, as quite out of the range of notions with which a lady

392

might be supposed to be familiar. *Her* intentions—she might have said, in the improbable circumstance of her getting into a conversation on the subject—her intentions had been honorable from the first: marriage, and nothing less, being the object. Of course there had been difficulties, there always were, times (she would have supposed) had changed, and such an extraordinary procedure as the winter just past, in the house on Long Island, would certainly never have been permitted when *she* was a girl—but times had changed. People were always getting divorced, these days, and no one seemed to mind; it was in the papers every day. The romance between Louisa and Mr. Alter had gone on, so far as a mother was concerned, in the most honorable manner possible under the circumstances—he had never concealed the unhappy fact of his marriage, and proclaimed, from the first time she had brought up the subject, his intention of doing the right thing. Any moral discomfort involved in the winter on Long Island, in Hugo's visits to the house during that time, had been quite swallowed up in the physical discomfort of the experience—it was really intended, that place, for a summer cottage, and a primitive one, at that—and in some remote corner of her mind Mrs. Leonard compared this period of nervous suspense to Washington's winter at Valley Forge.

As for the marriage itself, it was certainly very fortunate; but she did not consider that all its benefits flowed in one direction. The wealth on one side was amply compensated, in her opinion, by lineage, breeding, beauty, on the other; Mr. Alter—for after all, what was an Alter?—must surely realize how his position was being improved.

Hugo, as a matter of fact, had thought of no such thing. He was in love again, intensely, and with a faint consciousness of becoming, possibly, an object of ridicule; he was, after all, fifteen years older than the girl, and while that was not precisely November marrying May, nevertheless the phrase which kept occurring to him about his condition—"in the prime of life"—uncomfortably suggested hair-dye and a truss. But his heart, a rather boyish and earnest heart to begin with, was singing with the recovery of feelings he had been afraid might never be his again. So far as he thought of his prospective mother-in-law at all, it was with slight horror at her complaisance, which he considered did not show a sufficient care of her daughter's name. Hugo took both love and marriage most seriously; that he himself was as it were constitutionally incapable of fidelity to one woman did not seem to him especially relevant, because, really, he was a person altogether without pride, and convinced of being in this respect a poor sinner much as he might have been convinced on proper medical testimony of his having diabetes.

"It is just the way I am," he had once said to Julian. "Believe me, I'd be happier if I were like you." And he added, with an earnestness which quite canceled out anything epigrammatic in the remark, "They talk about *free love,* but, believe me, it is not even inexpensive." He was always somewhat out of date; Julian could not remember hearing anyone use the phrase *free love* since they were in college.

Hugo was a tall but stout person, whose round face, light complexion and blond hair gave him an appearance of perpetual youth; as his hair was now thinning noticeably, this appearance had become exaggerated, he looked less like a youth and more like a little boy; the concentrated center of that large, round face showed the wistful, petulant innocence of childhood. He was always wonderfully well dressed in a somewhat old-fashioned and countrified style, of which the most conspicuous elements were a Norfolk jacket and a vest and square-toed shoes with very thick soles. His manners were beautiful, he was amiable and very generous in a lordly way which was sometimes resented; he tended to press things on people whether they wanted these things or not: "Here, use my car if you like." "Why not stay here whenever you're in town?" "If you're free this weekend, you must take over my place on Long Island." This easy behavior gained him, beyond the resentment of some, a number of followers who, Julian thought, imposed on him; but Hugo was wealthy enough, it seemed, or possibly insensitive enough, on this one point, not to notice.

There was perhaps one element in his nature which led to viciousness; he had an extreme love, amounting almost to religious veneration, for happiness. Hugo liked to be happy himself, and found that it conduced to his happiness to be surrounded by happy people, or by people, at least, who had the manners to give that impression whatever might be their inward feelings; so that, while he was generous to a fault where there was no need, and often exercised his generosity so as to anticipate request, he made what could be called a moral point of refusing his aid where the need for it was made depressingly obvious, and he had majestically turned off friends of long standing for being, over any length of time, gloomy in his presence.

This trait had something to do, in Julian's opinion, with his friend's behavior to Alma in the recent crisis. For Alma had endured Hugo's affairs, over a dozen years, with a patience more than exemplary and somewhat resembling, to an unprejudiced view, co-operation: "Our Lady of Perpetual Forgiveness," as one person had called her. She had suffered not only his women, but—perhaps more important to her—the money they cost him; she had suffered not only the money, but—and this must certainly have been more painful—Hugo's periodic collapses, apologies, resolutions and struggles of conscience, when nothing would do but he must confess all, not without detail, and beg her forgiveness. Theirs had never seemed, exactly, a marriage designed to last, but it had come to seem, finally, a marriage more or less accidentally fallen into such a pattern as allowed survival. The precise sequence of events leading to its final collapse had never become quite clear to anyone; people told tales around the fringes and were silent at the center. But Julian saw, or thought he saw, that one person could not go on indefinitely eating another's sins without some reciprocal motion; whatever Alma had got out of the arrangement, and it must have been something, to have lasted her a dozen years, had in the end proved insufficient to her needs. It was difficult to say which had come first, the decision to divorce Alma, the idea of marrying Louisa, or Alma's falling ill, but Julian presumed on his knowledge of Hugo that it was the last of the three, and that the mainspring of the entire action was Hugo's intimate, possessive relation with the idea of happiness.

Julian frequently compared his own character with that of his friend, but never arrived at any finally satisfactory ratio. Sometimes it seemed to him that his own rather rigidly moral nature won the victory—it was better, after all, to live with one woman and keep out of trouble; nor did it escape him that Hugo's infidelities were budgeted on a scale which Julian himself could never afford. At other times, at times such as the present, when it had become with him more or less a point of honor to commit an act of infidelity (to have, as he put it, a secret life), he saw Hugo as roy-

ally courageous and himself as guilty of moral cowardice. Whatever Hugo did, Julian now thought, Hugo would never address to
himself pseudonymous letters designed to color his actions and
make them plausible; he might seek to excuse himself to others,
though not often, but he would never begin by deceiving himself.

But perhaps, on the other hand, Hugo had simply not got enough
imagination for anything so circuitous; and perhaps, again, the
moral deviousness with which the business was conducted would
be, for Julian, as it would not be for Hugo, the essential note, and
the adultery, carnally regarded, of quite a lot less importance.
After all, he now thought, it seemed very doubtful that Hugo
really had the happiness by which he set such store; the very fact of
his continually looking after strange women suggested a deficiency; very likely he was incapable of enjoying his many actual affairs
to the extreme degree that Julian, with nervous ardor, would enjoy
even one, even, perhaps, an imaginary one.

Julian and Sylvia, when they came home that afternoon, had
both been uneasy in their own minds to the degree that they failed
to notice each other's uneasiness. While getting ready to go to
Hugo's party, they engaged in the most animated and objective
conversation they had had for some time, each with the idea of
showing the other that all went along as usual; consequently they
quite enjoyed each other's company, and gained a fresh idea of
their happiness together.

Sylvia told Julian very circumstantially what it had been like to
visit Alma, and how the dogs had enjoyed the outing; Julian gave
Sylvia a witty account of his lunch with Mr. Archer More, adding
as an afterthought that he had walked home through the Park,
liked it quite well, and planned to do so more often during the
good weather. Sylvia, because Julian's animation in describing his
day seemed to her both natural and charming, felt certain that the
anonymous letter was a product of dream, just as Dr. Mirabeau
had said; Julian, on his part, became convinced by his wife's gaiety
and the nice way in which she laughed at his jokes that she could
not have seen the anonymous letter that morning, and he thought
complacently how, if all continued to go well, he would simply
intercept and destroy the next one, so that, after all, nothing decisive would have happened, the position would be as before. He

reminded himself with some severity that this was, however, not a definite decision; he promised himself to *think about it* before morning.

Sylvia kept telling herself that she need not feel guilty about Marius; only if she mentioned him at all she would be drawn on into explaining that she had spent most of the day in his company, that he had been in the apartment that afternoon, et cetera, all of which would be inconvenient; also it would mar the light tone of the conversation, which was raising her spirits and making her look forward to the party with pleasure. She would talk with Marius, she resolved, neither more nor less than with others, and she would keep out of those intimate conversations in dark corners which parties so frequently seemed to lead to.

It was nonsensical, Julian thought, to suppose that he really would meet that girl in Central Park at midnight. No doubt she was attractive, in a way, not a way he cared very much about, however; but what mattered was, chiefly, his not being the sort of person who did such things, which were suitable, after all, for college boys. To pick up a girl in the Park, of course, was amusing; it was, even, a flattering thing to think that one could, to have proved that one easily could. Even while he felt somewhat uneasy about it, he also felt rather proud of it. The action of that afternoon had about it a kind of criminal secrecy and gutter romanticism which was pleasing to consider: the prince and the flower girl. But of course it was the sort of thing that went no further; even if he did plan, on a suitable occasion, to take a mistress, she would not be the first one presented to his eyes by chance, and she would be—though this thought discomforted somewhat his liberal views—of his own class, or, better, his own *sort*.

Altogether, Julian and Sylvia, for these reasons and none better, pleased one another so much, their conversation and glances became so teasing and erotic while they were dressing for the party, that at last they felt impelled to spend a quarter of an hour together on the bed before going out. Julian was delighted to take his wife in such perfumed and silken circumstances—she was already almost dressed, and looking very fine—which suggested something romantic and clandestine; while Sylvia, too, was pleased with this sudden storm. Consequently they appeared at the party rather late, and in that rather smug, fat mood of good cheer which is often the result of such activities when legitimately engaged in, with the approval of church and state. It must be said, though, that as the erotic tension between them was thus relaxed, they charmed each other somewhat less than they had a few moments before; but that is natural enough, and each was privately willing to accept, for the time being, this compromise in which satisfaction was taken for love. This private and reserved area of experience, too, this little secret, did much to establish for each of them a benevolent superiority to the world in general and to the people at the party especially. It was like having money in the bank, Julian mused as they walked over to Hugo's house, and he wondered if one's pleasures past really could be added up into a substantial balance, or whether, once they were over, they simply and irretrievably vanished.

The party was large and gay and noisy. Hugo's apartment took up the whole top story of an old, graystone building, and had a terrace which overlooked the Park. When Julian and Sylvia came in, Hugo pushed his way toward them, bringing martinis.

"You already know Louisa," he said proudly, bringing her forward. "Here is Mrs. Leonard, Louisa's mother, and her sister, Elaine. You know everyone else."

It was always the fiction, at Hugo's parties, that everyone knew everyone else; Julian never failed to be amazed, however, at the extent of his friend's acquaintance; on a quick first look around he saw almost no one whom he knew. The invitation had been for cocktails, and read "five to eight o'clock," but the host typically in such a case provided an enormous buffet, and most likely no one who counted himself at all Hugo's friend had taken seriously the stipulation as to time, or provided himself with any other entertainment during the whole evening.

Louisa was slender-waisted and handsome, with very large, black eyes, and long, black hair falling free over her shoulders; a girl who wore massive, crude bracelets of hammered silver, and somewhat suggested a goddess of battles. When Julian had met her before, in less public circumstances, she had seemed subdued and rather maidenly, but now a certain wild emanation of power possibly without control frightened more than it charmed him, and he gathered that she was already a little drunk. He envied

Hugo his girl's youth—it was perhaps typical of Julian in his present state of mind to think of this marriage as in effect a transfusion of blood—while at the same time, youth or no youth, and through all the fine ripeness of complexion, sparkle of eyes and freedom of movement, he thought dourly that one detected already in the elder Miss Leonard the possibility and even the probability of Mrs. Leonard, with her pinched elegance and blue-gray hair, who was just now saying that Hugo had spoken so often about Sylvia and Julian, she had been longing to meet them. Now that she had met them, however, there seemed to be little more to be done about it, and Mrs. Leonard stood stiffly before them for a moment, then lunged away to the left with her cocktail glass extended. Hugo took Louisa suddenly away to be introduced to new guests, Sylvia too turned aside, rather because of the unwritten rule that one did not hang about one's husband than because she particularly wanted to talk to anyone else, and Julian was left in a little clear space with Elaine Leonard.

This girl was smaller than her sister, she came about to Julian's shoulder, and, in his opinion, which he gave himself as a connoisseur, quite pretty; the combination of black hair, cut short, and blue eyes, with intensely white skin and teeth, was pleasing, it had an extraordinary delicacy delightfully set off by a smile which was slightly crooked and eccentric, and which appeared and disappeared on her face with great suddenness, as though, behind the young lady which she of course was, there now and then looked forth another creature of *gamine* artlessness and honesty and, perhaps, impudence. All this Julian perceived with great objectivity, with aesthetic distance, and would perhaps have had no further interest in Elaine, whom he considered *too young,* had she not at once said something quite arresting to him.

"Do you know who you look like, very much?" And, as Julian winced slightly, "You must have heard this a hundred times before—you look exactly like Federigo Schwartz."

So, then, his name was Schwartz? With a certain superior irony Julian patted the right-hand pocket of his coat, and felt through the material the envelope of the first of Federigo's letters, which had been there since the morning.

"How do you know I'm not?" he asked, with a teasing smile. The girl looked at him steadily for a moment before replying.

"Oh, there are differences," she said. "You don't look as strict as Federigo, and your eyes—I think—are lighter."

"My eyes are quite dark," said Julian, a little piqued.

"But Federigo's are black, absolutely black. And anyhow, I don't believe you could be Federigo, because, you see, he's supposed to be off on a world cruise."

"Supposed to be—?"

"I mean, it's hard to know exactly, with Federigo," Elaine said seriously. "He is a secretive sort of person, and he'd as soon lie to you as not. Anyhow, about the world cruise, I didn't hear it from him, you know. Someone just said the other day that he had sailed. He has his own boat."

"Do you know him well, this Federigo?"

"Oh, no, I've just met him a few times. But you must know him, surely," she added, "he's your double, after all."

"It's a large city," said Julian. "I have heard of him but never met him."

"Probably," Elaine said, "he goes around pretending to be you, and getting you into trouble. It must be marvelous to have someone who looks exactly like you," she added.

Julian considered this statement with some care.

"Well," he said, "he hasn't signed my name to any checks, at least not so far."

"And have you signed his name to any?" asked Elaine.

The course of the party would imitate in little the growth and decay of civilizations, thought Marius as he stood on the edge of this one. In the beginning, a few isolated pairs and groups regarded one another suspiciously, like peoples whose sacred books tell them they alone were made by the gods, and who now have to account for the Ammonites and Edomites who surround them. Presently, a little commerce developed, assisted by the co-operations of hostility—for war was better than peace for the marriage of cultures—and larger groups began to form, with migrations from one part of the room to another. Then, as if on a signal, everyone began to co-operate on building the Tower of Babel; all conversations became one, and all conversations became unintelligible, often quite literally in a number of languages. There would follow a dispersion of the nations from this Plain of Shinar, and for a while all would be flux and chaos; the person with whom one believed oneself to be talking would suddenly no longer be there, would be replaced in mid-sentence by another or by several others, but all this would seem scarcely to matter, one ear being as good as the next. Then, slowly, more permanent arrangements and align-ments would develop; as the weak fell by the way, the nations whose name was History began to form the true, the intimate and mystical body of the party, from whose behavior general laws might be deduced; and it was at that time—still, for this particular party, a little way in the future—that the polyhistors, the great talkers and consecutive, traditionary thinkers, of whose number Marius accounted himself one, would step in to make continuity and a certain amount of sense of the business before an enthralled auditory. And then, once that great age had run its course, not without a further defection of the drunk and lecherous, would follow the *modern period* of arrogance, quarrels, fights (often enough) and rather pathetic, careless libertinism; until at last the pitiful remnant perceived itself to be huddled in isolation and silence among the ashes and cigar butts and the ruined glasses. Then—in the gray, cold light—everyone would go home, and that was a metaphor, thought Marius, for, quite literally, The Lord Knew What.

He made his way through the crowd to Julian Ghent and Elaine Leonard, who were now standing together as if they did not know why, in silence; to them he repeated the substance of what he had just thought concerning parties and world history. It fell quite flat. They smiled politely but without great interest, and Marius con-cluded they could not have heard all he said, the clamor around them was terrific. Still, the silence at the center of it, where they stood, became noticeable, and to make conversation Marius said: "I suppose Sylvia told you, Julian, we had a quite amusing after-noon driving out to see Alma." He turned to Elaine and added, "Mrs. Alter as is," to which Elaine replied, "I know." This little exchange gave Julian time to compose his face, which nevertheless looked a trifle grim.

"Yes, Sylvia said," he drawled with such ease and assurance that Marius at once perceived Sylvia had said nothing of the sort. The idiot, he thought, she wants to dramatize everything. He smiled boldly up at Julian, who was taller than he.

"Let me get us some more to drink," Julian said, taking their glasses, and he edged away through the crowd toward the bar.

"And you are the sister of the bride-to-be," said Marius, with calm and deliberative rudeness, to Elaine.

"I gather," she replied, "you are one of Hugo's loyal friends who believe he is making a dreadful mistake?"

"Oh, no," he said. "I don't make judgments."

"What do you do, then?"

"I watch," said Marius with great gravity. "I watch the comedy go by."

Elaine thought him an oddly pompous person, but at the same time felt some sort of alliance with him, perhaps because they were both younger than the general run of people there; also, of course, they were single, which in that gathering was not the usual thing to be. She could think of him as a boy, which of course was impossible with Hugo and Mr. Ghent and people like that.

"You wouldn't by any chance be one of the clowns yourself?" she asked, smiling her crooked and charming smile.

"You see through my disguise," he said, giving a little bow. "Underneath my breaking heart I have a wonderful time." What a delightful girl, he thought, and considered the likelihood of his falling in love with her there and then—for that smile alone, if for nothing else.

Julian now returned with the drinks. He was furious with Sylvia, also secretly pleased. There were secrets after all, then. Federigo, he told himself, was real. At the same time, looking at Marius rather carefully, he did not believe that this young man made love to Sylvia. A little pipsqueak intellectual, he thought, and poor at that. It was ridiculous. Nevertheless, Sylvia had kept it secret. Julian experienced a certain pride of power in the advantage he seemed to gain by knowing this small fact; he personally became the irony of fate, and felt, as he handed Marius a martini, as though the pearl onion in its depths had been poisoned.

Oh, dear, Marius thought as he accepted the drink, smiling again at Julian, is he going to become obstreperous? He determined to avoid Sylvia during the whole evening, not caring in the least whether this would allay her husband's suspicions or intensify them, but simply to punish her for this piece of what he called *romanticism*.

"Here's to us all," said Elaine, raising her glass and smiling impartially at both of them.

It was all very well, thought Sylvia with some annoyance, to decide that one would treat Marius with exactly the consideration one gave to others, not more and not less, but it was disturbing to have no opportunity whatever to put this excellent plan into effect. It was getting late, everyone had already eaten, and Marius, who by now had formed about himself a small cohort of people, out on the terrace, to whom he was being witty, had at most nodded twice to her across the room. She resented this rudeness on his part, and considered that if he valued her friendship, to mention nothing more, he had best be somewhat more demonstrative.

Sylvia, for all her recently developed line of psychiatric chat, was not a very light or easy person in society. She was rather slow, and did not like conversations which quickly broke off, or groups which constantly changed their composition while one thought what to say next. She preferred that stage, rather late in a party, at which it was possible to have a long, serious talk with some one agreeable person, a program which had only the one difficulty attached to it, that the gentlemen who most readily settled down to such a long, serious talk were also those most likely to want to take her off in some dark corner or down the hall to a bedroom.

For these reasons she had not, so far, been enjoying herself at all; she felt bored and very self-conscious, as though everyone would notice how much she stood alone. She was also drinking more than usual, perhaps for no better reason than that, where she was standing, there was no place to put down the glass, which accordingly she raised to her lips nervously every few seconds.

Hugo came over to her, and put his arm round her shoulder in a friendly way; she felt humbly grateful, and smiled up at him. Hugo was rather drunk, and leaned on her heavily.

"Having a good time, darling?"

"It's a lovely party, Hugo," she replied.

"It is, isn't it? Everyone happy, having a good time. No harm in that, is there?" he demanded sternly.

Sylvia was reflecting, rather vaguely, that this was the man, this one with his arm carelessly flung about her, who had first known her body. Here they were, eight years older, or nine years. It seemed horrible, and yet as though it visibly proved nothing ever mattered; she felt slightly faint, and as if she and Hugo were withdrawn into a space of silence amid the noise, a perceptible isolation. Something of this feeling must have transmitted itself to Hugo.

"We've never talked about that time," he said, somewhat aggressively.

"No," she said.

"You see, I knew what you were thinking," he said, though Sylvia considered this to be no great achievement; what else would she be thinking? But Hugo became very serious.

"I never would have forgiven myself," he said heavily, "if anything had happened to you then."

"Do you think that was nothing?" she bitterly asked him, thinking how odd it was that she and this large body next to her had together made a child, which of course could not be allowed to be born, much less to live, grow up, die—the wretched thing, whatever it was, and nameless at that, had not even had time enough to die. Likely enough she could never have another. Hugo thought that was nothing.

"I mean," he largely explained, with a gesture of the hand, as though this party itself were one of the results of their union, "it's all worked out, hasn't it? You and Jay, my dearest friends—you treat that Julian right, now," he admonished her. "He's a good man. And you're a good girl, Sylvia. Sometimes I think you two are the only really happy people I know. I hope it will be like that with Louisa and me."

"And Alma," Sylvia could not resist adding.

Hugo took his arm away and turned to face her.

"I know," he said mournfully. "You needn't push it. You couldn't make me feel more of a failure than I do already. Believe me, Sylvia, I know I'm to blame—but what can I do, what can I do about it now?" He looked down at her with an expression of pathetic and childish helplessness. "I just *am* that way," he pleaded, adding, with some smug satisfaction, "but my Louisa will keep me in line—look at her over there." He pointed out on the terrace, to the group around Marius Rathlin. "She's got strength enough for two, I count on that," said Hugo.

Sylvia watched Louisa drain the remains of her drink and hand the glass to a young man with a crew-cut who made off toward the bar. She was glad that Hugo could see this as a demonstration of strength of character.

"Tell me, seriously, Sylvia," Hugo said, "does Jay know what happened with us?"

"He has never known you were involved," she replied. "Of course, he had to know about the child—and I presume," she added with an angry smile, "he may have deduced some prior sexual activity from that."

"Don't joke, darling," Hugo said. "I've always felt badly about that. Sometimes I think I owe it to Julian to let him know, and you do, too. This way, it's like holding a dirty joke over his head—if you see what I mean."

"I really don't see what would be the point," Sylvia said, "now. They say," she added, "that every cell in one's body is replaced in a matter of seven years. The people we were then must be outlawed by the statute of limitations, or something."

"Believe me, Sylvia," Hugo said, "I've always been attracted to you. If I weren't a reformed character—" He broke off, laughing, and took her arm. "Let's go out on the terrace," he said, "and listen to Marius being witty, if that is what Marius is being."

"I'd really be just as pleased, Hugo," said Sylvia, "if you could control your sudden access of conscience to the point of not confessing to Julian. A wife's job is difficult enough without that."

They strolled together out on the terrace.

2

At eleven-thirty Julian abruptly left the party. He spoke to no one, and it did not seem likely that anyone had seen him go. If anyone had, that did not much matter either, for it was characteristic of Hugo's larger parties to proliferate, late in the evening, half over town; people went to nightclubs, for rides in automobiles, to other parties; then, sometimes, they came back.

Doubtless his lust for the strange girl Bianca had been developing unconsciously in him almost from the moment he had left his wife's arms several hours before. But this simple motive would not by itself have been strong enough to overcome the guilt it evoked, and therefore employed those hours in allying itself with con-

sciousness and reason, and building a complex structure of rationale whereby the act itself might be supported. By the time he left,
this rationale, for all practical purposes, had replaced in his mind
the motive of lust; to the extent that he told himself, in the elevator,
that he was merely going to walk once or twice around the block,
and not until he found he was walking rapidly down Fifth Avenue,
on the Park side, did he fully acknowledge again what it was that
he had set out to do.

In the first place . . . But there was no orderly arrangement of
reasons, they tumbled extravagantly one over the other like the
explanations of a guilty schoolboy who does not see that one
excuse is infinitely better than two. What it all came down to,
though, was that he was angry (Sylvia), drunk (himself) and bored
(the party).

He had been one of the group surrounding Marius Rathlin on
the terrace. It was true that Marius talked brilliantly and was
amusing, particularly when he became a little drunk. But what
was all this, thought Julian disgustedly, but talk talk talk? What
had it to do with anything that mattered? Sylvia had lied to him by
failing to mention Marius; this caused Julian a bitter satisfaction,
it represented an opportunity, the world implied so tenuously and
delicately in the anonymous letter began to exist. Here was Marius, now, talking (as though that world did not exist) about religion. Marius was wearing his lecturer's voice; thin, high-pitched,
with a reedy intensity that further annoyed Julian, who moved a
little away from the group and stood by the railing of the terrace,
where he abstractedly entertained for a moment the idea of throwing himself down on the street.

Beyond lay in silence Central Park, a darkness thinly laced with
lights; while he watched, a traffic light changed from red to green
out there in the black space. Bianca would be walking, perhaps,
toward the Zoo, toward the pool, where he imagined the seals,
silent and unwatched now, plunging swiftly through the opacity of
the waters.

He was bored. Out there, somehow, in the silent spaces of the
Park—where he had played as a child, and how far away that
was!—lay life, impulse, secrecy; while up here on Hugo's fine terrace there was talk. Marius was praising Catholicism now on aesthetic and—of all things—*hygienic* grounds; he developed the par-

adox that it was the most satisfactory religion "for a gentleman" because it was the most pagan of religions. Mythology, animism, "the nasty practices of the heathen," Catholicism did not deny these things but rather sanctified them, drew them up into grace; it gave the believer a wide and living world. Thus Marius. But Julian considered that all these fine ladies and gentlemen gathered here, listening to the fine talk, kept in their hearts the secret of lust, that their inmost thoughts were concentrated on sex, that madness thinly veiled possessed them all, the madness which all the forces of society seemed designed at once to provoke and restrain but never to allay.

"Therefore," he said to himself, "we live in hypocrisy. I am not alone, but I am merely bitten by the same great louse which crawls in the night from bed to bed." But this acknowledgment made him feel more alone than ever.

He was drunk, though only to that point at which he had a magnified view of his own powers and of what was possible. Because his thoughts were secret, he felt secrecy around him like a shroud, and he left the house.

Julian was fifteen minutes beforehand at the rendezvous; this annoyed him. Like a schoolboy, he thought. The loneliness of the Zoo frightened him somewhat; what seemed the laughter of beasts in distant cages intensified the silence which appeared to him to belong to his own moral isolation. Bright green leaves whispered and waved about the globe of a nearby lamp, and the sidewalk beneath reflected a million particles of gray, stone light; it might have been a landscape on the moon.

The dark waters of the seal pool rolled uneasily, the oily surface caught occasional ripples of light. A seal barked loudly close at hand, and Julian jumped. A policeman passed under the street lamp across the pool and seemed to be eying Julian closely, but said nothing and went on, the metal plates of his heels striking the pavement in a measured beat.

Perhaps she would not come? At this moment Julian hoped she would not. He allowed himself five minutes more, then he would take a taxi and in another five minutes appear at the party as though he had never left it. In the darkness behind him animals groaned and chuckled as though in uneasy sleep. Bianca came from the shadows and took his arm. She was wearing a white dress, sleeveless and loosely cut. Julian found his heart beating very rapidly, and he imposed upon himself feelings of desperate gaiety. At one instant he thought: no one will ever know. At the next instant he thought that it would always be possible to kill himself afterward.

"Where shall we go?" he asked, noticing that his voice shook in the attempt to keep its tone light and casual.

"I know a place," she replied almost in a whisper, and he allowed himself to be led away. They walked westward, out of the Zoo, through a tunnel smelling of urine, up a dark path. Julian put his arm around Bianca's waist, his hand slipped down to rest on the curve of her backside, which hardened and softened agreeably with the rhythm of her walking; he observed that she seemed to have nothing on under her dress, and he confirmed this observation by sliding his hand up to touch her breast, at which she leaned closer to him and rested her head on his neck so that he smelled again, in some excitement, the strong, raw perfume with which she seemed almost drenched. Julian's heart was pounding, his mind was shaken by a feeling of wild freedom in which nothing, not the most horrifying or perverse imaginings from dreams, would be forbidden him. The strange thought came into his head that he wished Bianca would resist so that he might rape her. Possibly he would kill her afterward.

Presently, in a place of darkness, she led him aside from the path. They clambered hand in hand up fairly steep slopes of rock, then into a grove of young trees. She turned to face him, and for a moment they stood apart.

"All right. Now," he heard her say in a new, sharp voice, and almost at the same moment felt himself seized from behind by an arm around his throat, while something else, harder than a fist, came at him from in front and smashed against his nose and mouth. He was thrown heavily to the ground and kicked once or twice, more with contempt, perhaps, than to hurt.

"Go over him good," the girl said. "The bastard's married, too." Great indignation in her voice, thought Julian, who did not altogether lose consciousness under several more blows in the face. He felt his coat wrenched around under him, the lining torn out. Someone with a flashlight looked into his wallet; an inadvertent motion of the light disclosed the two young men, the black and the white, who had been standing behind Bianca that afternoon at the Zoo. One of them, in darkness again, knelt and took Julian's wrist watch. Bianca whispered to them to hurry, he felt a final kick under the ribs, then there was silence and darkness.

After a few moments Julian sat up and took a deep breath. He hurt in a number of places, but was able to move all his limbs. The taste of blood was in his mouth, and he felt a trickle down his neck also; the place where he had cut himself shaving had been opened up again.

For all this, he felt strangely light and peaceful, almost amused. The suddenness of the attack had given him no time to be afraid, and the entire affair had been over very quickly. Of course, it was disagreeable to lose one's wallet and watch and be beaten up at the same time, but Julian's sense of a merited punishment, and one which, moreover, had both anticipated and prevented the crime it punished, gave him an odd feeling of relief. With his clothing torn, blood on his face and collar, he thought gratefully that he had done nothing wrong, that the situation had not changed, that inwardly, by the preservation of grace, he was still the man he had been.

A disagreeable thought struck him: would this assault be followed by blackmail? The wallet of course contained, in addition to some forty dollars, his name, address, et cetera. Suddenly he remembered the anonymous letter; to his great relief this was still in the side pocket of his coat. Probably, he decided, such people did not go in for blackmail; criminals, he had heard, usually stuck to one line of work; and perhaps these little wretches could not even write. This educated thought a little restored his confidence.

Just now Julian realized, in a moment of quiet terror, that he was not alone. Someone, a white jacket faintly glimmering, sat beside him on the ground. Out of the darkness a voice spoke.

"Poor dear," it said. "Poor lamb, you have had a bad time, haven't you?"

The voice—a man's voice—was gentle, caressing, faintly ironic at the same time. The expressions it employed seemed to Julian faintly effeminate, and suggestive of the character of a male nurse.

Now a hand with a handkerchief began to mop at his face. The handkerchief was wet, but smelled slightly also of some sort of toilet water. Julian pushed it away.

"I'm perfectly all right," he said severely, but discovered on trying to stand up that this statement was an exaggeration. The stranger gently and firmly helped him to his feet and supported him with an arm around his waist.

"Here, try to walk a step or so," the voice advised him. "I'll hold you."

With the stranger's assistance Julian was able to get on, limping slightly, and even to get down the rocks to the path. They walked on together.

"You must feel an awfully foolish boy," the voice said out of darkness, its tone both soothing and distantly amused. "You ought to have someone to take care of you."

"I appreciate your help," said Julian, "but, if you don't object, we won't discuss the matter."

"Embarrassment, oh, dear," said the stranger, and clucked with his tongue several times, most disagreeably to Julian. "You've made a positive ass of yourself, and you're afraid I know it." There followed on this a loud, rather too musical laugh. Then they came into the light of a street lamp. Julian, turning, looked into his own face, his own eyes. The stranger—if he could be called that—met his gaze steadily and coldly, with a smile which Julian was unable to return and which caused him finally to drop his eyes.

"Yes," said the other with an air of quiet self-satisfaction, as though it explained everything. "Yes."

For reasons which he could not fathom, Julian was not even surprised.

"You are Federigo," he rather muttered than said, his eyes still on the ground.

"Come, keep walking," the other said. "I think it's time we had a little talk, you and I, and I don't want to be forever about it. Besides, we must get you cleaned up and presentable."

Julian let himself be escorted, Federigo's arm linked in his, for some distance, to a paved stone circle in the center of which stood a fountain. The waters fell from a pitcher held aloft by three stone women closely grouped, and splashed into a surrounding trough, on the edge of which they now sat down. The entire area was dimly lit by street lamps placed around the outer edges, and Julian recognized the place as one where he had once gone roller-skating, around and around the fountain. He looked down into the waters, which were filthy with shredding cigarette butts, matches, candy wrappers, then at Federigo, who was dipping his handkerchief and wringing it out.

"Your intentions," said Federigo, "have doubtless been of the best all along. But you are, you know, a dreadful innocent. Here, hold still," and he began washing Julian's face and throat with the handkerchief.

"They said you were on a world cruise," Julian managed to say through the rather rough scrubbing he received. "But you don't surprise me, you know, I'm not surprised at all. It is quite surprising that I'm not, when you come to think of it." He felt that he was babbling most stupidly, but could not stop. "Did you know that I took your name in vain?" He giggled. "On a letter, it was, a ridiculous letter, though I don't know if it was so ridiculous after all, do you see?"

"Please hold still and be quiet," said Federigo.

He continued to scrub Julian's face vigorously, then rearranged as neatly as possible his shirt and tie, buttoned up his coat.

"A little awkward," he said, "but not too bad. If people do notice, you can always put on a haughty expression and tell them you'd rather not discuss the matter. Your haughty expression does really frighten people, you know; even if they see it is mere childishness, and laugh about it behind your back, they are afraid to say anything to you. Of course, they talk about it among themselves. . . . It's funny, isn't it, what a great deal of such hocus-pocus goes to making up a character, a personality, something that really, in the world's eyes, exists? *Pulvis et umbra,* darling, and yet—there it is, big as life, moving around, putting out pseudopodia in the direction of what it thinks it wants. How dramatic and really entertaining it all is! Which reminds me, my friend, what do you think of your little performance this evening?"

"I was an idiot," Julian said in a low voice; he felt as if he were back in grade school, and looked cautiously at Federigo to see if he had answered aright.

"Oh, as to that—it is not absolutely certain," said Federigo. "On the one hand, yes. And, on the other hand—hardly. So the phrase goes, among eminent educators, statesmen and divines. Operationally, it is hard to deny you've been a fool; yet, as I said, your intentions were sound."

"I don't know what it was I wanted," Julian said sadly.

Federigo, for answer, took Julian's hand, closed it into a fist, and rapped the knuckles painfully against the stone rim of the basin where they sat.

"That's your trouble," he said. "You don't really believe it's there till it draws blood. Of course you know what you want, only you're ashamed to say so. You want to know the worst."

Julian considered this statement in silence, looking at the slight cut on the knuckle of his middle finger.

"Yes, blood," said Federigo. "From your own private stock and individual blood bank. You have, I believe, some five quarts of it crawling around in you at approximately a mile an hour top speed, and only slightly faster than that in the heat—as you might call it—of passion." He smeared his own finger on the cut and daintily licked the blood from it. "Salt as sea water," he said, "which is very nearly what it is. It has built up that wall of skin and bone and brain which keeps you from being the All. All that a boy is he owes to his mother, it's a wise child, and so forth." He laughed, and put his arm around Julian. "Put it another way," he continued. "Did you ever stop to think, years ago, when you came out here to play—you roller-skated right around here a number of times—well, did you ever believe you would be here tonight?"

Julian tried to disengage himself from the encircling arm without openly using force, but found it impossible.

"You think you know everything, don't you?" he sneered childishly. "How could I have thought of any such thing?"

"How, indeed?" concurred Federigo, as though this explained everything. "And yet, you know, time is not the whole business. How many times, already, do you suppose you have walked over the very place where you will die?"

"This is ridiculous," Julian said, trying to get up but being heavily restrained by his own feeling of weakness as well as by the arm across his back. "I don't know you, and I don't believe I want to."

"Oh, now, I should scarcely say that," Federigo objected. "Who signed whose name to a letter—or two letters? Besides, I only want to help you to what you want. I'm not here for my own pleasure, you know.

"Look, let us consider it this way," he continued briskly. "As two men of the world, let us agree on one thing, that whatever it is you want, it is not simply to seduce one or two little girls, or for that matter a thousand and three little girls. Very likely one little girl is much like another, when it comes to that last dreadful scene on the bed—don't deny it, dear boy, you do think it's dreadful, I know you do. You are perfectly aware, are you not, that if it was your ambition to go to bed with this one and that one—if it was truly your ambition—it could be arranged quite easily, without this fuss over anonymous letters and strangers in the Park? That little creature, by the way, had clap anyhow, so you are better off than you realize. Or perhaps a touch of clap, a mild dose, is included among your secret desires? Perhaps that would have pleased your mighty righteousness very nearly as well as being beaten about the chops with a flashlight and robbed of your money? Who knows? I merely offer the possibility for your consideration.

"Oh, dear Julian, I've known so many of your sort in my time, you cold Rover Boys of the spirit. Perhaps you think you are the only man in the world who has had the idea of sending himself anonymous letters about his wife? You got the idea you were a pretty wicked lad, did you not? You were in a real tizzy of fright and delight. And yet the thing is done every day, a hundred times a day, the innocent postman—if even he is innocent, which I doubt— trudges along with fallen arches precisely from the weight of such communications, the world is full of people spying on themselves in this manner. Their typical weapon is the boomerang, and they almost never remember to duck when it returns; one suspects they do not even want to duck, it is themselves they have been aiming at right along, and they have tribally adopted the boomerang as their armament because it is the only thing one can hurl at oneself."

"But what does one do instead?" asked Julian, who had to admit to himself the disagreeable cogency of some of his companion's remarks.

"Instead? Instead? Why, look at it. The world is all before you, perfectly real, it all exists, stones, trees, running water, minutes, hours, bugs, mirrors—get out of yourself, and smell the bracing air of reality. That's what to do instead."

"Now you sound like a scoutmaster," said Julian.

"It all exists," said Federigo impressively, "and not only that, but—may it set your mind at rest—*nothing else does.*"

"Nothing?"

"Nothing whatever, a little dust, a little smoke, maybe. When you think that is God watching you, my dear, it isn't."

"Who, then?"

"It's only me from over the sea, said Barnacle Bill the sailor," sang Federigo, suddenly breaking forth in a loud voice, raucously gay, as he stood up. "Come, let us walk out of the Park."

As they went along, however, Federigo continued to expound to Julian his curious notions.

"It only takes a mite of courage," he said, "audacity enough to put on the point of a pin. You've lived a sheltered life, you were educated at the best schools, you know theoretically that bad things happen—so of course you can't believe in happiness, and you're perfectly correct. Happiness doesn't really exist, it is only the absence of everything you are looking for; you know, *reality:* filth. But you don't altogether want to find it, do you? Not that you don't look hard enough, but that you make sure every time of looking in the wrong place. You are like the man the policeman found searching for his watch under a street lamp. 'Where did you lose it?' asks the policeman. 'Over there,' the man replies, pointing out in the darkness, 'I'm looking here because the light's better.'" Federigo laughed with unnecessary vigor at his own joke.

"I was in the war," said Julian rather primly.

"Of course, of course, that's what you always tell yourself, you were in the war. You went out there and killed the enemy, didn't you—*out there?* But you hated the sergeant, the captain, the people on your own team? Of course you did! What did you think the war was trying to say, what does it ever try to say? Be your age!

"And that brings me to another thing. Age. You're not dead yet, you know, you have a number of years to stagger through. Well, don't pride yourself so much on your *maturity.* For whenever you do, you'll merely make an ass of yourself, as you did tonight. People don't really grow up, you know, they merely revolve. When you are mature you will realize it by noticing that somewhere along the steep gradient of moral effort you have died. In short, I advise you, my friend, to stop festering, and take a little honest pride in what goes on around you. Do you want love? Go right ahead, fall in love with the first little girl you meet. What's so terrible in that? And even if it were terrible—could it be worse than the way you are going on now?"

They had come out of the Park while Federigo was talking, and now stood on a street corner.

"We'll say good night now," Federigo said. "Don't resent it if I lecture you, I wouldn't do it if I didn't think it necessary. There, go ahead, live, be happy, you can do it. And remember, I'll be around if you want me."

Julian began to say something, but Federigo, squeezing his arm, swung him around facing the other way and sent him off with a coy yet forceful slap on the behind.

"Get on with you," he cried gaily, and Julian heard him laugh. He saw that he was standing at the entrance to Hugo's building. When he turned to survey the darkness outside the doorway there was no sign of his recent companion. The stone frame of the entrance, the glass in the door, the bronze handle, all seemed brilliantly real, the lights in the hallway nearly blinded him by their brightness; he felt like a tired swimmer coming up the beach out of the undertow of the last wave reaching after him.

There was a mirror in the elevator. He looked pale and fairly presentable, though there was a patch of blood which could not be concealed on his shirt collar. It was perfectly true, he decided, that Federigo's eyes were somewhat darker than his own.

3

The party was still going on, in a subdued way; it had considerably thinned out. The door of the apartment stood open, and Julian crossed the threshold just in time to meet Elaine Leonard coming from the kitchen. She stopped, they looked at one another for a moment, just long enough, as it happened, for Julian to fall in love with this girl, and for her to realize that he had. The glance between them wavered and changed its character several times during that moment; all Julian's free-floating speculation about the secrecy of the world, all his diffused lust, became concentrated upon Elaine's eyes; also, all the disgust, for himself and for others, which had been as it were held over from the episode of Bianca and scarcely allowed entrance into his feelings until now. Elaine, not knowing the how or the why of all this, nevertheless felt and responded slightly, tentatively, and with some unease, to the fact of its being so.

Just how this happened, how such things ever happen, would not be easy to say. She, coming from the kitchen and carrying two drinks, paused in his path and gave him, in the first place, a look intended to go with what she was about to say, namely that his absence had been noticed, not altogether with pleasure; she raised her eyebrows slightly.

He, in part because she knew, or knew of, Federigo, interpreted this glance as somehow involving them together in a conspiracy of undetermined object. He looked back at her with a gravity in which was also something ironical, and his eyebrows went up, too.

She took this as some sort of admission of his being caught, for some reason, red-handed, but with a gaiety attached to it that reckoned informally on her knowing how these things were; she noticed at the same time the blood on his shirt, and that his lower lip was somewhat puffed out. This last gave him an expression at once sardonically defiant and indescribably stupid. She replied by the merest hint of a smile—that smile so full of crooked honesty— intending friendly sympathy touched with sarcasm. This sarcasm, in her, seldom meant hatred or bitterness, but was the expression by which she seemed to understand quite well what she did not in fact understand.

"You've been missed," she said, with a nod of her head toward the further room, meaning to indicate at least that she was not the one who had missed him.

"Oh?" said Julian, and then, "Is one of those drinks for me?" Elaine gravely handed him one. "I was—just out," he said. "What happened?"

"I'm afraid your wife," she replied, "became, you might say, indisposed."

"Drunk?"

"You might say."

"Oh, dear," muttered Julian, summoning resolution. "Where is she?"

"Oh, she was taken home a while ago. Marius took her. There was some fuss over where you were while all this was taking place."

"I had a little trouble," Julian said, "in a bar."

Elaine smiled at him somewhat more broadly, meaning to say again that she understood with a superior sympathy touched to irony by her extensive knowledge of the world and its ways. This smile did not exactly, as the saying is, catch at Julian's heart; rather, it tore at his nerves. This girl of nineteen or so (and she knew Federigo) seemed to see him with a penetrative innocence, the calm of knowledge in her eyes. He felt sentimentally ashamed of himself, as though his presence at this moment visibly corrupted her, and she standing there like a martyr shot full of feathered arrows, taking it as easily as in an Italian painting. He saw himself now in her eyes as some kind of beast, a beast endowed with reason in order that it might make a fool of itself. Please understand, he wanted to say to her, I am not like this, really. I am unhappy. Of course, he could not say any such thing, and he instead gazed intently at her, as though he could make his eyes speak for him: forgive me, they would have said if they could—more like a beast than ever.

She however misinterpreted his long look to mean that he pitied her for being a young girl who did not understand as yet what this world was; accordingly her smile became more crookedly satirical and her eyes quite severe, as she said to him:

"I don't mean to mix in your affairs," with a slight emphasis on the final word. The strictness of her look, the kindness and scorn, both it seemed altogether objective, in her tone of voice, broke Julian down. He wanted to reach out and stroke her hair, thus coming, by a process of varied misinterpretations on both sides, to an expression and glance which Elaine, as she had been fallen in love with before, could quite well understand, as she showed by turning away, after a last smile of conspiratorial kindness which cost her nothing, and walking down the hall to the dimly lit room beyond.

Julian stood irresolutely in the narrow hall, and stared into his drink. He ought to go home, and it was the last thing in the world he wanted to do. He did not in the least believe he would discover his wife Sylvia in bed with Marius Rathlin, though he recognized, too, that he did not believe it only because his experience had not equipped him to believe any such thing, and for no more substantial reason. He did not want to go home to a discussion of Marius, a discussion of Sylvia, a discussion above all else, of himself. It was to be presumed, of course, that Sylvia, having been ("you might say") drunk, would be asleep. That made matters, almost, worse, since he would have to wait for morning with the threat of *explanations* pending; and he could sense already how dreadful, with a hangover added to everything else, he would feel in the morning. He desperately did not want to be told (being quite capable of telling himself, a dozen times a minute) that his behavior had been at least irresponsible, and probably something a good deal worse than that.

Some people can do it, he reflected, and others can't. Why was that? And how horribly unfair. Some people doubtless made a habit of leaving parties to visit a woman; they came back, no one had noticed, or those who did notice were such as would merely smile to themselves. *He* left a party—once!—and the world looked ready to fall on his head. The worst of it was that he blamed himself more than anyone else could—though it seemed likely that Sylvia, when she recovered, would at least compete with him in that line.

If he should be, for example, drunk—in a certain high and authoritative mood which drink at one stage induced—he had no doubt of his ability to explain everything, make everything all right . . . simply, of course, by lying, or by (let us say) dramatizing. With this in mind he drank off the drink Elaine had given him, and went into the kitchen to get another.

But it was impossible, for in the nature of things he would not be drunk at the time of explanation, for just the reason that while he was drunk he would feel no need to explain anything whatever; when he sobered up, though, and he supposed he must, sooner or later, the prospect of feeling guilty, the necessity of saying something to Sylvia, extended itself before him. Then again, how in the world was one to explain, even to oneself, Federigo? who seemed to Julian far more important, at this moment, than anything else which had happened during that time in the Park—not so much a time, it began to appear, as an abscess in time, a darkness, a vivid dream with irrevocable consequences still to be faced in waking.

Then there was Elaine Leonard, and for an instant he beheld his self-contempt reflected from her eyes, his corruption gaining pathos from her purity. The tenderness and abasement he felt swelled in him to a romantic, ardent sadness, and he had a maudlin wish to be nineteen again, with the open world of choice before him. Love, passionate and bitterly exclusive, love for this one girl, he saw, would redeem everything: Bianca, Federigo, everything, the anonymous letters, might be absorbed into the realm of intense feeling and converted, from casual lust and rage, into honesty again—if he loved Elaine.

In a flash he saw before him the dreadful scenes, the quarrels, the cold arrangement with lawyers, the divorce court, freedom . . . a vision of Sylvia, who looked more surprised than anything else. But, of course, Elaine must love him in return, or what would all this mean or matter?

"Julian!" It was Hugo's voice, loud and somewhat peremptory; his footsteps could be heard in the hall. "Julian!" He came round the corner into the kitchen. "There you are," he said, as though his friend had simply been misplaced, like a collar button. "I want to talk to you, Jay," he said earnestly. "Let's fix a drink, and we can talk right here."

Hugo fixed two drinks and handed Julian one, quite disregarding the fact that Julian already had one; his manner seemed to say that this would prevent their being interrupted. It was like the final conversation with an alcoholic—his friends give him one last round of his favorite drink, sit him down, talk to him seriously and more in sorrow than in anger . . . Hugo sat himself down on the drainboard, Julian leaned against the refrigerator facing him. Hugo was quite drunk and in a magisterial mood, nevertheless he seemed somewhat embarrassed to begin.

"Understand," he said after a space of silence, "I don't know, and I don't want to know, where you've been all this time. That's your business. But the things that happened while you were gone, here in my house—ah, Jay, I'm not going to lecture you, you know that. But you are my oldest and best friend, and I hope I'm yours—and just to prove it's still so, I want to ask you to be best man at my wedding. Will you do that?"

"Yes," Julian said almost inaudibly.

"Thank you," said Hugo with a kind of judicial satisfaction. "Now—about this other thing. There's something wrong between you and Sylvia? There must be. She's drinking a great deal. I've never seen her do that before tonight, Sylvia's not that kind of girl.

But that in itself wasn't anything, only—if you see what I mean—
you weren't there just when you were needed."

Oh, dear God, Julian thought with dreadful anticipations. It
must have been far worse than anything he had thought.

"If she had only got drunk and passed out quietly, you know,"
Hugo said, "that would not have been so terrible. We could have
put her in a cab with someone, Louisa could have taken her home—
she could have slept here, for that matter. But she made a fuss," he
said impressively.

"She made a fuss," Julian repeated.

"When she couldn't find you anywhere. She behaved rather
foolishly about it, I thought, she got all sorts and conditions of
people to look for you, it was like a kind of game for a while—
then, she was quite drunk, you must bear that in mind, she started
telling everyone, rather loudly, that you hated her, that you believed she was unfaithful to you but that you wouldn't speak to her
and wouldn't give her a chance to defend herself. Then she got
dreadfully angry and went about saying 'shit' to people, and so
forth, you know how it is when people get, well, intense—not very
pretty, and she kept on drinking through it all. Then finally she
announced to everyone present that she would goddamn well give
you something to hate about, and she collapsed on Marius Rathlin—more or less all over him."

"And?"

"And he took her home," Hugo said unhappily. "Oh, I'm not
suggesting there was anything sinister about that, he was terribly
embarrassed. But you weren't there, and—and, well, you see how
it went. Marius was elected. I'm afraid," he added stiffly, "some
people tended to make jokes about it."

"Oh," said Julian.

"I don't mean to put all the blame on you," Hugo said. "I'm
concerned, that's all. It'd look mighty odd for an ancient lecher
like myself to take a high moral tone with you, but there's also
manners, discretion, to be considered. I care for you and Sylvia
more than any friends I've got. You may not believe it, because I
don't ordinarily talk about such things, but your marriage has
always been a kind of ideal to me—the way I hope things will be
with Louisa and myself. I know you may have made a mistake,"

Hugo said with earnest heartiness. "My god, who doesn't, some-time or other? And you've been a kind of *preux chevalier* for so many years, haven't you? But if there's something wrong, Jay, for God's sake don't keep it all locked up in there, let me know what it is. I'll help you out, if I possibly can. But what you need is a man you can talk to—I know how that feels. So break down—here, let's fix one more—and tell Uncle Hugo what's gone wrong."

After Hugo had fixed fresh drinks and sat back again on the drainboard, Julian in a dramatic silence, because there was noth-ing else to do, handed him the anonymous letter. Hugo opened the envelope and looked at the sheet of paper long enough to read it a number of times.

"I see," he said to himself. "I see, I see." He looked decisively up at his friend. "Do you think this is true?"

"I don't know."

"Well, do you have any idea who would send such a thing?"

"No."

"Federigo, Federigo," Hugo observed. "Kind of a smart-alecky name to pick out. A wise guy." His voice had become very hard, and he clenched his fist suggestively. "Boy, if I were you," he said, "I'd take this kind of thing very seriously, very seriously indeed. There's nothing more rotten, more cowardly, in the whole world, than a man who won't sign his right name to a letter—whether it's true or not," Hugo added angrily.

"No," Julian dully agreed.

"Surely you have some suspicion, some idea?" asked Hugo.

"No, I don't," said Julian.

"Is this the only one of the things you've got so far?"

"Yes, the only one."

"There will be more," Hugo said with satisfaction of a sort. "These people are never content to stop with one. Take it from me, there will be more," he said somewhat smugly, "and sooner or later he'll give himself away. Listen, Julian," he added, "let me help you. What you need is professional work."

"Professional?"

"Detectives, boy, detectives. I'm going to hang on to this letter," putting it away in his pocket, "and I'm going to take you and it to some people I know. On Monday," Hugo added firmly, "we'll go

to these people, Pritchard, Ferriter & Magoun is the firm name—
why, I shouldn't be at all surprised they could find out right off
who sent this thing. They have methods, you know, science."

"I don't think you should go to all that trouble," Julian said
feebly. "If you'll just let me have the letter—"

"Don't be silly," Hugo said, "I know you, you'd put it away and
worry yourself sick. Jay, you need help. I can't see my old friends
made unhappy on account of some wretched son of a bitch somewhere. We'll get this all straightened away together; why, if you
like, I'll help you explain to Sylvia." He winked at Julian. "You got
upset, you were worried, you left the party and went to some bar
on Third Avenue, you got into a scrape with some drunk and he
beat you up a little but you ought to see what happened to him—
that's all." He winked again. "She has to accept that, don't you see,
because after all—there *is* this anonymous letter, and if that doesn't
account for a husband's reactions, why, what would?"

Hugo got down off the drainboard and patted Julian on the
shoulder.

"Go home and sleep," he said kindly, "your worries are over.
Only don't forget," he added, "if you get another of these lousy
letters, you let me know right away. And what's more, if Sylvia's a
bitch to you tomorrow, and you've got to allow she might be, just
tell her it will all be explained in a few days."

Hugo saw Julian out the door.

"I don't mean to throw you out, Jay," he said, "but probably
you've had enough party for one night, and anyhow, this one is
nearly over. Remember," he concluded, "on Monday—Pritchard,
Ferriter, Magoun. I'll call you up in the morning."

The apartment was dark, a little glow of moonlight or streetlight
touched a corner of the bedroom. Out in the hall bathroom the
dogs stirred slightly, turning over in sleep. Julian listened for a moment to his wife breathing heavily and evenly in sleep. He undressed
in silence, letting his clothes fall on the floor. As his eyes became
more accustomed to the dimness he saw that Sylvia was fully
dressed and lay on the coverlet. He tenderly pulled off her shoes,
thinking that here if anywhere was a proof of innocence, also that
Marius might have risked so much at least without becoming an
adulterer. Sylvia stirred uneasily, emitting a groan or a snore.

Julian got into his own bed and stretched out. There they lay, he reflected, in parallel, like figures on a tomb, or like an advertisement for pyjamas, except that neither of them was wearing pyjamas. Those figures on the tomb, where had they come from?

On their wedding trip, he remembered, that was where. In England, in some ancient abbey or other down in the west country. A knight and a lady lay, with grave and sharpened features, in a bronze silence atop their sarcophagus. Sylvia had said something, her hand entwined in his just as the knight's was with the lady's. What had she said?

"They must have loved each other well."

"For six or seven centuries," Julian had replied.

Fidelity and death, he now thought. There had been another tomb nearby, the product of a somewhat later period, where the sculptured emblem more realistically imitated the contents: a skull of bronze, through the empty eye of which a bronze and gleaming serpent crawled; that was austere, as Julian had remarked with satisfaction at the time, austere and witty.

"Witty?" she had asked, and he had been unable to explain, at least to his bride's satisfaction, just what it was he had meant.

He wondered now whether he would die in this bed, which rested, as it seemed, rather uneasily under his weight, and he saw this comfortable contraption suddenly for what it was, a waiting, patient animal. Or else it was a marsh, a mire, and he imagined how one day he would feel himself all at once sinking into its soft, yielding depth, stretching out both hands to the woman, the friends, the doctor—faceless, all of them—who stared down on him from above and watched him swallowed up.

And Sylvia? Would she die in the bed next to his? Had all this been arranged, irrevocably, some long time ago, so that there was now nothing anyone could do about it? Julian wondered whether he would be afraid to die. Perhaps he would, and he saw at the last instant Sylvia bending above him with a bitter and cruel smile, as though this—his being terrified to die—were the final secret, the one she would have waited many years, maybe, by that time, to discover and confirm. Or would she be the one, and he the watcher above the bed?

What was beyond? He considered the God in whom he did not believe, and Who was not therefore, it seemed, in the least prevented from existing, just at this moment. The anger of his conscience, which he could not turn away because it began within him, produced in him a vague, objectless terror, or a terror which had everything for its object, and which he could not escape because it caused everything in the world to reflect himself, so that everything in the world became fluid and unstable, there was no solidity anywhere, as in a dream the most trivial object became charged with feelings of despair and fear, while the world began to fall away as in a dream.

Sylvia for her part was not asleep. She pretended to be when her husband came home, out of shame and hatred. She felt him pull off her shoes.

Thank you very much, she thought angrily, and wanted to giggle. Her head had begun to ache terribly. Perhaps she had been asleep, after all, but now her head ached. If she got up, however, she would have to say something to Julian, which was impossible, so she lay there and added the headache, grain by grain, to everything else which was so hateful.

A blessed, drunken amnesia was not quite strong enough to prevent her from feeling ashamed, or from the knowledge that she had put on some sort of exhibition which it would be better not to know much more about; the details were under a sort of merciful narcosis, though Sylvia thought that if she remembered them her head might possibly stop pounding.

Marius had been, so far as she could recollect, a perfect gentleman. She did not even think he had tried to kiss her except in the taxi (which was all right). Of course, she must have made a splendidly attractive object to kiss, especially after having (she thought she remembered) been sick in the gutter just as they got out of the cab. Her mouth tasted as though she had been sick. Marius, it was to be presumed, then, had gingerly deposited her upon her bed, where she now found herself—not in it, mind—and he had retired, she supposed, upon such a strict observance of the situation as not even to have removed her shoes, which God knew he might have done. Still, a perfect gentleman.

And where had Julian been all this time? She did not know, and just now she did not much care, either; it was enough that he had not been there when it was necessary—if he had been there, it would not have been necessary for him to be there, because she would not have become drunk, so then he might have gone off wherever he liked . . . That seemed to move in a circle, rather. What was all this about? About Julian's having gone off somewhere—she merely wanted him to know she did not usually mind; she wanted him to have a certain freedom at parties and so forth, it was one of the things that kept a marriage going—nothing serious, only a certain light freedom—kissing other people's wives, just as their husbands kissed her. But it was inexcusable for him not to be there when whatever it was had happened.

That dreadful letter. At this moment, with a blinding headache, she could see it so clearly, on the dining room table, a plain white envelope such as might have been purchased in any one of a hundred shops. But it had been a dream. As Dr. Mirabeau said, a certain light freedom between husband and wife had to be allowed, these days. She herself used to be so strict about such things, like a girl in an invisible convent. With the thought of an invisible convent the pain in her head gave a fearful jump. But now she was relaxed, easy-going. That was the way, a little give and take. They had, she believed, a *modern marriage*; this was, however, the expression people typically used some twenty years ago; she had not realized that modern marriages could be as *démodé* as all that. What had the letter said? She could scarcely remember. All that fuss about it in her mind all day long, and now she could remember only that it was signed Federigo, and said something about being alone. It was strange how dreams faded from your mind. It was a plain, white envelope, and it lay on the dining room table, just as clear, as clear as the dream could make it.

BOOK TWO

But all the storie
of the night told
ouer,

And all their minds
transfigur'd so
together,

More witnesseth
than fancies
images,

And growes to
something of great
constancie;

But howsoeuer,
strange, and
admirable.

—Shakespeare

Chapter Five

THE second letter had been mailed late Friday afternoon, and did not appear in the Saturday morning mail; consequently, so far as Julian and Sylvia were concerned, nothing happened over the weekend. On Saturday they got up very late, not feeling well; there was not energy enough between them to begin a discussion of the previous night. Instead, they politely and distantly sympathized with one another, and recommended aspirins at odd intervals when the silence seemed to become unbearably intense. At four o'clock they encouraged themselves with cocktails until they could eat a light supper (Julian with a show of domesticity made an omelet) and went to the movies, then early to bed. On Sunday they read the papers thoughtfully for a long time, got out the car and took themselves and the dogs up into the country; the trees were a hazy, beginning green, flowers appeared, it began to rain. It did not rain hard, but steadily. They felt chilled and gray, and drove back to town. It was late afternoon, and they went to another movie. When they came out it was still light, still raining, they got sandwiches and beer from a delicatessen, went home, ate, Julian smoked a cigar, Sylvia did as much of the double-crostic in the *Times* as she could do without effort, and went to bed.

Nothing happened. . . . It was terrifying. At every moment it seemed something must snap, but nothing did, neither of them screamed or broke into tears and curses, or suddenly turned on the other with a knife, though each thought of such things constantly. They were both polite, good and, on the whole, kindly persons, who had been taught by their parents and at the best schools not to raise their voices, indulge in tantrums or make scenes; they were reasonable beings. Moreover, they loved one another. Their belief that they loved one another—love, on this view, became a slow-burning unhappiness—was the sacrifice imposed upon both of

429

them equally by pride; even at their worst moments in seven years of marriage they had never allowed to pass their lips that word *divorce,* which would have seemed to them both an admission of moral failure. The dogs, Troilus and Cressida, slept, were fed, moved gracefully around the apartment, and were silently, as possessions have the habit of being in these circumstances, a reproach, as though to say: How can you be unhappy with two such fine dogs? The furniture too rebuked them, entering into the spirit of the silence: the clean-lined, slender legs of the low, modern tables, the alert appearance of the couch with its square corners and straight back, the inquisitive curve of a lamp which bent its bell-head heavily from a corner; all these smart impersonal objects, as coldly reasonable here as they had been in the shops whence they came, all at once achieved the identity of unhappiness: if we thought you would be like this, they seemed to say, we would not have come here. Julian recognized this appearance from distant childhood; it was the critical look the Christmas presents began to have when one became ill-tempered and was punished in their presence.

The movies they saw were both murder mysteries, portraying a world of sinister gestures most of them meaningless, sleights of hand to defer the recognition of the really guilty person; detectives moved in a desert of clues, the camera picked up dramatic contrasts of light and shade everywhere, the characters loved and hated each other by turns on demand of the plot. In both stories the murderer turned out to be the girl who had hired the detective in the first place, and with whom he had been more than half— saving only his keen perception of evil in the heart—in love. To Julian, the reflexive idiocy of this arrangement, so fashionable in the detective novel, betrayed as though accidentally some real and intimate source of guilt; in one of the pictures there were even anonymous letters. He and Sylvia sat in the darkness to witness all these things, occasionally they even held hands, transmitting to one another by slight increases of pressure the most cryptic intimations of feeling. They were like two survivors clutching each other across a piece of floating wreckage in the midst of a silent and wide ocean.

Three or four times during the weekend occurred the following exchange.

"I love you," one would say, bestowing a light kiss on the other. "I love you too, darling," replied the other, with a little caress.

These words seemed to sink without resonance or reverberation into the wide silence. They sat in the living room, where from above the mantel of the empty fireplace Sylvia's portrait looked down. It had been done five years before, the painter had made Sylvia extravagantly slender (it seemed now) and with a look of wild innocence, in the style of Ophelia—in a white gown, clutching blue flowers with flashes of dark red—of which the intense poeticism disagreeably suggested insanity. Julian felt he wanted to tear this work off the wall and fling it on the floor in front of his wife, but was prevented from doing so in the first place because he did not know exactly what he would say after that. That picture, he thought—its eyes, for all their naïve and startled expression, covered the room like radar—is the most dreadful lie ever perpetrated. Covertly, by brief glances, he compared it with Sylvia, in whose comfortable, handsome body he found no trace of the thin, bitter, erotic ecstasy suggested in the canvas. How could she sit there with that dreadful reproach, that living lie, looking down on her from the past?

Sylvia looked up from the paper.

"What is the name of the disciple who doubted that Christ was risen?" she asked. "Six letters."

Julian did not know, and offered to look it up.

"That's not quite fair," she said, "but still—"

"It was Thomas," he announced after several minutes. "He wouldn't believe till he put his hand in the wound."

"Of course," said Sylvia, "*doubting Thomas.*"

This is what life is, Julian thought. We use the Bible to fill out crossword puzzles. The Word that died upon the Cross. It was a puzzle, certainly. He did not believe in God, yet it was quite true that he typically felt someone watching him, just as Federigo had said. Federigo? Was there any such person? Had he been there, that night in the Park? Julian uncomfortably remembered a few vivid details, the arm about his shoulder, the somewhat coy, bantering tone of sympathetic yet mocking amusement, the "boomerang"—had any of that taken place? And Bianca? He felt a sinking sensation of remorse, as if he were about to be sick to his stomach. It had all happened, it was all perfectly real—to the stomach; only the mind found it vague and unconvincing.

Federigo, he said to himself reasonably and in a convincing way, is either real or a hallucination. But here his mind began to boggle, since neither alternative could possibly be found acceptable.

If he is real, Julian quickly decided, he must be the Devil.

If he is unreal, I am going insane.

The Devil of course did not exist, for if the Devil existed, then God would have to exist—but did that necessarily follow? Or was it the Devil himself—whoever that might be—who alone existed, and alone sponsored, criticized and assessed the belief in God? So that God was the imagination of the Devil working on the world? This line of speculation impressed Julian as at once ridiculous and too deep to be followed any further, he simply became confused. Besides, considered as a real, objectively existing Devil, Federigo appeared absurd; he did not have enough reality.

Considered, on the other hand, as a subjective impression, he uncomfortably had too much; if Julian tried to think of him that way, it seemed he had unquestionably been *there,* no getting around it. But he was not going insane; he had read somewhere that the very thought one was going insane was one's best guarantee against it; insane people never believed they were. On the other hand, if it was only for that reason he believed he was not going insane, where did that take him? Confusion again.

The thought of insanity, however, fascinated him, it presented a way out. The prisoner pleaded insanity, he had committed his crimes while of unsound mind, therefore they were not his crimes. Of course, as his rigorously brought up mind had gathered from all its experience so far, this was a solution too glib for belief. On exactly the appropriate occasions, when one was ashamed, afraid, hoping somehow to avoid an onerous duty, one generally did not fall sick of consumption, break a leg, go raving mad, or simply explode into a thousand pieces; one faced up, and went on facing up, to whatever was going at the time. If somewhere in this life tragedy existed, this perhaps was where it might be found, in the enduring pain of responsibility which provided no such symbolic escape—in duty, shame, guilt, fear, without the alleviation of sickness, madness, death.

To live a clean, honest life . . . Julian knew quite well, in theory, that human suffering, misery and degradation were everywhere around. Civilization, on the other hand, was organized to the end that these phenomena should not obtrude themselves, that they should be as much as possible confined and segregated, and dealt with by people who qualified as technicians with respect to misery, suffering and degradation and could, therefore, handle the tabooed objects without fear and without revulsion. Others, though, would do well to walk quietly and with their eyes to the front. The blind beggar on the street, the crippled and drunken Legionnaire in the subway, the woman vomiting in the gutter between two parked automobiles: to acknowledge such things was to ask for trouble, it was, for a member in good standing in civilization, slightly subversive, and smacked of *making a fuss* which was neither necessary nor justifiable; even charity, when it was unofficial, became a political act.

Julian remembered having once seen a dead man on the street, a window-cleaner fallen from his ledge. A crowd gathered at a little distance. Women, with faces averted, went carefully around the body on clicking heels and continued on their ways. It had been beautifully delicate, the expression they unanimously wore, an expression of pride and the highest breeding which did not permit them, just at that instant, to look down. Nor had he himself done anything except feel an indescribable helplessness and lonely guilt, until a policeman and a doorman came running up, and the latter covered the body with a rubber mat taken from before the entrance of a building down the street. He thought now that the policeman and the doorman had been enabled to do this thing for no better reason than that they wore uniforms, and it went through his mind that Marius had said something similar about war: "It's splendid, because you can tell the good guys by the color of their hats."

As for Marius, now, did that young man, he wondered, have a real intention of having an affair with Sylvia? Julian reminded himself sharply that it was not impossible; it merely seemed impossible, or, better, very unlikely, because he implicitly tended to take it that Marius saw Sylvia just as objectively as he did himself, and therefore that Marius would not see in Sylvia anything so exclusively attractive, unless—which she was not—she was to be had for the asking. Then, too, apart from her being, so far as he knew, a chaste and modest person, and still a little frightened of pleasure, there was undeniably the fact that courting Sylvia, especially with any degree of secrecy, would be an expensive proposition, even if it meant no more than buying her occasional meals—she liked to dine well, did Sylvia, as her figure began to show—and now and then (Julian supposed) some little present or other. Of course, Marius might personally require a rather motherly type; and Sylvia, for that matter, someone who by his youth combined lover and child. This idea abruptly disgusted Julian, who believed accordingly that what he felt was jealousy. He glanced over at his wife, as though she must have followed his thoughts, but she continued imperturbably to bite the eraser of her pencil as she looked at the puzzle.

It's amazing, he thought, what things can go on in the human head, what battles and betrayals, all in utter, lonely security. He closed his eyes and deliberately began to think of Elaine with tenderness and lust; he discovered sadly that it took deliberation to do so, his mind kept slipping off to other things, her image even at his most intense concentration remained vague except for a rather crude intimation of what her smile was like. They were alone in an unidentifiable room; he put his hands on her shoulders, there was the smile again . . . he pulled the dress down over her arms, the same dress she had been wearing the other night, and then without interruption he was thinking of Federigo again, seeing his smile instead of hers. That this should be so provoked him to a slight anger based on the fear that he might be impotent—which is ridiculous, he added. But it bothered him, as though it were morally a reproach, that he could not concentrate even upon what he proposed to himself as supremely desirable; it was so, it seemed, only objectively, and his poor, reasonable mind was like an adult saying to a child, "What do you mean, you won't have chocolate ice cream? You know you *love* chocolate ice cream." It is old age, he thought sadly, I've had my time. Upon this consideration it became to him a point of honor to prove himself upon Elaine—upon her body and her spirit—because the victory would be won not only over her but also over death. Surely, he reflected, that was natural enough, Sylvia herself must understand that.

"I can't do any more, I'm going to bed," Sylvia remarked, standing up.

"I'll just stay here for a little while," he replied.

"You look sad," she said. "Is anything wrong?"

"I'm just thinking," he said with a certain heaviness.

"I thought maybe it was your headache again," she said, bending over to kiss him. "I love you," she whispered in his ear.

"I love you too, darling," he whispered back, raising himself up to kiss her softly behind the ear.

What went on in the human head, Julian decided, went on also, on a slightly larger scale, in the human apartment. Apartment, that is, where people keep apart; he had never thought of that before. Privacy—what it meant was secrecy, hypocrisy. Two people got married, they pooled their possessions—all their possessions— and sat in an apartment, where they were as dragons guarding some dread secret which they themselves could not understand. People came to the apartment to visit, they saw the thick carpets, the good furniture, the color scheme, the well-chosen prints and paintings, they moved over to ask mute questions of a row of books on a shelf—but all these things told them very little, they never saw the apartment at such times as the dragons sat alone, at such times as the secret itself became more terrible and burdensome than any threat to it from without the walls could possibly be. It was this, perhaps, which gave him the constant sensation of being watched, assessed, marked in some secret book—the idea that somewhere there existed a world which exactly replicated the way in which this world ought to go, and with which this world was steadily, point for point, being compared—conscience (he had read some- where this clever definition) was the still, small, inward voice which told you when someone was watching. But according to Federigo, no such other world—and therefore no such voice— existed; or if it seemed to, it was only Federigo himself, or, more strictly, Barnacle Bill from over the sea. Only?

It seemed to him now that his life was a kind of dramatic per- formance; all that happened appeared to have a singular quality of being witnessed and made prominent, as though on a stage or a movie screen. The cameras moved quietly, recording everything: *Sylvia, in nightgown, moves across left to kitchen for a glass of water; Julian looks up but says nothing; she returns, blows kiss, exits up right to bedroom.*

Julian was tired, and every time he shut his eyes for an instant the world of sleep, that lay so close behind the eyelids, persisted in throwing up to him its cynical and whirling hints; when he laid back his head against the chair he would at once see (how strange, to see by shutting the eyes!) men with the faces of bulldogs crawling about in snow, or children who were skeletons in dimity dresses; and then someone would throw a snowball at him and he would wake suddenly in horror with that icy lump imbedded in his brain.

I really must go to bed, he thought, and all at once he remembered what he had dreamed the night before.

He had been in bed (a curious place to be, in a dream), it was a warm night (as in fact it was) so that the covers were thrown back and he lay naked on the sheet (just so). Well, on this sheet crawled a reckonable number, say five or six, very little worms, about the size of nail parings (large ones) but dark and corrugated. As Julian watched, their tails, or at least one end of them, they didn't seem to have heads, kind of withered off until detached from the rest, whereupon each tail became another little worm; this began to happen with considerable rapidity, and there was soon a large number of worms. He noticed at the same time that his body was covered with red spots, which in the dream he sensibly took to be worm-bites. And he woke up. The momentary relief he experienced at seeing his body quite free from any red spots was soon replaced by a queer, remote depression which had stayed with him right through the day—different from, more basic than, his secular depression over marriage and life—as though something had gone wrong, either with the dream itself or with its relation to his waking life; as though, he put it to himself, remembering certain remarks made by Federigo on the subject of clap, as though he might in some obscure way have required those red spots to be really—really?—present on his body, for reasons too nefarious to be named.

Gets up from chair; moves away from camera to kitchen; returns with whisky and soda in glass; exits up right to bedroom; camera trucks slowly toward bedroom door.

Stimulated by her anxiety, Sylvia's dreams had already presented her with an anonymous letter, which thus gained the status of a recurrent image, a symbol, and would be presented to Dr. Mirabeau for inspection on the morrow. She had carefully copied out what she could remember of the dream:

> The letter lies on the dining room table; I try to pick it up, but it seems to be glued down. Anyhow, I know perfectly well what it is.

It is from Alma, I say, and suddenly notice a man sitting across the table from me. It is Federigo—I know this although he does not look at all like what I imagined. Instead, he is tall and fair-haired, and smokes a pipe; he says something about a walk in the Park. I know I must not go with him, and then I feel someone pulling my head back by the hair.

Sylvia placed a pencil and pad on the night table before going to bed, so that it would be convenient for her to receive any further revelation which might be granted.

2

Monday morning came; the anonymous letter lay on the table; Julian was determined to follow exactly the same procedure with the second as with the first. One must go through with what one begins, he thought, and took care, as he read the letter (with a delicate tremor of the hand) to make a long face and a small mouth.

"What is it?" Sylvia asked.

"It is nothing," Julian replied again, and presently took the dogs out for their morning walk.

Sylvia, who was so convinced of the first letter's being a dream as to have dreamed of it now twice running, stared at the new letter with some consternation; she saw Julian's hand tremble, as he made a long face and a small mouth and put down the letter on the table. She did not believe it, even the similarity of the envelope and the paper—no one she knew would use notepaper like that— failed to convince her, and when her husband departed with the dogs she sat for a couple of minutes without touching the letter. It cannot be, she thought at one instant; and at the next, suppose it mentions Marius, then what? Suppose it says something about Hugo, then what? what?

> SIR—
> Who is Sylvia, what is she? etc.
> FEDERIGO

Though she noticed that her hands were trembling, Sylvia felt on the whole relieved; this was not exactly nothing, but it was nothing *in particular.* Compared with the first, it was even rather

genteel; in becoming literary Federigo had sacrificed somewhat of
his tone, except perhaps for that sharp, rather sinister "etc." That
all our swains commend her? It seemed a sweeping statement, and
for that reason faintly ridiculous. On a sudden suspicion she rushed
over to the bookcase and spent several minutes hunting for the
song, which when she found it proved to contain little enough
cause for alarm.

"He is literate, this Federigo," she decided in an access of de-
tective-story vigor, "but not sufficiently so, or surely he would
have added the one telling line, 'Is she kind as she is fair?' Or
perhaps he was hurried?"

But chiefly she thought how, provided with the letter itself, she
would triumph over Dr. Mirabeau. "A dream, doctor? Are you
quite certain? Then how do you explain this?" she would say, producing the document. And she would of course sweep out of the
office then and there and for good. But as a precaution, Sylvia, still
holding the letter, pinched herself to be sure she was awake.

After Mirabeau, she decided, Marius must see this letter; he
might have some idea as to the identity of the writer, and better
even than that it would convince him of the existence of a certain
romance and danger in their relation—which of course must be
what the letters were about. If he continued after this to claim that
he loved her . . . the idea had its perilous charms.

As for Julian, poor thing—what did he imagine was going on,
what must he imagine? Still, it was contemptible, it was dishonest
of him, to think such things in silence. But would he be silent
when he returned this morning? Or would he say to her, Look
here, what about this? as any honest man ought to do. Or was that
what any honest man could be expected to do? Divorce? Death?
Horribly extravagant notions had entered her dining room. Surely
husbands did not murder wives over such things these days; even
the subtle *décor* of the apartment spoke out rather sharply against
the idea.

It now struck Sylvia that Julian's behavior in this business, beyond being contemptible, was also mysterious. On the one hand
he might have confronted her with the letters and demanded an
accounting; on the other hand he might have kept silence, she
would in that case never have seen the letters, and gone secretly
about preparing whatever action he proposed to take: detectives,

perhaps, with divorce or even death somewhere in the background. But he had done neither of these things, and substituted instead something oddly in between: she was allowed to see the letters, but that was all, there all communication stopped. Whatever this meant, and she had no idea at this moment, it was deep and subtle. Perhaps, in the case of behavior so deep and subtle as this, Julian himself might be quite uncertain as to where he stood, and, if neither player altogether understood the rules of the game, one might succeed as well as the other. Sylvia, imbued at this moment with the spirit of innumerable detective stories, cached the letter in the drawer of the desk where she kept six months' receipted bills and all the checks returned from the bank: a messy pile of papers of all descriptions; it would be like finding one particular leaf in a forest.

Julian came in with the dogs, which he unleashed. Sylvia was sitting over a cup of coffee at the dining room table, the newspaper spread out before her. He stood about uncertainly at his end of the table, looking down at the other three or four letters which had come in the morning mail.

"Is there something the matter?" Sylvia asked, and waited nervously. Julian looked down at her.

"There was another letter here, wasn't there?" he asked.

"I don't know," Sylvia replied. "I haven't looked at the mail yet. Maybe it got under the paper, though." And she made a show of looking under the paper, shaking it out, looking around on the floor. "It's not here," she said indifferently. "Who was it from?"

"That's very odd," said Julian, frowning, and added, "it wasn't important, only an old classmate of mine—I never really knew him well—who is getting married. It took him a long time to make up his mind."

"Who was he?"

"Ah, you didn't know him—as I say, we never really got to be friends."

"And who is the girl?"

"Oh, I've no idea about that," Julian said, "a name I'd never heard before, Jane somebody, I think. You're sure you haven't seen that letter?"

"Quite sure," she replied, "anyhow, you know I don't read your mail, darling. Probably it'll turn up stuck to the underside of a dish or something." In a burst of co-operative sympathy Sylvia lifted three or four plates. "Anyhow, as it's not important . . ." she said after a moment.

"Still, it is extremely strange," he said, shaking his head. "I mean, I don't have hallucinations, do I? And how could such a thing simply disappear?"

"I don't know why you're making such a fuss, darling," Sylvia said, and added, with a slight edge to her voice, "unless you're implying I have for God knows what reason concealed this trivial document while you were out."

Julian stared at her for a long moment, and Sylvia coldly stared back. There was after all something mean and petulant about his face, she decided, something childish between the eyebrows and in the pouting mouth; it emerged very clearly when he attempted to be ominous without saying so, like a hard type in a movie.

"No, of course not," he finally said. "Of course not. And anyhow, it is not important. Only strange." And with the customary casual kiss he left for the office. Sylvia sat for a long time, while the coffee grew cold. She felt she had clearly won a victory, for in some sense he certainly had backed down, but its meaning remained altogether obscure; what in the world was the battle about? It seemed as though they were engaged in some sort of bitter contest in separate sections of a revolving door; they put out their tongues at one another, and shouted things which the thick glass prevented entirely or made meaningless, and all the time, pushing as hard as they could, they went merrily round and round. Someone, perhaps, would fly out on the street in the end.

The office was dark, Sylvia could rather feel than see, above and behind her eyes, the edge of a circle of light which, like a magical precaution, surrounded the doctor and his note pad.

"Any more anonymous letters?" Dr. Mirabeau was jovial this morning. But Sylvia had no intention of playing her high cards off first; she had planned this scene, with dialogue, as carefully as an Elizabethan in a tragedy of revenge.

She humbly reported two dreams, the second of which had come to her only that morning in a delicious five minutes of renewed sleep. This second one was very brief: a strange man presented her with a calling card, which was, however, perfectly blank.

"So, so," said Dr. Mirabeau with satisfaction. "I could have predicted from your behavior last Friday that this image would come up again. Its insistence, by the way, is a very promising sign; certain resistances would seem to be dissolving, the materials of the dream become more pointed. Glued to the table, you said? Glued to the table in the first dream and in the second it is a blank calling card; notice that in both cases you are unable to read any message."

Sylvia noticed.

"I still can't help feeling," she said, "that the first one, the one I reported Friday, was real. Its *tone*"—giving the doctor his very own word—"was different, somehow."

"Can you think of any reason why that should be so?"

"Only," she said in a weak voice, "that it was real, after all, and that *it* started the dreams."

"Ah, Sylvia," said the doctor calmly, "we've been over that. No backsliding, now. You can see, can't you, how it would be to the advantage of the forces behind the dream to convince you of their reality, to get as it were a foothold in your waking life?"

"Then how do you account for this?" cried Sylvia in a somewhat coarser tone of triumph than she had quite bargained for. She sat bolt upright on the edge of the couch and spun the letter to him across the desk. Dr. Mirabeau's eyebrows went up, wrinkled, remained up as he drew forth the sheet and studied it, while Sylvia concentrated with fierce humor on the expression of his face, which otherwise, however, did not change in the least for several moments; then a wise, broad smile began to spread itself out— like sunshine on butter, she thought angrily, and wondered what wonderful thing he thought he had discovered now.

"Well?" she asked impatiently.

"The letters of which it is composed," said Dr. Mirabeau imperturbably, "are from *Harper's Bazaar*. My wife takes it, I was reading it only yesterday. The paper is right, and here, you see, is an initial S at the head of an article, which I particularly noticed because it was so very flowery. From a magazine read chiefly by women, you see," he observed with satisfaction.

"You mean," inquired Sylvia, "Federigo is really a woman?" But of course. Why had she not suspected a woman in the first place? Alma, possibly. To have used a man's name was the most elementary precaution.

"Yes," Dr. Mirabeau said in a strange, rather priestly tone, as though sorrowing over human frailty and at the same time seeing the sad humor of it. "Yes, a woman."

Sylvia began to recover her confidence in Dr. Mirabeau, who she considered was now demonstrating a plain, manly common sense which had taken her in a moment further along the road to a solution than she had thought it possible to get. She might have noticed, herself, about the slick paper, and herself identified the letters from *Harper's Bazaar,* which she read; and of course she might then have drawn the simple yet inevitable conclusion for herself: a woman.

"The same woman that wrote the first one," said Dr. Mirabeau, "if there was a first one, which I still beg leave to doubt. Sylvia," he said, with deep patience, "I'm surprised at you, I really am."

Observing her somewhat flabbergasted expression he held up his hand before she could find any words.

"Please," he said authoritatively. "You were tempted, and you fell. Of course. I can understand that, only it is a little late in the therapy—I had thought—for shenanigans of this sort. Am I a dummy, Sylvia? Is your physician a little boy, to be fooled?"

"What in the world do you mean?" she asked with indignation and bewilderment.

"Calm, Sylvia. Listen, I will tell you a little story. When Sigmund Freud first announced to the world his discovery that all dreams—absolutely *all* dreams—represented a wish fulfillment, this news was not received everywhere with screams of pleasure and delight, you know that. Not only psychologists stood up to say he was wrong, but even the unconscious of the patients set to work to denounce his theory. A young lady came to him with a dream in which disgusting but trivial things happened to her. 'Now,' she cried triumphantly, 'tell me if you can what wish is fulfilled in that stupid dream.' The Master merely looked at her, and he said, 'Why, dear lady, of course—the wish to prove that I am wrong.'

"And in the same way, Sylvia," he continued over the beginning of any protest on her part, "in exactly the same way . . . You leave here on Friday, you are still a little angry, it seemed so real to you"—he imitated in passing her pleading tone, adding a rather disagreeable whine—"so: what to do next? Why, of course! Give the poor old dummy a real anonymous letter. He thinks he knows it all, you'll show him he's not so smart. Dream, eh? I'll give him dreams. And you wrote it yourself. Didn't you?" He smiled at her to suggest he was being angry only as a friend, that professionally it was quite all right, was the sort of thing his poor, feeble-minded clientele did to him day in and day out.

"That is the most outrageous and absurd thing I've ever heard in my life," said Sylvia, standing up. "Don't imagine for one moment, doctor, that I am going to put up with this course of—of—nonsense," she sputtered, "for an instant longer. This is the end."

"Just one moment, Sylvia," said Dr. Mirabeau in a grave voice. He rang a buzzer on the desk.

"Nurse," he said as the door opened, "Mrs. Ghent has become a little overexcited, it is nothing much, but we want to see that she calms down before she leaves here."

The door closed; Sylvia heard it being locked.

"How dare you!" she cried.

"Sylvia, please try to get yourself under control; have a cigarette, sit down. You know," he added, "you make me a little concerned. To try to score off the doctor, that is one thing—but to take it in this way, with such vehemence, when you are found out; that doesn't show such a firm grasp on the real nature of things, does it? You seem to have reached a rather perilous degree of detachment. Tell me, apart from these dreams do you sleep well?"

"As well as I ever have," declared Sylvia, "but don't you delude yourself for one instant—"

"Have headaches? More than ordinary fatigue? Eyestrain?"

"Dr. Mirabeau! Just what are you getting at?"

"I am a little disturbed, as I told you. I may as well mention that your friend Alma began behaving in this fashion a few months ago, and I am wondering whether in your case an ounce of prevention might not be the best thing possible. If we could, as it were, isolate this local disturbance over the letter-dreams, let it have a chance to cool off . . ." He seemed now to be addressing himself rather than Sylvia, who accordingly became very frightened.

"Please tell me plainly," she demanded, "what you are trying to say. All this is utter nonsense, as anyone but a psychiatrist would have been convinced long ago—"

"Ah, it is nonsense, then."

"Not the letters, *of course*—but your ridiculous interpretation. And I will not stand for being detained in a locked room by anyone. Medical ethics, doctor—"

"Sylvia, if you do not take yourself in hand at once," he said with asperity, "I shall feel quite convinced that you must have a few weeks of rest and professional care, and as your physician I shall take steps to see you get it."

Sylvia, as much amazed as frightened, collapsed on the couch and began to laugh; her laughter became very nearly hysterical. She saw herself going the way Alma went.

"There, that's a good girl," he said soothingly, "laugh it out or cry it out—one's as good as the other, they're much the same thing, really." He came round the corner of the desk, patted her hair and dropped his handkerchief in her lap. She continued to laugh rather wildly for several minutes, choked, wept a little, and dried her face with the handkerchief. This seemed to her the most improbable thing that had ever happened to her, and she wondered whether she would simply be abducted through the back door and placed in an ambulance. Julian might not know for several weeks. . . .

"Now, that's better," said Dr. Mirabeau. "Maybe now we can talk it over sensibly. Come, tell me, what made you do it?"

"All right," Sylvia said, putting on an air which she hoped would be proper to the circumstances, something between sullenness and hilarity. "It was silly of me," she said, "I don't know what I wanted."

"Well, then, that's all I wanted to hear," he said heartily. "No need to apologize to me, you know."

"May I have it back?" she inquired in a small pathetic voice, stretching out her hand.

"Why don't I simply tear it up here?" he asked, "and we'll consider the matter closed."

Sylvia debated whether the letter were close enough to snatch; it was her sanity he was holding there, and about to tear it up, at that.

"I'd like to keep it, if you don't mind," she pleaded. "It will be a reminder to me."

"Very well," he said, relenting, and gave her the letter. "I see no harm in that. And now, you know, I don't think there is any point in going on with the session today. The time is almost up anyhow.

And I feel, in an odd way, that despite everything we have gained ground.

"Still," he added, pressing the buzzer which caused the nurse at once to open the door, "I'd like you to think over what I said about an ounce of prevention. If you're feeling some extra pressure these days, why not? What's to prevent your taking a few weeks of quiet in the country? You could join Alma."

"You make it sound positively tempting," Sylvia said as she left, "we could play gin rummy together.

"For weeks and weeks and weeks," she added when she was far enough down the hall to be out of hearing. The letter had become quite precious all of a sudden, and she clutched it very tight in her gloved hand as she emerged from the darkness of Dr. Mirabeau's basement office for, as she hoped, the last time.

It had not occurred to Sylvia that just on this morning, when she wished to consult him anyhow, and when as a result of what had just happened she needed someone to whom she might unburden herself, Marius might not be waiting for her. She stood on the sidewalk for a few minutes, looking indecisively up and down the street. Then she went to the drugstore on the corner and called him up.

"My dear," he said—his voice on the telephone was flat and small and brittle—"you must realize that with all the gallantry in the world I simply can't afford to buy your lunch as often as I would wish, unless we eat at the Automat. Accordingly, I offer you the Automat."

"Nonsense," Sylvia said impatiently. "I'll pay for the lunch this time. I want to talk to you."

As it was Monday, many restaurants would be closed; finally Marius mentioned one in the Fifties that they could agree on, and there they met. Sylvia, who was not characterized by any such oriental punctiliousness as would defer business to the end of the meal, showed Marius the letter at once, and gave him a brief history of the situation up to the present time.

"I mean," she said, "I've never been so frightened in my life, I almost thought my mind *was* going."

Marius, looking thoughtfully at the letter, heard her story to the end in silence. As he had no interest whatever in detective stories, no futile deductions from it occurred to him. "How very funny," was what he said when she had finished. "Yet how very serious, too."

"Well, which is it?" she angrily demanded. "Funny or serious? If you're going to be superior about it—"

"I don't see why it should not be both," he replied. "And why do you get so impatient? I am at least accepting, to begin with, your version of the business, and from what you tell me that is more than your witch-doctor did. After all, there are perfectly good motives available for your having written it yourself."

"Such as—?" she asked in a dangerously haughty tone.

"To be perfectly immodest," he said, "you might be designing to develop my interest in you by adding this element of peril and romance. There, there, don't get excited, I don't really think that. But even worse than that," he added, "would be the plausible idea that it was your husband's interest you were trying to attract— which would mean, once you got him to inquire somewhat into what you do all day, that I would be the first person he would come across. Presuming, that is, that there are not a great many others . . . ? All right, all right, I take that back," he said hastily. "But, you see, that is what made me so angry at you the other night— you didn't tell him we were together during the afternoon, in a perfectly innocent way through no fault of mine, God knows, so that when he finally found it out he naturally thought it was not innocent—what you keep secret never is, of course—and my telling him must have looked like bald-faced bravado. For a moment there I thought there might be a small scene—'I'll thank you, sir, to keep your hands off my wife,' is the way I imagined Julian saying it. And when it developed, later on, that Julian was nowhere about and you *devolved,* to say the least, around my neck in the presence of one million witnesses to whom you proclaimed that you were taking off to commit adultery—well, almost proclaimed—and I had to take you home . . . It is true that I got slightly worried, and it went through my mind that for no particular reason we would find Jay waiting for us in the bedroom with—I don't know what. I kept imagining a crossbow, or some other suitably primitive weapon such as a kris, somehow I don't see your husband handling a gun, do you? That's why I didn't stop even to take off your shoes, you know. I kept having the odd feeling that he was standing in the closet, so I fled like Joseph at my earliest convenience. Sorry."

"Oh, God," said Sylvia miserably, "was it as terrible as that?"

"It wasn't great," he said. "But never mind. Glad to be of service. And really, I guess, he was not in the closet."

"I'm sorry, Marius. I had no idea. I wish you hadn't told me."

"I hope you're not going to cry in here, Sylvia. They may think it is the food. It is true, though, that embarrassment is the most terrible of the emotions."

"What shall we do?" she asked him plaintively.

"*We*? Oh, dear, I might have known this would finish with me in the middle. The first thing to do, if you'll pay the man, darling, is to leave here. That is my opinion."

As they walked up the block toward Sixth Avenue they passed a record shop, from the open door of which several sorts of music flared out on the street.

"This is where I live," Marius said. "Upstairs. Would you like to see it?"

Sylvia recognized a degree of arrangement in all this, beginning with Marius's proposal of that particular restaurant; nevertheless, she wanted to be in a quiet place for a few minutes.

"'Where should this music be? In th' air or i' the earth'?" said Marius, giving Sylvia the strong impression that he said this to every girl who climbed these stairs. Indeed, the music—only slightly muted, and with some effect of distance—seemed to come from no particular source and surround them as they stood in the one bare room where Marius lived.

In one corner was a narrow cot covered with an army blanket. Opposite this, a small black desk and chair stood against a wall which was absolutely blank save for the dramatic exception of a large crucifix, a cheap one of black wood with a silver figure of the Savior drooping artistically on it. In one corner, behind a hanging, was a gas stove and small refrigerator; bathroom and closet completed the arrangements, which struck the girl as beautifully and yet rather pathetically austere.

"I'd expected more books," she said, looking at the small row at the back of the desk.

"Oh, I live in the public library," he said. "The goodness in poverty is not having to own the damn things. Now, Sylvia, if you feel like going to pieces, the house is yours."

Sylvia sat down on the chair at the desk. She did not exactly weep, but she bent her head in her gloved hands and bit her lip nervously. Marius stroked her hair softly, standing beside her. It was a scene of tender emotion, except that neither of them felt anything but rather confused.

"About the letter," he said, "I don't know what one does with such things. I could *think* about it for a bit, if you like."

"What good will thinking do?" asked Sylvia.

"Well, I merely meant that that's practically all I can do," he replied. "I am not a detective, you know." After a moment, he added, "You might simply confront Jay with the thing—here are the letters—what is going on?—that's one way."

"I suppose so," she said dully, "but I just don't want to."

"Why not?"

"There would be some sort of dreadful quarrel," she said. "I'd hate it, I always hate it when the weakness in people comes out, when they suddenly look like children who are going to cry. I just hate it."

"Be the best thing, maybe," Marius said. "Have it out. But maybe you don't want to have it out?"

"What does that mean?" she asked.

"Maybe you'd rather have it come true—now the letters have given it a kind of presumptive existence. This Federigo has offered you a suggestion."

"I don't know," Sylvia said. "I don't know what I want."

"You seemed to, the other night when you were drunk," he insisted. "The idea being that if your husband could believe such a thing about you when it was not true, there'd be a certain gaiety in making it come true."

"Don't remind me of the other night," said Sylvia in a small voice. "It will make me wish I was dead."

"Ah, Sylvia," he said. "Darling." He took her hands and drew her to her feet, into a kiss and embrace which lasted awkwardly between tenderness and passion until she found they were standing much closer to the bed than the desk.

"You're a very beautiful girl," he whispered to her. "I do love you, Sylvia, very much."

She permitted, and co-operated in, a number of caresses which rapidly became more ardent. They sat down together on the bed.

A march by John Philip Sousa stood out among the medley of musical sounds below.

"No," she whispered as he began to open her blouse. "No, dear. Not here, not now." She was staring at the hanging figure of Christ on the other wall; despite that she was not religious, or perhaps precisely because she was not, she was horrified to think they were desecrating that image.

"Why not?" he urged her, also in a whisper, then, his glance following hers, he saw the crucifix.

"Ah, that," he said brusquely, and going across the room he tore it from the wall and put it in the middle desk drawer, which he slammed. Sylvia was inexpressibly shocked.

"Marius! How can you do that? How can you dare do it?"

He stood facing her with a kind of defiance at once humorous and pathetic.

"My dear," he said, "it is my secret. I am not a Catholic at all. I only wish I were. Please don't tell this to anyone, Sylvia."

For her part, she could only stare at him.

"I've always wanted to be," he went on, wringing his hands together. "I think it is the most wonderful thing, I love all of it—the tradition, the ceremony, all the splendor and kindness. But I could never bring myself to join the Church. I just, you know, behave as if I were, I observe Lent, I observe all the feasts, I meditate on the Seven Deadly Sins, the Seven Sacraments, the Seven Penitential Psalms, the Four Last Things, I think constantly of Christ dying on the cross—"

"But you don't go to church?" Sylvia asked incredulously.

"I did, to learn the rituals," Marius confessed. "I still do, now and then."

"But no confession? No communion?"

"I couldn't," he said. "As St. Augustine tells us, it would be taking hell fire in my mouth."

"Oh, dear," said Sylvia very abruptly.

Marius sat down beside her again.

"You see, I don't believe in God," he explained, putting his arm around her again. But it was no good; he felt vulnerable and victimized, even though extremely tender toward the girl who had received his dreadful secret; while as for Sylvia, she had begun to giggle uncontrollably, she had never been so confused in all her life.

3

Julian's conspiracy against the world began to frighten him by the power it had, being itself in its inception unreal, of evoking perfectly real events in its wake. He felt bitterly ashamed of himself for his demeanor that morning at breakfast, but what else was he to have done? It was impossible for the letter simply to have disappeared in the brief time he was out, yet it was impossible too—for him—to say directly to his wife, What have you done with that letter? Secrecy condemned him to silence, silence to a world in which, it seemed, no objective evidence of anything existed—could he be absolutely certain he had written and mailed the second letter? He remembered his doubts about doing it, his determination to do it, remembered that he had sat right here at his desk and done it—but he could not achieve, try as he might, any convincing image of his having done it. Possible, after all, that he had dreamed the whole business? No, it was not possible. There was, in the first place, the first letter; he clearly had not dreamed that. He reached thoughtfully into his pocket, which was empty, and recalled in dismay that he no longer had the first letter either; Hugo had it. And Hugo was going to call in a company of private detectives.

But that too, if all had been a dream, could have been part of the dream. Julian did not think it likely, but he had, just now, sitting like a hermit in the midst of the vast silence, no way of demonstrating the reality of these events, of Bianca, of Federigo, of the letters. His face, of course, was still a bit bruised, though the swelling of his lip had gone down. There was the cut on his throat, but that originally happened while shaving, did it not?

The morning mail, when Miss Duddon brought it to him, included a small package which turned out to contain his wallet; there was, of course, no return address. The world, that greater anonymity, had spoken. Julian was relieved at the return of the wallet, which cut down on the likelihood of his being blackmailed by those people, and he was strangely charmed by the tact and courtesy of their having chosen, from the two addresses on the identity card, the office rather than the home; feebly, he even felt grateful to Bianca; the gesture savored, very faintly it is true, of Robin Hood. At the same time, it meant that everything was real, the existence of this objective communication from the outside inspired conviction also about the letters; it all must have happened.

Then the detectives too would be real. How terrible! One consequence produced another. Could they find out anything? It seemed doubtful, unless, as he suddenly realized, they would include him among the suspects merely as a matter of course. They could check on the office typewriter. But how foolish to think they would suspect him, Julian, the husband, recipient of the letters, and the very person, in the first place, who hired the detectives. And yet, he dismally acknowledged, this was exactly what happened in the movies, where it seemed that the criminal's first action after committing his crime was invariably to hire a private eye to trace himself down and turn himself over to justice. Did things really happen that way? Were people really so filled with guilt as to make such a thing likely—in real life? But real life, as it was called, continually imitated art, so that if the detectives of twenty years ago, say, would not have suspected the husband, these detectives—having been, of course, subjected to the movies—would certainly suspect the husband. And Federigo had told him that for a man to send himself anonymous letters, far from being so extraordinary as to be considered unique, happened with incredible frequency and was perhaps not even unusual. Federigo? There was another problem. Problems were everywhere.

In all this, Elaine proved to be the only agreeable thing to be thought about. Julian called up Elaine. Louisa answered the phone, and he spoke to her in a deeper voice than usual, not quite a disguise, in case she recognized him anyhow, but not quite not a disguise either.

"This is Julian Ghent," he said to Elaine when she got on the phone. "I'd like to talk to you, if I might—about our conversation the other night," he added.

"Yes, go on."

"I mean—if we might get together somewhere?"

"Oh. I see." Her voice was doubtful; a silence followed. Then she said, "I'm very busy."

"It's rather important," Julian said. "How about this afternoon?"

"Oh, I couldn't. I work in the Museum of Art in the afternoons. I paint," she explained.

"You paint," repeated Julian, somewhat put out by the introduction of this new element. "Well, might I come round to the Museum, maybe just before closing time—take you for a drink?"

After another silence, Elaine said, "You might."

"The Metropolitan?"

"Yes."

"Where will I find you?"

"I don't know, exactly," she said. "You'll just have to look around among the paintings. Don't come early, Miss Desmond doesn't like us to be interrupted."

"Miss Desmond?"

"The teacher."

"Oh. I see."

All in all, it was not a very warm or satisfying conversation. And what, actually, did he want to say to the girl when he got there? I love you? It did not seem likely.

To put these thoughts aside for a time, Julian concentrated with great determination, during the rest of the morning, on Dr. Thybold's campaign to rid the world of tobacco. That did not seem likely either, but he managed to devise what amounted to a threatening letter in the name of modern medicine, addressed to "intelligent men and women everywhere," and especially to parents. "Would you," it began, "deliberately inoculate your child with cancer of the lungs?" Julian fancied there might be a small picture for a letterhead, showing a naked babe on an operating table, and a surgeon—or possibly just the surgeon's hand—poised with the needle aimed at the child's breast.

When he had done this, not giving himself time to think of anything else, he drew the Bible to him and began to consider the campaign of Mr. Archer More. I AM THE LIGHT OF THE WORLD, he wrote in block letters across the top of his pad, then spent half an hour searching for the source of this expression, without success. He would have to ask Miss Duddon, or have her look it up in a concordance at the library. Let it go for the present.

With the Bible beside him, Julian began to compose a passage of several paragraphs on the state of the world. He depicted children dying everywhere (not of lung cancer)—some by bombs, some of famine, some on the bayonets of savage troops. It was quite hard, he found, to bring these scenes of carnage into a right relation with Faith; for he felt, personally, that exactly the same thing would be going on if people turned to God in great droves and filled the churches to overflowing at all hours of the day. But on the other hand, the somewhat swollen style demanded by this work— "the I-say-unto-you kind of thing," as he privately named it—came very easily to his pencil, only that it induced a certain self-hatred.

I must try to imagine, he told himself, what it would be like to be Archer More. His mind quailed before this idea.

The whole business, Julian began to believe, Thybold, More, the art of advertising itself, the entire world of demand and satisfaction, buying and selling, consisted to a dangerous degree in the production and communication of anonymous or pseudonymous letters. He took up the first magazine that came to hand and looked at the advertisements. Page after page, all the same. Everywhere people were speaking blandishments and threats, appealing with bitter persistence and ferocity to fear, shame, desire, guilt, despair—and always under a pseudonym which gave authority: in the name of science, in the name of God, the name of happiness, the name of love, the name of honor and the name of freedom from underarm perspiration. All this was deemed to be perfectly honorable, also necessary; if it did not go on, the wheels would stop turning. If the wheels stopped turning, then what?

Julian did not know what. He imagined the stopping of the wheels, the generators, dynamos, locomotives, the taxis in the streets below; there followed a confused vision of the gleam of metal fading, rust on a window frame, the huge city and the social fact filled with the sigh of a soft wind, and silence, silence, silence.

As for myself, he thought, I have written two anonymous letters, two. In them I did not speak as though I were God or the Government of the United States, I did not pretend to be Health or Morality or Industry or Labor or Management or Science or Fear of Death or Love or Conscience or any of those fine and wonderful things. I pretended to be Federigo, and look what is happening to me.

Hugo did not forget, he came to the office himself during the afternoon and dragged Julian by main moral force to the offices of Pritchard, Ferriter & Magoun.

"I don't want you to forget it," he said over his friend's protest. "I personally, as your friend, want to see this thing cleared up as much as you do. Or as much as you ought to do."

The detective firm was not far away, on the fifty-fourth floor of a skyscraper.

"This isn't the original Pritchard Ferriter Magoun," Hugo explained as they went up in the elevator. "These young fellows bought the name and the good will—the mailing list, you know. When they came out of the Army, it was. It's Mr. Bilsiter I want you to talk to, he's a good sort of man, he'll know what to do."

Mr. Bilsiter, whose first name turned out to be Chauncey, was a large, soft, fair-haired young man—the hair had also a graceful wave to it—with an egg-shaped face in which huge eyes carried out the egg-motif; there was also a very lofty forehead with some sort of eczema on it. He was on the phone when they were shown into his office.

"But darling," he was saying, "she *knows* already, that's exactly what I'm trying to tell you, she *knows,* and what's more she tore up the prints and laughed in his face and said he could show the negative to whomever he damn pleased. If I were you, Fred, I'd drop the whole thing right away—tell him we don't do business with people like that. There might be violence, anything can happen with that woman. I've met her, darling, *I know*." Mr. Bilsiter replaced the phone very decisively.

"Hugo!" he cried. "How nice of you to stop in. You haven't had any trouble, have you?" he asked, less cordially.

"No," Hugo replied. "My business has gone along fine, thanks. The decree is being granted this week. Your people did splendidly," he added, with some pompous embarrassment. He then presented Julian, stated succinctly what their business was, and handed Mr. Bilsiter the first letter from Federigo. Julian felt hypnotized, he thought this could hardly be happening to him. At the same time, he was a little less terrified than he had been, for Mr. Bilsiter did not look as though he could detect eggs at Easter. He was now staring owlishly at the letter through a magnifying glass.

"You poor thing, how disagreeable for you," he said to Julian. "Do you know this person Federigo, I mean do you know anyone of that name?"

"No," said Julian.

"Heard the name anywhere—read it in the papers, maybe?"

"No."

"Hummm. Foreign name, eh? Italian."

"I noticed that," Julian allowed himself to say.

"And no one has mentioned such a name in your presence recently?"

"No."

"I ask," said Mr. Bilsiter, "because in these matters, where a person doesn't use his right name, it almost invariably happens that he gives himself away by being clever, he uses a name which bears some allusion to his experience, to what he is doing—he doesn't simply lift one out of the phone book, which would be the sensible way."

"Really," said Julian, "it's not very important, and I don't suppose you can do much on the one letter. I don't like to take up your time—"

"You've received only the one letter?"

"No," said Julian, before he had time to think. Now I've put my foot in it, was what he did think when he got there. Hugo and Mr. Bilsiter were looking at him keenly.

"One came this morning," he confessed. "I'm afraid my wife took it," he added miserably. "At least I couldn't find it anywhere." He explained how he walked the dogs in the morning, and thought as he went along what a ridiculous figure he must be making himself out to be.

"So—Sylvia knows, does she?" said Hugo. "What did she say?"

Julian was forced to recount that disgraceful little scene as well.

"I'm afraid," said Mr. Bilsiter, "to be perfectly plain about it, sir, I am afraid you are growing a pair of horns. Or why would she deny it?"

Hugo hastily got up.

"I don't think I need to hear this, Jay," he said kindly. "You can count on Chauncey to help you see it through. I'll call you up to hear about how things are going along." He patted Julian's shoulder with funereal sympathy and took his leave.

"As I see it," Mr. Bilsiter said when he and Julian were alone, "the letters by themselves don't give us much to work on—unless, of course, you get more of them. Oh, we'll check what little we can, but if you've no connection whatever with anyone called

Federigo—if the name rings no bell in your mind—we're fairly stuck, you see, to begin with. We must play a waiting game," he said sagely. "On the other hand," he went on, "what we can certainly do is pin down the contents of the letters, establish the truth of the accusation they make—I'm afraid I have no doubt at all it is quite true—and collect the evidence, names, dates, places. . . ."

"Evidence?" asked Julian stupidly.

"For the divorce," Mr. Bilsiter explained. "You won't, I should think, have much trouble at all, it looks like being a perfectly clear case, perfectly lovely. The one thing I don't like, though, is Mrs. Ghent's knowledge that such letters exist. She may lay low for a while, not see the man." He frowned, then said in a brighter tone, "But they seldom do, you know. In my experience it usually turns out they somehow refuse to acknowledge that someone knows, they can't resist seeing each other just once more and then once more—and so it goes, as if they were invisible. You know, just the way people who pick their noses in public always think no one has seen them."

"But really," Julian found space to protest, "I don't want a divorce, I—"

"What you do with the evidence," Mr. Bilsiter said, "is naturally your own business. You may be the old-fashioned sort, I don't know. I don't want to know. We collect the evidence, and there our responsibility ends. We do divorce work, Mr. Ghent, we are not toughs or thugs in this firm. In plain English, if you decide to kill your wife, or, for that matter, yourself, kindly don't tell me about it."

When Julian left the office of Pritchard, Ferriter & Magoun he had rented the services of a private detective, who was to report to him upon his wife's actions daily for as long as was necessary, these reports to be made by mail to Julian's home. All this Julian did, or allowed to be done, not only because it was too late to turn down Mr. Bilsiter—it seemed as though that would be an open admission that Julian himself had guilty knowledge of the letters (which Hugo would of course get to know at once)—but also because he had become somewhat bemused and spellbound by the idea. He saw himself sitting at breakfast, over the coffee, reading about Sylvia while she unsuspectingly sat opposite.

Perhaps there's something in it, after all, he thought as he left the office. It will do no harm to find out, just as a point of academic interest, what she does all day long. It's funny how little I know of her life—or of her, for that matter. What does she think? What does she think about me? That is something no detective report can tell me, of course. Still, it is interesting simply to let things happen as they will. And of course I don't need to *do* anything with what I find out; unless, that is, the whole awful dream turns out to be quite true. . . .

"You certainly have started something now," said Federigo, who was walking along beside him. "Detectives and all. Probably blood-hounds next. It's a long boomerang that has no turning."

"I should think I've got enough troubles without you," Julian nearly snarled, as they walked uptown.

"Without me, my dear friend," said Federigo, "you wouldn't have the troubles. Without me," he added, "you'd be dead. Here, let's walk up through the Park." He took Julian's elbow and steered him across Fifth Avenue.

"'And Peter called to mind the word that Jesus said unto him,'" blithely said Federigo. "'Before the cock crow twice, thou shalt deny me thrice. And when he thought thereon, he wept.' Very beautiful, that, and so mysterious, don't you think? 'And when he thought thereon, he wept.' Julian, when are you going to weep?"

Julian maintained an angry silence.

"You believe," said Federigo, "that eyes are made for seeing, but I tell you—I say unto you, to give it the proper tone—I say unto you that eyes are made for weeping with."

They walked through the Zoo, Federigo chatting all the while.

"Tell me," Julian said at last, "what must I do to make you leave me alone? Do you want me to apologize for using your name? I'll do it, I'll swear never to think of you in the future, if that is what will make you leave me alone."

"To make me leave you alone," said Federigo, "you must be other than you are."

They walked, after this, up past the pond where children sailed boats, or at least where they had done so when Julian was young. As Federigo pointed out, however, there was now but one vessel in this entire water, its progress followed by two or three elderly men; it was a miniature submarine.

"It would solve all your problems, wouldn't it," Federigo then observed, "if she simply died this week. A natural death, of course."—

"Shut up, shut up," cried Julian in a childishly savage voice. "Keep your despicable thoughts to yourself."

"Oh, it hadn't occurred to you? I thought it had. Beg pardon," said Federigo mildly. "Just an idea," he went on, "just an idea. I was thinking chiefly of your freedom, after all, you can't blame me for that. I wonder what your detectives will find out. Will they realize how utterly strange it is for a man to get such letters and then allow his wife to see them, and even to keep one? If they think of that, dear, I shouldn't be surprised if it was all up with you— honor, morality, honesty, the whole works: pouf! And all for what? You haven't even been unfaithful. Ha ha, that started the whole silly treadmill revolving, and here you are, just what you were before, only a few days older. Except in thought, that is. And I say unto you again, whoso looketh after a woman to commit adultery with her, why, he might just as well go right ahead, isn't that so?" Federigo chuckled disagreeably, and pointed ahead up the path.

"There is the Museum of Art," he said. "School's out for today, my friend. Run along to the great masterpieces, let your conscience be your guide." He turned away.

"Stop! Wait!" cried Julian.

"I thought you wanted to get rid of me," Federigo called back over his shoulder; he ran down a small side path and through a tunnel, where Julian followed. On emerging and looking everywhere around he caught no sight of Federigo, but felt, nevertheless, as though that gentleman continued to watch him from a place of hiding.

Chapter Six

IT was characteristic of Julian, as a morally minded person, to view the world more or less entirely in terms of his own decisions; he implicitly believed that once he had made up his mind to be unfaithful, and had gone so far as to find the right girl to be unfaithful with, and even fall prospectively in love with this girl, she would at once fall into his arms, the way ahead would become clear, there would be easy sailing, et cetera. Things did not of course turn out in exactly this way; he found he had underestimated rather grossly the world's independence of his moral vision; furthermore, courtship took time, money and attention, all of which had to be provided without disturbance, at least in appearance, to the normal distribution of his time, money and attention.

As to time: he was fascinated, his entire sensibility was heightened; instead of a dull succession of moments along which he traveled like a bead on a thread, he began to see time as a house, an immense closed space of many mansions (like the Museum, in a way) with secret passages, hiding-places, alcoves, false partitions behind which whole rooms could be concealed without disturbance to the apparent dimensions as seen from outside. If one shaved fifteen minutes off here and ten there and another ten over here, if moreover one were then twenty minutes late getting home, there was very nearly a whole hour which seemed scarcely to belong to time, which afforded a delightful, cozy, though temporary shelter from the inexorable public succession of moments registered on clocks everywhere around it. In fancy he compared it with that model of an Egyptian tomb in which, on one rainy afternoon in the Museum, he first kissed Elaine; a brightly lit space with cold, smooth, pinkish walls and a sign which said:

TOMB OF PER NEB

"False door" through which it was believed that the deceased entered into the bliss of the other-world.

In order to secure this corner in time, Julian began to take taxis uptown, leaving the office twenty minutes early and saving also the half hour or so it would have taken to walk.

This cost money, and money was more inexorable than time; time, being manufactured, as it were, out of waste materials, out of moments which separately would have meant nothing and been useless but could be thus assembled into a spare hour, need not be regarded as literally being taken from Sylvia and given to Elaine; with money it was otherwise. They had, too, he and Sylvia, a joint checking account—which they could not be said to have, really, as regarded time—and any inordinate withdrawals on his part would be noticed at the end of the month. Julian resolved at first to spend very little on Elaine, transferring in this manner the guilt of his conduct from the moral to the financial realm; but guilt it remained, slice it how he might, with the result that now and then, in an access of disgust and contempt for himself, he would spend a great deal of money on her all of a sudden; which he would then regret. As a solution to both problems at once, of time and money, he devised a series of dentist's appointments—for it was quite true that his teeth needed attention—which out of consideration for his work he placed in the late afternoon, so that he could leave the office at four and attribute all extra expense to the dentist, whom he would claim to be paying in cash (he even went so far as to invent a personality for this dentist, to make him the sort of man who would have to be paid in cash, in case an explanation should become necessary). Then even this began to worry him, for the ridiculous and yet quite disturbing reason that he was spending money on Elaine which ought properly to go to the care of his teeth: images of death and slow decay—"I am killing myself for love"—gave a secret poignancy to his love, the more because their source was too silly to be mentioned or even coherently thought about.

Attention, however, or, more properly, the quantity of love or of feeling generally, disturbed him in quite another way; it did not at all appear to diminish by division as money did and as time would if he spent more of it with Elaine. On the contrary he came from a meeting with Elaine buoyed up and filled with affection, of which Sylvia received the benefit; Julian was more charming with her, more interested in her, and took her out to dinner more, than he had done in months. He recognized his feeling as in part a kind of obscure gratitude to his wife for not noticing anything, or appearing not to notice anything, and this gratitude, as it could have no direct expression, took the form of an increased tenderness and demonstrative pleasure in her company; even in bed, where Julian desperately thought of Elaine at all instants—and thought with terrible remorse that it was she whom he betrayed—it was, after all, Sylvia who received his passionate and treacherous ardor as sheer advantage.

Julian during this time had moments of the most intense wretchedness, but they alternated with moments of great charm—not necessarily, either, the ones spent with Elaine, but chiefly perhaps the moments of imagination; at least life became less dull. He thought longingly about the enchantment of a polygamous society; how easy and delightful it all would be. When he read in the newspapers some story of a man's having successfully led a double life for some years undetected, with two wives in the same town, he was extremely pleased at what he took to be a demonstration: neither woman dissatisfied, each with her own home and her own life and her own husband, and the man doubtless charmed with the essential element of secrecy and darkness in his life, which satisfied what Julian considered to be the basic, neglected element in the male character, the need to be at least two persons; as he named it, the *dramatic need*.

One such story in particular fascinated him. A young man in a Southern city had managed for over a year to be the husband simultaneously not merely of two but of three women—but that is a little too much, thought Julian, imagine the financial arrangements and the struggle to keep those identities fully separate. This situation, however, had a quite amusing finish; the young man finally was caught out over something trivial: he refused to take wife number three to the same double feature he had been forced to see with numbers one and two; the third wife was suspicious, in the first place, for no better reason than that she had wanted particularly to see this bill at the neighborhood theater, she began to think, she asked questions, she set on detectives, and the husband was caught. Before being put away by the iron indignation of an offended society (which nevertheless, according to the tone of the newspaper account, was laughing enviously up its sleeve) this extraordinary man admitted to being somewhat bored with the whole business, and glad it was over.

So affection seemed to expand, with Julian, as required, it rose to its occasions; the more love he needed the more he had. Somberly he recognized, however, that this happy state sufficed only for the beginning of the program; for just so long as love remained spiritual in fact, whatever it might be in intent, no wickedness appeared on the surface. But beneath the surface there waited, quite plainly, the brute sexual fact, where the principle of division obtained exactly as it did with money; shameful as it was to acknowledge, love's incarnation was corrupt while love's spirit was not; what was given to one woman in bed could not be given to another, nor was there here any way, such as an appointment with a dentist who did not exist, of fictitiously extending, so to say, one's capital. This worried Julian, though not, at this time, very much, for the good reason that he could not by any means be certain or even very confident of Elaine's soon becoming his mistress; that existed, if it did exist, at some remote crossroads not quite to be located in ordinary time, and as for the moment he felt borne along on a wave of precarious happiness he did not require himself to think very rigorously about the approaching time of decision.

On the day he first met Elaine in the Museum Julian had walked meditatively and slowly through the galleries; he wished to come upon her, if he did, as though by accident, for he was still full of the sensation of being watched, and even had the faint, absurd suspicion that the eyes of the portraits, which seemed to follow him along, had been slit open to admit in their places the eyes of Federigo.

He found Elaine seated before a huge canvas by Titian containing among other figures a billowy, naked courtesan the size of a taxicab or so, which she was copying, not very well, on her easel. He stood behind the girl for a few minutes in thought and a certain dismay; that she should paint was a sufficiently jarring note, somehow, and that she did it badly was almost intolerable; moreover, in flat heels and a smock she looked like a dreadful little schoolgirl. He very nearly dropped the whole affair at this time, but one thing alone kept him there, and this was the tenuous certainty, something in the straightness of her back, some highly accented concentration on what she was doing, that she was quite aware of his presence behind her. Julian came closer and stood there in a critical posture, his head to one side and hands behind his back. The girl turned slightly.

"There you are," she said. "I'm nearly through. Terrible, isn't it?" she indicated her canvas.

"It is a little, well, lumpy," Julian said, comparing it with the original and noticing at the same time that Elaine had a pretty smudge of white paint on one cheek.

"Mother likes me to do it," Elaine said. "Perhaps she believes it will keep me off the streets. I don't mind, really, though. Oh, Miss Desmond," she said with an air of pleased surprise, "this is Mr. Ghent."

Julian saw a fierce-looking old lady, very small, in oatmeal tweed and thick woolen stockings, who put one hand on the cameo at her breast and sighed flutteringly.

"That's all right, then," she said. "It is so hard to keep people from annoying the girls during the session—this place, you know, is a veritable wolf-haunt, ideal for pick-ups. You know one another, then. That's all right. But I must insist," she went on while shaking hands with Julian, "that you do not disturb Elaine during the hour, I will not have it. Do you paint, Mr. Ghent?" Miss Desmond began edging him slightly away from Elaine.

"No, I'm afraid I don't," Julian politely replied.

"Not at all?" Miss Desmond asked. "Not even a little bit?" She coyly held up finger and thumb close together, as though to show in how slight a degree it would be possible for Julian to paint.

"Not even that much," he said, and drew Miss Desmond further aside to say in a low voice, "I am sorry to interrupt in this way, but there is something important I must say to Elaine. She is my cousin, you know," he added.

"Not bad news, I hope?" Miss Desmond asked. "If you must, then, Elaine," she called, "you had better put away your materials and go with your cousin. But remember," she said severely to Julian, "this is an exception. It must not, must not become the rule."

"Why cousin?" Elaine asked after they had got away. Julian laughed. The success of even this slight deception, in which Elaine had co-operated passively at least, pleased him a good deal.

"Why not?" he asked lightly, taking her arm as they left the Museum. He led her to a bar nearby—there was not much choice in this neighborhood, and it was a disagreeably domestic and ordinary bar—but the waiter would not serve Elaine because she was too young. This amused Julian and accordingly annoyed her. They got into a cab and went downtown to a place on Third Avenue called the Delta Café, where there was not enough light in the booths for the waiter to make out Elaine's age, and where in any case he would not greatly have cared.

"I hope you solved your little difficulties the other night," said Elaine.

"Ah," said Julian neutrally, indicating either that he had, or that no solution was possible and that, in any case, the whole matter was beyond discussion.

"I think you've a lovely wife," Elaine then said without the least malice in her voice. "A perfectly beautiful girl. I wish I looked like that," she said simply.

"Yes," Julian said. "But Sylvia's not entirely well. She goes to a psychiatrist, you know."

"Oh?"

"This is a rather difficult time," he added, "I don't know if we will stay together, Sylvia and I." It was the first time Julian had phrased this idea aloud, and he felt ashamed of it. But there was also a kind of pleasure in his shame, and he thought that now he had begun to betray his wife he would go on to the end, probably a bitter end. "I'd rather not talk about it just now," he said.

"Why did you call me today?" she wanted to know.

"Because I felt lonely," he replied. "I wanted someone I could talk with."

"And you suddenly decided on me?"

"I've thought about you a good deal since we met the other night," he said. "I like the way you smile."

They looked at one another. In the semi-darkness of this place the slightest glance gained a conspiratorial character; they were like two spies, full of suspicion, inquiring for a password. They looked into one another's eyes, saying nothing but what could be

said for them by their eyes which were either windows of the soul
or mirrors on the world. Julian's glance intended earnestly what
he would not say, and hers inquired into its sincerity with a like
earnestness in which there was, however, some amusement. The
brief dialogue of these eyes ran something like this:

ELAINE: This is very nice, and even exciting. There are res-
ervations, of course.
JULIAN: I do mean it. I know exactly what I am doing, and I
know it is wicked.
ELAINE: I am free to do as I like. You, on the other hand—
JULIAN: I can't help myself, you can do with me whatever you
please now.
ELAINE: I may please and I may not, but thank you.

"I hope we can be good friends," Julian said, and took her hand.
"May I see you often?"

"I'm sure we'll be good friends," she said, gently disengaging her
hand.

They continued to meet at the Museum. Julian would arrive
toward the end of Elaine's painting session, and hang about evad-
ing so far as possible the eye of Miss Desmond; then Elaine would
put away her equipment, Julian following at some distance, and
they would meet almost as though by accident in some quarter of
the building where Miss Desmond had no business; among the
medieval armor, in the Egyptian collection or far away where the
Chinese jade and pottery lived. In this way Julian came to see his
friend against a number of exotic and diverse backgrounds, and
this effect of variety did not at all diminish her charm for him. He
was very happy at this time, though also somewhat apprehensive
of being seen by someone he knew. He had a curious double feeling about this; there was, first, the odd self-consciousness whereby
he *knew* at every instant that he was being watched, spied upon.
At certain moments he had the penetrative knowledge that he himself was doing the watching, that he stood back in a corner of the
gallery, slightly shielded by statue or glass case, and saw himself
over some little distance taking Elaine's arm, walking with her,
heard himself talking to this girl (his voice sounded very odd); at
these moments he watched with cynical doubt and a sneer how

their heads came close together as they looked at one or another exhibit—came together and casually, whisperingly, drew apart again without a smile, without a glance, with no acknowledgment of what they both knew.

On the other hand he was possessed by a supreme and unfounded confidence in either his discretion or his luck; for the very reason that he felt himself constantly observed by the critical eyes of his own guilt, he did not really believe it was possible for any other person to see him and Elaine together; he told himself that his friends were really not the sort to be found dead in any museum but the Modern Art. Then, too, there was recklessness; supposing anyone should see, what of it?

When, one rainy day about a week after their first meeting, Julian and Elaine entered the Egyptian tomb with the pinkish walls and found it empty and perfectly screened from observation, they were both quite aware of what was going to happen; each was quite aware, also, of the other's awareness, and yet perhaps not altogether certain, so that there existed a fine tension between them as they turned toward one another in the clean, empty tomb which the Museum authorities had illuminated very brightly perhaps against just such a contingency.

Elaine kissed him with amateurish and experimental ferocity, fastening her teeth on his lower lip; it was, for Julian, an uncomfortable business, which he felt she probably considered highly erotic from having read about it in a novel. Nevertheless, it was a clear triumph, and in pride he reminded himself that this was happiness.

After a moment in which they clung together she let him go, pushing him a little away, and stood back as far as the space of the tomb allowed. She laughed, beginning with that out-of-kilter smile which he found so terribly appealing.

"My dear," she said, "this is not a good thing for us to be doing."

"You are absolutely lovely as an Egyptian," Julian said.

But of course this kiss, this moment of clarity which divided so exquisitely the past from the future, entailed as a consequence long discussions; they were two civilized people, yes, that was agreed, but what exactly did being civilized include in such a situation as theirs? Julian said at one point—they had left the tomb and were strolling aimlessly around the monuments of Egypt, hand in hand—that they must be absolutely honest.

"We must know what we are doing," he said, and Elaine nodded gravely. They knew what they were doing to such a degree that very soon, having made the circuit of the hall, they found themselves again before the tomb, whereat they smiled at one another—"well, once more," whispered Elaine—and went in. They were unaware that at this time, and again as they emerged a few moments after, they were observed by Marius Rathlin, who was enraged at the sight of them.

It would not have been extraordinary for Marius to visit the Museum at any time in the course of his studies, but as a matter of fact he had come there because Elaine's mother told him on the phone that Elaine was to be found in the Museum. From some little distance, just as he had caught sight of the girl and been about to speak to her, he saw Julian come up and take her arm; Marius had more or less been following them since, with a grim smile of utter indecision on his face.

Marius had not seen Sylvia since the afternoon of his confession; her drastic response had, to say the least, somewhat clarified his feelings about her. After his humiliation he had felt very angry and had a vision in which he seduced Sylvia, there she was lying naked on his bed, and he laughed at her—in the vision he even spat on the floor—and walked out of the room (the vision allowed that he himself was fully clothed). He rated himself most severely for this feeling of vengefulness, which, however, he could not help having, and decided that the best thing would be never to see her again. Surely she must perceive, if she had—which he was not altogether sure she did—any delicacy at all, that he had given into her hands a certain power over himself, perhaps the greatest power one person can have over another in the limits of polite society, the power of making him appear ridiculous.

On the other hand, did he not have the same power over her? The situation of the anonymous letters, and the incredible attitude of Dr. Mirabeau, were sufficient subjects for humor. So that it was, for the time being, a stand-off between them, or they would be two blackmailers taking in each other's washing; the figure confused but the meaning clear.

He had decided finally to stand on his dignity; she would have to make the first move. And in keeping with this decision he had not seen her for a week or so. Then he had turned his attention to

Elaine, who was, he told himself, younger, more attractive than Sylvia, blessedly unattached, altogether more suitable; he even began to think of marriage.

And now this! It was like moving in a dream down one corridor after another, and finding at the end of each one Julian. Kissing in the tomb! it was horrifying—by which he meant as he honestly acknowledged that he was envious.

He debated whether he should scurry round to the other end of the hall and casually approach them so that they should pass face to face—if he did this, he would with generous irony and the most exact punctiliousness stare at Julian and fail to recognize him, thus in the one gesture combining scrupulous courtesy and sophistication with the cut direct. He did not do it, however, because while he would have loved to embarrass Julian he feared to offend Elaine.

Marius had spoken to this girl but once; she had no idea, could have no idea, of his possibly feeling anything in particular about herself; yet he already imagined himself in love with her, saw his pathetic figure skulking behind Egyptian statues as the rejected suitor, and attributed this chance revelation in the Museum to design, to her conscious cruelty; all this of course increased his sour love.

But if he did not approach them, then there was nothing to be gained by staying in the Museum. He watched them for a moment more, strolling hand in hand away from him just as though their being together were the most honorable and upright thing in the world. Marius hastened away with his secret knowledge, knowing he would use it—somehow, he did not yet know how—and regretting for an instant at the same time that if he used it he must thereby lose the precious detachment which made him the keen observer that he was.

"But that's nothing," he said as he went down the steps outside, "I am a suitor, I am entering the arena, this that is happening to me is love." He walked away in a confusion of feeling. "As for that Julian," he thought grimly, "he is living in a fool's purgatory."

2

All in all, Sylvia considered, things were looking up; for nearly a week she had not seen Marius, and during that time there had

been no anonymous letters. Could there be, perhaps, some connection? She had also deliberately missed two appointments with
Dr. Mirabeau, and was beginning to hope the doctor would simply and without comment of any sort submit his final bill at the
end of the month—for of one thing she was very certain, she was
not going back to him, not even for so long as it would take to
explain that she was not going back. Perhaps it had been Dr.
Mirabeau who was really her trouble all that long time? Not that
she believed he had sent the letters, no, she would not go so far as
to think that even of him—but might it not be true, at least in the
odd world of the psyche, not that one went to the doctor because
one was sick, but that one was sick because one went to the doctor? It might well be, look what had happened to Alma.

It even seemed to her that her husband was becoming kinder
again, more attentive and loving, even erotically interesting, all of a
sudden; this too had happened since she left off going to Mirabeau.

Sylvia liked to think that things solved themselves the easy way
if given the chance; she began to see the tension between herself
and Julian, accordingly, as "one of those times that come up in
every marriage," while as for the anonymous letters, though she
remained puzzled, she decided at the end of a week without them
that this was one of the things it was unprofitable to puzzle about.
Something nasty had undoubtedly happened, and been felt, reflected, in her behavior and Julian's; but she would be willing to
settle for its being over, even if this meant she never would understand exactly what had happened. Had she known the letters
would stop, she reflected a little angrily, she never would have told
Dr. Mirabeau and consequently she would not have been subjected to the humiliation of being thought insane. But then—looking on the bright side—she would never have had, either, the nerve
to break off the treatment, never would have discovered in a sufficiently convincing way how blind that treatment could be to whatever happened from the outside, how it refused to believe in anything not inwardly provided for. So it was an ill wind which had
blown this much good at least. Again, she would not, had she
known there would be no more letters, have told Marius of them
either; but then neither would she, probably, ever have come to
know in return Marius's own delicious (and extremely odd) secret,
which put her on even terms with him. She hoped, even so, that

Marius was not vastly offended over his confession and her uncontrollable response—surely he must be able to see the enormous humor of it?—and determined, though she would not be the first to break the silence, that when next they met, which would most likely be at Hugo's wedding a few days hence (the divorce-bak'd meats, you might say), she would be very kind to Marius, and say something—she did not know exactly what—which would indicate sympathy and secrecy; and to which he must reply (of course!) with like indications about the confidence she had placed in him. Doubtless the *whole thing,* as Sylvia vaguely phrased it, was going to die down and be forgotten; whatever Julian may have been thinking it was evident that he had now changed his mind—whatever had happened, for example, during Hugo's party, would not now be brought up as a reproach to anyone.

The point was, she now saw, to live a full, busy life; it was only in idleness that one became infected with dreams in which life might be otherwise. One could, of course, continue in the most innocent way to be good friends with a young man like Marius, if that were an arrangement in which he would sensibly co-operate. But anything else, so far as she was concerned, would be out of the question, though perhaps with regrets. Of course it would be nice, in some ways, to have an affair; but things simply were not constituted in that way these days (she had a moment of doubt here; were they not?), and the point about taking marriage seriously meant above all that one did not, absolutely did not and must not, make trouble. She resolved that some time soon she would have a friendly explanation with Marius on this score. "Of course we are tempted," she would say in her new wisdom, "it is part of the game. Ideally, my dear, I should be delighted to go to bed with you, I'm sure we should have a splendid time together—but one simply does not do such things." In imagination she saw Marius nodding gravely and tenderly his assent to this proposition, which combined romantic charm with moral security; and Sylvia believed that if he were any sort of man at all he would care for her more deeply than ever—she would even say as much: "If you are as intelligent and kind and good as I know you are . . ."

Sylvia's full, busy life at this moment centered around the preparations for Hugo's wedding. Exactly what it would center around after that event she had not yet considered. There were numbers of things to be done in a short time, for the date had been set rather suddenly and late on account of the divorce. Sylvia still did not altogether approve of this marriage, it is true; yet she was by nature incapable of remaining apart from "making arrangements." She helped Mrs. Leonard with the invitations, she went with Louisa to give advice about what clothing would be suitable for England at this time of the year; she arranged by herself the catering for the *bon voyage* party in the stateroom.

"You know, suddenly I'm very happy again," she said to Julian one evening.

"Ah, darling," he said, with a kiss, and stroked her hair.

"For a while I thought we were going to have a perfectly furious quarrel," she confessed, "but love wins out again. I hate quarreling, I guess I'm just not the violent type. I'd rather just have everything go along smoothly. Real happiness is kind of quiet, just like this, sitting here with you, not saying much."

"Ah well, every marriage has its ups and downs," Julian replied, his feeling of unredeemable shame mixed with secrecy and triumphant contempt producing, with some effort, a commonplace.

"Those horrible letters—!" Sylvia said boldy. Julian smiled in what seemed to her some physical discomfort, and raised his eyebrows.

"Yes, the letters," he said.

"Darling, you didn't really believe there was anything wrong, did you?"

"I was a little uneasy," he said in a joking tone, "you're a damn' attractive wench, you know. But then I decided I was being silly— you'd be incapable of keeping a secret for twenty minutes, wouldn't you?"

"But who is Federigo?" she asked with a great sense of relief that these cards though face down were finally on the table. "Do you know?"

"I've no idea," Julian replied. "That was the most horrifying thing—that feeling that we were being watched over by some stranger, or even by one of our friends posing as a stranger."

"You haven't got any more of them?" she hesitantly asked, very much wanting not to know.

"No," said Julian. "I guess whoever it was gave it up as a bad job. If I ever catch up with him—" he added significantly, making a fist.

"Well, if you do," said Sylvia sensibly, "I hope he's not bigger than you are."

This was the end of the discussion; they were like two people examining an infected wound and pretending to each other that the hard, inflamed spot which covered it represented the formation of new, healthy skin; they probed very tenderly indeed around the edges, and if the one winced the other pretended not to see. Even Julian began to believe that this was a new life, if not necessarily a more honest one than the old, and that whatever happened with Elaine would at least have no connection with the letters of Federigo, which had served their purpose (along with, perhaps, other, unforeseen purposes) and were definitely at an end. He reminded himself, however, that the activities of the detectives were not at an end; the most recent report let him know how Sylvia had spent Friday: she had gone shopping with Louisa, with whom she then had lunch and went to a movie; the evening she had been with Julian himself, who thus appeared like a stranger (an odd feeling, again as if he were in a play or movie) in the report directed to himself. All this, if dull in the reading, was impeccable domestically. Ah well, he supposed he must keep these bloodhounds on the track—at rather considerable expense—until Hugo left with Louisa on his honeymoon; then he would tell Mr. Bilsiter it had all been a mistake, or at any rate that he did not want the trailing continued, and the whole matter would be forgotten by the time Hugo returned from England.

There was, meanwhile, one little thing that troubled Sylvia, though she talked of it with no one, and this was the odd feeling which overtook her now and then, wherever she happened to be during the day, that someone had his eye on her; she could sense it, there was a spot on the back of her neck that seemed to be receptive to a stare. But however often and suddenly she turned around, in a crowded restaurant or walking down the street, she was unable to identify her follower, if she had one, which she came finally to believe she had not. "Now this," she told herself, "would be the ideal tale to put before Mirabeau, who would call it entirely subjective—and in this instance he'd be entirely right, too. It is the beginning of a mild form of persecution-feeling; I was worried and guilty over things last week, and this is a kind of psychical hangover from that time. If I simply relax, and realize it is my own conscience which is following me around, everything will be all right." The uncomfortable feeling persisted, however, or at least it returned intermittently during each day, and Sylvia bore it stoically.

One evening, when as it happened Julian was out—it was the second time in the week that he had to work late, for as he told her, his vacation was coming soon, and there was a good deal to clean up before he could leave—Sylvia had a phone call from Hugo, who said he would like to have a talk with her.

"Why don't you come over here?" she said, thinking this must have to do with the arrangements for the wedding; and Hugo promised to come.

"Where's Jay?" he asked, and when Sylvia told him that Jay, poor thing, had to work late, Hugo raised his thick eyebrows.

"His vacation is coming soon," she explained on seeing this expression.

"Where do you plan to go?"

"No idea," she said. "We haven't even thought of it yet."

"Ah." Hugo was not a man who could be comfortable in the possession of secret knowledge; his awareness that Sylvia, who was possibly unfaithful to her husband, was being shadowed by detectives which Hugo himself, moreover, had been responsible for hiring, made him feel quite ashamed, for he really did like Sylvia as much as he claimed to do; so he reminded himself that he personally, Hugo, wanted this question of the anonymous letters cleared up, it was all—detectives, that is—for their own good, it was his business to see his friends happy again, which was as a matter of fact the errand he had come here on.

"Look, I have a notion," he exclaimed, as if it had just come to him. "Why don't you just take over my place on Long Island for your vacation? At Lantern Point."

"Oh, Hugo, we couldn't do that," said Sylvia, thinking that this might be very nice indeed.

"And why not? Do you both good to get away from—well, to get away from civilization for a bit. It seems to me you've both been under some strain, these last weeks."

So it had showed? But of course it had, Sylvia reminded herself.

How couldn't it have showed, considering her behavior at Hugo's party, Julian's absence . . . ? A moment of anxious doubt overtook her, and she smiled gaily.

"Every marriage has its ups and downs," she said.

"Sylvia," Hugo said earnestly, "I want you to tell me one thing—are you and Jay—are you, that is, breaking up, have you thought of doing that?"

"Darling Hugo," she replied, "you of all people must surely know that married couples *do* now and again think of such things—that's one of the thoughts that keep them going."

"Ah, then it's not serious," he said heavily. "I'm so glad. You two, you know, are just right together, never let anyone tell you otherwise. And if you ever have any little troubles, why, I hope you'd let me know before you do anything, well, anything odd."

"Hugo, what are you trying to say?"

"Sylvia, I hope you haven't been having any—wrong ideas. About Julian the other night."

"Wrong ideas?"

"Such as—well, you know what I mean. I happen to know," Hugo said impressively, "that Jay left that party only because he was unhappy and wanted to be alone for a while. He went to a bar and while he was there he got into a fight with some drunk. So if you've been thinking anything else, Syl, get rid of it right off."

"Hugo, how do you *happen to know* all this?"

"Because, of course, Jay confessed it to me. I can tell when a man like Jay is telling the truth and when he's not, I've known Jay for longer than you have."

"And did he also confess," Sylvia asked, "what he was unhappy about, that he had to leave the party to be alone?"

"Well, I didn't want to push it too far," Hugo said, "but after all, you know, you were giving one or two fairly good reasons, yourself, why he might have been."

"Yes," said Sylvia, frowning. "I'm sorry I was a fool at your party, Hugo."

"Oh, that." He waved it away. "Don't think of it. I only wanted to be sure everything was all right between you two."

"We did have a few bad days, you know how it is," Sylvia said, "but everything's fine now—so far as it's your business, darling," she added sweetly, but Hugo was not embarrassed.

"Of course it's my business," he said, "when my friends are unhappy. But whatever it was," he went on after a pause, "I'm delighted you've cleared it up. I've always thought about you two, you know, that there are faithful types and unfaithful types—you and Jay are faithful types, you couldn't do anything out of line if you had to. It would hurt too much. With me," he added reflectively, "it's different. Even now, you know, and I'm terribly in love with Louisa, I can see the time coming when I shall want someone else, it's just my nature. But I suffer for it, Syl, you know that."

"Hugo, I'm sure you do," said Sylvia, "even if," she could not resist adding, "it must be great fun to suffer in just that manner." She softened this remark with a smile, which Hugo returned.

"Now then—what about the place? Say you'll take it, Sylvia, it will give me pleasure to think someone's getting a bit of use of it— Elaine and her mother wouldn't think of going up there again, I don't believe they liked it one bit and I can't say I blame them, in the winter at any rate. It's primitive, you know, I've deliberately kept it that way. Out on this lonely point on the dunes, it looks over the sea—it used to be a smuggler's hide-out, the original house, you can still see the foundations. They used to light bonfires there to deceive ships into wrecking on the shoal, and then they'd plunder the wreck. Mooncussers, they were called, because they hated the full moon that gave them away. There's a wood stove and fireplaces, you'll find plenty of wood left. No electricity, of course, and you get the water from a well, you pump it up. I think you and Jay would enjoy it. Be fine for you, too."

"It sounds wonderful," Sylvia said, dubiously imagining herself drawing water from a well. "I'll think about it, and talk it over with Julian."

"Nonsense, surprise him," Hugo said. "Look, I've brought you the key. Just pack him into the car and take off, you'll both love it. Do say you'll have it."

Sylvia accepted the key, reflecting that they might actually go up there. To live the simple life, she thought, to get away from things for a while . . .

Hugo kissed her at the door before leaving. This kiss began as a friendly salute, which he with some force prolonged and finally attempted to convert into something quite different; Sylvia pushed him away rather angrily.

"There are faithful types and unfaithful types, just as you say," she reminded him, and he laughed.

"I don't know why I wanted to do that," he said. "For old times' sake, maybe. We're getting older, darling, we're all getting older. I could love you again, Syl," he added, "I could ask you to go to bed with me again just for that, because we're getting older and, after all, what else is there for people in this life? Or maybe," he continued, philosophically rubbing his behind against the edge of the door which was swinging back and forth, "maybe it's more that I want to betray Louisa even now, already, or that I just dread getting married again even if I do love her. There's a lot of hate in love, isn't there, you get a kind of need to do the dirty on someone just because you love her. The first time I was unfaithful to Alma, you know, I kept thinking about her all the time. It was like slapping her face and saying over and over, 'Take that, and that, and that.' Like in the movies." He laughed again. "It was more like sleeping with Alma than sleeping with Alma was."

"Are you saying," Sylvia asked dangerously, "that you felt that way with me?"

"No, this was well before your time, darling," said Hugo, rather delighted with himself; then seemed to see that this was going too far, according to Sylvia's expression. "It's just the kind of rotten no-good I am," he said apologetically.

"That doesn't need much further demonstration," Sylvia said.

"Syl, one more kiss, darling," he said. "For old times' sake, and to say the world's not worn out yet. Another couple of days, you know, and I'm lost forever."

Feeling a certain wry, inward humor in all this—that it would be all right to do very near anything so long as you felt you loved only your own husband—Sylvia accorded Hugo this farewell kiss. She felt herself caressed as from a great distance, a distance of more than seven years, and it seemed not to matter at all. These fumbling hands and squeezing fingers, the soft lips and behind them the hard teeth, what were they searching for in her body? She seemed to be standing back and looking at this body receiving those caresses as though it were the body of another person, for whom she felt both pity and contempt.

"Darling girl," muttered Hugo as she pushed him away. He

sounded drunk, though he was not; that was what the body did, the empty body with no one at home inside.

"It would have been fun," he said, recovering himself and smiling down at her.

"Yes, I'm sure it would have been great fun," said Sylvia, and closed the door firmly after him.

3

The wedding of Hugo Alter and Louisa Leonard took place in church, very solemn and ceremonious; everyone was beautifully dressed and took a serious if not a reverent interest in all that went on. Julian Ghent, being best man, had a close view of the proceedings, and as he did not bow his head more than a little at the appropriate moments, found himself regarding the combed and plastered silver hair of the minister from a distance of only a couple of feet during a considerable part of the service. This ancient and reverend head bowed over its book seemed to focus for Julian agreeable feelings of righteous displeasure which mingled with his conventional wishes for Hugo's (and Louisa's) happiness and with the emotion, not religious in form but connected commonly with all the higher and mightier observations of the passage of time, which he felt no less than most who were present, and which even brought tears to his eyes. He morally resented the authority over love which everyone was compelled to assume in the minister as the witness of church and state; he resented the power which must be really present in the business to bring him close to tears; he resented the rich, golden and vested hypocrisy which in a muted voice sanctified by compulsion. Julian did not weep, but he felt the tears in his eyes and the slight trembling of the chin which had always warned him, in childhood, that he was going to cry. Instead, so as not to, he fiercely concentrated on the bowed, silver hair before him, and wondered whether clergymen were trained to use a special sort of hair-cream, to anoint themselves formally with it, in the hope of achieving just this dull silvery luster which seemed, for himself at least, the quintessence of past time together with the seriousness and sorrow of life. As he handed Hugo the ring Julian was reminded that his grandfather, who died in Julian's childhood, had had just such silver hair, metallically combed and plastered and stiff, thin enough to allow a view of the skin of his head; this grandfather died in the winter, and because he used to winter in Florida the story given to the child Julian was that Grandfather had gone away to Florida. Julian had been sent out to the Park to play, he remembered it was a bitter cold, dark day with which he always associated a sepia picture of Florida on a post-card—a picture of the Everglades, a writhing of rich vegetation and one passage of reflective, shiny water in the foreground, all of it of course in the dark rotogravure brown which was then the fashion. Here, then, in the minister's bowed head, in the firm but thin strands of hair through which the scalp gleamed, this returned to Julian, not flooding suddenly back like a revelation but slowly spreading and sinking like a stream released over soft ground: how the name of death, when he learned it, had taken on that chocolate brown together with the smell of the postcard itself, which was in turn associated with the characteristic smell of Florida—where he had never gone, perhaps because Florida and the Everglades were the names of death—and which carried with it the forbidding bitterness of that afternoon in Central Park, with the keen wind which had brought the tears to his eyes and numbed his fingers. Standing here beside Hugo and Louisa Julian suddenly felt sorry for his grandfather who was more than a quarter of a century in his grave, alone and unthought of by anyone save, for this instant, Julian himself, who seemed to enter for a moment the cold, bitter Everglades of the mind.

It was strange that the celebration of happiness should bring with it this ancient image and the cloudy thought of death; yet even the celebration of happiness mentioned the name of death, reminded of it and of the provisional nature of the happiness whose relation to time was here being so seriously remarked. Oh, my friends, he thought, I do hope you will be happy. But even the thought carried with it all unlikelihood, and induced in Julian's mind a sophistication quite the reverse of what his inward exclamation sincerely intended; he saw the marriage as mockery, all its implications of virginity and freshness amazed and made the best of by an old gentleman in an odd costume whose silvery hair had the dull gleam of a counterfeit half-dollar, or for that matter a real one.

Louisa was very handsome in a gown of heavy white satin. Hugo looked solemn, imposing, somehow ever so slightly pathetic as he gave the appearance of listening to the words of the service with great attention—as though he might put them down in a notebook and check his daily conduct against these recommendations which smoothly flowed from the minister's mouth.

Mrs. Leonard wept happily and with loud sobs throughout the service and after, in the taxi on the way to the boat, and throughout the nervous, rather dreary party which occupied the two hours or more before sailing time.

On account of the confined space of the cabin—a quite capacious one for ordinary purposes—the party was small and gave the impression of being enormous: "Not more than three hundred most intimate friends," Marius observed to Julian; moreover, pieces of hand-baggage were everywhere, and presents—flowers, baskets of fruit and baskets of bottles of whisky—continued to arrive the whole time. Everyone was standing up, talking, smoking, drinking; for a background, which one became aware of only intermittently, there was the slight, preparatory trembling of the vessel itself, the humming sound that went with it, now and then a huge blast of the horn which caused all the guests to pick up their belongings and look nervously around, and the purposeful rush of all sorts of people, including officials, past the open door of the suite. Through the urgent, loud conviviality could be detected another sort of urgency, as the time of departure brought to the surface people's worst anxieties about a possible failure to get off the boat before it left—an anxiety which punished, Dr. Mirabeau might have said, their dream-like wish to remain on the boat and sail off forever; there were arguments about the time, and a sentence frequently repeated was: "Don't worry, they'll warn us when it's time to go." All this was very fatiguing to the nerves, not least because prolonged farewells tend to lose their character in a few moments, leaving what remains to betray itself finally as an uncontrollable wish to escape.

At the center of all this, a peculiar force of secret awareness, which might be given very generally the name of love, related several of these people in a network of unequal tensions: the exclusive character of these relations was witnessed by a superficial gaiety spread among them all, which disguised, or at least intended to disguise, isolated and secret communications of some urgency.

Sylvia, for example, was aware as Louisa was not—not in particular, anyhow—of "the kind of person" Hugo was so far as this related to herself; she could even perceive this honeymoon voyage not as a setting forth into the new and the unknown but as an interlude in a possible, highly theoretical relation, not yet by any means over, between herself and Hugo; this thought formed a kind of revenge, very remotely, for the sake of Alma, so that Sylvia could look on the new bride with superior pity, poor thing. This awareness of hers was concealed also from her husband Julian, who did not know either the quality of Sylvia's relation with Marius—what it had been, what it now was, what it might be—nor the secret of Marius himself for that matter, whose elegant, learned, altogether fictitious affectation of Catholicism made for something esoteric and aristocratic in his presence.

Marius, Sylvia saw, was talking with Elaine, over near the window. Now *that* would be a very fair match, she considered. Of course, Marius would have to give up his rather bohemian ways and take a job, but if he did he and Elaine might make a lovely couple; both quite small, thin, highly bred (all this in appearance, anyhow) and charmingly young. Sylvia imagined herself as the Older Woman, *stepping out of his life* with a gracious smile and the hint of tears, to whom the young people would owe their happiness; all this, of course, as she realized with a slight start, began with the assumption that she had first been the young man's mistress, otherwise it would lack its romantic significance. If Marius had not chosen that moment, the other day, for his confession, if it had not struck her as so ridiculous—if, if, if—who knows what might have happened? It was so easy to make a mistake.

Marius, who would in a few minutes tell Elaine of his love for her—would he tell her of his having seen her with Julian in the Museum?—at this moment savored with delighted detachment the last rewards of irony. He saw Sylvia—looking at her with keen, neutral attention across the stateroom, a tall, serenely beautiful woman in a severely cut suit of navy blue—as eaten inwardly with doubt and self-distrust and unhappiness over the anonymous letters which, with Dr. Mirabeau, had very nearly driven her into adultery with Marius himself; and as invincibly ignorant, at the same time, of the real occasion available for her despair to feed upon; that her husband was deceiving her with Elaine, who looked at this moment the picture of pretty innocence as she smiled at something he, Marius, had just finished saying. As for Julian himself, whom the anonymous letters must have worried—not quite needlessly, it would seem—about the conduct of his wife, Julian seemed at this moment the ideal victim, being as he must be at once worried and happy, scared of unknown and generalized danger but meanwhile quite foolishly secure in the secrecy of his passion which was not secret. Marius felt as though even the deep trembling of the ship beneath his feet were part of the exultation of his power, and knavishly concluded that if he could at one and the same time make Sylvia and betray Julian to her, this power would have wrought its beautiful utmost; after which—and even through which—he would love only Elaine.

Elaine for her part regarded Sylvia with what is usually called honest pity—a misnomer, since this virtue is almost by definition excluded from the feeling of pity. She felt quite attracted to Julian, and she loved situations of a certain danger; they were, in fact, the only things she did love. Her feelings for Julian were experimental, but boldly so; not unlikely she would go to bed with him, some little time after he asked her to, *if* the adventure could be kept light, casual, charming; there was a regrettable tendency she had noted in Julian, he wanted to *be in love,* with all the serious, irrevocable and somehow disconsolate connotations of the idea. Elaine was quite delighted with what she thought of as her own toughness, a kind of knowingness about the world which should (and did) surprise gentlemen of thirty-five or so in a girl of twenty, and an ability to take excellent care of a self which, whatever else she gave or seemed to give, kept its privacy and sufficiency. Looking over now at her lover's wife, Elaine was like the executioner whose superlative technique can detach the head from the body so suddenly that the victim mercifully will have—so far as human beings can tell—no time in which to feel pain. As for Marius, with whom she was talking at this moment, he was a sweet boy who transparently was going to tell her in a few minutes that he loved her; Elaine had no real objection to his doing so at all, but hoped he would not be pathetic, if only for his own sake, since what she admired happened to be strength and a certain ruthlessness—the thing, perhaps, which attracted her to Julian, whom ordinarily she would not have suspected of strength, was the engaging carelessness he displayed about his poor wife, and this carelessness more than anything else would prevent her from ever getting to know, since it was as a rule, she believed, when people became serious and sad in love that they made fatal errors. Love was most charming when it involved deceit.

As for Julian, he too was possessed at this moment with a delighted awareness of his superior power in having at the same time in the one room his wife and the girl with whom he was in love; it was like seeing two express trains which seemed to be rushing toward one another at a great speed of closing but proved at the last possible instant to be on separate tracks so that they passed one another in perfect safety, with the appearance of accident, of luck, yet with the consent in reality of forethought and plan. And no one knew! He smiled at Elaine, who happened to glance his way, and she smiled back; the secret seemed to shuttle palpably through the smoky and crowded room. Only one thing at this time disturbed Julian's Machiavellian pleasure, and this was the momentary thought of Federigo, who remained to him, it appeared, as a kind of legacy left over from the anonymous letters. He is the Devil, Julian thought, and, simultaneously: I am insane. But both these thoughts, deep in the silence of his body—he felt them, as it were, in his stomach rather than his head—rather increased than diminished his feeling of reckless, arrogant mastery over the nature of things. He smiled at Sylvia, who was not looking at him; this smile might have gone between her ribs and killed her. He was even willing to smile at Marius, that poor, prissy little gentleman, who was talking so earnestly—doubtless wittily as well—to Elaine, not knowing of course that this was Julian's Elaine whom he tried so hard to impress. Marius returned the smile somewhat angrily, he thought, and Julian decided this smile might refer also to Marius's having attempted Sylvia's virtue and found it—as the detective reports would seem negatively at least to show—unassailable; and Marius, unable to make his friend's wife, was unaware of turning now toward his friend's prospective mistress. Julian's feeling of towering, isolated strength increased until it seemed it might topple from an insane height.

Hugo, who was becoming more drunk than anyone present, felt grateful to everyone indiscriminately; everyone seemed to cooperate in making his life charming and happy. He was, in a way, honest with everyone, so that they all must love him for exactly what he was, which he supposed to be something of a minor villain; whatever anyone of his acquaintance did, so far as marriage was concerned, he could always compare himself to his own advantage with Hugo. Therefore people did not want him to change, they needed him just as he was, and it was as if Louisa somehow embodied the expression of their gratitude to him. She was beautiful, and her beauty was enhanced in the light of his own licentiousness; she was not merely married but as it were sacrificed to him. He sought out Julian and tried to express to him something of this feeling of being, as he said, "like a God." Julian nodded rather distantly to all this, and Hugo remembered that his friend had troubles of his own; he inquired about the progress of the detective reports.

"Nothing," said Julian, "perfectly clear."

"I knew it," Hugo cried enthusiastically. "What did I tell you—you've nothing to worry about."

"Except, of course," Julian added, "she had a visit from you the other night—you were there for a little over an hour, according to the report." He laughed. "Are you the man, Hugo?" Then he added, "I think probably the best thing to do is drop the whole business. There have not been any more letters. And this Bilsiter is being so absurdly thorough, he called up and asked me how long we'd been married, had there been anything in the past, had I ever been away for any length of time—that sort of thing."

"Oh, really, you don't say?" said Hugo, with an abrupt change of expression.

Marius meanwhile had told Elaine bluntly that he was in love with her, and now sought some means of demonstrating his knowledge without altogether giving it away.

"Do you see much of our friend Ghent these days?"

"No, of course not," Elaine replied, "is there some reason why I should?"

"No reason at all," Marius said with dark significance, "absolutely no reason. I just thought I'd ask," he added. "He's in rather a bad spot, you know, these days."

"Oh, really?"

"Yes, it seems he gets these anonymous letters suggesting his wife is unfaithful to him. Letters signed by someone who calls himself Federigo."

"Why, I know a Federigo," Elaine exclaimed in pleased surprise. "But it couldn't be that one, that's Federigo Schwartz, for he's away on a world cruise and besides, he doesn't know Julian, I don't think. He is Mr. Ghent's double, did you know that? The spit of him, like twins."

"Oh, is he, indeed?" Marius smiled a sinister smile indicative of more understanding than he actually at this moment was in possession of. Here was a strange new piece of information to be deeply considered; there was a Federigo, he was the image of Julian Ghent; what did one make of that, now? He looked very intently at Elaine.

"Is she, do you think," asked Elaine, "unfaithful, I mean?"

"All I mean is," he said to her, "that because of this situation in which our friend Ghent finds himself, his tastes may be a little capricious just now, and one ought not to take very seriously, for example, his interest in Egyptian art."

Elaine beautifully showed no surprise; Marius thought she was wonderful at this moment.

"My dear, don't threaten me," was all she said.

"Are you in love with him?" Marius asked in a low voice.

"Of course not," Elaine replied with a little laugh. "And you mustn't be so serious, yourself, either—if you love me," she added, "you must please me a great deal and make me happy. No romantic sulks, now."

So the party continued for some time; everyone had a secret from someone and for this reason believed himself powerful, sometimes this belief was erroneous. A was victorious over B, B over C, but when it came to the end of the alphabet, A would be found to have been conquered by Z. Finally the visitors were warned that it was time to leave the ship and they collected their belongings and began confusedly straggling out on deck.

Hugo went as far as the gangplank with Julian, holding his arm, in fact. At the last possible moment, drunk, blushing, and speaking very fast in a low voice, he told his friend that he had been the man who, seven years before, had got Julian's wife Sylvia with child.

Julian stopped walking and simply stared at Hugo stupidly.

"I suppose I should tell you to hit me," Hugo said, a helpless expression on his broad, red face. "Go ahead, it's your right," he added, more or less thrusting his face forward to be hit, and help-fully adding, "I won't hit back."

Julian was unable to do anything at all, he stood there as if paralyzed.

"This way, please," an officer cried. The crowd moved, swayed, sifted down the gangplank carrying Julian mercifully along with the others; Hugo himself was very nearly taken off the boat in this manner. There followed a tiresome period during which all Hugo's friends stood on the pier waving their handkerchiefs, though Julian, who had not recovered from the shock he had just received, could not be certain whether he was waving farewell or simply shaking his fist with a handkerchief in it. To be on the safe side, he did a little of both, and hoped that it left Hugo in doubt too.

Chapter Seven

JULIAN Ghent, when young and a single man, had been quite unsuccessful with women. He betrayed himself time after time by being evidently too eager when he should have been restrained, a little aloof, or even downright disdainful. Some older and more adept ladies would even tell him about this fault, making an artifice and a convention out of what they were supposed to feel in the course of nature, but even guided by this good advice Julian continued to be too candid in revealing his desire, so that nearly all ladies, however much they liked and even (some of them) loved him, continued to deny the final gift of their favors. For the first axiom in love is that whoever does not despise is despicable; love is, like chess, a contest in which tolerance is impossible, lucky accident unlikely and a draw very infrequent except between grandmasters.

The most poignant thing was that the young Julian had known all this quite well in theory, but was always afraid to put it into practice to the extreme degree that would have been necessary. His love affairs always began well, for when his feelings were not involved beyond admiration and desire he possessed naturally a fine arrogance which made it seem as though the advances were being made from the other side; but as soon as he saw the overwhelming effect he was having on the girl of his choice he would respond helplessly by falling in love (perhaps with the image of himself which he saw reflected in her eyes), and he would say to himself: "All right, then, she loves me, let us drop the pretense." A fatal error, since it was certainly with the pretense that the girl had been in love, and she, her own ambition to servility and degradation thus put off, would take her revenge by a mocking coldness, a light-tempered carelessness, the appearance of perfect freedom from the pains of love as soon as she saw that these pains could be

486

suffered instead by Julian. And this attitude of hers, which he as much as anyone had created, would further inflame in the young man an unhappy passion, or a passion perhaps for unhappiness, which increased as the chances of satisfaction diminished; he would grow bitter and disagreeable, until quite soon even the friendship which was tacitly supposed to replace love would become unendurable to the girl, and all was over.

This flaw in Julian's nature would perhaps never have been overcome by any internal resources; he would be, it was possible to predict, all his life a failure at the edge of success, a perpetually bitter optimist. Yet his weakness—of inveterate pride, vanity, sentimental greed—had oddly been made over into strength by his marriage. Not only did the satisfaction of the immediate desires of the flesh allow him to be less urgent about woman generally, but also the jealousy of his wife, by making an affair with another woman very nearly unthinkable, provided Julian with exactly that aloofness and restraint necessary to let his more attractive qualities shine forth, so that at parties other women were frequently found trying to get him off into corners and sometimes making improper suggestions to him. The dignified coldness of his response humiliated and further inflamed these women, so that Julian perceived now how successful he might have been had circumstances not made success impossible to take hold of.

What he did not perceive was the paradox, that this success he could not take hold of was owing entirely to his wife Sylvia, who thoughtlessly, by the reflection in him of her jealousy and strict views, made her husband attractive to other women. Had his marriage been suddenly annulled, Julian would doubtless next day have relapsed into his weak-willed, pleading ways, and been spurned again by everyone.

These considerations lead to the further thought that it is, after all, virtue which seduces to love. Thus the high price placed on virginity warrants a certain reticence which is lovable because it is in the first place contemptuous of love and can therefore incite the lover to humiliation and hurt. The whole proposition is morally wicked, perhaps economically unsound, but, however, erotically and abysmally virtuous.

Julian's relations with Elaine Leonard developed, according to the familiar pattern (with certain technical differences on account of his being married), in the direction of unhappiness and began to exchange their original freedom for bondage. The charm of leading a double life, in the first place, began to go sour on him; moreover, he realized it could not be kept up for very long; something was bound to give, one way or another. There was even a danger that Elaine, who was perhaps not so much cruel as young and thoughtless, and who, whatever else she was, happened not to be a coquette or tease, might become bored and consequently explode the whole business herself—for fun, as she put it on one crucial occasion.

Sylvia had gone to the movies and Julian, telling himself that the time had come, pretended to be tired so he could stay home. In fact he was tired, but this did not prevent him from at once phoning Elaine to suggest, with a show of carelessness, that he was alone and she might if she liked come over for a drink; she had never before been in his apartment. He regretted this step as soon as he hung up the phone, and twenty minutes later Elaine arrived.

She was dressed, with a kind of sacrificial simplicity, in black, without jewelry or any accent of ornament, and this costume, together with a kind of quiet tension in her demeanor, informed Julian plainly that she had come to him as his mistress. This was so, as even he had to admit, as a result of his own intentions, his own actions; he was delighted, of course, in a certain highly theoretical way, also frightened, but not merely in theory. At once he imagined Sylvia, bored with the movie, returning early. His own hypocrisy repelled him, but the idea of ignominious discovery (and possible violence—"I'd kill her," Sylvia had said so long ago, "and possibly you as well") inspired a kind of nervous terror.

While he fixed drinks in the kitchen, Elaine wandered around the living room, looked at the books, the furniture, the pictures (there was the picture of Sylvia, too, gazing around as if suspiciously) and said "What a lovely place." The dogs, Troilus and Cressida, frisked around her, and she admired the dogs ("What lovely dogs"). Julian brought in the drinks and suggested she might like to see the rest of the apartment. Elaine agreed, and they spent a few minutes in this way ("And this is the kitchen" . . . "Here is the bedroom") but as it was a small place there was not a great deal to be shown; also the furniture appeared to Julian to be staring at him in a peculiarly disagreeable and *knowing* fashion.

Elaine conventionally admired everything; finally they returned to the living room, where she turned to him and said, with a grave sweetness:

"You asked for me, and here I am." And she put up her face to be kissed. Julian obediently took her in his arms. Out of the corner of his eye he saw Sylvia staring out of the portrait. The kiss was prolonged, and became quite impassioned; it represented to Julian a new depth of self-disgust and, perhaps for this very reason, an intensification of pleasure; treachery, violation, hatred even, were the things which gave point to his love for Elaine.

"I love you, darling," he whispered, with an eye to the portrait.

"Do you want me?" she whispered back, and he replied "Of course I do." They embraced again. Through the charming, somewhat alcoholic and bitter fragrance of her perfume Julian unwillingly became aware of the sour smell of her body in heat; this is reality, he thought in desire and wild fear, and let her go.

"Not here, darling," he said. "Not this way."

"Oh, and why not?" She smiled at him her wicked, crooked, innocent smile. Julian glanced up at the portrait.

"She might come back," he said. "And anyhow—it wouldn't be fair."

"Who wants to be fair?" she lightly asked, turning her back on him.

"I love you, Elaine," he offered again, somewhat helplessly.

"Well, then . . . ?"

"We must be honest—that's the thing."

"And what does that mean?"

"Elaine, darling, if I told her—if we were perfectly honest about this—there's no shame to falling in love, is there? Would you marry me if I were free?"

The girl, her face still averted, was silent for a moment.

"No," she said then, in a tone of judicious reflection. "No, I very much doubt I would."

Julian stood aghast and frightened. She seemed to be leaving him alone in a house which they had robbed and ruined together.

"I don't love you, darling," she went on. "I don't want to talk about love. This is fun, or it was supposed to be. The last thing I'm interested in is breaking up one happy home"—she laughed angrily—"and starting another. That's not my dish at all."

"But I'm in love with you," Julian repeated.

"And here I am," said Elaine. "What do we do about it?" She turned back to face him, and there would have been perhaps another embrace, but Julian was becoming thoroughly miserable.

"Not here—not in this house," he said with somewhat absurd firmness, the picture of a man putting his foot down and finding bubble gum under it.

"Your delicacy is marvelous," she said. "Sylvia would be delighted."

"Please don't say her name," Julian said between menace and appeal. Elaine looked at him with a remote, objective curiosity.

"Don't you believe I have some right in this?" she inquired. "I thought it was all so simple—you wanted me, you were attractive, I decided I wanted you—and now where are we?"

"Yes, darling, but not this way," he exclaimed. "Not with her looking on . . . and she might come back, there's that, isn't there?"

"Yes, there is that," Elaine admitted. "This is being damn badly managed, isn't it?" She seemed to consider for a moment, then asked. "Tell me, Jay, will you go away with me—will you meet me somewhere for the weekend?"

This proposition struck Julian as the perfect solution. *Away,* so long as it was anonymous and without particular character, and as it perfectly put off the embarrassment of the moment, appealed to him enormously.

"I'd have to make some excuse," he cautiously said even so, "tell Sylvia something, I don't know what. Where would we go?"

"I'm going to Hugo's place anyhow," said Elaine, "out at Lantern Point. If you want to come along—so. If you don't—so," she added carelessly. "I leave Friday. Tell Sylvia it's a business trip—I believe that's what people commonly do, isn't it?"

"But I never take trips in my business."

"Then this will be the first time, won't it?" she said sweetly. "She'll suspect, of course—won't she? But what's that? And we'll have a few days. We might even send her a postcard saying 'wish you were here.'"

"Don't, please don't be like that," he begged her.

"I only mean to say you must make up your mind." Elaine picked up her gloves from the coffee table before the sofa, looked up quizzically for an instant at the portrait of Sylvia, and said,

"I'm leaving on Friday. You've got a couple of days to make up your mind and tell her some story or other. But it's got to be by then—or else never. If you came along," she added, "I might, I just barely might, decide to forgive your rudeness now. Don't imagine it's so pleasant for me, your conscience—such as it is."

"Darling, I'll think of something," Julian promised. "I'll call you Friday morning."

A kiss, somewhat grudgingly and coldly given, was his reward for this pledge, and then Elaine, to his great relief, left.

Almost as soon as the door closed behind her Julian began to wish things had been otherwise; now he felt not only guilty but humiliated as well, and this humiliation, he dimly recognized, increased his love for Elaine, and satisfied something in his nature which went deeper than his desire to be unfaithful to his wife. Thinking it over now, he found his original motives almost impossible to recapture; what he had started out to do, possess (as he called it) another woman, could be viewed in several ways: as a simple desire for sexual experience elsewhere (but it was certainly not simple, whatever it might be); as an assertion of freedom; as an expression of contempt for Sylvia (that one hurt, it hit close to home); as an enlargement of his own importance; as a wish for secrecy and even criminality; as curiosity about what evil was and where its place in the world; finally, as a wish to be punished, caught and punished—a wish to find, or if necessary create, an objective situation consonant with those feelings of guilt and insufficiency with which he had begun. The verdict of guilt had been delivered first, so long ago; what had to be discovered was the crime.

Like a murderer silently cleaning up the scene of his fatal action, Julian took both their glasses into the kitchen and washed them; he also scrubbed the lipstick off his face. Then he realized it would not look natural for him to have sat home all evening without a drink, so he made himself a highball which he did not want and took it into the living room.

"You're not going to offer me one?" asked Federigo, who was sitting on the couch looking at Sylvia's portrait. Julian gave a slight start, but only from the suddenness; it really frightened him that as a matter of fact he was not in the least surprised to see his curious acquaintance sitting there in the living room; also, while he was disturbed (naturally, who would not be disturbed?) he even, in a way, felt grateful for the presence of another person—especially one who was neither Sylvia nor Elaine.

"So it's you again," he said rather curtly, and made another drink for Federigo, who took it without saying thank you, and began to sip in an extraordinarily delicate way, as though he were not used to drink. Federigo was dressed casually in slacks and a shirt open at the throat; he also wore sandals instead of shoes, and looked very much at his ease; even impudently so, thought Julian—like a proletarian poet or some such individual.

"Now what is it you want?" Julian asked, determined upon boldness.

"I? I don't want anything, I'm perfectly content," said Federigo, looking indeed the image of a man satisfied with himself. "You're the one, my dear, who wants things." He laughed. "Though the Lord alone knows what it is you want, when all's said and done. As a lover, Julian, you'd make a wonderful real-estate agent—'and this is the kitchen, this is the bedroom, here is the bathroom . . .'" Federigo imitated Julian's voice very accurately, with overtones of sarcasm at the same time. He laughed again. Julian was infuriated, out of sheer embarrassment.

"Damn you," he cried, "how do you know that?"

"Oh, I've been here right along," Federigo said, "only you overlooked me—as well you might, I suppose, under the circumstances. Julian, you remind me of a funny story. Do you want to hear a funny story?"

"No, I do not want to hear a funny story," Julian said between his teeth; but Federigo went right ahead anyhow, and Julian listened.

"There was this man, this drunk, at a bar—I'm sorry it begins in such a common way, but there it is, no help for that—and he made friends with a party of strangers. He fell more or less in love with them, the way drunks will, and when the bar closed he took them back to his house for one more drink. But when they got there he first insisted on showing them over his home. They were unwilling, but they went along for the drink, and he showed them everything in the most boring detail—here is the living room, here is the hall and this is the closet, here is the kitchen . . . I won't take you through it all, I don't want to bore you, Julian. Finally he led them upstairs into the bedroom, where he turned on the light. 'And here is our bedroom,' he told them. 'That woman in the bed' (pointing at her) 'is my wife, and that man lying next to her—that's me.'" Federigo laughed at his joke, but Julian did not.

"I don't see anything so funny in that," he said with grumpy dignity, "and I don't see that I'm very like it, either."

"Oh, you don't?" asked Federigo. "Well, then, perhaps you're not—how should I know?" He looked curiously at Julian. "What are you like, then, do you think?" he inquired.

"If you know so much," Julian replied, "I suppose you know that, too."

"I've a fair idea," admitted Federigo, "but have you? There's the point. Have you ever used a camera with one of those split-image range-finders?" he asked. "The sort where you see two images of what you aim at, and you turn the knob until at the right focal length the two images coincide and become one? To me," he said, "you are a man looked at through such a camera, not at the right focal length."

"Looked at," Julian said doubtfully, "but by whom?"

"By yourself? By God?" Federigo spoke in a bored voice. "Who cares about that?"

"I care. Listen, Federigo," Julian said earnestly, "tell me this plainly. Are you the Devil?"

"My dear boy," drawled Federigo, relaxing on the couch, "that is your trouble, an all but incredible naïveté. Supposing I were the Devil, and you asked that, what sort of answer would you get— 'tell me plainly, be honest with poor me, dear Mister Devil'—how silly can you get? And even if it became quite clear to you that I was the Devil, what then? That's only a name, you would still have to ask what devil would so particularly belong to you. All this dramatic *me retro Satanas* kind of thing may be very well for the Saviour, but for you—no. You don't want him behind you, after all, behind you is the direction of danger and the unknown—a fact which, by the way, also makes toilet training such a profound influence on the Idea of the Good. And by the odd irony of history the great Descartes, inaugurator of the reign of reason, located the soul back there, behind the head in the pineal gland which is supposed nowadays to be the atrophied relic of a third eye which warned of danger from the rear. No, Julian, on the whole you had better have your devil out in front of you, in full view—like myself, for example."

"I knew that about the pineal gland," muttered Julian. "It was in Philosophy at college."

"Of course it was," Federigo easily agreed. "And now you are playing with the notion that I am some sort of subjective hallucination, because I know only what is known to you. Well, that is a nice notion, I suppose, and quite comforting even if it does suggest you are not quite right in the head, because it is better to be a little queer, isn't it, than to be diabolically possessed? Though some say, of course, that the two things are one. After all, the inner and the outer reality are very oddly married, aren't they? The outer reality has never been seen except by the inner one and according to its own rules—at least, so all reasonable people agree—in these *modern* times," he added sarcastically, "therefore you can see only the external world which is made a part of your internal world—so that knowledge becomes a kind of cannibalism, you digest the virtues of your enemy and they become you in the process—the courage of the warrior and the goodness of the missionary, all one in the stew. But of course even cannibals must be careful of whom they eat; you might bite on a coward, a lecher, a thief or murderer, and become that—if the analogy is not getting a little too far-fetched to be followed."

"Then you are me?" Julian asked.

"I haven't said that either," said Federigo. "You're far too intellectual for your own good. Hasn't it ever occurred to you that this world is a real world, and that things are profoundly and beautifully, sometimes, just what they seem to be? Be more simple, Julian." Federigo stood up. "Come with me," he said, "for a walk in Central Park. There's something I want to put before you."

"But my wife," Julian objected, "she'll be coming back, she will worry . . ."

"You are admirably considerate," Federigo said. "Nevertheless . . ." And for reasons he could not compass, Julian felt impelled and even willing to follow, taking only one precaution before they left, which was suggested to him by the thought of Central Park at night: he left behind his wallet, thinking in confused shame that if his dead body should be found out there in the morning it would be difficult if not impossible to identify. Federigo noted this and seemed to approve it, though somewhat satirically, saying:

"I think you are wise to leave behind that little artificial heart (you notice men typically carry their wallets in pockets so placed as to suggest a right-handed heart balancing the one on the other side?)—not on account of the money, but the various civil identities it proclaims, the one hundred and one license plates which you usually wear on your public person. It is funny," he added, "you were robbed of your watch, now you leave behind your wallet. It suggests the not absolute impossibility of your ever learning from experience."

They walked together into the Park. Federigo insisted on linking his arm with Julian's in a disagreeable sort of intimacy, but on the other hand Julian felt quite safe with Federigo at his side. They skirted the dark bulk of the Museum of Art and climbed a small hill.

"This is Cleopatra's Needle," said Federigo, pointing to the little obelisk at the top, "but of course—I'd forgotten—you know rather a lot about Egyptian monuments by now, don't you?"

Julian did not reply.

"You will remember," said Federigo, with something of the lecturer's manner, "that this field over which we look was once water?"

"Yes, it was the Old Reservoir when I was a child," said Julian.

"Close your eyes," Federigo said, "Now look again."

Julian opened his eyes and looked. There before him was the Old Reservoir again, with its low retaining wall of rough stone. He stood on the path and marveled; it seemed to be daylight all around him.

"Over there, to the left, where the Old Fort is—that's where you used to play, most often," Federigo said. "Come, let's walk over that way."

They came to the place, which was full of nursemaids, children, baby carriages—exactly like real life, Julian thought, save that they seemed to see it from a great, empty distance. After a moment he realized this was so because of the silence; it was all exactly like real life except that nothing made any noise; there between the Reservoir and the playground, under the shadow of the Old Fort, he stood in mysterious and silent daylight, unseen by anyone, and watched the children at their play.

"That one in the brown corduroy shorts," Federigo observed, "that is you, Julian."

Julian looked at the little creature who at this moment was sitting in some dirt beside the path. He remembered those brown corduroy shorts, which for some reason made him want to cry. Now a governess, whom he remembered quite well though he could not come up with her name, walked over and picked the little Julian bodily out of the dirt and slapped him. There was an expression of absolute rage on her somewhat shriveled face.

"This is Miss Collis," said Federigo. "She was with you for a long time, and loved you quite well, really, little horror that you were. She is still alive, did you know that? She slapped you in Central Park and she is still alive. She is in an asylum for the insane in upstate New York. It's odd, isn't it, what becomes of people?"

Julian heard all this as from far away. He began to cry, in part angrily because it seemed as though Miss Collis had really slapped him, hard, only an instant ago, and in part sadly because Miss Collis—he looked sorrowfully at her angry face in the playground—would one day be committed to an asylum for the insane. This feeling he had, of knowing the future, and knowing it also as the present, seeing all things, past, present and future, as one, was a feeling of strange power but also of reverence; he seemed to hear himself saying, "You see, one looks at these things, but one doesn't touch them." A moment later he realized this had been said, however, not by himself but by Federigo.

The little Julian had by now stopped bawling over the slap; he was playing in the midst of other children: Tommy Burns, Edward Cohn, Alexander something or other, a little girl named Genevieve, and two others whom Julian could not remember. Federigo supplied their missing names.

"Rita Larson," he said kindly, "whom you were going to marry when you grew up. No, don't worry, she is still among us, she married quite well—a banker in Trenton, New Jersey—she has several children, the eldest daughter looks rather as she did then— or does now, if you'd rather put it that way. The little boy you don't remember for a rather good reason; it was he who taught you about masturbation, you finally founded a sort of social club for the purpose and had an excellent time until the governess—not Miss Collis but another one—found you all in the bushes one afternoon. That little boy is Raymond Berenger, of course, and he now teaches at a prep school in New England somewhere, though unhappily he will soon be fired for homosexual practices with the students—you see, Julian, you had quite literally a hand in that as well.

"Alexander Hanson, now," he went on, "died in the war, at Bastogne. Edward Cohn never got that far, poor thing. Only a few days after what you are looking at now he came down with mastoiditis, was operated on and died in the hospital. You forgot about him, as children will, in a few days."

This seemed to Julian the most frightful and cruel outrage of all, though he did not see why. Tears of sorrow and long put-off mourning rolled down his cheeks.

"There, that's right," Federigo said, "you are weeping, aren't you, Julian? Tommy Burns is doing quite well, you'll be glad to know, as a certified accountant in this city. He never married, though. Elaine Leonard, by the way," he added, "has not yet been born."

Julian silently looked on at the scene below, watching the children playing in the shadow of the Old Fort which seemed to be also the shadow of futurity over them.

"I'm sorry," he said, still weeping. "Oh, I am awfully sorry."

He shut his eyes tightly for an instant of remorse and regret; when he opened them again the scene had faded. It was night, the playground stretched out where the Old Reservoir had been, but the Old Fort still stood on the rocks above. Julian turned to Federigo, but no one was there, and he had to find his way out of the Park alone.

As he went home, with eyes still wet, be began to lose the sense of what he had felt; secular considerations also obtruded themselves. Immense lengths of time seemed to have passed, Sylvia would have come home, she would be suspicious—unjustly, he cried in silence, unjustly—but there would be two glasses standing there because of that wretched drink he had made for Federigo. The silence of the house, and those two glasses, would surely betray him.

"He is the devil," said Julian of Federigo. "Only a devil could do such things as he did tonight."

And indeed it seemed as though Federigo must be a devil, or

have some supernatural power, whether for good or ill, since when Julian arrived home he found that practically no time had elapsed whatever, since Elaine's departure. Sylvia had not returned from the movies, and two glasses, it was quite true, stood on the coffee table, but one of them bore distinct traces of lipstick.

The Devil, thought Julian, as he washed the glasses.

2

Sylvia meanwhile, instead of going to the movies, was visiting with Marius in his room above the record shop, which was now, of course, quiet. It was an impromptu call, and not prearranged, she really had intended going to the movies, but when she arrived at the nearest theater she felt bored with the idea, in need of company, and rather resentful of Julian for being too tired to come with her; also, now that the wedding was over, her full, busy life seemed a little to have collapsed on her hands. Accordingly she decided that, as she had found no opportunity to tell Marius as yet the things she had thought during the party, now would be as good a time as any, so she phoned him and found him at home. It amused Sylvia, as with great poise she made herself comfortable facing Marius—she even sat boldly down on the bed—that the crucifix was not in sight on the opposite wall; she wondered whether he had removed it permanently or merely taken it away for the period of her call. In any case, she did not refer to it. What she had come for, she said, was to talk to Marius *sensibly*.

The substance of this sensible talk amounted to this, that Sylvia and Julian had been going through a critical time in their marriage—"the sort of thing that all married couples have to face sometime"—but that this time now was over. Anything Sylvia had said during that period, anything she had almost done, must be put down (of course) to her worry over the domestic situation (which conditioned, said Marius to himself, her foreign policy)—she had been almost mad with anxiety and doubt. But things had, as things will, righted themselves almost overnight; Sylvia wanted no uncertainty to remain in Marius's mind concerning her loyalty to her husband.

"Of course," she said lightly, "I should have been delighted to run away with you to some secret place for a mad weekend of delight—but you can see what my motive would have been, even then, I should only have been revenging myself on Julian."

"I see," Marius said, trying to look properly glum and rejected, while in reality he was almost hugging himself with glee, as people will whose exclusive possession of knowledge lets them play for a moment the role of destiny in the affairs of others. "What about the anonymous letters?" he casually inquired.

As for the anonymous letters, Sylvia said, that was something she did not understand, nor yet—she supposed—did Julian. Marius raised his eyebrows practically to his hairline. Doubtless some person had thought it a good joke, though the Lord alone knew who among their acquaintance owned so perverted a sense of humor; at any rate, there had been no more letters for some time, and Sylvia, in her new security, very much doubted there would be any more. "We've heard the last of Federigo," she said, and added that she hoped Marius would do her the favor of forgetting he had ever heard of such communications, implying that she in return would never mention to anyone any confidences Marius had imparted to her on the subject of religious faith (allowing her eyes to rest for a moment on the absence of the crucifix on the opposite wall). Of course, Sylvia concluded, she and Marius would remain good friends, and she would always be grateful for his having stood by her in the time of trouble.

"Sylvia," said Marius seriously, "supposing you should discover you are quite mistaken, and that the trouble is not over after all— imagine, for example, that Julian is actually deceiving you—what then?"

"Ah, no," she replied. "I worried over it—I thought that if he believed those ridiculous letters he might set out to show me that two could play at it—but I don't really believe he would. He does love me, and he is not a hypocrite—and besides, where would he find the time? I'd undoubtedly know about it at once."

"Undoubtedly. But still, supposing . . . ?"

"Why, then—" she laughed—"then, darling, I should fly for refuge to your arms. I'd leave him at once," she added more seriously.

At this moment the phone rang, and Marius, answering, was shocked to hear Julian at the other end; it seemed impossible that neither he nor Sylvia could detect each other's presence in the situation, and Marius believed at first that Julian must have known his wife would be here. Instead, however, it turned out that Julian, speaking in a rather troubled voice, wanted Marius's help and advice "about a religious matter," and could Marius meet him for lunch next day?

"Yes, I suppose I could," Marius replied. "What do you mean, a religious matter?"

"I want to ask you something," Julian said seriously, "about the Devil—I thought you'd be the only person I know who would have a, well, a professional qualification . . ."

Marius, amazed, allowed Julian to set a time and place for their meeting, then hung up.

"Just a fellow I know," he said in response to Sylvia's slight, questioning glance.

"I didn't mean to pry into your life," she quickly replied. Nevertheless, she then went on to tell him, speaking as the Older Woman, that she thought it was time he married and settled down. She mentioned the name of Elaine Leonard tentatively—"for instance."

"I hardly know her," Marius said, adding with beautiful irony, "you know her much better than I do."

"I mean, of course," Sylvia continued, "you would have to give up your way of living, you would have to take a job—"

"But Elaine might not care to marry me," he objected, "she may have in mind to marry quite another person."

They talked for a few minutes about Elaine, agreed she was a charming girl; then Sylvia got up to leave.

"Julian thinks I'm at the movies," she confessed, "and I must get back at about this time."

Marius saw her downstairs and even to the corner, where he got her a taxi. Sylvia had, more strongly than ever, the feeling of being watched; but she did not think it right to involve Marius any further than she already had in the subjective problems of her psyche.

The matters of Dr. Thybold and Mr. Archer More, which had begun on the same day, the day of the first anonymous letter, as Julian recalled, settled themselves also on the same day, very abruptly. Julian had scarcely got settled in the office when there came a phone call; he heard a low, hoarse whisper at the other end.

"This is Doctor you-know-who," the whisper said. "Are you alone?"

"Doctor who?"

"Doctor—you know—lung cancer," the voice mysteriously went on.

"Oh, Thybold," Julian cried, "what can I do for you?"

"You can please not mention my name," said the doctor furiously. "Are you alone?"

"Yes."

"I'm phoning from a pay station. I daren't go home."

"You what?"

"I've received an anonymous letter," Dr. Thybold said in a quavering voice. "I'm afraid the cigarette industry is after me."

"An anonymous letter?" cried Julian in exasperation. "Oh, nonsense, doctor. You know perfectly well people don't do that sort of thing these days."

"Don't tell me, young man," the doctor said, "I have the letter right here, I'll read it to you."

In amazement Julian heard Dr. Thybold's voice, with an appropriate dramatic ominousness, read the following message:

> It is not too late to mend. Retract your advertisement at once. Do not go to the police, you are being watched. If you go ahead with your plan consequences follow at once. You have been warned.

"Isn't it signed at all?" Julian asked.

"It is signed," said the doctor, "'Nicotine the friend of man.'"

Julian controlled an impulse to laugh, not because it would be unseemly but because the laughter already felt hysterical in his throat.

"What do you want me to do?"

"Burn the letters," Dr. Thybold replied promptly. "I know when I'm beaten, I can't fight the cigarette kings."

"But some of the letters have already gone out," Julian objected. "Besides, as you said, you have to be prepared to suffer for your beliefs."

"Well, I gave up smoking, didn't I?" Dr. Thybold demanded. "But this is serious. Look, I can't talk any longer. A man is watching me. Please do something."

And on this the phone went dead. Julian sat for a few minutes feeling dazed, then gave instructions through Miss Duddon that no more of Dr. Thybold's circulars should be mailed until further notice.

"There are two men here to see you," said Miss Duddon, "a Mr. Archer More—he says you will remember—and friend."

"Send them in," said Julian.

Archer More was cold sober, and consequently looked frightful, with sagging cheeks and dilated eyes so bloodshot the pupils were nearly obscured. His relation to the gentleman with him was that of a prisoner to a policeman; the other man, holding him by the arm, pushed little Mr. More into the chair opposite Julian, but himself remained standing.

"How far has this ridiculous outrage gone?" he demanded.

"Just what outrage do you mean?" Julian countered.

"This—this advertising campaign," sneered the gentleman, "about love!"

"Nothing has been published yet," Julian replied, "I have the copy here waiting for Mr. More's approval."

"Mr. More will approve nothing," decisively announced the other man. "I am Mr. More's lawyer, my name is Henry Pratt, and I am delighted to be in time to prevent Mr. More from getting himself into serious trouble."

"The love of Christ Jesus," said Mr. More faintly, "serious trouble. Martyrdom. My head hurts."

"You may take it as a definite order," said Mr. Pratt, "that these advertisements are to be canceled—as of now. It is very fortunate that this got to my ears in time."

"I'm afraid I don't understand what this is all about," Julian said.

"The law, the law," said Mr. Pratt impatiently. "Surely you don't imagine Mr. More has any right to go around spending his money, much less throwing it away? Mr. More, sir, owes alimony to eleven women. These eleven women have eleven lawyers. If this nonsense about advertising became public these eleven lawyers would slap eleven injunctions against Mr. More before you could say—well, before you could say whatever you thought of saying. This gentleman," the lawyer continued, "exists, you might say, in order to go on paying alimony to these eleven women. If he died, that would be perfectly all right, quite legal, because the estate would be split up among the eleven former wives; if he married again, that would be perfectly all right, so long as he could show, if necessary, that he could support another wife without reneging on the alimony payments. Mr. More," he concluded, "is neither more nor less than the living result of his actions, and he must take the consequences. That is all there is to it. Your firm, sir, may put in a bill for whatever expense this business has put you to; if it is reasonable, it will be paid. If it is not reasonable, you may go whistle for it. Good day."

The lawyer bodily pulled Mr. More to his feet; Mr. More groaned, wobbled slightly, steadied.

"Consider the lilies of the field," he cried as he was more or less dragged through the door.

These two crises, happening on the one morning, left Julian bemused by the idea that life was one grand theatrical performance. I live, he thought, in a world operated by Federigo; and he began to think that the actions of Dr. Thybold and Mr. More had run their courses together not as a result of coincidence but rather, though in an obscure sense, as demonstration: Dr. Thybold in his silly way a moralist, wanting to reform the world by works, and Mr. More in his silly way a mystic, wanting to redeem the world by advertising, which was after all a species of prayer.

"And I too," he reflected, "I wanted to change the nature of things, and I wrote anonymous letters. And now I don't know whether I'm coming or going."

This doubt whether he was coming or going formed the subject of his discussion with Marius Rathlin at lunch. Julian flattered himself that he conducted the inquiry at such a high theoretical level as to arouse no suspicion about his particular actions; he mentioned no names, neither of Federigo nor of Elaine.

The information which Marius already had, however, enabled him to see rather more than Julian imagined he saw. He knew, for example, about the letters, and he knew that Federigo exactly resembled Julian. The only thing that badly puzzled him was this, that Julian described his double (not mentioning the anonymous letters, of course) in such a way as made it seem this person could be no more than a hallucination, a *Doppelgänger* in fact; but Elaine had testified on the other hand—and if she were hallucinating, it would surely not be with this particular hallucination—to the real existence of a person with the odd name of Federigo, who, however, could not in her opinion be responsible for the letters, being away—and if that were true, neither could he be the person who haunted Julian.

"You know the thing that troubles me most?" Julian said. "It's that I am not even frightened when he appears, not even surprised, really. Sometimes I get angry with him—but I ought to be terrified, isn't that right?"

"If you want my honest opinion," Marius said, "it sounds more like incipient schizophrenia—you *know* the world is full of invisible enemies out for your blood, but at the same time you *know* that they can't hurt you, so as a result you're not even frightened."

"Oh." Julian took this information in reasonable calm, but was of course a little disconsolate. "You think I'm going insane, then?"

"Well, I don't exactly *think* so," Marius said. "You behave all right, though you look sort of pale and tired. It's not what I would think by myself, but it is certainly what is suggested by your story."

"But I chose you to tell it to," Julian explained, "because you're probably the only person I know at all well who really believes in the Devil—your religion does require you to believe in the Devil, doesn't it?"

"You mean you chose me to tell it to," said Marius, "because you believe I am a credulous and superstitious imbecile?"

"No, really," Julian assured him, "there's no need to be offended."

"But after all," Marius said, "what the hell would the Devil want with you?"

"Meaning I am damned already?"

"Meaning at least," Marius replied, "that it would not take any special concentration of effort on the part of His Sinfulness."

"You know," Julian said thoughtfully, "sometimes he seems to be a very nice fellow."

"Of course—I imagine his appearance wearing your face has predisposed you in his favor. I can only think, Julian," Marius added, "that you have done something so dreadful you refuse to face it, and finally it has caught up with you; the objective equivalent of your guilt is meeting you face to face."

"Oh—you think that?"

"I've no way of knowing what it is, of course," said Marius

smugly. "Perhaps it's an analyst you need, not a priest. You might have an interview with Sylvia's man Mirabeau, who I believe is very hot on subjective impressions and fantasies and all that. You might become a classic in the literature of the subject," he concluded helpfully.

"I thought you might be able to tell me something," said Julian, "but never mind. I hope you won't mention this discussion to anyone?"

"The only advice I can give you," Marius said, "is, Be good and it will go away. As for your secret, it's safe with me—I shall be as the tomb, as the tombs of Egypt." He was unable to resist this final flourish, which he thought he had put in very aptly, and watched with a bland smile Julian's suspicious glance get nowhere and disappear.

Reflecting on this interview, Marius did not come explicitly to the conclusion that Julian had written those letters himself; nevertheless, he now decided upon his course of action, which struck him as villainous but irresistibly to the point: the letters had gone one way so far, now let them go the other way.

As he sat at his desk, occupied in the unfamiliar and tedious task of cutting snips of paper from the *Journal of the History of Ideas* and pasting them together, he smiled sourly, having thought of a charming parallel from history; when the young Louis XIV wished to impress Mlle. de la Vallière, he engaged M. le Marquis de Dangeau, a witty and eloquent man, to write his letters to her; the lady, duly impressed, thought herself insufficiently educated to write a proper reply, and in her turn engaged M. de Dangeau to write her letter to the King. Not a parallel, perhaps, perhaps a bit oblique, but at any rate (thought Marius) it must have been extremely amusing for M. le Marquis de Dangeau.

After what Marius had said Julian was more confused than ever, and it seemed the mere operation of fate that Dr. Mirabeau should call him up at the office during the afternoon.

"Is your wife quite well?" asked the voice, after introducing itself.

"I suppose so," Julian said doubtfully. "Why shouldn't she be?"

"Well, she has skipped a number of appointments with me, just after one rather crucial session."

"Oh, I see."

"And I wondered if it would not be wise for you and me to have a little talk about the situation?"

Somewhat numbly, Julian heard himself agree to a time late in the afternoon; it was with considerable nervousness, never having before been to a mind-doctor (as he put it) that he presented himself at Dr. Mirabeau's office.

Not being a patient (not being a patient as yet, Dr. Mirabeau's attitude proclaimed) Julian was not required to lie on the couch but sat facing the doctor across the desk; nevertheless the atmosphere was hypnotic and mystifying, all the room being darkened save for the single circle of light in which their four hands rested on the blotter, and Julian could see out of the corner of his eye *the couch* of which one heard so much and which gained, although an ordinary enough piece of furniture, something of the technical, scary mystery of medical equipment generally.

"To bring you up to date," said Dr. Mirabeau, "it all began over a question of anonymous letters—I take it you did actually get to see these letters?"

"Yes, I did," said Julian noncommittally.

"Ah. Now I must say that I at first made a mistake, a quite natural mistake. Mrs. Ghent did not actually bring the letter, the physical piece of paper, here to the office. From the way in which she spoke of it, I naturally concluded she had dreamed the whole improbable event, and she came in the course of the session to agree with me.

"But then," said the doctor impressively, "there came a second letter, and this one she brought to me. Of course I saw where I had gone wrong at once."

"You did?"

"Yes. For reasons which we need not go into, technical reasons having to do with the analysis, it became quite clear that Mrs. Ghent had written this letter at least, possibly the previous one if there was a previous one—"

"Oh, yes. There were two."

"Yes—had written them, as I say, herself. Now, Mr. Ghent, it may be—none of us is perfect—that I made a further error here, a serious one, by treating your wife's relation with me as her primary motive in these communications. It occurs to me now that if that had been so she need never have brought you into it at all. But as you can testify yourself to the existence of these letters, it strikes me now that their major object was not merely an effect of the transference (which secondarily it was nevertheless designed to strengthen) but their major object was to involve you, to focus your interest and attention on whatever Sylvia—Mrs. Ghent—had done or was about to do.

"Now, Mr. Ghent, what I want you to tell me, in perfect confidence, as speaking to your own medical adviser, is this—is your wife faithful to you or not? That is, has she actually committed herself—in reality—to the fantasy proclaimed in the letters?"

"I don't know," replied Julian, "but I have reason to think not."

"Reason?"

"Detectives. I was, of course, bothered by those letters."

"Naturally, one would be bothered."

"Naturally."

"And you think there's nothing to it?"

"No."

"Ah," said Dr. Mirabeau, "I was afraid of that. It makes our problem more acute."

So this was psychoanalysis. Julian already had an impulse to confess everything, but he manfully resisted, though the sweat began to break out on his brow. He wondered, as though from a great distance, whether he would go with Elaine for the weekend at Lantern Point, and, if so, what excuse he would make to Sylvia.

"More acute," Dr. Mirabeau continued, "because, you see, if she had in fact been unfaithful to you—these things do happen, do they not?—there would have been at least *some* connection with ordinary reality. As it is"—shaking his head sadly in the gloom back of the lamplight—"as it is, I must tell you that Mrs. Ghent is showing a detachment from the world, an apathy toward the daylight so to say, which I find professionally frightening. It suggests, even, incipient schizophrenia. And her refusal to return here after our last session seems, does it not, to support that judgment? She simply won't face up to the reality of her situation."

"No," said Julian simply in order to agree; he scarcely knew what he was assenting to, and only wanted to get out in the fresh air.

"Now I cannot force her to come back," said Dr. Mirabeau,

spreading his hands in a gesture of easy helplessness, "but just there I think you might be able to help, if you are willing. Pick a time when she seems in a good, or at least not a bad mood; talk reasonably to her, do not appeal to her emotions or become emotional yourself—be rational. In such cases as these, we frequently find, the emotions are curiously uninvolved, stubbornly remote, while the reason itself is extremely susceptible of conviction, it follows and assents to even most ridiculous chains of evidence simply because they have the appearance of being rational rather than emotive. It is an odd condition in which, you might say, the loss of reason presents a symptomatic appearance which is more reasonable than reason itself, the patient will spend long hours analyzing causes, motives, and so forth. Do you see?"

Julian said he saw, and upon his promise of co-operation, over a manly handshake, was permitted to depart. In another moment, he thought, his head might have left his neck and gone spinning skyward, gently and slowly, like those children's balloons he had seen at the Zoo in Central Park.

Chapter Eight

F EDERIGO'S third letter, which arrived in the morning mail Friday, outwardly resembled the other two save in one particular: it was addressed not to Julian but to Sylvia. Julian, who the previous evening had told his wife that he would have to spend the weekend in Philadelphia (why Philadelphia? He did not know) where the firm was planning to open an agency, and who accordingly would phone Elaine later in the morning to say he was going with her, did not even notice the arrival of this letter or Sylvia's reception of it, because he was engrossed in his own mail. This included a report from Mr. Bilsiter's office, that on the other night, when he had entertained Elaine and, later, Federigo, when that odd thing had happened in Central Park, Sylvia had been not at the movies but with Marius Rathlin at his apartment.

So! he was thinking, at just the moment that Sylvia opened her letter, so there is something in it after all. How fortunate that he had not called off those detectives. In order to keep the savor of his triumphant secrecy he looked at his wife, who all unaware was reading a letter. Julian felt, for her, pity and contempt—how secure she must imagine herself!—and, for himself, justification. Everything, complex as it was, had worked out; the idea of the anonymous letters finally justified itself in the only way possible, by being right, by referring to a real situation; his going away with Elaine Leonard likewise justified itself by means of what these letters brought to light.

Sylvia looked up from her letter, and said in a neutral voice, "Why don't I walk the dogs this morning, darling, and you finish your coffee?"

"Of course, anything you say," Julian replied. Their eyes, however, did not meet. And when Sylvia had got dressed and put Troilus and Cressida on their leashes and left the apartment, the letter was prominently displayed on the table where Julian must presently see it.

Sylvia, with a grim expression on her face, immediately walked the dogs to the nearest drugstore, where she telephoned to Marius. It was difficult to do, as the door had to be left open and the dogs kept trying to drag her out of the phone booth.

She could see it all now, of course; and the worst thing in it, perhaps, was her own blindness and ridiculous sense of security, the feeling that the anonymous letters were past and gone, love reestablished (when really it had been an armed truce) and life ready to go on in the normal way. She imagined Julian and Elaine laughing at her, and this idea horrified her so much that she could scarcely speak when Marius answered the phone.

He, having expected this result, had difficulty in sounding properly surprised, and then a more unexpected difficulty in sounding properly gratified, when it turned out that Sylvia would go away with him that very day, that she knew the place where they would go, that she realized (as she did not, in her extremity, fail to remind him) that he loved her whatever happened, and that she was coming at once to his room.

Do I love her? he asked himself while waiting, and had to allow that he did not.

"Still," he said, "it will be charming—if only it can be kept that way."

Sylvia in twenty minutes appeared, dragging the dogs upstairs.

"Queen and huntress chaste and fair," elegantly said Marius, for whom it was perhaps never too early in the morning.

"Listen to me," she said breathlessly, "and don't be silly. Listen—Marius, do you love me?"

"Of course, darling," he said lightly, and put his arms around her, "you know that."

Sylvia, however, having received this assurance, backed away and drew from her handbag a single key, which she presented to him. He stared at it doubtfully.

"It is the key to Hugo's place out at Lantern Point. We'll go there—it's lonely and beautiful. Marius—I want you to go out there first and wait for me. I'll come out later, but first I must go home to pack, and"—grimly—"have words with my wretched husband."

"This is all so sudden," said Marius. "What's happened between you two?"

"Oh, I'll tell you later, when I get out there. It was Elaine, all that time—do you know, he's actually going to Philadelphia with her, on *business*; he told me he was going to Philadelphia on business, and I believed it. Then, this morning, that letter came—I'll give him *business*!"

"Sylvia," Marius said, "are you going with me for love or revenge?"

This brought her to a stop for a moment.

"You don't know how it's made me feel," she said, "how horrible, how dirty it is."

"Ah, there," he said to comfort her, and put his arm round her shoulder.

"But it's not just revenge, Marius," she said. "It is you, truly it is."

"Of course," he said. The dogs had by now twisted the leashes quite around them both.

"Marius, it will be fun," she whispered. "But promise—I don't know, I'm still ashamed—promise it will be dark, and without saying anything."

"I promise," he gravely assured her. "In darkness, silently—like strangers."

"Silently, like two strangers in the night."

Julian meanwhile had called Elaine.

"I was just about to leave," she said. "Are you coming?"

"Yes," he said into the cold phone. "Yes, darling."

"You'd better get over here in five minutes, then."

"Oh," he said. "I couldn't leave so soon. I'm not packed, and really I'd better be at the office during the day—Sylvia's got the idea I'm going to Philadelphia on business, you see."

"Why, you clever lad," said Elaine, without admiration. "Imagine thinking up a thing like that."

"Darling, don't—I love you, darling. Let me drive out, I'll be there and meet you by early evening."

"You know, dear, I doubt you will," was the reply. "I think you'll back out at the last moment. But it's your picnic. I'll be there, and if you are not, that's the end. Understood?"

"I love you," said Julian into the phone which had gone dead.

Nervously he walked about for a few moments, went to the dining room table and poured himself more coffee. So it was all going to come true at last! At this moment his eye fell on the letter, which so exactly resembled in appearance the ones of his own composition. With shaking hands he opened it and was shocked to read:

> MADAME:
>   Elaine the fair, Elaine the loveable,
>   Elaine the lily maid . . . ?
>   FEDERIGO

For a moment Julian was capable of only one thought: I never wrote that. He sat down and looked incredulously at the letter, as though expecting it to dissolve in his hands and be no more. This was what it felt like to receive an anonymous letter; just so Sylvia must have felt.

Reality had spoken. At this moment Sylvia returned.

"So!" she said, upon seeing the letter in Julian's hands.

"So!" replied Julian, but less dramatically.

Because they were both highly moral, or moralistic, persons, an argument necessarily had to take place. This argument became passionate at times, at times bitter, at times, also, ridiculous (there was a passage of debate about who was to take the car, the dogs, et cetera); but this argument was on both sides corrupted by secrecy at the root, and by the uncertainties of desire, so that very little truth resulted from it. Julian, for his part, felt a sneaking gratitude at being caught out; the entire escapade with Elaine was by this means wrought up—a little hysterically—into honesty, he was no longer skulking behind Sylvia's back, everything was now brought out in the light of day (except, of course, the letters). And Sylvia in the same way felt a certain relief; it was now possible to have an affair without betraying anyone; she told Julian she was leaving him, what she did after that would naturally be her own business. Beneath their disagreeable tones, beneath the real but imperfectly apprehended consternation over parting, both were experiencing the same furtive jubilation, the random feeling of freedom and emptiness together; it is also likely that neither believed their separation would be permanent.

She loves me, after all, thought Julian. When she returns things will be as I wish. And he pictured himself as planning rationally with a much-chastened Sylvia the *modern marriage,* marked by occasional light infidelities, which would exactly suit his requirement.

He can't live without me, after all, Sylvia thought. When he comes to heel, after a few days, I shall outline exactly what can be permitted and what cannot.

There were tears, a few, on her side; sullen gloom on his. At last they subsided into a kind of sad rationality (like civilized people, as Julian stuffily said) and Sylvia began to pack. Perhaps their closest appreciation of what was really happening came when they accidentally began to talk about their possessions.

"Since I'm the one who's leaving," Sylvia said, "I should have the car."

"I'm sorry," he replied, "I need the car, and besides it is registered in my name."

"I said I want the car."

"And if you take it, I shall report to the police that it has been stolen; instead, I give you all the furniture"—with a large gesture. "I'll put that in writing."

"What do I want with all the furniture—do I carry it away on my back?"

"The money in the bank belongs to you as much as to me. I can't stop you from buying another car—I regret to say."

"All right, but one thing I insist on—if I haven't the car, you must take the dogs."

"I don't want the dogs," said Julian. "I've never wanted the dogs. Hugo gave them to you, really."

"Hugo gave them to both of us, for a wedding present."

"And I know why," said Julian with a sour smile.

It was decided upon this that if Julian had the convenience of the car he should also undertake the inconvenience of the dogs, who at this moment were walking aimlessly around the apartment trailing their leashes which had not been removed.

"Where will you be, if I should have to get in touch with you?" Julian asked Sylvia. He had determined not to be the first to ask, but when Sylvia, with a suitcase, approached the front door in a decisive silence, he gave in.

"I don't see that is any of your business," she replied. "I won't be hiding, I assure you. You can find me if you want me badly enough."

"That's not what I meant at all," he said heatedly. "I meant, to arrange about the separation—lawyers, and so forth."

Neither Julian nor Sylvia had ever had any extensive dealings with the world of litigation and the courts; even the word "lawyer" frightened them both a good deal.

"We'll settle all that another time," Sylvia said. "But meanwhile, I think we ought to agree on one thing."

"And that is?"

"That neither of us will draw out all the money in the current account, or deliberately spend an extraordinary lot just to inconvenience the other."

"Well—I won't if you won't," Julian agreed. "But what is an extraordinary lot?"

"I merely mean," Sylvia said with excessive sweetness, "don't set up your precious little whore in the Plaza. Find her a cold-water flat, or let her live here so long as she doesn't use *my furniture*." Sylvia perhaps would have had a good deal more to say on this theme, once started; on the other hand, a better exit might be hard to find, and consequently the door slammed with dramatic finality on the word *furniture*.

As soon as his wife had gone Julian phoned Elaine, but found she had already left. He then phoned Mr. Bilsiter of the detective agency, whom he informed of what had happened.

"You suspect she is going to Mr. Rathlin, yes," said Mr. Bilsiter patiently, "and you want evidence, yes, of course. It shall be done, I'll see to it myself if possible. Now tell me Mr. Ghent, do you want us to phone you—quite plainly, do you want to be in at the death?"

"Certainly not," Julian cried.

"Well, some do and some don't," said Mr. Bilsiter carelessly.

"I merely meant," Julian added, "that I shall be away myself this weekend. You may simply send the results here to me by mail, as you did the reports."

"You shall have them, sir, if they are there to be had," Mr. Bilsiter promised. "Testimony and, to clinch it, photographs."

This last, which had not occurred to Julian, horrified him; he imagined himself staring, under Mr. Bilsiter's gaze, at a flashlight picture of his wife in bed with Marius Rathlin, and he shuddered. When one thought of it that way, the whole business took on a quite loathsome reality. But while he was shuddering, Mr. Bilsiter had said good-by and hung up.

Now there was no one left to phone. There was no one left. Julian had the apartment, save for the two dogs he did not like, to himself. Later in the day, to be sure, he would be with Elaine, and time would resume; but he stood now in an abscess in time where there existed only, it appeared, the fact of his being alone. He walked slowly but nervously around the room; the dogs walked around the room their leashes rattling on the legs of tables and chairs. Exasperated, Julian unsnapped the leashes, collared the dogs and locked them in the hall bathroom, turning on the light because they were afraid of the dark and whimpered if left that way. Now he felt more alone than ever, and confronted by the monstrosity of his nature. The accusations of the world were one thing, and occasioned mere secular anxieties; but the accusations from within, being inescapable, had a religious and exalted character, so that before he knew it he was pacing up and down like an orator on a platform.

The curtains were still drawn over the windows, for Sylvia had not pulled them back. Julian remembered reading that in a closed room one could have no way of knowing that the world still existed outside, and in a sudden access of anxiety he strode over and drew back the curtains; it was a gray, rather misty day, but the world, or at least this street of it, perceptibly existed.

An early fly crawled on the window pane and flew against it buzzing; for no other reason than that he felt miserable and full of guilt Julian devoted some time and attention to pinning this fly against the corner of the frame and squashing it. In disgust he rubbed its small black remains, with a little red blood (Sylvia's?) from his finger. Of course, the poor thing (he thought) had not suffered, there had not been time. But he could not, on consideration, admit this comfortable notion, for, how could he know what time might be to a fly? Perhaps that instant, in which his fat finger had descended on its life, had amounted, when gauged in fly-time, to some six weeks in agony in a hospital with, say, cancer, in human time. What was the world? In the bathroom, with the lights on, the dogs whimpered even so, and Julian walked the empty apartment.

The world went around, and he with it. His nearest evidence at
this moment of the world's (and his) incessantly going around was
the electric clock on the bedside table (he had wandered into the
bedroom and stood abstractedly regarding the unmade beds).
This clock read about a quarter to eleven and emitted a light,
humming tone which he had always taken to be the domestic
image and idol of the power behind the world going remorselessly
about its interminable business. This clock was a machine more
mighty, sacred and dreadful than any rosary, for example, or
prayer wheel of the Buddhist; under the appearance of an innocent, convenient recording device it exercised an absolute compulsion upon the waywardness of life; at this very moment, while he
watched, it was going about its work of making him older, even
while with the same three hands it brought some into the world
and pushed others out, made this one punctual to tea and that one
late for a plane in which he would have been destroyed. Everyone
in society, it would be not too much to say, possessed a clock, or
was possessed by one; portable models were also available, and
their association with strap or chain was not accidental, for did
they not everywhere demonstrate servitude? (Julian was reminded
that he no longer had a watch; also that so far as marriage was
concerned he had, more or less, his freedom; these observations
failed somehow to impress him favorably.)

He sighed, he was alone. Sylvia's photograph on the dresser
followed him with eyes of a terrible and accusing candor as he
guiltily left that room.

The living room was of course no improvement, for there again
was the portrait of Sylvia which he himself, Julian, had caused to
be done, a long time ago, by a young artist who, for all the appealing expression he had caught, or put, in the face, had given the eyes
a cold glitter and the mobility of swivel mountings. Was there not,
he asked himself as he went on through to the kitchen, something
morbid, something presumptively commemorative, in this making
of images? Did it not—by its intention of preserving the past—
give away the selfishness beneath its tender pretense? as in the
anecdote which Marius had told him as coming from, of all people, Sigmund Freud, of a young man who sighingly remarked to
his pretty wife, "Do you know, my dear, if either of us should die I
think I would live in Paris?" But if some such wish lay concealed in

the black inward of the camera, in the mind which set the painter on about his business, the eyes took their revenge. "I know what you are thinking," was their word whatever one was thinking, and whatever one was thinking when suddenly made aware of the eyes, they were right, or at any rate convincing.

In the kitchen, where he went without any clear idea of what to do when he got there, he heard the subtle hum of the refrigerator, the domestic imitation of silence. Another emblem, this, of the power streaming ceaselessly through all things, the violent fluidity which itself enabled the world to look relatively solid and stable. He opened the door and stared objectlessly into the cold, lighted box, which contained a neat and sparing arrangement of foods, none of them at this moment very interesting to him: a package of bacon, a box of eggs, a bottle of milk which was paradoxically of all things in the world the coldest-looking and most forbidding; a thin, tall bottle of Niersteiner, and this he doubtfully reached for, held to the light, began to return to its place, and finally put down on the drainboard of the sink. This move brought him face to face with another electric clock: eight minutes to eleven. The sweep second hand moved with a dreadful smoothness.

There were sixty seconds in each minute, thirty-six hundred in each hour, thirty-six times twenty-four was already incalculable without pencil and paper, the result of that multiplied again by three hundred and sixty-five would be a staggering figure whatever it was, and, finally, *that* times an indeterminable (at present) number put by some authorities at seventy would be, leaving leap years out of consideration, the enormous number of seconds involved in measuring out a long human life, if anyone wanted to know. Julian observed with a sense of irritated anxiety that this problem had already cost him some fifty seconds in the computing; moreover, about half his hypothetical number of seconds had already been used up. Of course, he might become a centenarian, or he might fall down dead in, say, twelve more minutes. The first possibility was statistically unlikely, the second did not seem probable under the circumstances unless he killed himself, which he now realized was what he had been thinking of doing.

He poured the wine into a squat, ordinary kitchen glass and returned with bottle and glass to the living room, where he sat down on the couch before the ornamental, empty fireplace. The eyes of his wife Sylvia looked down at a difficult angle, over her cheekbones, at the top of his head.

It was almost with gratitude that he saw, a few minutes later, Federigo standing rather shyly in the corner of the room, as though he had come through the door only a moment ago. Nevertheless, he put up a show of anger, and said:

"You had to send that letter, didn't you? I hope you're pleased."

"Ah, darling, I didn't send it," Federigo said, smiling.

"Don't call me darling, please," said Julian fiercely and with a surprising blush.

"I didn't send it," Federigo repeated, "and yet, you know, I thought you rather wanted some such thing to happen. It's been at the back of your mind for a few days, hasn't it, that the next thing on the program was to get caught off base, somehow-anyhow? Are you quite sure," he added, "that you didn't send this last letter as you did the others? You might have made it up and mailed it and then forgotten."

"No," said Julian, nearly in a shout. "That's ridiculous. You did it, you must have done it."

"I don't *do* things," said Federigo with a kind of disdainful dignity. "If I had, believe me, I should have chosen a different quotation from Lord Tennyson—whose reputation, I believe, is going up these days:

His honour rooted in dishonour stood,
And faith unfaithful kept him falsely true.

Practically metaphysical, isn't it, with all that back and forth in the words; confusing."

"It's obvious you did it," cried Julian. "You knew it was Tennyson."

"They're very well-known lines," said Federigo evasively. "Still, that's not here nor there. The point is, what next?"

"I don't know," Julian sullenly replied. "And I don't much care."

"Go to Elaine? Kill yourself? Take a world cruise? Live elsewhere under a new name? Redeem yourself by missionary work in a malarial swamp?" Federigo presented these alternatives, if that is what they were, rapidly and in a neutral voice, adding in conclusion, "How far can you go by Ferris wheel?"

"I'm going to Elaine," Julian said. "After that—we'll see."

"Spoken like a little man," said Federigo. "As for myself, I'm delighted to see you do something straightforward. I'm sure it will work out for the best—so sure," he added, "that I've come to say good-by."

"You are leaving me? Now?"

"It's what you wanted, isn't it?" Federigo approached Julian casually, and before the latter was aware of his intention, heartily and disgustingly kissed him on the mouth, then quickly backed away toward the bedroom, with Julian angrily following.

"I'll just use your bathroom before I go," said Federigo, pretending to be unaware of Julian's fierce expression; and he disappeared, leaving Julian to walk up and down the floor until his exasperation lapsed in moody inattention and sullenness.

He must have remained in this state for some minutes; he was never certain whether he had heard the toilet flush or not, but when he finally knocked on the bathroom door and then, hearing no answer, opened it, his strange companion was nowhere to be found.

"He must have slipped out while my back was turned," Julian decided as he packed an overnight case. His last action before leaving the house was to open half a dozen cans of horse meat, which he disposed at various points about the house, so that the dogs, liberated from the other bathroom, should not starve. But the image of them prowling the lonely rooms, and perhaps a certain vivid reminiscence of the smell of horse meat, remained with him all the day and night in resentment and reproach.

2

Far out on the northeastern end of Long Island Lantern Point jutted into the Atlantic; it was a desolate, haunted kind of country on the best of days, a land of shifting dunes and twisted, stunted pines, and today a thick fog from the sea rolled cold and gray over it all; out here, on a knoll which doubtless in good visibility overlooked the water—one could hear the waves through the fog—Hugo Alter's house stood alone.

Marius received directions at the station and decided, as he had plenty of time and not much money, to walk out; he invested a

small sum, however, in provisions, reminding himself that even
adultery marches on its stomach. The sand road off the highway
was clearly marked, and the distance from there only about a
mile; even despite the fog Marius became quite cheerful as he
swung along carrying a bag in which were eggs and sausages and
coffee and bread—there was a kind of biblical and ancient freedom about his having suddenly entered, only a couple of hours
from the city, this loneliness.

This pleasant mood changed rapidly, however, on his entrance
into the house. In the first place, the front door was not only not
locked, it stood open; nothing could more have resembled a trap.
Marius imagined that a party of tramps, escaped criminals, mad-
men, might have taken advantage of the loneliness of the place to
hide out here. He reconnoitered, listened at the door, heard nothing, then at last took his courage and stepped inside.

Here it was very gloomy and cold, not only from the character
of the day but because the windows were boarded up; the very air
had that refrigerated stillness and staleness which suggested the
tomb, the whitewashed walls were bare and dismal, one of them
bore a calendar which had not been turned since February. It was
the kitchen he had entered on, and here he stood for several minutes, while his hands and feet grew cold, looking at the black iron
bulk of the wood stove and thinking that he ought to get busy at
once cutting some kindling and lighting a fire; but he suddenly felt
so depressed as to be unable to move. There was no doubt at all in
his mind that Sylvia was a foolish woman; surely they could have
arranged something more sensible than this? He himself would
not have wanted a hotel room, for hotel rooms seemed to him, for
such purposes as this, like re-usable coffins—but what in heaven's
name would have been wrong with his own room, poor but cen-
trally heated, and with the blessing of electricity? Marius imagined how cold it would be in this house come night, and how
utterly, utterly dark—how desolate. "I have my love to keep me
warm," he murmured sullenly.

At this moment he heard a noise, a kind of scratching and dragging, from another room. He stood as if petrified. Human beings?
Mice? He decided finally on mice, but the idea did not much comfort him. The noises began again—he imagined mice five or six

feet high—then resolved into footsteps; a door swung toward him creakingly; Elaine Leonard came into the kitchen.

During a moment of astonishment, neither spoke, for each determined not to be the first to show surprise (*nil admirari,* Marius told himself proudly; one so seldom met situations surprising enough to let this motto be serviceable), and at the end of this moment each was ready with a *clever remark*.

"Dr. Livingstone, I presume?" said Elaine.

"A small world, is it not?" said Marius.

"You are aware, I guess, that this is private property?"

"I just happened to be passing by, and thought I'd drop in."

Another silence followed, then Elaine said:

"While you're here, you'll find some kindling in the shed round the corner to the right as you go out; also an ax and some logs. If you will first bring the kindling and then go off rail-splitting, I'll try to see that we don't freeze to death."

Marius did as he was told, with some difficulty; he even brought an ax, luckily wedged in a chunk of wood, down on his toe, but without serious harm since he had already got too tired to hit very hard. He also, at Elaine's instruction, pumped water up from the well. In half an hour or so they had the kitchen warming up to a reasonable temperature and had even made coffee. During this time they scarcely spoke; each was wondering what was to be done with this odd situation. They drank coffee and smoked cigarettes; the kitchen was quite cozy, and (thought Marius) as full of suspicious tension as it would have been had they been married and living there for months.

"I could have the police come over and get you out of here," Elaine observed in a highly theoretical tone, not moving from her chair.

"Isn't that sort of elaborate?" he asked, as though also prepared to theorize. "There's no phone, you'd have to walk down to the village—I mean, you could hardly send me, could you? If you're very determined, probably you could persuade me to leave—but I wonder if there isn't a better way?"

"I wonder," said Elaine, and a moment later proposed they take a walk on the shore. "I am afraid," she said, "we are going to have to explain ourselves, or each other, somehow."

Down on the shore, below the dunes, the fog was close and cold about them. The waves washed with a sound of sandpaper at their left as they walked along; it was possible to see barely twenty feet out on the black calm of the water and the breaking white of the small waves; not even a bird cried in the calm.

"Like the beginning of the world," she said.

"Or the end of it," said Marius, feeling however that this was not so much a difference as an agreement between them. He boldly took her hand, which she did not remove, and they dawdled slowly down the shore, idly swinging their linked hands.

"Do you love him?" Marius presently asked; Elaine looked up at him and grinned.

"You seem to know a great deal," she said. "But, as I told you the other day—no, I don't. This was designed, sort of hopelessly, for pleasure. And you—you followed me out here, I guess?"

"Well, as a matter of fact—no," Marius said. "You see," he began to explain, "we seem to have got hooked up on the same circuit. Sylvia's coming down, too."

"Oh, my God," Elaine said. "And he told her he was going to Philadelphia on business." After considering this for a moment, she began to laugh.

"I think you couldn't have heard the latest," said Marius. "The Philadelphia version has been seen through—your friend Federigo," he added with conscious malice, "has struck again." And he explained what he had heard from Sylvia that morning, reporting the text of the letter as if she had told it him but not by any means admitting his fateful rôle in the business. "Elaine the fair, Elaine the loveable," he said, partly to see her blush and partly for the pleasure simply of saying this to her, "Elaine the lily maid—and there, with a question mark, it ends."

"It does, does it?"

"Yes, and I very much fear that in the sequel the Ghents have broken up. At least," Marius added, "Sylvia gave me that impression this morning."

"So that Julian, when he gets here, if I know Julian, will be desperate with *love*. Oh, dear," Elaine sighed. "With large, moony eyes and a serious expression and talk about honesty and wanting to marry *me* to make everything all right again. Oh, dear."

"I think," said Marius, "that Sylvia has some such notion about me. I got the idea this morning that love alone would save everything—it also seemed, and this was not so nice, as if she was retreating on prepared positions, and I was to be the prepared positions."

"You mean she arranged this with you before she broke up with him?"

"I am afraid there was this element of calculation in it," Marius said. "But it didn't seem right for me to back out just then."

"Oh, dear," Elaine said once again. "Do you suppose it is marriage makes people like that—or are they that way to begin with?"

"Maybe they get married because they are like that," said Marius.

"Of course, you led her on," she said. "That was wicked, wasn't it?"

"Let not the pot and the kettle begin slanging one another," Marius reminded her. "You are here, too, you know."

They became aware just then of a strong, disagreeable smell. Just before them on the sand lay a big, dead fish with a huge head of which the lower jaw protruded in a kind of grin studded with sharp, uneven teeth. Flies flew about intensely buzzing, violent with black life in the midst of the calm of the fog. On seeing this sight they both turned in silent agreement to walk back the way they had come, and as they turned Marius took Elaine by the shoulders and kissed her, with consent. Then, hand in hand once more, they walked away.

"What's to be done?" he asked.

"We might simply run away," said Elaine. "After all, if this is funny for us, think how it will be for them to find each other here."

"Yes," Marius agreed. "Quite literally, the bonds of matrimony."

"Are we, do you think, wicked people, you and I?" Elaine asked. "Or are we only younger and a little more gay?"

"I simply don't know," Marius replied. "I suspect we're wicked enough to live. Probably it would be best to run away—that is, you're not dead set on meeting him, are you?"

"No," said Elaine, "I think I could live without."

"I feel the same way about her."

They walked in silence for some minutes. When they had almost reached the break in the dunes which led to the house, Marius said:

"There is another way, you know. It's difficult, and it's devious,

but it has a certain decisive charm—as we are, you and I, difficult
and devious persons. As I imagine it now, things would go roughly
like this . . ."

3

Human actions, of course, are natural and realistic—or are
they? The things which take place in our lives take place from, we
presume, the more or less accidental complicity of purpose and
accident; we may believe the result to be predestinated by powers
watching over us, or we may believe the result to be consequent on
our own rational cleverness, or we may believe things happen
mostly by chance. In any case, we seldom and only under special
conditions—ranging in kind from jokes to tragedies—believe our
actions, which so resemble products of freedom and the free operation of our wills, are in fact compelled, ourselves all ignorant, by
other human wills; and if we believe it seldom, we never believe it
willingly. Such things have to be forced upon our notice: a man
moving across an open field, under the open sky, naturally refuses
to believe he is moving through a dark, narrow tunnel from which
there is no escape; yet frequently, so far as his will is concerned,
the latter is the more accurate version.

What Sylvia saw, what Julian saw, what they saw who watched
behind the scenes, or knowingly and with a charmed sense of
power acted a part upon the scene—as a matter of fact, no one *saw*
a great deal, for the greater part of the action was acted after dark,
Marius and Elaine had hidden all but one lantern in order to simplify the plot, and this darkness, it ought to be remembered, was
the darkness that was before electricity, the divine and awful darkness which people who live in cities experience only in the midst of
a war, and which they otherwise tend to forget about, telling
themselves (if they think of it at all) that it could not be, really, so
terribly dark—but, of course, it is.

Already when Julian came on the scene, in the late afternoon, he
had the headlights on, mostly because of the fog—but the fog
seemed to bring the night down earlier. As he stepped from the car
he saw Elaine emerge from, oddly enough, not the house but a
clump of trees. She greeted him with a kiss, and he began to feel
better, a little, than he had at any time since early morning. It was

still with a reckless and glum sense of desperation, however, that he returned her kiss, thinking dismally that he felt, absolutely and physically felt, that he was being watched, probably by Sylvia, absurd as it was to think so. He wondered where she was.

While Elaine led Julian into the house—he proudly showed her the bottle of whisky which he had been sensible enough to bring—Marius dutifully trudged back to the village of Lantern, where he met Sylvia, who arrived on the only train it had been possible for her to get, the last one of the afternoon.

"Oh, dear God," she thought miserably as she stepped down on the platform and saw her lover, "dear God, this is really happening. My marriage is over, seven years are gone, now I am doing *this*." She embraced Marius with considerable fervor in order to conceal this feeling, and at this sight Mr. Bilsiter, standing in the vestibule and preparing to dismount with two cameras and a black valise, turned to smile wisely at his assistant, and wink.

Marius had decided, he told Sylvia, that it would be best to dine in the village, which they accordingly did. Marius was tender, charming, even rather sentimental than witty; also, he paid the check. Sylvia began to feel somewhat more secure, though this probably was as much as anything a result of having dinner. She felt also, and accordingly, as though she had arrived at the end of a road; this, whatever it turned out to be, was the place of decision; and she was free for the first time in days of that annoying sensation of being followed. From time to time, however, she wondered bitterly about Julian and his Elaine in Philadelphia—how could he, knowing that she knew, go on with such a thing?

Elaine, carefully watching the time, cooked Julian a thin sort of supper, with which, however—or more likely with the mere spectacle of her domesticity—he was charmed. She then insisted on making him go for a walk along the shore, in the course of which she said to him:

"Julian, please promise me, when you come to me tonight, it will be dark, and you won't speak?"

Julian expressed surprise.

"Please, darling, let it be that way. I am not so used to these things," Elaine added, "as you are."

This unlooked-for hint of innocence—and indeed, Elaine seemed, out here in the lonely wilderness beside the sea, less sophisticated than he had thought—quite charmed Julian, who tenderly promised they should be silent.

"There is a dead fish somewhere about," he said, sniffing. "Let us turn back." He kissed Elaine as they turned, and had the weather been much warmer a complication might at this point have developed in the scheme; as it was, however, they slowly walked back toward the house, where Marius and Sylvia, a few minutes before, had arrived by means of the single taxi operating from the village of Lantern. (Mr. Bilsiter and his assistant at this moment awaited the return of this same taxi; they stood shuddering with cold in the shadows of the station platform, while they munched sandwiches they had thoughtfully purchased before leaving New York City.)

"I lit a lamp in the kitchen," Marius said, "thinking it would be dark by the time we got back." He also pointed out the open bottle of whisky on the table as evidence of his solicitude.

"There is a smell of cooking," Sylvia said doubtfully, looking around into the deep shadows cast by the lantern.

"I made myself lunch when I got here, darling," Marius told her, "and brought stuff for breakfast as well." With the lantern he showed Sylvia into the bedroom down the hall, away from the kitchen. "There is only the one light," he said, "but that is as you would have it, isn't it?" And he respectfully withdrew, saying he would come to her in fifteen minutes. "Silently," he added, giving the girl a light kiss and hug.

Marius replaced the lantern on the kitchen table, and left the house.

("It is Mr. Alter's place," Mr. Bilsiter was saying to his assistant. "Give them another hour, I'd say." And he arranged accordingly with the driver of the now-returned taxi.)

"There's the house," Elaine said, seeing the light in the kitchen. "We almost lost it, I thought for a moment."

"Darling," Julian whispered as they entered the kitchen. "Darling, I love you. Do you love me?"

"Of course I do," she whispered back. "Remember—silence," she added, still whispering, and pointed down the hall. "Come to me in ten minutes," and, taking the lamp with her, she vanished toward the bedroom. Sylvia, lying tensely alone in the bed, heard footsteps; she shivered, perhaps as much from cold as apprehension, but the footsteps went on. Sylvia sighed; the time was not yet.

Elaine passed the bedroom as softly as possible, stepped out the side door at the end of the hall, and blew out the lantern.

"How goes it?" whispered Marius from the pines.

"It goes," she whispered back.

"Should we take their car?"

"It would make too much noise."

"It's a long, long walk to the station." And they vanished silently down the path.

Julian stood alone in the kitchen. He had taken off his clothes, and it became very noticeable that the kitchen stove was going out. Surely ten minutes are up now? he thought, but between eagerness and doubt he gave it a moment or so more. It was cold, and dreadfully dark except for the slight glow from the rim of the stove-plate; he wished Elaine had left him the lamp.

At last he tiptoed down the hall to the bedroom, opened the door, tiptoed across the floor, and drew in his breath sharply as he hit his bare toe on the bed post. Very creditably, he refrained from saying anything, and got into the bed all naked as he was, and lay beside the cold, naked body he found there. They both lay quite still for a few moments.

Scruple, doubt, unwillingness, guilt, anxiety, are all very human; but what presently followed went according to nature, which is perhaps not so human as all that. The thoughts of the two persons in the bed—two persons whom it would be very difficult, at this moment, to name accurately—were, allowing for differences in the pronouns, as though thought by the same mind; a mind with two backs.

The night was deep, dark; the waves washed ceaselessly up and down, back and forth, on the sandy, stony shore; the dead fish on the beach, as the tide moved in, was nudged uneasily, stirred back and forth—the flies departed—turned over in a lifelike motion, and taken back into the sea which had tossed it up.

She found herself thinking fiercely, with an effort of concentration, of Julian; just as Hugo had told her he likewise had thought of Alma; it was a slap in the face and a revenge.

He thought of Sylvia, rather miserably it is true; at the same time he knew she could not compare with the beautiful young girl who now lay in his arms. They both found each other highly satisfactory, and, being prohibited from the release of talk, all their concentration went physically into this act of darkness which they committed, even while mentally it turned back so that each fed fiercely on the matter of his own mind.

"Darling," he whispered at last, and she too broke the silence to whisper, "Darling." The two characterless and disembodied ghosts of voices met in the stillness and hung there. She thought of Julian, and he of Sylvia.

So this is what it is, thought the single mind between them. This is the great secret that everyone knows, this is the Whore of Babylon, the pleasure of Judas, the object of all the movies, the space between the lines of newspapers and the silences of mother and father; what is wicked is the wish to be wicked, and this, this, is wickedness.

The silence was broken by the sound of footsteps, creaking of doors, muffled voices. The bedroom door flew open, a flashlight directed itself imperatively at the couple in the bed, a voice was heard to exclaim "This is them" and, almost immediately, there followed—as Julian and Sylvia sat bolt upright in bed—two blinding flashes of light, as if the heavens had opened and judgment day peremptorily been declared. Then darkness descended, there came the noise of feet running, a terrible thud as someone bumped into a door, a dirty word loudly shouted, footsteps vanishing, silence again.

Even then, in panic and consternation (looking for a match), they each suspected any and every incredible thing except their own continued—and, it seemed, compulsory—innocence of any infidelity save that of the mind; which some strict authorities have declared to be equal and tantamount, as sin, to that of the flesh.

Among other things, they discovered that Marius and Elaine had vanished—not, perhaps, as though they had never been; but sufficiently vanished. They stared at one another, Julian at Sylvia and Sylvia at Julian—across the small, new flame of the match.

This is a very old story, and when it used to be told in what may have been in some respects a simpler age, it would have ended, perhaps, like this: ". . . and the married couple, when they perceived how astoundingly and justly they had been diddled"—or "saved," depending on the sort of person narrating the tale— "resolved ever after to be true to one another."

We no longer dare to say so much; that "ever after" phrase does not come easily to us. Yet it remains to sum up the short-term results, so to say, of this witnessed action, which took place not so very long ago:

Julian and Sylvia Ghent are still together, without being altogether certain why; though it is true that there was born to them a child, whose creation could have been dated to that night. This child was a boy, whom they named Peter. Mr. Bilsiter, by the way, sent Julian prints and negatives of the photographs taken in the night; there was no comment, but the bill, while it could not under the circumstances be called blackmail, was extremely high. It seemed to bear out the truth of Hugo's aphorism about free love; that love was never free, and seldom even inexpensive.

Marius and Elaine were so charmed with the cleverness and success of their plot that they were unable to resist getting married themselves, and are now experiencing some of the delights and difficulties of that state. On this account, and because of the child, the Ghents were able a little to revenge themselves on the new couple, to whom for a wedding present they gave the dogs Troilus and Cressida. This might have offended Hugo, but Julian and Sylvia decided not to care, and at all events Louisa had made Hugo settle down in Italy, where it is regrettably true that she betrayed him with one gentleman after another, and some not so gentle.

Mr. Archer More, it appeared in the papers, took his twelfth wife amid great celebrations, and divorced her one year after. Of Dr. Thybold, nothing so happy can be reported: Julian's attention was caught by a small piece in the paper about a man answering his description who had been found shot to death in what was called a "hide-out" in Canarsie; the victim had evidently been chain-smoking for several days before his demise, which was ascribed to gangland warfare—but Julian looked up the account in several papers, which reported the poor man's name variously as Dybold, Dybbuk, and Dr. Hy Ball, and was sadly satisfied that it had been indeed his late client, caught up with at last by the cigarette kings.

Of Federigo, nothing more was heard after Sylvia had asked once, "But who was Federigo?" and Julian had replied, "Oh, he died during the war, in the Coral Sea"—actually filling his mind, at that moment, with the peace of that translucent coral image.

Yet Julian saw him once again. It was at a party, in a brilliantly lighted room with crowds of people. They came face to face.

"Federigo Schwartz," Julian said boldly; but the other, looking him straight in the eyes, said: "I beg your pardon, you must be mistaking me for someone else." To which Julian replied, quite gaily: "Oh, very well, if you want it that way. Incognito again, I see. But," as he turned away, "I understand now what you meant." And this phrase might have covered a multitude of sins.

ACKNOWLEDGMENTS

All of the works collected in this volume are copyright © Howard Nemerov, with the exception of the following, which are used by permission:

"Bottom's Dream: The Likeness of Poems and Jokes," *Virginia Quarterly Review* (Autumn 1966).

"The Bread of Faithful Speech—Wallace Stevens and the Voices of Imagination," copyright © 1963 by Rutgers, The State University. Reprinted with permission of Rutgers University Press.

"Composition and Fate in the Short Novel," *The Graduate Journal* 5:2 (Fall 1963), copyright 1963 by the Board of Regents of the University of Texas.

"Everything, Preferably All at Once: Coming to Terms with Kenneth Burke," *Sewanee Review* (Spring 1971).

"Figures of Thought," *Sewanee Review* (Winter 1975).

"James Dickey," *Sewanee Review* (Winter 1963).

"On Metaphor," *Virginia Quarterly Review* (Autumn 1969).

"Preface" and "In Conclusion" from *The Oak in the Acorn,* copyright © 1987 by Louisiana State University Press.

"Randall Jarrell (A Myth about Poetry)," *Kenyon Review* (Fall 1969).

"Some Minute Particulars," copyright 1979 by the Pulitzer Publishing Company.

"The Swaying Form: A Problem in Poetry," *Michigan Alumnus Quarterly Review* (Winter 1959), copyright 1959 by the Regents of the University of Michigan. Reprinted in *To the Young Writer: Hopwood Lectures,* second series (University of Michigan Press, 1956).

INDEX OF WORKS

Poems by Titles

Short Stories